DREAM

ROUTES OF THE AMERICAS

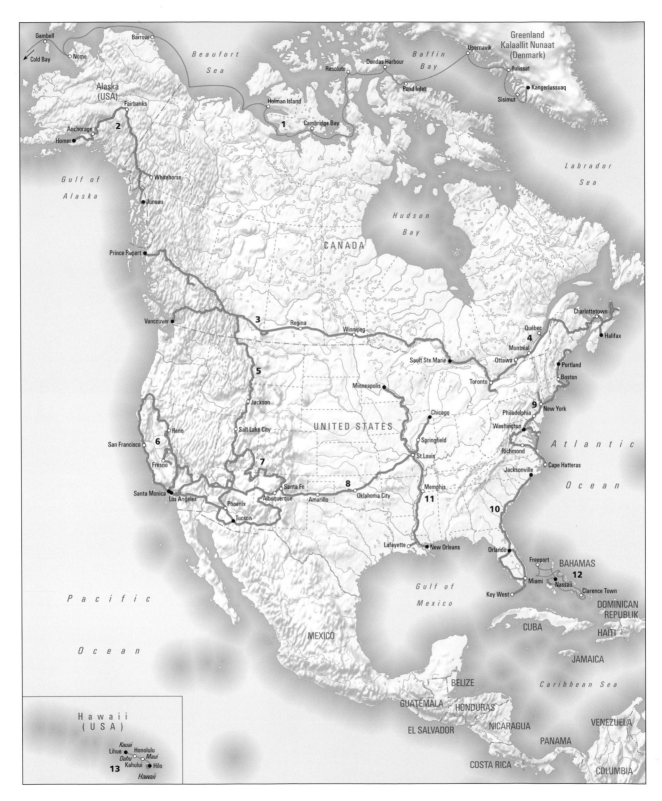

Gambell
Cold Bay
Nome
Barrow
Beaufort
Sea
Greenland
Kalaallit Nunaat
(Denmark)
Upernavik
Ilulissat
Baffin
Bay
Resolute
Dundas Harbour
Kangerlussuaq
Pond Inlet
Sisimut
Alaska
(USA)
Fairbanks
Holman Island
1
Cambridge Bay
Labrador
Sea
2
Anchorage
Homer
Whitehorse
Gulf of
Alaska
Juneau
Hudson
Bay
CANADA
Prince Rupert
Vancouver
3
Regina
Winnipeg
Charlottetown
Québec
Halifax
Montréal
4
Sault Ste.Marie
Ottawa
Portland
5
Toronto
Boston
Minneapolis
Jackson
Chicago
9
New York
Reno
Salt Lake City
UNITED STATES
Philadelphia
Washington
San Francisco
6
Springfield
Atlantic
Fresno
7
St.Louis
Richmond
Santa Fe
Jacksonville
Cape Hatteras
Ocean
Santa Monica
8
Memphis
Los Angeles
Albuquerque
Amarillo
Oklahoma City
11
Phoenix
Tucson
10
Lafayette
New Orleans
Orlando
Pacific
Freeport
BAHAMAS
12
Miami
Nassau
Gulf of
Key West
Clarence Town
Ocean
Mexico
DOMINICAN
REPUBLIK
CUBA
HAITI
MEXICO
JAMAICA
Caribbean Sea
BELIZE
GUATEMALA
HONDURAS
VENEZUELA
EL SALVADOR
NICARAGUA
PANAMA
COSTA RICA
COLUMBIA

H a w a i i
(U S A)
Kauai
Lihue
Honolulu
Oahu
Maui
Kahului
Hilo
13
Hawaii

UNITED STATES

Sargasso Sea

Gulf of
Mexico

BAHAMAS

Havana **17** CUBA

MEXICO **14**

León

Mérida

Cancún

DOMINICAN
REPUBLIC

Mexico City

Santiago de Cuba

HAITI

Puerto Rico

San Juan

ANTIGUA AND BARBUDA

Oaxaca

15

BELIZE

JAMAICA

ST.KITTS AND NEVIS

Mexicali

Acapulco

GUATEMALA

HONDURAS

Caribbean Sea

SAINT VINCENT AND
THE GRENADINES

DOMINICA

18

SAINT LUCIA

Ciudad de Guatemala

16

NICARAGUA

BARBADOS

EL SALVADOR

Coro

Saint George's

GRENADA

Cartagena

Maracaibo

Caracas

TRINIDAD AND TOBAGO

COSTA RICA

PANAMA

Cumaná

19

Panamá

Ciudad Bolívar

VENEZUELA

GUYANA

Bogotá

Parque Nacional
Canaima

SURINAM

French Guiana

Cali

COLOMBIA

20

Quito

ECUADOR

Galápagos Islands

Genovesa

21

Santa Cruz

Guayaquil

Loja

Piura

Trujillo

BRAZIL

PERU

Lima

Cuzco

Salvador

22

Nazca

23

BOLIVIA

Cuiabá

Brasília

Arequipa

La Paz

Cochabamba

Tacna

Sucre

26

Arica

Ouro Preto

Iquique

Antofagasta

PARAGUAY

São Paulo

Pacific

Foz do Iguaçú

Rio de Janeiro

Ocean

24

CHILE

La Serena

Córdoba

Valparaíso

Mendoza

URUGUAY

Santiago de Chile

ARGENTINA

Atlantic

Temuco

Valdivia

Puerto Montt

San Carlos
de Bariloche

Ocean

25

Coihaique

Perito Moreno

Puerto Yungay

Falkland Islands

Stanley

Punta Arenas

Ushuaia

Cape Horn

South Shetland Islands

27

Elephant Island

Antarctica

Port Lockroy

Atlantic

Ocean

5

Introduction

The 27 carefully researched routes in this book will take you to the most fascinating destinations in the Americas, through magnificent scenery and unique cultural sites, to bustling cities, quiet, sleepy towns and last, but not least, to dream beaches.

The routes range from the Alaska Highway in the north of the continent to a cruise to the world's most southerly continent, Antarctica.

The route descriptions:

An introductory section in each chapter provides a summary of the route and introduces its scenic and cultural highlights. This is followed by a description of the important towns and sights along the route, together with road information and directions – all consecutively num-

bered and cross-referenced with the maps at the end of each chapter and illustrated with lavish color photographs. Extra pages featuring detailed comprehensive information are dedicated to the cities and national parks through which the routes pass.

Each journey has an information box with important travel tips regarding the length of each route, how much time to allow, local traffic laws, weather, the best time to travel, and useful links and addresses.

The touring maps:

Special touring maps at the end of each chapter chart the course of each route and highlight the most important cities and sights. The main route is clearly identified and complemented with additional

suggestions for interesting detours. Eye-catching symbols (see list opposite) mark the location and the type of attractions along each route. There are short intros in the margins of each map presenting interesting facts and superb color photos highlight particularly fascinating destinations.

Remarkable landscapes and natural monuments

- Mountain landscape
- Extinct volcano
- Active volcano
- Rock landscape
- Ravine/Canyon
- Cave
- Glacier
- Desert
- River landscape
- Waterfall/rapids
- Lake country
- Geyser
- Oasis
- National Park (fauna)
- National Park (flora)
- National Park (culture)
- National Park (landscape)
- Nature Park
- Cultural landscape
- Coastal landscape
- Island
- Beach
- Coral reef
- Underwater Reserve
- Zoo/safari park
- Fossil site
- Wildlife reserve
- Whale watching
- Protected area for sea-lions/seals
- Protected area for penguins
- Crocodile farm

Remarkable cities and cultural monuments

- Pre- and early history
- The Ancient Orient
- Greek antiquity
- Roman antiquity
- Etruscan culture
- Indian reservation
- Indian Pueblo culture
- Places of Indian cultural interest
- Mayan culture
- Inca culture
- Other ancient American cultures
- Places of Islamic cultural interest
- Places of Buddhist cultural interest
- Places of Hindu cultural interest
- Places of Christian cultural interest
- Places of Jainist cultural interest
- Places of Abor. cultural interest
- Aborigine reservation
- Phoenician culture
- Prehistoric rockscape
- Early african cultures
- Cultural landscape
- Castle/fortress/fort
- Palace
- Technical/industrial monument
- Memorial
- Space telescope
- Historical city scape
- Impressive skyline
- Festivals
- Museum
- Theatre/theater
- World exhibition
- Olympics
- Monument
- Tomb/grave
- Market
- Caravanserai
- Theater of war/battlefield
- Dam
- Remarkable lighthouse
- Remarkable bridge

Sport and leisure destinations

- Race track
- Skiing
- Sailing
- Diving
- Canoeing/rafting
- Mineral/thermal spa
- Beach resort
- Amusement/theme park
- Casino
- Horse racing
- Hill resort
- Deep-sea fishing
- Surfing
- Seaport

The Northwest Passage

Through the North American Arctic

The navigation of the Northwest Passage cost the lives of many sailors and Arctic explorers and is still a fascinating adventure today. This legendary sea route along North America's coastline leads through fields of sea ice, pack ice, and icebergs on its way from the Atlantic to the Pacific.

Soon after the discovery of America by Christopher Columbus in the late 15th century, seafarers were already boldly making their first attempts to sail northward around the New World in search of a sea route to East Asia. At the beginning of the 16th century, in appalling conditions, explorers like Gaspar Corte-Real and Sebastian Cabot reached the islands of the Canadian archipelago. However, all attempts to find a route through the maze of narrow sounds and fjords failed, the way often blocked by impregnable pack ice; yet even the ill-fated 19th-century expedition led by English explorer John Franklin, which cost the lives of the whole crew, did not discourage others from making further attempts.

The subsequent decade-long search for Franklin's missing expedition contributed considerably to what was known about the Far North. The first person to prove the existence of the Northwest Passage was Norwegian explorer Roald Amundsen. With just a tiny ship and a small crew he successfully navigated the northern coast of the American continent between 1903 and 1906. However, the conquering of the passage, during which Amundsen and his crew spent two winters stuck in the ice, did little to lessen its dangers. It was not until 1942 that a second expedition, led by Henry Larsen, an officer of the Royal Canadian Mounted Police (RCMP), aboard the St Roch, succeeded in navigating the route, this time in the opposite direction, sailing from west to east. Nowadays, modern technology and navigational aids allow a safe passage, though only for a few weeks each year, and even then there is no guarantee that it will be possible to follow the planned route. The first voyage with a cruise ship took place in 1984.

The Northwest Passage has never become important commercially because its navigation is still difficult and plagued by un-

A young Inuit from Victoria Island.

Huge icebergs float south from Disko Bay. Around nine-tenths of the ice mass is hidden underwater.

The 1,800-km (1,200-mile) Iditarod dogsled race takes place in Alaska every year.

certainty today, although use of the passage has become a necessity for the mining industry, which exploits many of the natural resources that are found in the Canadian Arctic. Even so, the number of mining companies using the passage is limited to isolated examples, such as the Polaris Mine on Bathurst Island, where lead and zinc ore are extracted. In contrast, the oil from the Prudhoe Bay oilfield is transported by pipeline.

For indigenous people in the far-flung settlements of the North, the arrival of a ship is a special event; but although there are no roads to connect the region to southern Canada, the settlements are no longer as cut off from the rest of the world as you might expect. Almost all research stations and Inuit settlements are within reach of South Canada by air. It is true that modern technology has helped make life and travel in the Arctic easier, but the magic of the landscape, the solitude, and the peace remain undisturbed.

It is not just the sparkling surface of the sea ice in the estuaries and fjords, the strangely shaped icebergs, and the towering pack ice that make this place so fascinating and beautiful, the tundra also blazes with bright hues during its short flowering season. The play of shades from violet to pale pink across the night sky is also an incredible sight. As the nights grow longer and darker, the haunting glow of the Northern Lights appears: flickering shards of light filling the sky.

Even today, despite all the recent technological advances, life in the far north remains indisputably hard. The biggest challenge of all is the inhospitable climate. In winter, temperatures can be expected to drop to around -40°C (-40°F) or lower, and even in May, when the sun reaches a higher point in the sky, the thermometer only just manages to struggle above freezing. Spring is often considered the most beautiful season.

A snowy owl in its ground nest watches over its numerous offspring.

1

The cruise begins in Greenland and crosses the Canadian Arctic to the point where the Norwegian explorer Roald Amundsen began his successful navigation of the Northwest Passage. It then continues to Alaska and ends in the Aleutian Islands on the border with Russia.

❶ **Kangerlussuaq** This town has the largest airport in Greenland and is the arrival point for most visitors. The cruise through the islands of the Arctic departs from the Kangerlussuaq Fjord, which is approximately 170 km (106 miles) long. The route then passes numerous glaciers that drop abruptly and steeply into the estuary. Extending from the Greenland Ice Cap, they cut deep into the rock, carving out a path into the fjord.

❷ **Sisimiut** When open sea is reached at the mouth of the fjord, the route follows the rocky coast northward. After crossing the Arctic Circle, the small town of Sisimiut soon comes into view. The fish factory and cold-storage buildings

around the port leave you with little doubt as to how the local population earns its living. A particular export are the highly sought-after Greenland crabs, which are sold to countries all over the world. Back in the 18th century, Dutch whalers established a base here, as did the Danish missionary Hans Egede, in 1724. The current settlement, originally named Holsteinsborg, was founded four decades later under the patronage of Count Ludwig Holstein. Living in an urban environment necessitated a big lifestyle change for the local Inuit population, but nowadays most enjoy the comforts that modern life brings.

❸ **Ilulissat** Previously known by its Danish name of Jakob-

Travel Information

Route profile
Length: approx. 2,500 km (1,554 miles)
Duration: approx. 4 weeks
Start: Kangerlussuaq (Greenland)
End: Cold Bay (Alaska)
Itinerary (main locations): Kangerlussuaq, Sisimiut, Ilulissat, Upernavik, Pond Inlet, Dundas Harbour, Beechey Island, Resolute, Franklin Strait, Cambridge Bay, Ross Point, Holman Island, Herschel Island, Barrow, Point Hope, Diomede Islands, Nome, Gambell, St Paul Island, Dutch Harbor, Cold Bay

Travel tips
The Northwest Passage followed here may only be explored with an organized cruise (see information for cruise companies).

When to go
The Northwest Passage is only navigable for just a few weeks in summer and even then cruise companies may need to adapt the route to take into account the prevailing conditions and the amount of ice that is around. Expect swarms of mosquitoes if you make any day trips into the tundra during summer and be sure to pack some insect repellent. It is also a good idea to take high-necked, windproof clothing so that you can keep covered up as much as possible.

Tourist information
www.greenland-guide.gl (Greenland Guide Index)
www.hl-cruises.com (Hapag-Lloyd Cruises)
www.alaska.com

shavn (Jacob's Harbor), this settlement, the third largest in Greenland, is one of its most popular tourist destinations. Ilulissat (meaning "the icebergs" in Inuit) is a very appropriate name as the surrounding landscape is dominated by these white giants, floating slowly from the fjord into Disko Bay. The Greenland Ice Cap, up to 3 km (2 miles) deep in places, ensures a steady supply of ice. Propelled by the force of its own weight, the ice cap glides into the fjord via one of its many outlet glaciers. When the ice reaches the open water of the bay it breaks up, forming icebergs.

④ **Upernavik** The municipality of Upernavik (Springtime Place) is made up of several small groups of buildings hugging the jagged cliffs of Greenland's north-west coast, and has a total of around three thousand inhabitants. The main settlement, with around a thousand inhabitants, is located on one of the many small rocky islands off this part of the coast. The area around Upernavik, especially the nesting cliffs of Apparsuit, offer an excellent opportunity for watching the local wildlife: the tundra landscape of the Svartenhuken Peninsula is home to herds of reindeer and musk ox. The landscape to the north of Upernavik is even wilder, with a glacier flowing directly into the sea.

For the people of Upernavik, the sea is the basis of their existence, and even today most families still earn their living from fishing and seal-hunting. The most northerly open-air museum in the world has been set up in the buildings of the former Upernavik trading post to inform visitors about the development of the town and the traditional life of the Inuit people.

⑤ **Pond Inlet** The route now leads through the narrow Pond Inlet to the settlement of the same name in the north of Baffin Island. Here, in Eclipse Sound, the route enters Canadian territory for the first time. Founded just a few decades ago and named after an English astronomer, Mittimatalik means "the place where Mitima is buried" and is Pont Inlet's Inuit name; Inuit form the majority of the 1,300 inhabitants. A whaling station was established here at the beginning of the 20th century but abandoned after just a few years.

Despite the inhospitable climate, people have been living in the region around Pond Inlet for at least four thousand years. Archeologists have found evidence in the area of both the Dorset culture and the later Thule people, who were the ancestors of the modern Canadian Inuit. In 1929, two missions, An-

1 Icebergs off western Greenland.

2 Glaciers in the Ilulissat Fjord.

Walruses are the largest species of seal in the northern hemisphere. They inhabit the waters of the Eastern Canadian Arctic and Northern Greenland. These giant semi-aquatic mammals do not eat fish but dive for mollusks which they dig out from the sea bed with their canine

teeth, and then suck out the meat, pressing on the shell with their powerful upper lip. They also forage for starfish, sea urchins, and worms on the sea floor. Their tusks can grow up to 1 m (40 in) in length and the males usually have larger tusks than the females

glican and Catholic, were established in the settlement to foster and support Christianity in the region.

As with most of the settlements in the Arctic, the scattered buildings of Pond Inlet are plain and functional, with little architectural charm. However, this simplicity only serves to make the location of the settlement, with its spectacular mountain backdrop, all the more impressive. To the south, the peaks climb to over 1,500 m (4,922 ft), while to the north, on the towering Bylot Island, the peaks are just as steep and even higher at over 2,000 m (6,562 ft). Pond Inlet is the source of several vast glaciers, which surge inexorably toward the sea.

Both Eclipse Sound and the nearby Pond Inlet, which separates Bylot from Baffin Island, are littered with icebergs and sea ice even during the summer months. It is not only the views of this Arctic landscape that will fascinate you, the wildlife of the estuaries is also captivating. Beluga, narwhals, and occasionally even Greenland whales can be seen in the waters nearby, and sperm whales and orcas are

also sighted occasionally. Other marine mammals worth looking out for include walrus and various types of seal, including the ringed seal.

Most of Bylot Island is within Sirmilik National Park, one of Canada's newest national parks, established in 1999. The island is well-known as a bird sanctuary: hundreds of thousands of thick-billed murres and black-legged kittiwakes nest on its cliffs, and there is also a large population of greater snow geese. Bird- and whale-watching excursions leave from Pond Inlet and boat tours for anglers are also on offer, as well as trips by snowmobile and dogsled during the spring. You can learn more about the bird sanctuary on Bylot and the Sirmilik National Park at the Nattinak Visitor's Centre in Pond Inlet.

6 Dundas Harbour The route continues along the rocky west coast of Bylot Island through the narrow Navy Board Inlet to the north of Lancaster Sound, the 80-km (50-mile) wide main entry point to the Northwest Passage. The channels of the passage rarely exceed 300 m

(984 ft) in depth, so at a depth of over 1,000 m (3,281 ft) this represents the deepest section of the route.

A little further on you reach Dundas Harbour, located at a northerly latitude of nearly 75° on the south-east coast of Devon Island, the largest uninhabited island in the world. The RCMP opened up an outpost here in 1924 as part of a government move to curb foreign activity, including whaling, but abandoned it in 1932. Inuit families were relocated to the island in 1934, but although they chose to leave in 1936, finding the conditions too harsh, sovereign rights to Dundas Harbour are still disputed to this day. The

area to the north of Dundas Harbour reaches altitudes of 1,900 m (6,234 ft) and is completely covered by glaciers. Prehistoric finds dating back to the Dorset and Thule cultures have been discovered in the coastal region, proving that it has been inhabited for thousands of years.

Dundas Harbour is the ideal place to learn about Arctic wildlife. Walruses and seals on the coast and musk ox on the land make for impressive photo opportunities. It might be a good idea, however, not to get too closely acquainted with the polar bears that also live here, though these dangerous predators are rarely seen on land as

3

most of their prey lives on the eternal ice.

🄻 **Beechey Island** This island, in Wellington Channel, was discovered in 1819 by the English seafarer William Edward Parry and named after Frederick William Beechey, an officer from Parry's crew. Beechey Island played an important role in the history of exploration in the Canadian Arctic. In 1845, the polar explorer John Franklin thought the island's protected port would be a good place to anchor his ship for the first winter of his expedition, but it ended in tragedy. When rescuers arrived in 1851 they discovered the graves of three crew members marked with stones but no clue as to the fate of the remaining crew.

In the 1980s, the remains of the three men, which were well-preserved in the permafrost, were exhumed and scientifically examined. It emerged that the men had probably died of lead poisoning: the cans of food that they lived off for months on end had been poorly soldered with lead. Evidence of lung disease was found too, which also could have proved fatal.

In 1979, Beechey Island was declared a site of territorial historical significance by the government of the Northwest Territories. Today, like most of Northeast Canada, it belongs to the territory of Nunavut, formed in 1999. The graves of the three sailors are still a special point of interest for visitors to the Arctic.

🄼 **Resolute** Located on Cornwallis Island at the northern end of Resolute Bay, the so-called "hamlet" of Resolute is one of the most northerly settlements on earth and has around 250 inhabitants, the majority Inuit. Despite the small size of the settlement, its airport is big enough to cater for large planes and acts as an important hub for air traffic in the Canadian Arctic. Resolute is a reminder to visitors of how difficult life was in the region before the Northwest Passage was finally opened. The town is named after HMS Resolute, one of the many ships that took part in the search for the missing Franklin expedition. The Resolute was locked in the ice for two winters; in order to avoid a third winter of darkness and cold, Captain Belcher took the decision to abandon ship and the crew returned to England aboard a rescue ship. The Resolute was found in good condition by American whalers in 1855 and freed from the pack ice.

The hamlet of Resolute is important as a location for weather and research stations. The Canadian government assumed control of the original Inuit settlement only in the 1950s and 1960s. Today, Inuits live alongside scientists and engineers in the hamlet, and can still hunt according to their traditions. During the 1960s and 1970s, the Magnetic North Pole was located on the nearby Bathurst Island, only 150 km (93 miles) to 200 km (124 miles) west of Resolute. This made the town an excellent base for research teams investigating the earth's magnetic field. Since then, the magnetic pole has moved north beyond the latitude of 80°.

Despite this, weather stations and geophysical research facilities continue to be located in Resolute, which is now also the starting point for both the biennial Polar Race and the annual Polar Challenge, in which teams race to the Magnetic North Pole. Resolute also gained importance as the transport and provisions base for the Polaris Mine on Bathurst Island, for a time the most northerly ore mine in the world. Non-ferrous metals such as lead and zinc were extracted here until the mine be-

1 Nomadic polar bears searching for prey.

2 A big event for the whole village: cutting up a Beluga whale.

3 An Inuit fishing in the ice.

1

came non-profitable and closed in 2003.

⑨ Franklin Strait This strait is named after the explorer John Franklin (see page 34), who led an expedition into the islands of the Canadian Arctic in 1845 while attempting to prove the existence of a sea passage between the Atlantic and the Pacific. His ships, HMS Erebus and HMS Terror, commanded by Captain James Fitzjames and Captain Francis Crozier respectively, were sighted north of Baffin Island by whalers, but were soon lost in pack ice. Several expeditions set out to search for the missing crews, but their sad fate was not known until 1859 when a diary was found. It emerged that Franklin and his crew spent the first winter near Beechey Island and then sailed to Peel Sound and Franklin Strait. In September 1846, the ships again became trapped in the ice, this time in

Victoria Strait. While attempting to head south on foot, all members of the expedition perished.

The route continues past King William Island. The Northwest Passage Territorial Historic Park at the settlement of Goja Haven reminds visitors of the history of exploration in the passage and surrounding area with information boards and artifacts. The town is named after Gjøa, the vessel in which Roald Amundsen navigated the passage for the first time between 1903 and 1906. Amundsen found it an ideal place to drop anchor and conduct research into the earth's magnetic field. The historic park provides visitors with an insight into the life and work of the famous polar explorer, who spent three winters here.

⑩ Cambridge Bay Cambridge Bay, named for the English Duke of Cambridge and also known as Ikaluktutiak ("place of many big

2

fish") is on the south coast of Victoria Island and, thanks to its sheltered position at the end of the bay, offers good anchorage. The small settlement, with around 1,500 inhabitants, mostly Inuit, has developed into a center for arts and crafts. The Nunavut College of Fine Arts offers courses in the techniques and styles of Inuit art to inhabitants and tourists alike. Jewelry production is also popular, using mostly local stones such as the easily worked serpentine and the bones of marine mammals. Copper, found in some parts of

the island, has also been used traditionally by the Inuit and other metals and modern materials further enrich Inuit art.

In the area around Cambridge Bay, visitors can see the remains of old Inuit dwellings, built out of rock and earth and known as quarmaq.

One of the sights of the bay itself is the wreck of the Maud (named after the Queen of Norway and later renamed the Baymaud), the ship built for Amundsen's second Arctic expedition, which was sold to the Hudson's Bay Company in 1925

and sank in 1930. A lighthouse has provided safe passage into the bay since 1947.

Originally a trading post for the Hudson's Bay Company and a small police station, Cambridge Bay was developed in the 1920s as a Canadian government post for this part of the Arctic.

The Inuits, previously widely spread over the area, did not settle here until the 1950s. Cambridge Bay is an ideal place to learn more about the unique Arctic flora and fauna. Venturing onto the slopes in an off-road vehicle, you might be lucky enough to see whole herds of musk ox.

⑪ Ross Point The route westward along the southern coast of Victoria Island heads through Dease Strait and Coronation Gulf. If you have a chance to go ashore at Ross Point, take the opportunity to fit in a short walk around the area, far from any kind of settlement, to see some of the plant and animal life of the tundra. The most impressive animal you could see here is the musk ox, which frequently roams in small groups or even entire herds.

⑫ Holman Island After some 250 km (155 miles), the route, often narrow in places, opens out into the Amundsen Gulf, marking an end to the most difficult section of the Northwest Passage. This area is also the border between the Canadian Inuit territory of Nunavut and the Northwest Territories. The community of Ulukhaktok is home to the most northerly golf course on the planet, and welcomes international competitors every summer when it plays host to its own tournament. Despite its remote location, the island has become a magnet for artists, who are especially attracted by the traditional Holman Art Prints. Lithographs, etchings, linocuts, and other graphic techniques are used to create motifs symbolic of the Arctic world. Dancing and drumming are also important elements of community life in Ulukhaktok. Before the current settlement was established, the area was a trading post and some buildings still remaining from this time can be visited on Read Island.

⑬ Herschel Island The route continues through the vast Amundsen Gulf to the Beaufort Sea, passing the delta formed by the Mackenzie River before reaching Herschel Island. Lining the coast are great piles of driftwood bleached pale gray by the salt water of the sea. The driftwood, which is pushed northward from Canada's forest region across the Mackenzie and out into the sea, is a precious source of timber for building and burning in this area, which is barren of trees.

The local name for Herschel, Qikiqtaruk, means simply "island" in Inuit. During the short summer, the tundra here is a blaze of color. Though just a few square miles in size, the island with its sheltered port was regularly frequented by whalers and scientific researchers, and, with an Inuit settlement already in existence there, became a supply center for the entire region.

1 Musk oxen can often be seen in the Canadian Arctic.

2 Icebreakers in the Beaufort Sea.

14 Barrow The line of longitude 141° west is crossed at Barrow 80 km (50 miles) west of Herschel Island, marking the border between Canada and Alaska. People began arriving at Prudhoe Bay to look for crude oil as early as the 1940s, but it was not until 1968 that exploitable sources were discovered. The crude oil is pumped across almost 1,300 km (808 miles) to Valdez on Alaska's southern coast through the Alaska pipeline, which was completed in 1977.

As the largest settlement on the northern coast and the USA's most northerly city, Barrow is an important supply town for oil fields in the area. In summer, the pack ice briefly retreats from the coast, allowing boats access to the port to offload goods and supplies for the settlement.

Some 15 km (9 miles) north of Barrow is the headland known as Point Barrow, or Nuvuk in the local language, the USA's most northerly point and the departure point for many historic Arctic expeditions reaching back as far as 1576 when pioneers dared to face the cold climate.

15 Point Hope Point Hope is perched on a headland that juts west into the Chukchi Sea. The small town has a population of less than a hundred people, mainly Inuit. Among the attractions here are beautiful cult objects carved out of whalebone. From here the route continues south to the Bering Strait, which, along with the Bering Sea, Island, Glacier, and Land Bridge, was named for the Danish-born sailor Vitus Jonassen Bering (1681–1741), who explored the area. Cape Prince of Wales, the most westerly point

of the entire American mainland, is a mere 100 km (62 miles) from Cape Deshnev, the easternmost point of Asia.

16 Diomede Islands The two countries of Russia and the USA almost meet here. At the closest land approach, the two rocky, tuya-like islands of Little Diomede (American) and Big Diomede (Russian) are just 3 km (2 miles) apart. It is the only place where the two nations share a border. The International Dateline also bisects the channel between the two islands.

17 Nome This town played an important role in Alaska's history during the gold rush. Word got around quickly when gold was discovered in nearby Anvil Creek in 1898, and prospectors came from all over the world, hoping to strike it lucky. Today, Nome is most famous as the destination for the Iditarod Trail Sled Dog Race, held in honor of the dogsled team that brought the serum to bring to an end the 1925 diptheria epidemic among the Inuit.

18 Gambell Lying on the northwestern tip of St Lawrence Island, Gambell is almost wholly inhabited by Siberian Yupik, the indigenous people of the northeast Russian Federation.

19 St Paul Island St Paul is one of the four Pribilof Islands situated in the Bering Sea between Alaska and Siberia. Like

1 Ice floes drift in the Bering Sea.

2 Two teams from the Iditarod dog-sled race make a stop in Unalakleet.

The tufted puffin (Lunda cirrhata), which is common along the American Pacific coast from Alaska to California, is very closely related to the Atlantic puffin. Its most striking feature is its breeding plumage: pale yellow tufts of hair protruding above its eyes.

Dutch Harbor, the center for the fishing industry on the Aleutian island of Amaknak, is connected to Unalaska by a bridge. Unalaska, at the end of the Aleutian Chain, counts over four thousand residents. A busy fish_____ seafood processing port, Dutch Harbor is also a

tourist destination, with sportfishing, bird and wildlife viewing, cultural and historical exploration, or hiking and beachcombing awaiting the adventurous traveler. The harbor has been ranked no. 1 port of the nation's seafood volume and value since 11 years

most islands in the region, they are volcanic and provide breeding grounds for seabirds and seals. The Pribilof Islands are inhabited by Aleuts, whose homeland also includes the Shumagin and Aleutian islands and the western part of the Alaska Peninsula.

⑳ Dutch Harbor The small town of Dutch Harbor lies on the Aleutian Island of Amaknak and is connected by a bridge to the adjacent Unalaska Island.
The Russian Orthodox Church in Unalasaka is worth visiting. It is protected as a cultural monument dating back to the time when Alaska was part of Russia. The Aleutians came under Russia's influence in the 18th century when Russian fur trappers established settlements on the island, brutally oppressing and sometimes murdering the inhabitants. Missionaries from the

Russian Orthodox Church arrived later and built their first church here in 1825.
Despite being somewhat removed from world affairs, the Aleutians did not escape the effects of World War II. While the USA tried to protect the islands by building military bases, they could not prevent attacks by Japanese fighter planes, and on the morning of June 3, 1942 Japanese aircraft attacked Dutch Harbor.

㉑ Cold Bay The passage continues from Unalaska, past the Krenitzin Islands to Unimak Island, the largest of the Aleutian Islands. Pavlof, a huge volcano and one of many on the Alaska Peninsula, towers a vast 2,862 m (9,390 ft) above the bay, though it is often obscured by mist.
Like the islands in the area and vast regions of the Peninsula, Unimak is protected as a Na-

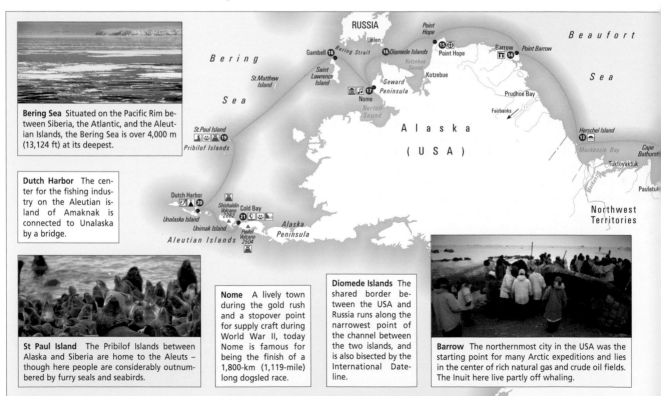

Bering Sea Situated on the Pacific Rim between Siberia, the Atlantic, and the Aleutian Islands, the Bering Sea is over 4,000 m (13,124 ft) at its deepest.

Dutch Harbor The center for the fishing industry on the Aleutian island of Amaknak is connected to Unalaska by a bridge.

St Paul Island The Pribilof Islands between Alaska and Siberia are home to the Aleuts – though here people are considerably outnumbered by furry seals and seabirds.

Nome A lively town during the gold rush and a stopover point for supply craft during World War II, today Nome is famous for being the finish of a 1,800-km (1,119-mile) long dogsled race.

Diomede Islands The shared border between the USA and Russia runs along the narrowest point of the channel between the two islands, and is also bisected by the International Dateline.

Barrow The northernmost city in the USA was the starting point for many Arctic expeditions and lies in the center of rich natural gas and crude oil fields. The Inuit here live partly off whaling.

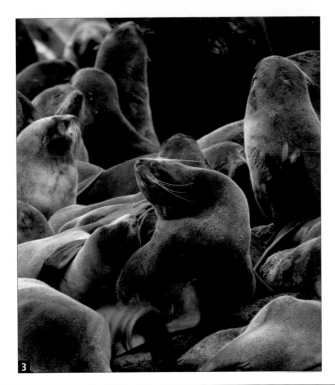

tional Wildlife Refuge. Many North American animal species can be found here, ranging from the enormous brown bear to the silver fox. Cold Bay lies at the outermost end of the Alaska Peninsula, with its airport an important transport hub for the south-western part of the state. The town's development was closely linked to the local airport. It was built during World War II for better defense of this isolated part of the USA against Japanese attack. At that time, it was also used as a stopover point for the transportation of cargo between the USA and Soviet Union.

Today, the town of Cold Bay is mainly inhabited by employees of the airport, military aerial surveillance, and meteorological service. With its offshore islands, mighty volcanoes, and rocky coasts rich in coves and bays, the area surrounding Cold Bay is home to some of Alaska's most impressive scenery.

Pavlof has erupted some forty times in the last 200 years and is one of the most active volcanoes in Alaska. The Izembek National Wildlife Refuge is a special animal haven, containing several lagoons that form the habitat of wild geese and migratory birds.

The adventurous cruise through the North American Arctic comes to an end in Cold Bay. Many passengers make the return journey from here by plane.

1 The American Pribilof Islands in the Bering Sea.

2 A Russian Orthodox church on St Paul Island.

3 A colony of furry seals on the Alaskan coast.

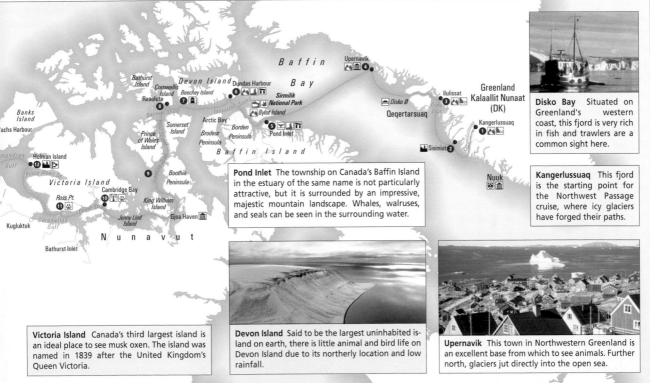

Disko Bay Situated on Greenland's western coast, this fjord is very rich in fish and trawlers are a common sight here.

Kangerlussuaq This fjord is the starting point for the Northwest Passage cruise, where icy glaciers have forged their paths.

Pond Inlet The township on Canada's Baffin Island in the estuary of the same name is not particularly attractive, but it is surrounded by an impressive, majestic mountain landscape. Whales, walruses, and seals can be seen in the surrounding water.

Victoria Island Canada's third largest island is an ideal place to see musk oxen. The island was named in 1839 after the United Kingdom's Queen Victoria.

Devon Island Said to be the largest uninhabited island on earth, there is little animal and bird life on Devon Island due to its northerly location and low rainfall.

Upernavik This town in Northwestern Greenland is an excellent base from which to see animals. Further north, glaciers jut directly into the open sea.

Alaska

Far North on the Alaska Highway

Americans like to call their 49th state "The Last Frontier". In Alaska, seashores, rivers, forests, mountains, and glaciers remain almost untouched, brown bears fish for salmon, sea lions fight for territory, and herds of caribou trek across the tundra. But even this far north the cities are expanding, oil production is becoming a hazard for the wilderness, and civilization is encroaching slowly but steadily on the landscape. Fortunately, several national parks have been established, and this route takes you there.

When William Seward, the US Secretary of State, acquired Alaska from the Russians for two cents per acre in 1867, this vast empty expanse of land was quickly derided as "Seward's folly" because it was believed foolhardy to spend so much money on the remote region. But the billions of barrels of oil that have since flown through the Alaskan Pipeline have more than earned the initial purchase price he paid. In Alaska, there are eight national parks protecting the state's valuable natural resources. By area, the Alaskan peninsula in the north-west of the American continent is the largest state in the US. It measures 1.5 million sq km (579,153 sq mi), easily big enough to fit Western Europe into it. From the Canadian border, which is 2,500 km (1,550 miles) long, the peninsula stretches nearly 4,000 km (2,480 miles) to the furthest of the Aleutian Islands on the western tip of the state. To the north of Alaska is the Beaufort Sea, to the west the Bering Straits, and to the south the Pacific Ocean.

The Pacific coast is broken up into innumerable islands, peninsulas, and deep fjords that reach far into the interior.

Mount McKinley is North America's highest mountain at 6,194 m (20,323 ft), and Juneau is the only state capital that is accessible only by boat, via the Alaska Marine Highway, or by plane.

Of its highland plains, 40,000 sq km (15,000 sq mi) are covered by glaciers. North of the Arctic Circle, the permafrost soil only thaws to a maximum depth of half a meter (18 in), but agriculture is still possible in the Matanuska Valley.

A walrus herd on the Alaskan coast.

Mount Wrangell (4,317 m/14,164 ft) is an extinct volcano clearly visible from Glenn Highway, which connects Tok Junction with Anchorage.

Mount McKinley, North America's highest mountain, is mirrored Wonder Lake, carved out of glaciers.

Until 1942, there was no way to get to Alaska by land, and only when the Japanese threatened to close in on Alaska did the US government decide to build a road connection through Canada. On 9 March 1942, a total of 11,000 people began construction on this road, about 2,300 km (1,430 miles) long, between Dawson Creek in Canada to the south and Delta Junction to the north. Despite the huge difficulties encountered, this pioneer route was in use by 20 November 1942 after an impressively short construction period of only eight months.

After the war it was handed over to the civil authorities and gradually improved. Today it is open year-round and in all weather conditions. It remains the only land connection between the USA and Alaska, and despite a tarmac surface along its entire length, the highway is indeed still a challenge. Be prepared for summer snowstorms, mud-slides, and washed-out bridges. The challenge has its rewards, however. Unforgettable scenery awaits you, often right by the roadside, where you occasionally see bears with their cubs, or elks with giant antlers. Fairbanks and Anchorage are modern cities, but even here the wilderness comes right to your doorstep. A trip into Denali National Park with the mighty Mount McKinley (6,194 m/20,323 ft) is a challenging and unique experience for any visitor.

If you want to get even closer to the "real" Alaska, you can fly from Anchorage to King Salmon in the west and then take a hydroplane to Katmai National Park and Preserve. In July you can watch bears catching salmon from incredibly close range, a world-class sight. Alternatively, pay a visit to Kodiak Is-land with its massive Kodiak bears, also known as the Alaskan grizzly bear, that weigh up to 500 kg (1,100 lbs) and reach heights of up to 3 m (10 ft). This is wilderness in its purest form.

The Arctic tundra is home to small herds of shaggy musk oxen.

The bald eagle was chosen June 20, 1782 as the emblem of the United States of America, because of its long life, great strength and majestic looks, and also because it was then believed to exist only on this continent. The national bird mainly lives in Alaska, and with

its 2,40 metre (7.87-foot) wing span it belongs to the most impressive animals in the North. The Eagle appears in the Seals of many US States, on most of the country's gold and silver coinage, and is used a great deal for decorative patriotic purposes.

1

Our Alaskan dream route begins in the capital, Juneau. After a boat trip across to Haines, we take the Haines Highway to the Alaska Highway as far as Border City Lodge, where the route goes through Canada. Back in Alaska via Fairbanks and Anchorage, the route takes us to Homer on the Kenai Peninsula.

1 Juneau Alaska's capital is located on a narrow stretch of coastal plain between Gastineau Channel and the steep slopes of Mount Juneau (1,091 m/3,580 ft). Right outside town are the towering Coast Mountains with spectacular glaciers.

In 1880, gold diggers Joe Juneau and Dick Harris first found gold in what is now the town's river. By World War II more than 150 million dollars' worth of the precious metal had been discovered in the area.

As early as 1906 the Alaskan state government was moved to this northern El Dorado. The mines have long been shut down now, and Juneau has become a quiet governmental town. More than half the town's population is involved in running the state.

Both of the town's most important sights are located on Franklin Street, the town's main road. One of them is the Red Dog Saloon, which was already infamous during the gold rush. The other is the Russian Orthodox Church of St Nicholas, which keeps a close watch over the moral fibre of the townsfolk. The church was erected by Russian fur traders in 1894, making it the oldest Russian church in the south-eastern part of Alaska. Another must-see is the Alaska State Museum on Whittier Street, with an exhibition of indigenous Native American culture and a bit of history of the white settlements in the area.

Travel Information

Route profile
Length: approx. 3,000 km (1,850 miles), excluding detours

Time required: 3 weeks

Start: Juneau
Destination: Homer
Route (main locations):
Juneau, Glacier Bay National Park, Skagway, Haines, Haines Junction, Whitehorse, Kluane National Park, Tok Junction, Delta Junction, Fairbanks, Denali National Park, Eklutna, Anchorage, Portage, Seward, Kenai, Homer

Traffic information:
Drive on the right in the USA. Speed limits in towns are 25–30 mph (40–48 km/h), and outside towns 65 mph (105 km/h). You must stop

when you see a school bus with the indicators on.
In Canada, distances are indicated in kilometers, in Alaska in miles. Side roads are commonly unsurfaced – watch out for airborne gravel.

When to go:
The best time to go is from mid-May to late September. The road into Denali National Park is only open from mid-June.

Information:
Alaska general:
www.alaska.com
www.travelalaska.com
Ferries in Alaska:
Alaska Marine Highway
www.dot.state.ak.us/amhs
Alaska Ferry
www.akferry.org
National Parks:
www.us-national-parks.net

The terrace on the State Office Building offers the best view of Juneau, the straits, and Douglas Island, which lies just off the coast. An excursion to Mendenhall Glacier, about 20 km (13 miles) north of town, is a must. This glacier calves out of the 10,000-sq-km (3,650-sq-mi) Juneau Icefield, with a face 2.5 km (1.6 miles) long where it breaks off into the lake.

The visitor center offers comprehensive documentation on the glacier, and you can go hiking along its edges.

❷ Glacier Bay National Park You should not leave Juneau without taking a boat or plane trip to this national park 85 km (53 miles) away. Giant glaciers detach themselves directly into the sea here, and giant ice floes descend from mountains that tower above 4,000 m (13,000 ft). No fewer than sixteen glaciers terminate in this large bay,

which was completely covered in pack ice as recently as a hundred years ago. Since then, the ice has receded by more than 100 km (62 miles), faster than anywhere else on earth.

These days, seals lounge on the ice floes of Glacier Bay, and humpback whales and orcas ply the chilly waters, breaching, hunting, and carrying on.

From mid-May to mid-September you can take day trips and longer excursions both by boat and by air from Juneau to Gustavus, a small settlement at the entrance to this huge bay. From Haines or Skagway you can also take scenic flights over Glacier Bay. The first leg on our route to the north is completed by boat.

❸ Haines This town at the northern end of Lynn Canal used to be a Chilkat settlement. The Chilkats are a sub-tribe of the Tlingit Indians who traveled along the Northwest Coast upwards behind the receding glaciers . Worth seeing are the old

military outpost "Fort William H. Seward", the Chilkat Center and a reconstructed Tlingit tribal house.

Before carrying on, you should take the ferry across to Skagway (1 hour) at the end of Taiya Inlet and visit the former gold-diggers' settlement there.

❹ Skagway When gold was discovered on the Klondike River in October 1897, the population of Skagway grew to more than 20,000 almost overnight as most gold seekers landed here before hiking along the Chilkoot Trail to the Yukon River. Between 1897 and 1898, a Wild-West-style town developed

1 Mendenhall Glacier feeds off the massive Juneau Icefield (10,000 sq km/ 3,860 sq mi). Its glacial tongue is 2.5 km (1.6 miles) wide.

2 Haines is located at the end of Inside Passage, where the Chilkat River flows into Lynn Canal, a fjord that stretches 145 km (90 miles).

Glacier Bay gives you a view into the history of the North American continent. Just one hundred years ago, the giant bay in which sixteen glaciers calve was completely covered in ice. Since the end of the 19th century, however, the ice sheet has been retreating rapidly

as it did at the end of the Ice Age – but over a significantly shorter time span. Today, the bay is a meeting place for humpbacks, killer whales, walruses, and seals. To experience the true raw beauty of the region, charter a boat or plane from Juneau,

1

that has remained almost intact to this day. The town's Broadway Street is now a historical park. You can't miss the impressive Arctic Brotherhood building, with more than 20,000 wooden sticks decorating its facade, or the Red Onion Saloon, where the floor is still covered in sawdust. Every evening a play is performed in Eagles Hall, bringing the time of the gold diggers to life.

Although the gold rush was past its peak by 1900, a narrow-gauge railway was constructed in that year across White Pass, between Skagway and Whitehorse. The most scenic stretch, up to White Pass at 889 m (2,917 ft), is now maintained as a heritage railway and will give you some unforgettable views of this wild and romantic landscape. The different climate zones produce myriad vegetation, ranging from wet coastal forests right up to alpine tundras at the top of the pass.

⑤ Haines Highway/Haines Junction From Haines, the Haines Highway winds its way across the foothills of the Alsek Range. At Porcupine it crosses the border into Canadian British Columbia, and just after that you get to Chilkat Pass at an altitude of 1,065 m (3,494 ft).

West of the road, the Tatshenshini-Alsek Preserve connects Glacier Bay National Park to the south and Kluane National Park in the north.

Heading north, the nature reserve joins Wrangell-St Elias National Park back in Alaska. People on both sides of the border have worked together to create this park, the largest protected area on the North American continent. As the crow flies, it stretches more than 700 km (435 miles) from Gustavus at the southern tip of Glacier Bay National Park to Richardson Highway in the north. There are no roads anywhere in the park, only mountains up to 6,000 m (19,500 ft), massive glaciers, and pristine forests.

The town of Haines Junction has 500 inhabitants and originally developed from what was once

2

a soldiers' camp during the construction of the Alaska Highway. Here, the Haines Highway meets the Alaska Highway coming from Whitehorse, which itself is also worth an extra detour (111 km/69 miles).

⑥ Whitehorse This is where the exhausted gold diggers would arrive after crossing White Pass. Downriver from the large rapids they were able to take a paddle steamer further north along the Yukon River.

When the Alaska Highway was being built, Whitehorse developed into the largest settlement in the territory.

Today, at the McBride Museum you can see old gold-digging and mining equipment as well as First Nations arts and crafts. Old Log Church, built in 1900, houses an exhibition on the Yukon Territory's missionary history. The paddle steamer permanently moored at the southern end of Second Avenue is called the "SS Klondike". During the

There are very few places on the Alaska Highway to access Kluane National Park on foot, and you can never go any further than to the foot of the icy giants. As an alternative, it is well worth taking a scenic flight across this breathtaking mountain landscape. Small aircraft take off from the town of Burwash at the northern end of Lake Kluane.

Or maybe you are into old ghost towns? At the eastern end of Lake Kluane, a short access road takes you down to Silver City on the lakeshore. This old trading post, long since abandoned, re-

gold rush, it regularly plied the Yukon between Whitehorse and Dawson City.

Back at Haines Junction you take the Alaska Highway to Kluane Lake at the eastern end of Kluane National Park.

⑦ Kluane National Park
North of Haines Junction the road rises up to Bear Creek Summit at 997 m (3,271 ft) shortly before coming to Boutillier Summit at 1,000 m (3,281 ft). Just beneath the pass is Kluane

Lake, the largest lake in the Yukon Territory at 400 sq km (155 sq mi). The highway runs along its western shore.

The national park covers an area of 22,000 sq km (8,492 sq mi) and has plenty of untouched nature including high peaks, huge glaciers, and sub-Arctic vegetation. At 5,959 m (19,551 ft), Mount Logan is Canada's highest mountain.

Down at more "moderate" altitudes there are large populations of black bears, brown

bears, wolves, mountain sheep, caribou, and elk. Further to the west are the inaccessible Icefield Ranges. From the air these look something like a giant lunar landscape made of ice and snow.

Given its extraordinary dimensions, it is hardly surprising that Kluane National Park was declared a UNESCO World Heritage Site as early as 1980, alongside Wrangell-St Elias Park, which borders it to the west.

1 The icy world of Wrangell-St Elias National Park is only visible from a helicopter or glacier plane.

2 A reflection of Mount Huxley (3,828 m/12,560 ft) in a temporarily ice-free pond in Wrangell-St Elias National Park.

3 Ice on lakes such as Kathleen Lake in Kluane National Park does not melt until late in the spring.

Wonder Lake is right in the center of Denali National Park. It is 6 km (4 miles) long and 85 m (280 ft) deep, and has a wealth of fish including lake trout, pike, and eels. The imposing Mount McKinley in the background rises 6,194 m (21,320 ft) into a cloudless blue sky above.

the lake. It is not only the highest mountain in North America, it is a full 5,500 m (18,000 ft) above the plateau from which it rises, far higher than Mount Everest, the tallest mountain in the world, rises above its base. Native Americans call it Denali – the Great One.

1

ally does give you that "ghost-town" feel.

From Burwash Landing, the Alaska Highway winds its lonely way through a largely pristine landscape of mountains, forests, and tundra, all in seemingly endless repetition. Towards the west there are some impressive views of the mighty St Elias Mountains, Canada's highest mountain range. The road first crosses Donjek River, then White River and finally, just before you get to the Alaskan border, there is Beaver Creek, Canada's west-ernmost settlement with rough-ly 100 inhabitants.

In October 1942 the last section of the Alaska Highway was com-pleted here.

8 Tok Junction Our first stop back in Alaska is Tetlin Junction, and after another 19 km (12 miles) you get to the small town of Tok.

Founded in 1942 as a soldier's camp when the Alaska Highway was being built, Tok is consid-ered to be the gateway to Alas-ka. From here, Fairbanks and Anchorage are the same dis-tance away.

The visitor center at the cross-roads has an interesting exhibi-tion of stuffed animals from Alaska, and Tok is also a center for husky breeding. Dog-sled races start here in winter and in the summer you can see teams training on a 20-km (12-mile) track that runs parallel to the Alaska Highway.

From Tok Junction, the remain-ing 111 m (69 miles) of the Alas-ka Highway follow the mighty Tanana River. The broad flood plains on either side of the road remind us that the glaciers of the Alaska Range once extend-ed all the way down to here.

9 Delta Junction We have now reached the northern end of the 2,300-km (1,430-mile) Alaska Highway. The terminus is located at the junction with

2

Richardson Highway, where a visitors center offers all kinds of information about the construc-tion of the highway and the Trans-Alaska Pipeline.

At Delta Junction the pipeline crosses the Tanana River in a wide arc and it is quite a sight in its own right. Its construction became a necessity when, in 1968, the USA's largest oil fields were discovered north of the

Brooks Range in Prudhoe Bay. Starting in March 1975, about 22,000 workers were involved in the two-year construction of the line, which now extends 1,280 km (795 miles) straight through the heart of the penninsula and down to the port city of Valdez. Half the pipeline was installed underground and the rest – nearly 700 km (435 miles) of it – is supported by a system of

78,000 stilts. The pipeline has to be continuously cooled in order to keep the 60°C (140°F) oil from destroying it. Another 153 km (95 miles) down Alaska's oldest highway, the Richardson Highway, you come to Fairbanks.

⑩ Fairbanks This city on the Tanana River owes its existence to the 1903 gold rush. Within seven years 11,000 people had set up shop on its primitive campsite. During World War II, large military settlements and the construction of the Alaska Highway fostered an economic boom in the town. After 1974 the construction headquarters of the Trans-Alaska Pipeline were relocated here. Today, Fairbanks is a modern city.

The Otto William Geist Museum tells you everything about the history and culture of Alaska's indigenous people.

Before carrying on, take the opportunity to relax and enjoy Chena Hot Springs about 100 km (62 miles) east of the city.

⑪ Denali National Park Our next destination is the highlight of the whole trip – Denali National Park. To get there take the George Parks Highway from Riley Creek. If you want to see the 24,000 sq km (9,265 sq mi) of the park and the highest mountain in North America (Mount McKinley), you have to take one of the shuttle buses operated by the park authority. These regularly run the 140 km (87 miles) into the park to Kantishna at Wonder Lake. The trip takes eleven hours, and if you picked a sunny day you will even get a glimpse of Denali, the High One, at a glorious 6,194 m (20,323 ft). The road runs through some hilly tundra with mountains in the 2,000 m (6,560 ft) range.

At the park headquarters you can visit the dog pens where the park rangers breed huskies. During the summer they train them as sled dogs for winter, when that is the only mode of transport allowed in the park.

The George Parks Highway now takes us towards Anchorage. Roughly halfway along it you get to the picture-book town of Talkeetna. You get yet another view of Denali from here. It is also the take-off point for scenic flights around the national park.

⑫ Eklutna About 33 km (20 miles) outside Anchorage you pass the Native American village of Eklutna. St Nicholas Russian Orthodox Church is oddly located right in the middle of a Native American Cemetery. There is also a Siberian chapel.

Bright wooden houses are set on the graves here, their eaves lavishly decorated with wood-carvings. The Native Americans believe they house the spirits of the dead. Just south of Eagle River, it is worth taking a 20-km (13-mile) detour to visit Chugach State Park. From here you can follow hiking trails to the glaciers further up country.

1 Denali (Mount McKinley) has a higher rise than Mount Everest: 5,500 m (18,000 ft). The peak is at 6,194 m (20,323 ft) above sea level.

2 A solitary grizzly bear roaming the autumnal tundra in search of food.

1

Denali

Mount McKinley towers above the jagged peaks of the Alaska Range, and at 6,194 m (20,321 ft) is the highest point in the United States. The Native Americans called it "Denali", the "High One", and since 1980 the national park has taken the same name.

In 1980, the former Mount McKinley National Park was extended to include the southern side of the mountain as well as a few peaks in the Kichatna Mountains. Mount McKinley, and the glaciers, forests, and lakes that come with it, was first placed under protection in 1917.

In those days there was no road between Anchorage and Fairbanks and only a few adventurous souls could enjoy the park's beauty; but once the Denali Highway was completed in 1957, tourists discovered Mount McKinley and flocked to this mighty mountain in the heart of the Alaska Range. However, even this flood of tourists has been unable to change Denali National Park's unspoilt scenery, a state of affairs principally due to the ban on private cars, which may drive no further than the Savage River, 18 km (11 miles) from the Visitor Center. In summer you can only continue on foot or take one of the shuttle buses connecting Riley Creek Visitor Center with Wonder Lake, 136 km (84 miles) further on, from which there is a stunning view of Mount McKinley. The return bus journey to Wonder Lake takes about 11 hours, and you can ask to be dropped off en route. Good places to visit on the way include the Tklanika River, a typical glaciated river in the Alaska Range; Sable Pass, where grizzly bears can often be observed in the soft tundra grass; and Highway Pass, with its breathtaking view of South Peak and other snow-capped summits.

1 In the park you will find 430 species of wild flowers; grizzly bears, elks and caribous.

⑬ Anchorage This city owes its existence to the construction of the railway line between Fairbanks and the ice-free port of Seward on the Kenai Peninsula. Originally a builders' settlement established in 1914, Anchorage eventually developed into a modern aviation hub. It is now home to half of Alaska's entire population. As you enter the city via Glenn Highway you'll see thousands of aircraft of small and medium size parked at Merill Field. Lake Hood is one of the largest hydroplane airports in the world.

⑭ Portage After 60 km (37 miles) on Seward Highway, you come to this town at the end of Turnagain Bay. At Girdwood,

just before you get to Portage, is Alaska's northernmost alpine ski resort, at Mount Alyeska (1,201 m/3,940 ft). Take a chairlift up to 610 m (2,000 ft) and enjoy a view of the Chugach Mountain Range glaciers.
At the end of the bay is Portage Lake. There are usually some oddly shaped ice floes bobbing on its deep-blue waters. On the far side, Portage Glacier drops into the lake like a giant wall.

⑮ Seward The natural deep-water port here is the economic engine of this town. The most important annual event is the Silver Salmon Derby in August, a salmon-fishing competition. You'll most likely want to check the Kenai Fjords National Park

Visitor Center for information on the 780-sq-km (300-sq-mi) Harding Icefield.
Leaving Kenai you first take Seward Highway back towards Anchorage before turning onto Sterling Highway at Moose Pass.

⑯ Kenai In 1791 the Russians built their second Alaskan settlement here. After 1846 it became the center of the Russian Orthodox Church in Alaska. The Holy Assumption Church and its three onion-domed spires are icons of the period, along with an old bible. The bible, like the other equipment in the church, was brought to Alaska from Siberia. The Kenai Peninsula is home to both the Sargent Icefield and Harding Icefields and

numerous glaciers that spawn off them.

⑰ Homer On the south-west side of the Kenai Peninisula is the "Halibut Capital", Homer. In this town at the end of Sterling Highway, it's all about fish. A giant fleet of vessels is always ready to set off for the next catch. If you are into fishing, you can rent a boat here or book one of the numerous deep-sea fishing tours.

1 Portage Glacier calving into the lake of the same name all year round.

2 The snowy mountains behind the Anchorage Skyline. The wilderness starts right outside the city.

Kodiak Island This island is home to the famous Kodiak brown bears, the largest carnivorous land animal in the world. They can weigh up to 500 kg (1,100 lbs).

Kenai Peninsula There are some large lakes on this mountainous peninsula, which extends 200 km (135 miles) into the Gulf of Alaska.

Homer This port town on the Kenai Peninsula at the end of Highway 1 is a mecca for deep-sea fishermen.

Denali National Park The heart of this park (24,000 sq km/9,265 sq mi) is Denali (Mount McKinley) at 6,194 m (20,323 ft). There are about 430 species of wildflowers here along with grizzlies, moose, and caribou.

Anchorage The skyline of this boom town looks a lot like other American cities. Half of Alaska's population lives here and its airport is the eighth largest in the USA. Planes are an indispensable mode of transport in the remote regions here. Many people even have their own.

Chena Hot Springs This oasis of relaxation is located 100 km (62 miles) east of Fairbanks on Steese Highway amid the dense forests of the Chena Valley. A small access road takes you to the sulphur springs where you can enjoy the healing waters. But be careful of any black bears that might be in the car park.

Portage Glacier This glacier south of Anchorage has a giant wall calving right into Portage Lake. Below the green mountains, bizarrely shaped ice floes with a bluish hue float aimlessly on the lake.

Wrangell-St Elias National Park Two mountain ranges are protected by this park – the volcanic Wrangell Mountains and the St Elias Mountains with the striking Mount St Elias (5,489 m/18,009 ft).

Kluane National Park Huge glaciers, sub-Arctic vegetation, bears, wolves, caribou, and moose are all integral elements of this park in the Yukon Territory around Mount Logan (5,959 m/19,551 ft).

Glacier Bay National Park In Alaska's southernmost national park there are no fewer than sixteen glaciers terminating in Glacier Bay. The bay is over 100 km (62 miles) long and has only been free of ice for the last 100 years.

Mendenhall Glacier This glacier, 20 km (13 miles) north of Juneau, Alaska's capital, is part of the gigantic Juneau Icefield, which measures almost 10,000 sq km (3,860 sq mi). The glacier tongue calves at a width of 2.5 km (1.6 miles) into Mendenhall Lake.

Haines This town at the mouth of the Chilkat River is an area where the Native Americans are famous for their totem poles.

Canada

On the Trans-Canada Highway from Vancouver to the Great Lakes

Built in 1962, the Trans-Canada Highway sweeps through Canada, the second-largest country on earth, for 7,821 km (4,860 miles). The western section, running from Vancouver Island to Lake Superior, passes through a variety of scenery, ranging from rainforest on the Pacific coast and magnificent national parks in the Rocky Mountains, through endless prairies to the "shining waters", as the Iroquois called the Great Lakes.

A journey from west to east through south-western Canada will take you through four different kinds of scenery, with the first, the 800-km (500-mile) expanse of the Rocky Mountains, being the most impressive. The greatest concentration of national parks is also to be found here, around the peaks of Jasper and Banff. Fertile, sedimentary soil abounds where the Great Plains of East Alberta, Saskatchewan, and West Manitoba join the Rocky Mountains to the east; these plains are all that remain of the Ice Age lakes that once reached as far as the prairies of America. The Canadian Shield, a pre-Cambrian volcanic formation consisting of some of the earth's oldest rocks, begins east of the Great Plains, near Winnepeg. Parts of it are 3.6 million years old. Its current form was shaped by Ice Age glaciers, which also gouged many lakes between the low granite peaks. The plain of the St Lawrence River, which begins near the Great Lakes in southern Ontario, exhibits similar glacial features.

Canada is famous for its endless forests, which cover more than half the country (4.5 million sq

A First Nations dancer with a headdress and ceremonial garb.

Lake Superior is the westernmost navigable lake for St Lawrence River traffic.

The Royal Canadian Mounted Police proudly display their traditional scarlet jackets on horseback. The police unit has a long tradition, having been founded in 1874.

km/1.75 million sq mi). With the exception of a few areas in the south, this is all evergreen forest, made up of larch, Douglas fir, spruce, and pine. In the far west, there used to be expanses of rainforest with giant Douglas firs, Sitka spruce, and Canadian hemlock. How things looked before the days of the chainsaw and deforestation by the logging companies is amply demonstrated in the Pacific Rim National Park on the west coast of Vancouver Island, the starting point of the Trans-Canada Highway.

The montane forest of the Coastal Mountains and the Rocky Mountains, stretching out further to the east, is home to many wild creatures, including moose, black and brown bear, red deer, Dall sheep, and moun-tain goats, all of which you might be able to spot from the car, if you are lucky.

As paradoxical as it might seem, the closest approximation to the ideal of Canada's wilderness is to be found in the national parks. There are as many as seven to be found along the border between British Columbia and Alberta, including the Mount Revelstoke, Glacier, Yoho, Banff, and Jasper National Parks. The last three, which make up the Canadian Rocky Moun-tains National Park, have been declared a UNESCO World Heritage Site. Despite preserving nature in the raw, Canadian national parks have an excellent infrastructure, including dedicated scenic routes as well as marked hiking paths and camping grounds in the most remote places.

Sunrise over Mount Assiniboine Provincial Park near Calgary.

Canada is a feast of high mountains, giant glaciers, virgin forests, endless wheatfields, and incomparable lakes; there are mountain villages and vibrant cities, too, and all of these are to be found along the 4,000-km (2,485-mile) stretch of the Trans-Canada Highway between Victoria and the Great Lakes.

Kilometer 0 of the Trans-Canada Highway (Highway 1) is located at the south-western end of Beacon Hill Park in Victoria on Vancouver Island. Ferries running between Swartz Bay, about 30 km (19 miles) north of Victoria, and Tsawwassen, south of Vancouver, provide a link to the mainland across Georgia Bay.

1 Vancouver (see pages 48). From Vancouver, follow Highway 99 (also known as the "Sea to Sky Highway") along Burrard Inlet. All along the way are stop-off points offering one marvelous view after another. The route from the Pacific to the mountains of Garibaldi Provincial Park crosses five vegetation zones.

2 Garibaldi Provincial Park About 80 km (50 miles) north of Vancouver, Garibaldi Provincial Park – whose highest point is Mount Garibaldi at 2,678 m (8,786 ft) – covers an area of 1,950 sq km (750 sq mi). The ski resort of Whistler has been spreading across Blackcomb Mountain on the northern edge of the park since the 1960s. After 310 km (190 miles), the Sea to Sky Highway reaches its northern end at Lillouet; 75 km (46 miles) further on, Highway 99 meets Highway 97, which will take you past Kamloops Lake into Canada's "Sunshine Capital".

3 Kamloops The Shuswap Indians once called the town Cumloops ("where the waters meet"),

Travel Information

Route profile
Route length: approx. 4,000 km (2,500 miles)
Time required: 4 weeks
Start: Victoria or Vancouver
Destination: Sault Ste Marie
Route (main locations): Vancouver, Revelstoke, Lake Louise, Banff, Calgary, Regina, Winnipeg, Sault Ste Marie

Traffic information:
Long stretches of the Trans-Canada Highway (TCH) are a similar standard to European motorways, although some sections are only two-lane. There are two marked routes through the prairies: in Portage la Prairie the southern route (described here) runs from Regina via Calgary into the Rocky Mountains; the northern route – the Yellowhead Highway (Hwy 16) – runs via Saskatoon and Edmonton to Jasper National Park. The Highway is consistently signposted with a green and white maple leaf.

Information:
TCH: *www.transcanadahighway.com*
British Columbia: *www.hellobc.com*
Alberta: *www.travelalberta.com*
Saskatchewan: *www.sasktourism.com*
Manitoba: *www.travelmanitoba.com*
Ontario: *www.ontariotravel.net*

as it stands at the confluence of the North and South Thompsons. The Secwepmec Native Heritage Park, a reconstructed First Nations village, will tell you everything you need to know about

2

Glacier National Park The park boasts any number of pristine high peaks, with wild and jagged glaciated summits reaching heights of 3,390 m (11,120 ft). Up to 20 m (66 ft) of snowfall can be expected annually on the park's 422 glaciers, and 10% of the park is covered with snow and ice throughout the year. Until 1962, when the Trans-Canada Highway was built, the park was only accessible by rail. The scenic route crosses the park for 50 km (31 miles) and almost all of the park's hiking routes begin from this road. Loop Brook Interpretive Trail (1.6 km/1 mile) includes some beautiful views.

Yoho National Park The little town of Golden is the gateway to this national park on the western slopes of the Rockies. From Highway 1, which crosses the park, there is a narrow side-road leading down into the Yoho Valley, which ends at the impressive 254-m (830-ft)

Takakkaw Falls. The end of the valley is surrounded by the impressive icefields of Mount Yoho, Mount Gordon, and Mount Daly, and above Mount Field there lies the Burgess Shale, where spectacular fossil finds have provided important insights into the flora and fauna of the Cambrian period; for all these reasons, Yoho National Park has been declared a UNESCO World Heritage Site. The observation terrace has a spectacular view of the Yoho Valley and the Spiral Tunnel. Highway 1 crosses Kicking Horse pass at a height of 1,627 m (5,330 ft) before descending into Banff National Park on the way to Lake Louise.

1 Lying between the mountains and the lakes, Vancouver is one of the world's most beautiful cities.

2 Mount Revelstoke National Park is noted for its lush Alpine flower meadows.

the Shuswap tribe. Heading further eastwards on Highway 1, it is worth taking a detour to Monte Creek to visit the O'-Keefe Historic Ranch of 1867, before entering the Rocky Mountains and the first of a series of national parks.

Mount Revelstoke National Park The little town of Revel-stoke is the starting point for exploring the eponymous

national park. There are two routes through the park: the "Meadows in the Sky Parkway" is 26 km (16 miles) long and takes you to Mount Revelstoke (1,943 m /6,375 ft), although the last stretch must be covered by a shuttle bus taking you to Balsam Lake.
The alternative is the mountain road over Rogers Pass (1,327 m/4,354 ft), one of the world's most spectacular passes.

The turquoise-coloured water of Garibaldi Lake provides a beautiful contrast against the background of the dark and jagged mountain ranges. On the 9 km (5.59-mile) Garibaldi Lake Trek you can discover the fascinating landscape of the park by hiking. Nestled between

alpine mountains and a spectacular glacier, Garibaldi Lake is one of the most scenic destinations in British Columbia. The campsite at Garibaldi Lake is popular in the summer and can be a great point to access longer hikes to Black Tusk or Panorama Ridge.

Vancouver

With a population of some 2 million, Vancouver is British Columbia's largest city. The core of the town lies on a peninsula, and a unique panorama is formed by the Pacific bays that reach deep inland on one side and the snowcapped peaks of the surrounding Coast Mountains on the other.

Its location is not the only reason Vancouver is considered one of the most beautiful cities in the world; modern shopping malls and skyscrapers offer a charming contrast to the more traditional districts of the city, and Gastown, the old quarter, has been a conservation area since 1971. The steam clock on the corner of Cambie and Water Street, which has become a symbol of the new Gastown, has weights which are raised up every five minutes by a steam engine. Canada Place on Burrad Inlet, a futuristic-looking convention complex with a luxury hotel and other amenities, is worth a visit and the art deco Cathedral Palace office tower, built in 1991, has become a new symbol of the city.

However, the heart of the city is at Robson Square, where a man-made waterfall splashes through lush vegetation amid the concrete, a green island between modern office blocks and historic buildings. Granville Square and the Pacific Railroad station, where there is a revolving restaurant with a fantastic view of the city, are also worth a visit. North America's second-largest Chinatown has grown up east of the old quarter and the streets are a riot of neon signs with Chinese characters, jewelers, souvenir sellers, bookstores, laundries, fantastic dragons, and porches and telephone kiosks decorated with pagodas. A visible sign of the close relationship between the Canadians and the Chinese is the classical garden of Dr Sun Yat-Sen, laid out behind the Cultural Centre by Chinese artisans from Suzhou in Vancouver, a peaceful oasis in the chaos of the city.

1 The view of the Vancouver skyline from the quayside.

7 Lake Louise The Stoney Indians called Lake Louise the "lake of little fishes" and its azure waters reflect Mount Victoria, whose glaciers stretch almost from the shores of the lake to a summit of 3,469 m (11,350 ft). The Grand Hotel Château Lake Louise, situated at the top of a terminal moraine, is no less impressive.

The top station of the cable car on Mount Whitehorn (2,034 m/ 6,675 ft) has a magnificent view of Lake Louise, Victoria Glacier, and the rows of peaks forming the Continental Divide.

A 13-km (8-mile) mountain road leads to the peace of Lake Moraine in the romantic Valley of the Ten Peaks; to reach Banff, 50 km (31 miles) away, visitors should take the Bow Valley Parkway (1A), which runs parallel to the Trans-Canada Highway and offers better chances to observe wildlife.

8 Banff National Park The magnificent mountain scenery of Canada's oldest national park boasts peaks rising to 3,500 m (11,500 ft), glaciers, Alpine meadows, and waterfalls. The main attractions are its lakes and caves, however, such as Castle-guard Caves. Banff, at the southern end of the park, is famed for its hot springs and historic hotels, such as the Banff Springs Hotel. The Banff Park Museum and the Whyte Museum of the Canadian Rockies are dedicated to the flora and fauna of the surrounding parks. The best views are from Mount Norquai (2,135 m/7,005 ft) and Sulphur Mountain (2,270 m/7,450 ft), both of which are accessible by cable car. The next whiff of city air is not for another 140 km (87 miles) to the east, at Calgary.

9 Calgary The "Manhattan of the Prairies" grew up out of a market town for farmers and

1 The glittering turquoise of Peyto Lake in Banff National Park.

2 The Takakkaw Falls in Yoho National Park, where meltwater from the Daly Glacier falls from a height of 254 m (835 ft).

1

ranchers. Nowadays, the best view over this big, modern city is from the 191-m (625-ft) Calgary Tower. The high point of the year comes in July with the Stampede, the greatest cowboy show on earth, and all roads in the 24-ha (60-acre) Stampede Park, on a bend in the Elbow River, lead to the Saddledome, which seats almost 20,000 people. Fort Calgary Historic Park, situated at the confluence of the Elbow and Bow Rivers, commemorates the first post established by the North West Mounted Police (NWMP) in 1875. Still scarlet-clad, they are now called the Royal Canadian Mounted Police (RCMP), and during the summer they perform a daily presentation of their proud past as "living history". Calgary Zoo and Prehistoric Park on St George's Island in the river is worth visiting. The prehistoric theme park has models of dinosaurs that lived in southwestern Canada.

⑩ Dinosaur Provincial Park About 200 km (125 miles) east of Calgary on Highway 1 you reach Brooks, which takes you on a detour to the Dinosaur Provincial Park. The park's scenic prairies and badlands are impressive, but the main attractions are the dinosaur fossils that have been found here (see left sidebar).

⑪ Cypress Hills Interprovincial Park A winding 200-km (125-mile) detour through the Cypress Hills provides for an attractive change from the much bigger Highway 1. Fifty km (31 miles) east of Medicine Hat, Highway 41 turns south towards the spa town of Elkwater. The Blackfoot tribe called this uniquely varied plateau and mountain landscape Ketewius Netumoo, meaning "the hills that shouldn't be". Fort Walsh National Historic Park, a reconstructed fort telling the story of the NWMP and the original na-

2

tive population, is not too far from Elkwater. Farewell's Trading Post is one of the infamous "whisky forts" where unscrupulous whisky traders would barter alcohol with the First Nations people for skins and furs. The network of traders was broken only with the involvement of the Mounties, today the Royal Canadian Mounted Police, which still rides on horseback.

Highway 21 leads back to Highway 1 via Maple Creek.
Saskatchewan's prairie scenery takes on quite different shades, depending on the season: the blue and yellow of the flax and rape fields predominate in the early summer, and the wheat is golden in late summer. Huge red grain silos – the "cathedrals of the prairie" – can be seen from a distance.

3

4

⑫ Regina Saskatchewan's capital is situated in the middle of endless wheatfields, and even today the Saskatchewan Wheat Pool, one of the world's largest wheat producers, has its headquarters here. Regina's expansion began in 1882 with the construction of the Canadian Pacific Railroad, and the RCMP, the successor to the NWMP, was also based here until 1920. The RCMP's national training academy, which has its own museum, is still on Dewdney Avenue. The Sergeant Major's Parade (daily Monday–Friday) and the evening Sunset Retreat Ceremony (every Tuesday in July and August) always draw a crowd. Wascana Lake, a man-made lake in the middle of the city, and its 1,000 ha (2,400 acres) of grounds together form one of the largest municipal parks in the world. The Royal Saskatchewan Museum has geological and paleontological exhibits, as well as examples of dinosaurs and finds from First Nations culture. The Regina Plains Museum, telling the story of the Plains Indians and their encounters with the first white settlers, is the right place for historians and enthusiasts.

⑬ Brandon This wheat town, about 300 km (185 miles) further east on the Assiniboine River, is Manitoba's second-largest city. The B.J. Hales Museum of Natural History has a display of more than 200 stuffed local bird species. Part of the museum is also dedicated to local First Nations culture. It is worth making a detour to visit the steep rock formations and rolling prairies of the Riding Mountain National Park, about 100 km (62 miles) north of Brandon. There are another 200 km (124 miles) of end- less wheatfields to be passed on Highway 1 before you reach Portage La Prairie, just before Winnepeg.

⑭ Portage La Prairie The Fort la Reine Museum and Pioneer Village, an open-air museum with 25 buildings, is to be found at the junction of Highways 1 and 26, where you can visit a schoolhouse, church, shops, and

1 Calgary, once a cattle ranchers' market town, now boasts an impressive skyline.

2 When the First Nations ruled the prairies, there were no horses; these arrived only with the coming of the white man.

3 The still waters of Lake Manitoba, north-west of Winnipeg.

4 Many waterfowl, such as the bald eagle, have found a home on the shores of Lake Winnipeg.

Mountains, glaciers, caves, and lakes – national and provincial parks in the Rockies

The Canadian section of the Rocky Mountains is one of North America's most striking mountainous areas and is covered by a string of National and Provincial Parks, which were declared World Heritage Sites in 1984 and 1990 respectively.

□UNESCO's decision to include the National Parks of Jasper, Banff, Yoho, and Kootenay and the Provincial Parks of Mount Assiniboine, Mount Robson, and Hamber as World Heritage Sites rested on their geological significance, conservation of the local rare flora and fauna, and the extraordinary beauty of the scenery. The important fossil site at Burgess Shale in Yoho National Park was also a contributory factor.

Visitors to the parks are greeted by imposing mountain scenery, with peaks rising to 3,500 m (11,600 ft), glaciers, ice fields, waterfalls, canyons, caves, hot springs, and Alpine meadows. Three zones of vegetation have formed, according to their elevation: montane forest, sub-Alpine forest, and a zone of Alpine tundra. Influenced by its milder, Pacific climate, the south-western tip of Kootenay Park has some semi-arid features. Trees common here include hemlock pines, Douglas firs, cedars, pines, and spruce. Many different animals have been observed here, including marmots, beavers, deer, moose, mountain goats, bighorn sheep, coyotes, wolves, lynx, pumas, black and grizzly bears, and many species of birds.

The infrastructure in this beautiful landscape is perfectly arranged: there are thousands of miles of winding but well-maintained scenic routes which cross spectacular passes and provide links to hiking trails and accommodation suited to every level of comfort.

1 A striking view of the summit of Mount Assiniboine, which has been called Canada's Matterhorn. Mount Assiniboine Provincial Park in Alberta is part of the Canadian Rocky Mountain UNESCO World Heritage Site.

2 At 3,954 m (12,972 ft), Mount Robson, situated in the provincial park of the same name, is the highest point in the Canadian Rocky Mountains. Its massive, angular form looms over the valleys at its feet.

houses from the time of the settlers. The museum and the village commemorate the 18th century, when Portage La Prairie was an important French trading post; the original fort was built by the French explorer Pierre Gaultier de la Vérendrye in 1738. The museum also has a comprehensive section devoted to the railroad, and exhibits include a private railway carriage from 1882 which once belonged to Sir William van Horne, the director of the Canadian Pacific Railway Company.

⓯ Winnipeg Situated to the south of Lake Manitoba and Lake Winnipeg, Manitoba's capital city represents the geographical halfway point of the Trans-Canada Highway between the Pacific and the Atlantic. Once called "win nipi" ("muddy waters") by the local population, Canada's eighth-largest city is now home to more than three dozen ethnic groups, who all arrived at the beginning of the 20th century as the transcontinental railroad opened up the west of this gigantic country.

Winnipeg's core stretches along the north bank of the Assiniboine River to its confluence with the Red River. The engine sheds and marshaling yards around Union Station, a beaux arts building from 1911, have been turned into a heritage park and some fortifications dating back to the Northwest Company and the Hudson's Bay Company have been preserved. The city's most prominent building is the Legislative Building (1919), whose mighty cupola is the seat of the 4-m (13-ft) "Golden Boy".

Winnipeg Art Gallery has one of the best collections of Inuit art. The Manitoba Museum of Man

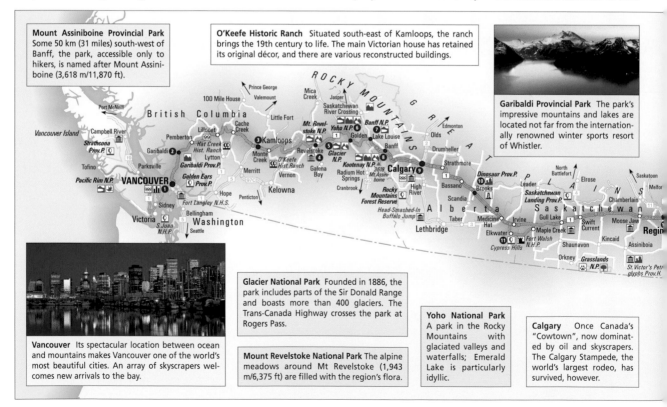

Mount Assiniboine Provincial Park Some 50 km (31 miles) south-west of Banff, the park, accessible only to hikers, is named after Mount Assiniboine (3,618 m/11,870 ft).

O'Keefe Historic Ranch Situated south-east of Kamloops, the ranch brings the 19th century to life. The main Victorian house has retained its original décor, and there are various reconstructed buildings.

Garibaldi Provincial Park The park's impressive mountains and lakes are located not far from the internationally renowned winter sports resort of Whistler.

Vancouver Its spectacular location between ocean and mountains makes Vancouver one of the world's most beautiful cities. An array of skyscrapers welcomes new arrivals to the bay.

Glacier National Park Founded in 1886, the park includes parts of the Sir Donald Range and boasts more than 400 glaciers. The Trans-Canada Highway crosses the park at Rogers Pass.

Mount Revelstoke National Park The alpine meadows around Mt Revelstoke (1,943 m/6,375 ft) are filled with the region's flora.

Yoho National Park A park in the Rocky Mountains with glaciated valleys and waterfalls; Emerald Lake is particularly idyllic.

Calgary Once Canada's "Cowtown", now dominated by oil and skyscrapers. The Calgary Stampede, the world's largest rodeo, has survived, however.

scenery. There are just a few small towns on the highway, which is now entering a large region of lakes.

At Vermilion Bay, the highway swings north into Pakwash Provincial Park and on to Red Lake and the Woodland Caribou Provincial Park. Further to the east you can take a detour to the heavenly lakes of Quetico National Park.

16 Thunder Bay The westernmost port on the Great Lakes and St Lawrence River that is still accessible for ocean-going boats lies here on the northwestern shore of Lake Superior; much of the grain from the prairies passes through this point. The most important tourist attraction is Old Fort William (see sidebar), and the best view to the south of the town is to be had from the 180-m (600-ft) Scenic Lookout at

and Nature, telling the story of the Hudson's Bay Company, is also worth a visit.

Highway 1, now bearing the number 17, continues to Ontario, but not only the nomenclature is different – the Canadian Shield begins here and there is a significant change in the

Mount McKay. The effort of reaching it is rewarded with a panoramic view of the whole of Thunder Bay.

17 Sleeping Giant Provincial Park East of Thunder Bay, a peninsula juts out far into lake Superior; the "Sleeping Giant" is a series of ridges 11 km (7 miles) long and in places 335 m (1,100 ft) high at the tip of the peninsula. There is a gentle hiking path to the panoramic view at the summit. The canyons and forests of the park are home to black bears, deer, lynxes, foxes, and beavers.

From here, Highway 17 passes Ouimet Canyon, rounding the northern tip of Lake Superior on the way to White River.

18 Pukaskwa National Park South of the village of White River on the north-eastern shore of Lake Superior, this national

park is reached via Route 627. The Visitor's Center at the northern edge of the park will tell you about the flora and fauna in the virgin forest, which includes moose, bears, and wolves, and three nature paths also begin here. The 60-km (37-mile) Coastal Trail is suitable for hikers with outdoors equipment.

19 Sault Ste Marie Highway 17 crosses Lake Superior Provincial Park on the wild and romantic eastern shore before reaching its destination at Sault Ste Marie (see eastern section of "Trans-Canada Highway" Route).

1 The Pukaskwa National Park on the north bank of Lake Superior is set in extensive primeval forest landscape that remains undeveloped. Here the landscape of pine forests becomes marshland and lakes.

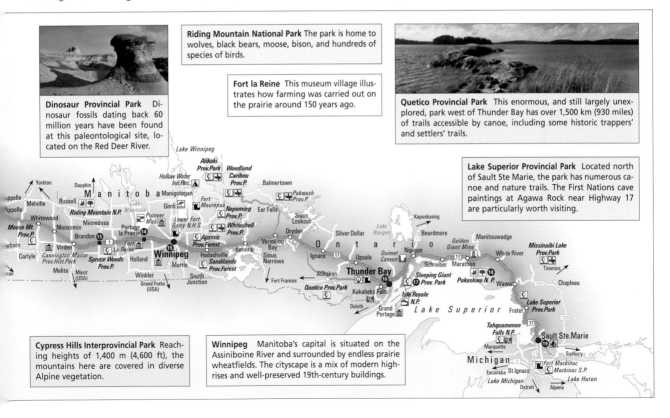

Riding Mountain National Park The park is home to wolves, black bears, moose, bison, and hundreds of species of birds.

Fort la Reine This museum village illustrates how farming was carried out on the prairie around 150 years ago.

Quetico Provincial Park This enormous, and still largely unexplored, park west of Thunder Bay has over 1,500 km (930 miles) of trails accessible by canoe, including some historic trappers' and settlers' trails.

Dinosaur Provincial Park Dinosaur fossils dating back 60 million years have been found at this paleontological site, located on the Red Deer River.

Lake Superior Provincial Park Located north of Sault Ste Marie, the park has numerous canoe and nature trails. The First Nations cave paintings at Agawa Rock near Highway 17 are particularly worth visiting.

Cypress Hills Interprovincial Park Reaching heights of 1,400 m (4,600 ft), the mountains here are covered in diverse Alpine vegetation.

Winnipeg Manitoba's capital is situated on the Assiniboine River and surrounded by endless prairie wheatfields. The cityscape is a mix of modern highrises and well-preserved 19th-century buildings.

Canada

On the Trans-Canada Highway from the Great Lakes to the Atlantic

Eastern Canada is the country's historic core and heart of the nation. The French founded North America's first cities in Québec province, while modern Canada was launched on Prince Edward Island, which means that a trip through Canada's eastern reaches is also a journey through 250 years of history, not to mention some fascinating scenery.

When journeying from west to east through south-eastern Canada, you cross three vast and diverse regions. Initially you pass through the southern edge of the Canadian Shield, consisting of Precambrian volcanic rock interspersed with myriad lakes and smooth granite domes. The stone is up to 3.6 million years old, and owes its present-day appearance to glacial activity during the Ice Age.

The St Lawrence Lowlands, which start near the Great Lakes in southern Ontario and stretch as far as the mouth of the St Lawrence River into the Atlantic, were also shaped by the Ice Age. The easternmost reaches of this vast and distinctive area are formed by the Appalachian Mountains. They are the reason the coastlines of Nova Scotia and Cape Breton Island have so many tiny bays and cliffs reminiscent of places like the west coasts of France and England.

European fishermen came to the east coast and to the St Lawrence River as early as the end of the 15th century to take advantage of the summer catch, but it was not until 1534 that Jacques

A grazing moose in Cape Breton Highlands National Park in Nova Scotia.

The thundering torrent of water at Horseshoe Falls, the Canadian side of Niagara Falls.

The Parliament Building, the "Canadian Westminster", sits proudly over the Ottawa River, near Alexandra Bridge.

Cartier flew the French flag in present-day Montréal. It was actually the beaver, or more precisely its fur, that inspired the real development of permanent settlements in this region. Since every fashionista in Europe in those days wanted to wear a beaver-fur hat, Québec was founded as a fur trading center in 1608, and France's Finance Minister Colbert finally arranged New France as a royal colony modeled on the mother country.

As is often the case, however, the success attracted competition. In 1670, the British circumvented the sovereign French territory on the St Lawrence and founded the Hudson's Bay Company in the north.

It soon became the continent's most famous fur-trading company. Following the Seven Years War, the Paris Treaty of 1763 forced France to cede New France to England. After that, the French language was still spoken along the St Lawrence, but the French no longer had influence over Canada's political structure. Today, although there are ongoing attempts in French-speaking parts of Canada, i.e. in Québec province and the adjacent regions of Ontario and New Brunswick, to secede, they are actually only a means of strengthening their own position. The accomplishments of secessionists thus far include a successful campaign to ensure French was declared the only official language in Québec in 1977.

For visitors coming from the west, it is always fascinating to observe how the first French traces suddenly appear in Ontario. Place names now sound French and, when in the Old Town quarter of Québec, you feel as if you're no longer in North America. It bears the features of Old Europe.

The 14-m-high (46-ft) Big Tub Lighthouse is on the Bruce Peninsula.

1

The journey from the west bank of Lake Huron along the St Lawrence River to Nova Scotia is a journey through the land of "shimmering water" and heads beyond Québec to the craggy cliffs on the stormy North Atlantic. Although the trip passes through the most densely settled regions of Canada, the wilderness is never far away.

1 Sault Ste Marie This "twin city" is located in both Canada and the United States, on a narrow promontory between Lake Superior and Lake Huron on the St Mary's River. The height difference between the two lakes is overcome by two locks dating from 1887, which are now listed as historic monuments.

After a small detour to Tahquamenon Falls National Park in the west, your route follows the coast of the North Channel. At Sudbury, the Trans-Canada Highway, which is the world's longest natioal road, branches off in two directions: Highway 17 heads directly to Ottawa while the south-western branch (Highway 69) runs along the east coast of Georgian Bay.

2 Midland This small town has three main tourist attractions. One is Sainte-Marie among the Hurons, a Jesuit missionary station established in 1639 for the purpose of Christianizing Huron Indians. Laid out in the style of European monastic settlements, the mission has been restored to its original state. The second is Penetanguishene Discovery Harbour, a marine base that has also been partially restored. The third is Georgian Bay Islands National Park in the middle of the Thirty Thousand Islands (visitor center is in Honey Harbour).

A worthwhile detour now takes you from Midland around the southern tip of Georgian Bay to the Bruce Peninsula National Park (Highway 6). For Toronto, leave the Trans-Canada Highway and take Highway 400.

Travel Information

Route profile
Length: approx. 3,500 km (2,175 miles)
Time required: 3 weeks

Start: Sault Ste Marie
Destination: Halifax
Route (main locations): Sault Ste Marie, Toronto, Ottawa, Montréal, Québec, Charlottetown, Halifax

Traffic information:
Two different lines of the Trans-Canada Highway (TCH) run through northern Ontario: the northern line, which connects the most important mining and resource centers, and therefore leads through the breathtaking scenery of the Canadian Shield, with wild rivers, untouched lakes, numerous small pioneer settlements, and endless forests with their wealth of wildlife; and the southern line, which runs largely parallel to the US border along the Great Lakes (Lake Huron, Lake Superior).

Information:
Ontario:
www.ontariotravel.net
Québec:
www.bonjourquebec.com
New Brunswick:
www.tourismnbcanada.com
Nova Scotia:
www.novascotia.com
Prince Edward Island:
www.gov.pe.ca

3 Toronto (see page 60 to 61) From Toronto you should make the day trip to Niagara Falls,

The most fascinating technological attraction here is the lock staircase of the Rideau Canal, with a height difference of 25 m (82 ft). The Musée Canadien des Civilisations is also a must.

7 Parc de la Gatineau This vast park, with sixty species of tree, is on the north-western edge of Hull. There are beautiful walks here during the Indian summer, and 200 km (124 miles) of cross-country ski trails attract visitors in winter. Continuing along Highway 7, with a constant a view of the Ottawa River, you arrive in Montréal after roughly 200 km (124 miles).

8 Montréal (see page 62 to 63). The city of Québec is 250 km

about 130 km (81 miles) away on the US-Canadian border. Take Highway 400 to get there.

4 Niagara Falls The Niagara River plunges 50 m (164 ft) over a 675-m-long (2,215-ft) fracture line on the Canadian side; on the US side it is 330 m (1,083 ft) wide. Good observation points are Table Rock, to the west near the horseshoe-shaped waterfall, or the Minolta Tower. Flow is greatest in the daytime during peak tourist season (June, July, and August). Once back in Toronto, the route heads along

highways 401 and 115 to the Trans-Canada Highway 7.

5 Peterborough The biggest attraction in this city on the Kawartha lakes is the Hydraulic Lift Lock from 1904. The gigantic lock is made out of a lock basin that can be pushed up or lowered 20 m (66 ft) together with the vessel.
The Lang Pioneer Village is a reconstructed 19th-century pioneer village, while the Petroglyph Provincial Park features more than nine hundred First Nations rock drawings that are

between five hundred and one thousand years old.

6 Ottawa Canada's capital is happily mocked as the "Westminster in the Wilderness". The parliament building in English neo-Gothic style is the dominant edifice in Ottawa, and its 90-m (295-ft) Peace Tower has a carillon made up of fifty-three bells. The tower's impressive observation deck makes the city look like a miniature of itself. The second icon of Ottawa is the Château Laurier Hotel, built in 1912 by Grand Trunk Railway.

1 Toronto: View of the Skydome and CN Tower.

2 From the air you can see the Niagara River, Horseshoe Falls, and Niagara Falls.

Toronto

This metropolis on the northern shores of Lake Ontario owes its cosmopolitan character to the large number of immigrants who came here after World War II, and who gave the city its European-Asian composition.

Toronto is an extraordinarily lively city. Bustling Yonge Street is considered a shopping paradise and bold construction projects signal dynamic development, while traditional buildings such as the Holy Trinity Church are listed historic monuments.
Be sure to see: Ontario Place, a futuristic recreation center on Lake Ontario with varying exhibitions, an IMAX cinema, and an ultra-modern children's playground; the Harbourfront Centre; the converted warehouses on the piers with shops, restaurants, waterfront cafés, art galleries, and theaters; and Queen's Quay and York Quay boardwalks.
Toronto Islands, connected to the city via a ferry, is a quiet refuge with tranquil canals, footpaths, and a historic amusement park for children.
The CN Tower was the highest freestanding building in the world until 2007. Its viewing platform provides a spectacular view from 447 m (1,467 ft). The museums in town include the Art Gallery of Ontario, a modern art museum with the most famous works by Canadian artists, the Henry Moore Sculpture Centre, and classic paintings from Europe. There is also the Royal Ontario Museum, the country's largest museum with a wide variety of international exhibitions and a replica of a bat cave. The George R. Gardiner Museum of Ceramic Art specializes in pottery and porcelain, and is the only one of its kind in North America.
Other highlights are the Eaton Centre, one of the largest shopping malls in the country and Yorkville, the "Greenwich Village" of Toronto.

1 Toronto: looking out over the modern skyline by night.

Montréal

Canada's second-largest city was founded by French Catholics in 1642. Due to its ideal location at the confluence of the St Lawrence and Ottawa rivers, Montréal rapidly grew to become a bustling trade hub.

Vieux-Montréal, the picturesque Old Town quarter, has numerous historic buildings and narrow alleyways situated on the southern slope of Mont Royal, which visibly remind you of the city's distinctly French character. In winter, locals flee to the Ville souterraine, the underground city with a network of tunnels, passages, and shopping centers. You can reach most of the inner-city hotels from the central train station without even having to go outside.

Sights worth visiting here include the Catholic Basilique Notre-Dame, an ornate church actually built by a Protestant Irish-American architect named James O'Donnell around 1829; the Pointe-à-Callière with the Musée d'Archéologie et d'Histoire, which remembers the site of the first settlement; and the Hôtel de Ville, the town hall built in French Empire Style, dating back to the year 1872.

Notre-Dame-de-Bonsecours Chapel is the sailors' church, as indicated by the many model ships hanging from the ceiling. The Musée des Beaux-Arts was opened as a museum for fine arts back in 1912, while the Biodôme de Montréal is housed in the former Olympic velodrome and provides information on various ecosystems.

The Jardin Botanique, created in 1931, is an impressive botanical garden with 26,000 plant species. Other attractions include the award-winning Musée d'Art Contemporain, the only museum in Canada exclusively dedicated to modern art, and the cultural complex of Place des Arts with concert and theatre venues.

1 View of Montréal's skyline from the port.

(155 miles) from Montréal, and Auto-route 20, which is part of the Trans-Canada Highway, heads along the southern side of the St Lawrence River.

⑨ Québec (see page 65)
From Québec, Autoroute 20 runs parallel to the St Lawrence River before the 185 branches off to the south at Rivière-du-Loup and becomes the Trans-Canada Highway 2 in New Brunswick. The lovely scenic route initially follows the St John River Valley where fields and pastures characterize the landscape. Arriving at Grand

Falls, west of Mount Carleton Provincial Park, the St John crashes 25 m (82 ft) over a precipice.
The next stop is the Hartland Covered Bridge, the world's longest at 390 m (1,280 ft).

⑩ Kings Landing The openair museum at the St John River displays 19th-century life using thirty reconstructed buildings. Apart from various farmhouses and residential homes, there is a print shop, sawmill, blacksmith's shop, mill, and a theater.
You arrive in the capital of New Brunswick 40 km (25 miles) later.

⑪ Fredericton This tranquil regional town at the lower reaches of the St John River was founded by French immigrants in 1732. The most important public buildings and the most beautiful Victorian houses are clustered around Queen Street and King Street. Learn about its history in the York-Sunbury Historical Society Museum.
Follow Highway 2 to the east until Route 114 branches off south toward the Bay of Fundy just beyond Sussex.

⑫ Fundy National Park The Bay of Fundy extends nearly 300

km (186 miles) into the country's interior and separates New

1 The first-class Hotel Château Frontenac, perched high above the St Lawrence River, is the icon of Québec and one of the city's best addresses.

2 At 390 m (1,280 ft) in length, the Hartland Covered Bridge is the longest covered wooden bridge in the world.

3 High tide in Fundy Bay has formed the sandstone cliffs at Shepody Bay Beach.

Québec

The capital of the province of the same name is the heart of francophone Canada. More than 90% of its 167,500 inhabitants speak French, and the townscape has also maintained its European flair.

Québec City is the only North American metropolis with a city wall, and the Old Town quarter's narrow alleyways even evoke a few memories of old Paris. Québec City has in fact been a UNESCO World Heritage Site since 1985. The settlement was founded here on the banks of the St Lawrence River back in 1608.

After the houses under Cap Diamant were repeatedly burned down, citizens of Quebec retreated to the hill and created the "Haute-Ville", the "Upper town". The upper and lower towns are connected by a cog railway.

Worth seeing here are the Escalier Cass-Cou, or "Breakneck Staircase", which connects the Haute-Ville with the Quartier Petit-Champlain in Basse-Ville, and Place Royale, the former marketplace in the lower town. The Musée de la Civilisation provides an insight into the city's development.

At the eastern end of the city wall in Haute-Ville is La Citadelle from the early 19th century. The Cathédrale Notre-Dame was built in 1647, and reminds visitors of French rule, while the Maison Chevalier shows how the wealthy families of the 18th and 19th century lived in Quebec.

The luxury hotel Chateau Frontenac, built in 1893, looks like a large European castle. The Parc des Champs-de-Bataille is today one of the largest parks in North America, and the tiny Rue du Trésor alleyway brings Parisian charm to Canada, which invites to a stroll through the city.

1 The narrow alleys of the Old Town feature the architectural heritage of Old Europe.

The Cape Enrage Lighthouse sits on top of a high sandstone cliff and helps to secure navigation in the Bay of Fundy. The beacons are particularly necessary here, because the colossal, 300-km-long (186-mile) bay between New Brunswick and Nova Scotia not only looks like a

funnel, but also acts like one at the shifting of the tide. Heading north-east, the bay becomes flatter. During the rising tide, around 100 billion tonnes (110 billion tons) of water surge into the bay and raise the level by up to 16 m (52 ft) – the highest tidal change in the world.

Brunswick from Nova Scotia. Its unusual funnel shape produces the world's largest tidal range, which can shift up to 16 m (52 ft) at the end of Cobequid Bay. At the northernmost arm of the Bay of Fundy is the national park of the same name, with its jagged coast cliffs. The sandstone formations at Cape Enrage are especially beautiful.

Back on Highway 2, you pass through Moncton and reach the star-shaped complex of Fort Beauséjour (Exit 513A at Aulac) at the northern edge of the Cumberland Basin wetland about 55 km (34 miles) away. The next stop is the Confederation Bridge, roughly 60 km (37 miles) down the road.

13 Confederation Bridge This bridge opened in 1997 and connects Prince Edward Island, also referred to as "P.E.I.", to the Trans-Canada Highway. It is the world's longest bridge over an ice-covered waterway at 13 km (21 miles). At a height of 60 m (197 ft), the crossing takes roughly ten minutes.

14 Charlottetown This hilly island is almost treeless, but green pastures and fertile farmland line the road. The small regional Charlottetown exudes Victorian charm and is considered the "Cradle of the Confederation", as it was here that the decision to unite Canada was made in 1864.

15 Prince Edward Island National Park The country's smallest national park is 24 km (15 miles) north of Charlottetown. As the St Lawrence River is only 15 m (49 ft) deep here until far out into the sea, the water along the 40-km (25-mile)

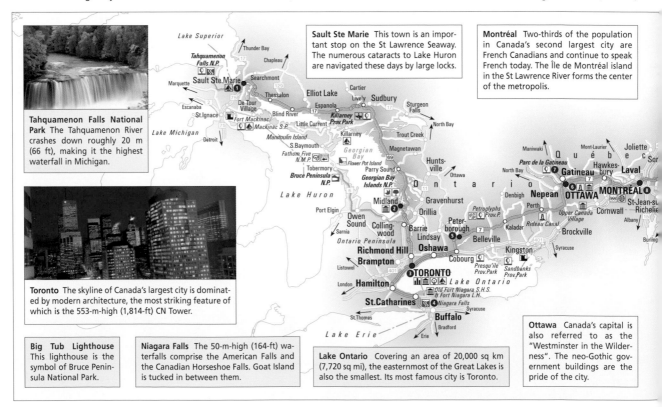

Tahquamenon Falls National Park The Tahquamenon River crashes down roughly 20 m (66 ft), making it the highest waterfall in Michigan.

Toronto The skyline of Canada's largest city is dominated by modern architecture, the most striking feature of which is the 553-m-high (1,814-ft) CN Tower.

Big Tub Lighthouse This lighthouse is the symbol of Bruce Peninsula National Park.

Niagara Falls The 50-m-high (164-ft) waterfalls comprise the American Falls and the Canadian Horseshoe Falls. Goat Island is tucked in between them.

Sault Ste Marie This town is an important stop on the St Lawrence Seaway. The numerous cataracts to Lake Huron are navigated these days by large locks.

Lake Ontario Covering an area of 20,000 sq km (7,720 sq mi), the easternmost of the Great Lakes is also the smallest. Its most famous city is Toronto.

Montréal Two-thirds of the population in Canada's second largest city are French Canadians and continue to speak French today. The Île de Montréal island in the St Lawrence River forms the center of the metropolis.

Ottawa Canada's capital is also referred to as the "Westminster in the Wilderness". The neo-Gothic government buildings are the pride of the city.

2

Sydney it's another 45 km (28 miles) to Louisbourg.

⑯ Louisbourg This small town on the east coast was the first French hub of power in the New World. Tucked behind the 8-m-high (26-ft) walls of Fortresse de Louisbourg are around fifty historic buildings, from the governor's house to the soldiers' barracks. The road then heads along the coast past Sydney and St Ann's through the mountains of the island's north-west and into the most beautiful national park of the Atlantic provinces.

⑰ Cape Breton Highlands National Park This impassable mountainous region with peaks up to 554 m (1,818 ft) immediately evokes images of Scotland. For hikers and mountaineers there are numerous trails and routes, while the 300-km-long

(186-mile) Cabot Trail, a spectacular coast road around the peninsula, is a joy for drivers. Back on the mainland you follow Highway 104 and then Highway 102 from Truro to Halifax.

⑱ Halifax The Port of Halifax is the most important in the Atlantic provinces, and the Province House, completed in 1819, is the seat of parliament. Perched high up in the west is the old citadel, whose forts were completed in 1856. The city's main landmark, however, is the clock tower from 1795.

1 A fishing village on Prince Edward Island. With the Gulf of St Lawrence, the best fishing grounds are literally at your doorstep.

2 The fort of Louisbourg, built by the French around 1740, has been restored to its original condition.

park coast is a pleasant and moderate temperature.
Less than 30 km (17 miles) east of Charlottetown, you can learn all about the lifestyle of European immigrants in the 19th century at the Orwell Corner Historic Village. From Wood Is-

lands you head back to Caribou, Nova Scotia on the mainland by ferry and from there along Highway 104 to the Canso Causeway, the road connection to Cape Breton Island. Highway 105, which is part of the Trans-Canada Highway, crosses the island, and from

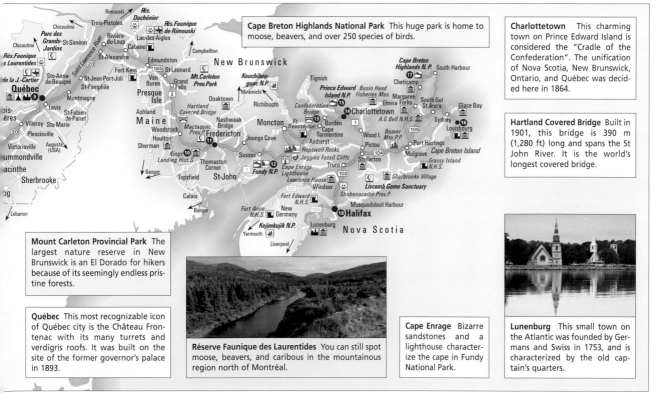

Cape Breton Highlands National Park This huge park is home to moose, beavers, and over 250 species of birds.

Charlottetown This charming town on Prince Edward Island is considered the "Cradle of the Confederation". The unification of Nova Scotia, New Brunswick, Ontario, and Québec was decided here in 1864.

Hartland Covered Bridge Built in 1901, this bridge is 390 m (1,280 ft) long and spans the St John River. It is the world's longest covered bridge.

Mount Carleton Provincial Park The largest nature reserve in New Brunswick is an El Dorado for hikers because of its seemingly endless pristine forests.

Québec This most recognizable icon of Québec city is the Château Frontenac with its many turrets and verdigris roofs. It was built on the site of the former governor's palace in 1893.

Réserve Faunique des Laurentides You can still spot moose, beavers, and caribou in the mountainous region north of Montréal.

Cape Enrage Bizarre sandstones and a lighthouse characterize the cape in Fundy National Park.

Lunenburg This small town on the Atlantic was founded by Germans and Swiss in 1753, and is characterized by the old captain's quarters.

Canada and the USA

On the Pan-American Highway from British Columbia to New Mexico

A journey through the North American West is a journey of contrasts. The route passes through mountain landscapes and open plains, pine forests and vast deserts, mining villages and megacities, and illustrates the impressive diversity of this enormous continent.

The full diversity of North America reveals itself in its entirety along the wide open stretches of the Pan-American Highway. From its begining on the Canadian Pacific coast to its end near the border between the USA and Mexico, this route travels initially in a south-easterly and then in a southerly direction. The roads on this long route are in exceptionally good condition but some of the side roads can be closed during the colder times of the year, especially in the north.

The northern section takes you through the Canadian provinces of British Columbia and Alberta as well as the US state of Montana. Larger towns are the exception here and the individual towns are often separated by large distances. Newer settlements originally developed from either trading posts or supply centers for the white fur-hunters. There are also a number of old gold-digging locations along the Pan-American Highway, where visitors are taken back in time to the gold rush of the 19th century. In some places there are also remnants of Native American Indian cultures, such as the impressive

Mount Assiniboine with fresh snow

totem poles, longhouses, and pueblos.

The Canadian part of the route is loaded with absolutely breathtaking natural landscapes. Majestic, snowy mountains reflect in the shimmering turquoise hues of Rocky Mountain lakes. To the east of the highway Mount Robson rises to 3,954 m (12,973 ft) above sea level, the highest peak in the Canadian Rocky Mountains. Glaciers and waterfalls drop powerfully to great depths from high cliffs.

The Pan-American Highway is also lined with vast expanses of forest. In a number of areas such as Banff National Park, the oldest National Park in Canada, the natural environment is protected from development and the dangers of mass tourism.

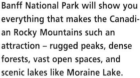

Old farmhouse in Grand Teton National Park in the north-west of the state of Wyoming.

Banff National Park will show you everything that makes the Canadian Rocky Mountains such an attraction – rugged peaks, dense forests, vast open spaces, and scenic lakes like Moraine Lake.

Further south the scenery changes. In the distance you see the skyscrapers of Calgary, a modern metropolis built on wealth generated by oil and natural resources, and given a makeover for the 1988 Winter Olympics. Some three hours from Calgary are the spectacular lakes and mountains of Waterton-Glacier International Peace Park, a union of Glacier and Waterton National Parks.

The route continues through Idaho, Wyoming, Utah, and Arizona. There are a number of remarkable contrasts here as well. Remnants of Native American cultures and the Spanish colonial era mix with modern cities and skyscrapers, and extensive forest areas stand in contrast to desert landscapes. Along the route variety can be enjoyed.

A major highlight of this particular section of North America is Yellowstone National Park in Wyoming. Salt Lake City, the capital of Utah and the center of Mormonism, is also an Olympic city, having hosted the 2002 winter games. In the vast desert expanses of Utah and Arizona the light and landscape change dramatically with the movement of the sun, producing impressive interplays of colors and shadows, and the rocky landscape of the Colorado Plateau is also impressive in places like Bryce Canyon National Park. The Grand Canyon, stretching over 350 km (217 miles) of magnificent desert, is one of the most visited sightseeing attractions in the USA – some 4 million people come here every year.

Sunset Crater, the youngest of Arizona's volcanoes, can be seen near Flagstaff and is today a training area for astronauts. In the adjoining "Valley of the Sun" to the south the towns appear like oases in the desert. The exclusive golf courses and fields exist only due to artificial irrigation. Phoenix, the capital of Arizona, still has a slight touch of the Wild West to it, but shines as a center for aircraft and high-tech industries. Tucson, the "City of Sunshine", has 350 days of sunshine a year.

Spirit Island in Maligne Lake in Jasper National Park.

The North American section of the Pan-American Highway leads from the Pacific coast via the Rocky Mountains to the arid regions of the American south-west. The route is lined with natural beauty that is protected in a series of spectacular national parks.

1 Prince Rupert The Pan-American Highway comes up with important cultural and historic sights right from the start. The creative carved totem poles of a variety of Indian tribes can be found all over the port town, and the pristine wilderness in the province of British Columbia awaits you just outside the city limits.

Highway 16 initially takes you through the Skeena Valley. At Hazelton it is worth taking a detour to the Gitksan Indian villages.

The Ksan Native Village is an open-air museum with several longhouses. In Kitwancool you can see what is alleged to be the largest standing totem pole. After 242 km (150 miles) a small road branches off at Vander-hoof towards Fort St James to the north (66 km/41 miles).

2 Fort St James National Historic Site On the eastern shore of the more than 100-km-long (62-mile) Stuart Lake is Fort St James, a town developed from what was originally a trading post founded in 1806. Actors re-enact scenes from the lives of 19th-century fur hunters during the annual summer festival in the reconstructed fort. For fishing enthusiasts there are a number of isolated lakes nearby to drop a line.

3 Prince George The Pan-American Highway crosses the Cariboo Highway (Highway 97) here. Once a satellite of Fort St James, Prince George grew into

a lively town in the 19th century with the construction of a railway that brought new settlers and adventurers. The Railway Museum has a historic steam train on display.

4 Bowron Lake Provincial Park A little detour leads you through Quesnel and Barkerville (the hub of a gold rush here in the 19th century) on your way to the wilderness around Bowron Lake. The adventurous drive over a gravel road at the end can be somewhat tedious and tiring but the effort is re-

warded with fantastic pristine landscape.

The eleven lakes in the area are a major attraction for fans of canoeing. You can paddle through the entire lake landscape in the course of eight days. Back on the Pan-American Highway, after driving 270 km (168 miles) through Fraser Valley, you reach Tête Jaune Cache, the gateway to the lovely Mount Robson Provincial Park.

5 Mount Robson Provincial Park The highest mountain in the Canadian Rocky Mountains

is Mount Robson at an impressive (3,954 m/12,973 ft). It is the king of this unique protected area (2,200 sq km/1,367 sq mi) and is beloved among hikers and mountaineers.

High altitude glaciers, crystal-clear mountain lakes, tumbling waterfalls, and exhilarating pine forests characterize this jewel of the Rockies.

After 100 km (62 miles) on Yellowhead Pass you reach Jasper in the Jasper National Park.

6 Jasper National Park The huge mountains here tower ma-

jestically over what is the largest national park in the Canadian Rockies, covering a total area of 10,878 sq km (6,760 sq mi). You get closest to the natural beauty of the park either on foot or in a canoe, the latter being perfectly suited to the 22-km-long (14-mile) Maligne Lake.

The Icefields Parkway (Highway 93) is the next portion of the route and is a highlight of the Pan-American Highway. It runs 230 km (143 miles) along the gorgeous panoramic route at the foot of the glacial ridge of the Rocky Mountains and past the Columbia Ice Field, which is the largest ice field in North America. The Athabasca Falls and the Sunwapta Falls are also worth seeing.

1 A mountain lake in Jasper National Park.

2 Boating on Maligne Lake in Jasper National Park.

Jasper National Park

Jasper National Park, less over-run with tourists than Banff National Park and Lake Louise, boasts unspoilt Rocky Mountain scenery.

Jasper National Park lies on the state border with British Columbia and its area of 10,878 sq km (4,170 sq mi) makes it one of the biggest national parks in the Canadian Rocky Mountains. Mount Columbia is 3,747 m (12, 290 ft) high and the Columbia Icefield extends almost to the Icefields Parkway. There are more than 800 lakes within the park boundaries, mostly fed from the surrounding glaciers; nearby Maligne Lake is considered the most picturesque and is one of the most photographed areas of the Rockies. Lac Beauvert, a jade green glacial lake, is very near the city, and Jasper Park Lodge, the old Grand Trunk Railroad's answer to the Banff Springs Hotel in the adjacent park, was built on its shores.

Jasper grew up out of a trading post for trappers, hunters, and prospectors and only became accessible to tourists when the Canadian Pacific Railway reached the town in 1911. The little town is less crowded than Banff – this is also true of the hotel – and the trails in the wilderness will allow you to explore the wonderful scenery of the Rockies in peace. There is a funicular railway connection to Whistler Mountain with breathtaking panoramic views.

1 You may even run into a coyote in the wilderness of Jasper National Park.

2 The alluringly unspoilt scenery in the wilds beyond the tourist cities of Banff and Jasper.

3 There are several waterfalls, falling into deep chasms such as the Maligne Canyon in Jasper National Park. Trails and narrow bridges have made this wilderness accessible to tourists.

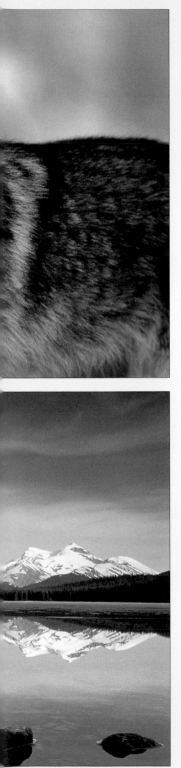

75

Broad plains stretch between the mountain ranges of Banff National Park, and lush vegetation thrives in the summer wherever the land-scape is protected from the cold winds of the north. But the growth period is short in these high mountains due to heavy snow volumes

Visitors to Banff National Park can choose between a hike to Mount Tuzo (top), to Vermillion Lake (2nd from top), or a drive along Icefields Parkway (2nd from bottom). Bottom: A popular photograph in Banff is of snow-capped peaks, hereirrored by Herbert Lake.

7 Banff National Park The road then takes you past the smaller Yoho National Park and on to the shimmering turquoise waters of Lake Louise. Nearby Moraine Lake is somewhat quieter. There are more than twenty-four 3,000-m (10,000-ft) peaks in this national park. Highway 1 turns off westwards near Lake Louise and heads over the Rogers Pass towards Glacier National Park.

8 Calgary The largest city in the area is Calgary on the western edge of the vast prairie. The approach from the west is especially impressive on days when the Chinooks – warm, dry autumn winds – are blowing down from the Rocky Mountains. They ensure grand views of the peaks towering behind the city and create the bizarre illusion that you could reach out and touch the mountains.
The largest city in the province of Alberta can be seen from far away. The downtown high-rises,

largely housing the offices of oil companies, banks, and insurance companies, rise grandiosely against the backdrop of the mighty Rockies. The city has developed from an agricultural center to a modern metropolis that attracts a great deal of foreign capital. A milestone in this development was the hosting of the 1988 Winter Olympics. Isolated though it may be in the middle of Alberta, Calgary is well on its way to becoming a million-strong metropolis and is an important inter-regional traffic hub.
Landmark, symbol, and the most important orientation point in the city is the Calgary Tower, standing at a proud 191 m (627 ft). The Olympic Saddledome ice sport arena provides an architectural link between tradition and modernity, and is one of the most advanced of its kind in the world. The design of the arena in the shape of a saddle also reflects the spirit of the Wild West, which is really brought back to

life in July every year during the hugely popular ten-day Calgary Stampede, when the ten-gallon cowboy hats, cowboy boots, and blue jeans dictate the dress code throughout the city. Rodeos and covered wagon races bring back the "good old days".
Heading south again, after 170 km (106 miles) you reach Fort Macleod. About 18 km (11 miles) north-west of the Fort is the World Heritage Site of Head-Smashed-In Buffalo Jump (see left sidebar). From here,

choose between Highway 6 (via Pincher) or 5 (via Cardston) to reach Waterton, the entrance to another breathtaking Canadian national park.

9 Waterton Lakes National Park There are two national parks near the border between Canada and the USA – Waterton Lakes National Park in the Canadian province of Alberta, and Glacier National Park in the US state of Montana. In 1932 the two were combined as the Wa-

3

terton-Glacier International Peace Park. For local Indians the entire area has always been known as the "Land of the Shining Mountains".

Just after entering the park from the north-east (Highway 5 and 6) you reach Bison Paddocks. A few kilometers further down, a narrow road branches off to the west towards Red Rock Canyon, named as such due to the red sedimentary rock in the area. The route continues to the 2,940-m-high (9,646-ft)

Mount Blakiston, the highest peak in the Waterton Lakes National Park. The Prince of Wales Hotel is one of the most striking buildings in the reserve, with stunning views of two lakes, Middle and Upper Waterton.

Access to Glacier National Park is via the Chief Mountain International Highway which travels along the eastern side of the park. The road was built in 1935 and is in good condition but is only passable between mid-May and mid-September.

⑩ Glacier National Park Mount Cleveland, at 3,185 m (10,450 ft) the highest mountain in the national park (not to be confused with the park of the same name in Canada), slowly comes into view after crossing the border. Dense pine forests in the low-lying areas are home to elks, grizzly bears, pumas, and lynxes.

Shortly before reaching St Mary, the road, which is closed in winter, branches off to Many Glaciers. The scenic landscape here,

with a total of fifty glaciers, is criss-crossed by hiking routes. The 4-km (2.5-mile) Swiftcurrent Lake Nature Trail is especially impressive.

An 80-km-long (50-mile) road takes you from St Mary over the Logan Pass at 2,026 m (6,647 ft) to West Glacier. The route, which is only passable between June and mid-September, is considered one of the most beautiful mountain routes in the whole of North America.

The journey then continues via Browning to Shelby. From here it is a further 82 km (51 miles) on Highway 15 to Great Falls.

1 An ideal location – the historic Prince of Wales Hotel in Waterton Lakes National Park.

2 Sinopah Mountain in Glacier National Park is an almost perfect pyramid.

3 St Mary Lake in Glacier National Park, Montana.

Glacier National Park

Glacier National Park comprises some 3,885 sq km (1,500 sq mi) of mainly unspoilt wilderness. In 1932 the park was combined with Waterton Lakes National Park over the Canadian border in nearby Alberta to form the Waterton-Glacier International Peace Park, with a total area of 4,630 sq km (1,790 sq mi).

Mighty glaciers roll down from the summits, carving glittering paths through the jagged mountains. Dense pine forests surround the rocky walls, and above the treeline there is only deserted tundra. A poetic soul once called the national park the "crown of the continent" after seeing the jagged mountain range silhouetted against the dark sky. Leading up to the continental divide and Logan Pass (2,025 m/ 6,650 ft), the aptly named "Going-To-The-Sun Road" is one of the most beautiful in the world, but is open only during the summer. The 52-km (32-mile) road was opened to traffic in 1933, after some 20 years of construction. Passing majestic forests, icy glaciers, and emerald-green lakes, the road descends to picturesque Saint Mary Lake in the eastern part of the park. The snow-capped summits of the surrounding mountains study their reflections in the water and tiny Wild Goose Island is the only hint of variation to break up the monotonous dark green of the lake. Chief Mountain International Highway will take you to the Canadian National Park, passing through the Blackfeet tribe's reservation; although the parks are notionally divided by the international border, the scenery is uninterrupted. In the 19th century, the area was still part of the hunting grounds of the feared Blackfeet Indians.

1 For Americans and Canadians the Waterton Lakes are a symbol of peace between the two nations. The picture shows Lake Sherburne in Glacier National Park.

Yellowstone National Park

This 9,000 sq km (3,475 sq mi) national park in north-western Wyoming is the result of a massive eruption which took place here 600,000 years ago.

John Colter, an explorer and trapper who had left the Lewis and Clark Expedition in 1806, was the first white man to set eyes on Yellowstone. He reported seeing hot springs shooting from the ground, bisons, and bears, and praised the land as one of the greatest paradises in the American West. People in the east, knowing how prone trappers were to exaggeration, were surprised at how little the westerner had overstated the case when the first tourists arrived and reported back. Yellowstone National Park is a majestic wilderness of mountains, rivers, and lakes, with more than 300 geysers.

The earth is in turmoil within the park's borders. The Grand Canyon of the Yellowstone River and the bubbling geysers are both reminders of past volcanic eruptions. Cold water seeps down to hot chambers some 2 km (1.2 miles) underground, boils, and is then forced to the surface through narrow fissures as steam or superheated water. Protected walkways run through the steamy landscape, seemingly losing themselves in the stinking, sulphurous smoke from the geysers.

The idea of turning the area into a national park was first mooted by the Washburn-Langford-Doane expedition, which explored the Yellowstone River in 1870 and gave "Old Faithful" its name. N.P. ("National Park") Langford, the first superintendent of the park, was a member of this team, which spent five years alone in the wilderness. Yellowstone was finally declared the USA's first national park in 1872.

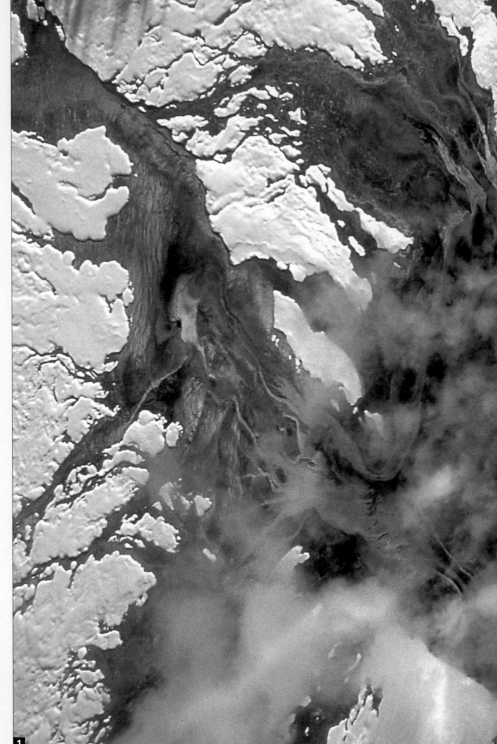

1 The microorganisms in the Grand Prismatic Spring make the many colours shine.

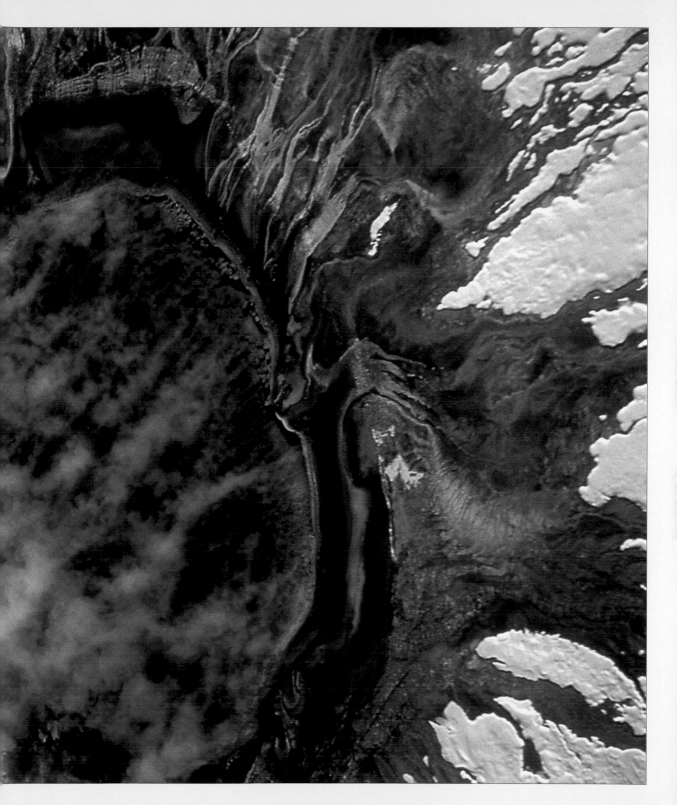

⑪ **Great Falls** The city's sight-seeing attractions include the Giant Springs, one of the largest freshwater springs in North America, and the Lewis and Clark National Forest, named after the explorers who traversed much of western North America at the start of the 19th century. About 44 km (27 miles) northeast of the city is Fort Benton, founded in 1846 as a trading post on the upper reaches of the Missouri River. Continuing south you pass more springs, including White Sulphur Springs. Continuing to Yellowstone National Park, it is worth taking a detour near Livingston to the battle-field of Little Bighorn 110 km (68 miles) away.

⑫ **Yellowstone National Park** From Montana you continue along the Pan-American Highway to the state of Wyoming, which boasts one of the continent's main attractions. Yellowstone National Park is indeed in a league of its own, not least because it is the oldest and largest in the USA. It receives around 3 million visitors a year, and it is easily accessible by car, although some entrances and roads are closed between November and April.

The Grand Loop Road meanders 230 km (143 miles) through the park. If you are approaching from the north it is worth making a short stop at Mammoth Hot Springs where information material and updates on the current passability of the side roads are available from the park office.

The significance of the reserve (8,983 sq km/5,582 sq mi) in the midst of the Rocky Mountains and the Grand Tetons was recognized early on as a natural treasure and was declared a national park in 1872.

Mother Nature shows her most spectacular side on this high plateau, which ranges from 2,100 to 2,400 m (6,890 to 7,874 ft). The forces of the earth's core come to the surface in the Yel-

lowstone National Park where the world's most impressive and powerful geysers can be seen. The highest of the roughly 300 geysers is named Steamboat. Approaching from the north you first reach the Norris Geyser Basin where, in addition to the Steamboat, the Echinus Geyser also puts on a show from time to time. A short distance further on to the south-west you reach the Fountain Paint Pot, a basin of bubbling red-brown mud. Upper Geyser Basin has the most

geysers in the whole of the national park. It is therefore no surprise that this is where the highest number of visitors will be found. You can even set your watch by some of the geysers and can plan your arrival accordingly.

Old Faithful is one of the most "punctual", displaying its skills almost every 80 minutes for a few minutes at a time, sending huge quantities of water about 50 m (164 ft) into the air. Other well-known geysers are Giant

Geyser and Castle Geyser. And it's not just a visual experience. The accompanying noises as you approach are also fascinating. Make sure you stick to the marked pathways at all times as the unstable ground bubbles and hisses at many places in the park. Steam clouds sometimes even reach as far as the Grand Loop Road.

All of this is evidence of volcanic activity within the park. Violent volcanic eruptions are not to be feared, however, as the last ma-

1 Yellowstone River near the 94-m-high (308-ft) Lower Falls.

2 The tranquil river landscape is ideal bison territory.

3 In summer, bison graze on the wide open spaces of the park.

4 Old Faithful Geyser in Yellowstone National Park.

5 A 34-km (21-mile) shoreline road provides access to Yellowstone Lake in the south-west of the park.

jor eruption took place around 600,000 years ago.

The waterfalls along the Yellowstone River in the south of the park are another striking attraction. At Upper Falls the river drops 33 m (108 ft) over the cliffs. At Lower Falls – only a few hundred meters away – the drop is as much as 94 m (308 ft). The viewing points in the Lookout Point and Grandview Point parking areas offer especially dramatic views.

⑬ Grand Teton National Park From Yellowstone National Park, John D. Rockefeller Jr. Memorial Parkway takes you to a much smaller park, Grand Teton National Park (1,257 sq km/781 sq mi), which is often overshadowed by its more famous neighbor. This is unjustified to say the least, however, as it also has a number of attractions on offer and is a more relaxed experience altogether.

The jagged peaks of the Teton Range, dominated by Grand Teton at 4,197 m (13,770 ft),are accompanied by glaciers that extend far into the steep valleys. The park's main axis is Jackson Hole, an 80-km (50-mile) valley through which the idyllic Snake River passes on part of its 1,670-km (1,038-mile) journey to the Columbia River, which eventually flows through Idaho, Oregon, and Washington into the Pacific. There are also a number of lakes in the valley.

Teton Park Road takes you from Jackson Lake to the south-east, the panoramic road offering continuously lovely views of the mountain landscape.

Jackson Hole can claim one superlative in particular. In 1933 the lowest temperature ever recorded in Wyoming, -54°C, was measured here. Even though it can be very cold in winter, such temperatures are obviously not typical. This park is open all year and the best time to go is between June and September. Most of the tourist facilities are closed in the winter but winter sports are popular here.

⑭ Jackson Situated on the southern rim of Jackson Hole, this is the ideal starting point for hikes in Grand Teton National Park as well as for white-water rafting on the Snake River. And, with its Wild-West-style saloons and bars, Jackson is more than just a tourist staging post. The place retains an authentic Wild West atmosphere and can be a lot of fun.

The Wildlife of the American West Art Museum has a good collection of paintings featuring the region's wild animals. The cultural history of the local Native Americans is illustrated in the Teton County Historical Center.

A few kilometers south of Jackson, a turn-off near Alpine heads west towards Idaho. Idaho Falls are a good distance beyond the state line. In addition to a Mormon temple that is worth seeing, the city is home to

the Intermountain Science Experience Center, a first-class natural history museum.

Back on Highway 89, you continue south from Montpellier through the Wasatch Mountains, which emerge abruptly from the plains. The area, at more than 3,500 m (11,484 ft), is covered in snow all year and is a popular winter sport area for residents of Salt Lake City. One of the main attractions here is the large salt lake to the west of the road, which you can reach by making a detour on Highway 80.

⑮ Salt Lake City The capital of Utah is one of the largest cities along the Pan-American Highway. Initially it seems an intimidating location for a city, with the Great Salt Lake to the west, the Wasatch Mountains forming a natural border to the east, and the Great Salt Lake Desert stretching west to the horizon.

However, in the middle of the 19th century the Mormons were in search of just this type of environment, remote and inhospitable, to face the wilderness.

Yet the gold rush and the completion of the transcontinental railroad brought more and more people to the town, which had developed into a lively city by the start of the 20th century. A century later, in 2002, the city received further impetus from the Winter Olympics.

The classical Capitol building (1915) is visible from afar and is the city's primary landmark, but Temple Square is really where things happen here. The 4-ha (10-acre) square is considered to be the Mormons' "holy square" and the temple is accessible only to members of the Mormon church.

The city's highest building at 128 m (420 ft) is the Church Office Building, also a Mormon building, which houses the central administration of this religious community. The view from the platform on the 26th floor is especially popular with visitors to the city.

⑯ Timpanogos Cave National Monument On the northern slope of the 3,581-m (11,749-ft) Mount Timpanogo are three caves that have been formed over a long period of time due to the porosity of the limestone that is characteristic of the area. The bizarre stalactites are a real sight to behold. The three caves are connected by a man-made tunnel and can be viewed as part of a guided tour. Due to its extraordinary nature the entire area has been declared a National Monument in the heart of the Wasatch mountains.

⑰ Capitol Reef National Park The Pan-American Highway is well-maintained in Utah. After having covered more than half of this state you will reach some of the absolute highlights along this dream route. Leave Highway 15 at Scipio and turn off onto Highway 50 for around 30 km (19 miles). Highway 12 turns off at Salina to the next national park.

The Capitol Reef National Park is characterized by a colorful cliff face towering above the Fremont River. The Fremont River has cut its way deep into a geological shift known as the Waterpocket Fold. Parallel ridges rise out of the desert sands here in a wave formation over a dis-

1 The Snake River flows through Grand Teton National Park.

2 Salt Lake City, the capital of Utah founded in 1915, lit up at night against the background of the surrounding mountains.

Grand Teton National Park

Grand Teton is located a few miles south of Yellowstone in north-western Wyoming. The parks are connected by the John D. Rockefeller, Jr Memorial Parkway.

The steep summits of the mountains in Grand Teton National Park are silhouetted against the sky like the teeth of some mighty shark; all are over 3,000 m (10,000 ft) high, but their steep sides make them appear even higher. Grand Teton and Mount Moran are by far the most impressive. White flecks of glaciers can be seen between the peaks and in spring the Alpine meadows are covered in bright wildflowers.

Jenny Lake is the most beautiful of the six lakes that stretch like a string of pearls through the park. Only a boat hire business and a few cabins betray the presence of man here. Four other lakes lying between the mountains – Leigh, Bradley, Taggart, and Phelps – have remained completely untouched. An asphalt road runs through the national park, but at no point do visitors have the feeling of being overrun by other people. The shores of Jackson Lake, the largest of the six lakes, follow the road between Yellowstone and Grand Teton; the lake is fed by mountain streams and the mighty Snake River. The park's Visitor Center is also here, and since 1906 the giant lake has been held in check with a dam – the only blemish in the park. The winding surfaced road from Moose Junction to Teton Village, Jackson Hole's ski resort, is open only during the summer.

1 2 Grand Teton National Park, with some of the most beautiful scenery in the American West, was established in 1929 and is located south of Yellowstone in north-western Wyoming. The park includes the 4,000-m (13,000-ft) peaks of the Teton Range, sticking out of the jagged landscape like teeth, and the extended valley of the Snake River.

Landscapes of this kind evoke the eternal dream of the Wild West: the fogswept Snake River in the heart of the Grand Teton National Park once was home to trappers and Indians. The source of the mighty river is in Yellowstone National Park and it flows into Jackson

Lake in Grand Teton National Park. Grand Tetons are America's quintessential mountain range, rearing up with sawtooth like exaggeration crowned by the 4197 m-high (13,770-foot) Grand Teton. By length the Snake River is the thirteenth largest river in the United States

1

tance of 160 km (99 miles). Water and wind have fashioned the unique shapes, which invite comparisons with chimneys, roofs, and even whole fortresses. There are also rock paintings from the Fremont Indians, which frequently depict animals.

Continuing along scenic Highway 12 you will reach Escalante where the road turns off to the south, heading towards the Grand Staircase Escalante National Monument.

⑱ Grand Staircase Escalante National Monument Those in search of pristine nature will not be disappointed by this reserve between Bryce Canyon National Park to the south and west, the Capitol Reef National Park in the north, and the Glen Canyon National Recreation Area to the east. The National Monument was named after four towering layers of rock. The beauty of the landscape is characterized by gorges, rows of

cliffs, and plateaus and is best experienced from the dirt roads off the main highway.

The drive along the 200-km (124-mile) Burr Trail Loop weaves its way through the entire area. Initially a tarred road, it takes you along Deer Creek and then through the rocky labyrinth of Long Canyon. It later becomes a bit more challenging but is easily done with an off-road vehicle.

Back on Highway 12 head towards Bryce Canyon Airport. Shortly thereafter, Highway 63 turns off right to the Bryce Canyon Visitors Center.

⑲ Bryce Canyon National Park Unlike the rest of the landscape in the region, Bryce Canyon is not a canyon in the strict sense of the word but rather a series of crevices and smaller eroded gullies, some more than 300 m (984 ft) deep.

A lovely panoramic route takes you 30 km (19 miles) through the park, which was founded in

2

1928, and leads to the southernmost point, Rainbow Point. The drive and its many vista points constantly provide splendid views over the park's dense pine forests.

Many of the orange, salmon-pink, or red rock formations have characteristic names, such as Sunrise Point, Inspiration Point, Thor's Hammer, or Chinese Wall. The landscape is other-worldly and is especially impressive at sunset or sunrise.

After Bryce Canyon it is worth making a detour some 100 km (62 miles) to the west to the Cedar Breaks National Monu-

ment. The turn-off to Cedar City is a few kilometers after the junction of Highway 12 and Highway 89.

⑳ Cedar Breaks National Monument Founded by the Mormons in 1851, Cedar City's Iron Mission State Park and Museum, with more than three hundred old vehicles, documents the pioneering spirit of the Mormons. The Shakespeare Festival also takes place here every summer in the Globe Theater. The National Monument's dimensions may be somewhat smaller than those of Bryce

Canyon but the hues are just as enticing.

The next stop is Zion National Park, which is reached from the turn-off at Mount Carmel Junction (Highway 9).

㉑ Zion National Park This area was declared a national park in 1919 and has several entrances. The most important attractions are found in the southern part, and the Zion-Mount Carmel Highway (9) takes you via the plateau at the East Entrance 600 m (1,969 ft) downhill to the more desert South Entrance.

The Canyon Overlook provides one of the best views of the heart of the national park, Zion Canyon. This was created by the Virgin River, a tributary of the Colorado River.

A tunnel built 255 m (837 ft) above the valley floor makes the drive to the Zion Canyon Visitor Center all the more dramatic. From here the Zion Canyon Scenic Drive follows numerous serpentine bends of the winding Virgin River for 12 km (7.5 miles). The most well-known hike in the park, the 2-km (1.2-mile) River Walk, starts at the end of the road and leads to the

600-m (1,969-ft) canyon walls. The waterfalls on the Emerald Pools Trail are also worth seeing, as are the Hanging Gardens, a cliff overgrown with vegetation. If you have time, take the park's southern exit and return via the Pipe Spring National Monument and the Pan-American Highway where the A89 turns off from Highway 89 at Kanab heading south.

At Jacob Lake a side road leads to the northern entrance of the Grand Canyon (North Rim); alternatively, you can continue along the A89 to the next stop, Marble Canyon.

㉒ Marble Canyon Close to the town of the same name in the far north of Arizona is Marble Canyon, a prime example of the state's diverse natural beauty. The canyon is traversed by the Colorado River and is spanned by a road bridge. Turn onto Highway 89 where it joins the A89 and drive a short distance north towards Page. From here you can either continue to Glen Canyon Dam or make a detour to Antelope Canyon.

㉓ Lake Powell Since 1963 the Glen Canyon Dam has held back the Colorado River to create the

1 Walls of rock in Capitol Reef National Park.

2 The Colorado River cuts through the horizontal layers of fascinating Marble Canyon.

3 A bold bridge over Marble Canyon.

653-sq-km (405-sq-mi) Lake Powell, built to generate hydro-electric power.

The lake is now a haven for water-sports enthusiasts. There are also splendid views of the sandstone formations whose perfectly flat plateaus look like they were measured with a ruler. On the southern shore is the nearly 90-m-high (295-ft) Rainbow Bridge, considered the largest natural bridge in North America. The area around the lake was declared the Glen Canyon National Recreation Area in 1972.

㉔ Grand Canyon National Park You can reach this world-famous national park from the north via the turn-off at Jacob Lake and from the south via Cameron (Highway 64) or Flagstaff (Highway 180), both of which lead to the South Rim. The northern side of the canyon, which is 30 km (19 miles) at its widest point, is about 360 m (1,181 ft) higher

than the southern side and the canyon walls drop nearly 1,800 m (5,906 ft) to the Colorado River here.

As the northern Kaibab Plateau is significantly higher than the southern Coconino Plateau, the North Rim provides a completely different perspective of the canyon landscape than the South Rim. Bright Angel Point provides a fantastic backdrop near the Grand Canyon Lodge. Shortly before this viewing point there is a 35-km-long (22-mile) road that branches off to the north to Point Imperial which, at 2,683 m (8,803 ft), is the highest point in the national park.

The southern part receives considerably more visitors. Grand Canyon Village is recommended as the starting point. From here a panoramic route provides access to West Rim Drive and East Rim Drive.

㉕ Flagstaff The drive from Cameron to Flagstaff passes the

Wupatki National Monument with more than 2,000 historical sites once inhabited by Hopi Indians. Just outside Flagstaff is the 120-m-deep (394-ft) crater created in 1064 by a volcanic eruption. The volcanic cone is called Sunset Crater Volcano because of its color.

The center of Flagstaff is characterized by red-brick buildings.

It is worth paying a visit to the Lowell Observatory from which scientists discovered Pluto in 1930. The cultural highlight is the Museum of Northern Arizona with archaeological and ethnological displays.

㉖ Walnut Canyon South of town close to Interstate 40/Route 66, head west to Walnut Canyon with its famous Sinagua Indian dwellings. More than twenty of the dwellings open to visitors were built into the cliffs in the 12th and 13th centuries, and some of them are in especially adventurous locations.

㉗ Montezuma Castle National Monument This Indian site close to the town of Cottonwood was declared a National Monument in 1906. It comprises the remnants of a Sinagua Indian dwelling that was fitted into the recess of a rock face 30 m (98 ft) high. The Sinagua built twenty rooms in the dwelling more than 600 years ago and used ladders for access. An exhibition in the visitor center beneath the cliffs documents the Sinagua culture. The trailhead along Beaver Creek is also here. From Cottonwood it is around 80 km (50 miles) to the junction of Highway 89 and Highway 60, which takes you to Phoenix.

㉘ Phoenix In Phoenix you join Interstate 10 going towards Tucson. The last stop before Tucson is an American Indian memorial.

㉙ Casa Grande Ruins National Monument Agriculture has been carried out in the Gila River Valley south of Phoenix for thousands of years. Local Hohokam Indian culture was already cultivating the land in this area in 200 bc using sophisticated canal systems.

The most important remnants of this culture include the Casa Grande, or "Big House", a four-storey clay building constructed at the start of the 14th century, the last period of the Hohokam. With walls 1.2 m (4 ft) thick it is more like a fortress, but was abandoned in the 14th century. The building can only be viewed from the outside.

㉚ Tucson After about three hours on the road you reach Tucson, the "City of Sunshine". The approach is an experience in itself. Once you have crossed the last chain of mountains outside the city, gleaming sky-scrapers appear, towering out of the Santa Cruz River valley.

The colonial era neighborhood lies in the shadows of these massive buildings and gives Tucson much of its charm.

Due to its climate and mountainous surroundings, the city is a popular winter sports destination, especially during the "cold" season when the temperature is a consistent 20 to 25°C (68 to 77°F).

Tucson is situated in the Sonoran Desert where the Saguaro cacti reach heights of 10 m (33 ft). The contrast between the end of the North American portion of the Pan-American Highway in the desert and its start in the cold coastal forests of Canada's Prince Rupert could hardly be greater. A dream route with a plethora of natural wonders for all seasons, not be missed!

1 Grand Canyon – view of the canyon from Toroweap Point.

2 Montezuma Castle Valley and the ruins of an Indian pueblo.

Grand Canyon National Park

"Don't spoil this great beauty" declared US president Theodore Roosevelt in 1903, "this is a view that every American should enjoy!"

The Grand Canyon National Park was established in 1919. The mighty canyon of the Colorado River is a natural wonder of overpowering beauty, cutting a gash over a kilometer deep through the red-brown wilderness of the Colorado Plateau. The rock strata are up to 250 million years old.

Tourist activity is concentrated on the South Rim, with numerous hotels and good viewing points. The best views are to be had from Grandview Point and Moran Point. Bright Angel Trail will take you first to Indian Gardes and then on to the Colorado River on the floor of the canyon. A hike such as this – which climatically is like walking from the north of Canada into the desert – is the best way to admire the canyon's treasures: the countless rock strata, the abundant plant and wildlife (there are over 60 mammal and 180 bird species in the Grand Canyon) and the river, winding like a green ribbon through the canyon. Guided mule-back tours are available from Bright Angel Lodge to Phantom Ranch, and these should definitely be booked in advance during the holidays.

Another way of exploring the Grand Canyon is by helicopter or by white-water rafting through the rapids on the Colorado River. Flights take off 13 km (8 miles) south of Grand Canyon River, and here a half-hour film about this natural wonder can be seen on the giant screen of the new Imax Theater. The film relates how the giant chasm was discovered by the Spanish, who barely noticed it as they were so intent on finding the legendary treasures of the seven golden cities of Cibola.

1 The Grand Canyon – always an overwhelming sight.

1

Over millions of years Colorado River has been carving its way through the rocky landscape to create the deepest, longest and largest canyon of the world. One of the big attractions is Whitewater Rafting. Experienced guides manage to steer their rafting boats over the

wild rapids of Colorado River past steep-rising cliffs (here at Horseshoe Bend). More than 70 cataracts await the adventurous travellers all along the gorge. Horseshoe Bend is the name for a meander of the Colorado River located near the town of Page, Arizona.

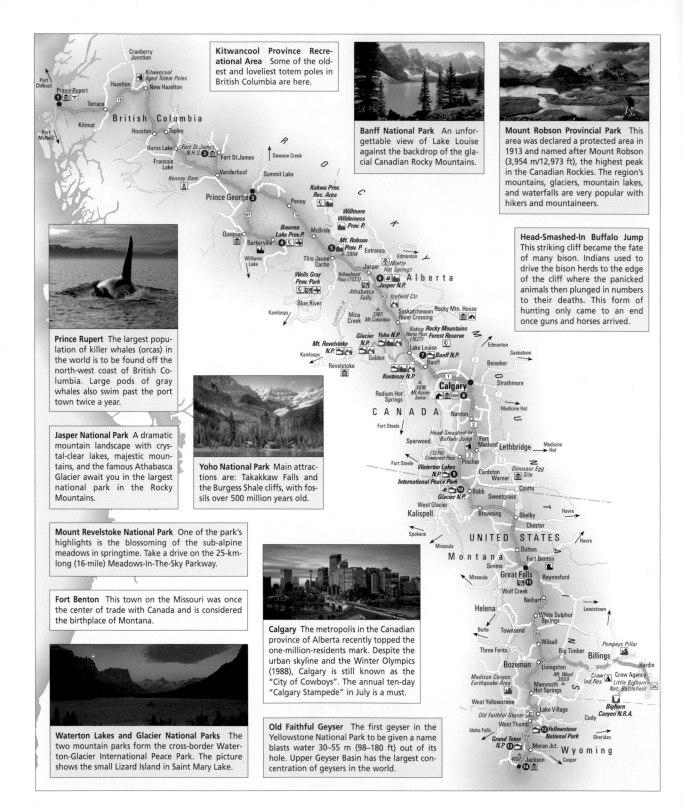

Kitwancool Province Recreational Area Some of the oldest and loveliest totem poles in British Columbia are here.

Banff National Park An unforgettable view of Lake Louise against the backdrop of the glacial Canadian Rocky Mountains.

Mount Robson Provincial Park This area was declared a protected area in 1913 and named after Mount Robson (3,954 m/12,973 ft), the highest peak in the Canadian Rockies. The region's mountains, glaciers, mountain lakes, and waterfalls are very popular with hikers and mountaineers.

Head-Smashed-In Buffalo Jump This striking cliff became the fate of many bison. Indians used to drive the bison herds to the edge of the cliff where the panicked animals then plunged in numbers to their deaths. This form of hunting only came to an end once guns and horses arrived.

Prince Rupert The largest population of killer whales (orcas) in the world is to be found off the north-west coast of British Columbia. Large pods of gray whales also swim past the port town twice a year.

Jasper National Park A dramatic mountain landscape with crystal-clear lakes, majestic mountains, and the famous Athabasca Glacier await you in the largest national park in the Rocky Mountains.

Yoho National Park Main attractions are: Takakkaw Falls and the Burgess Shale cliffs, with fossils over 500 million years old.

Mount Revelstoke National Park One of the park's highlights is the blossoming of the sub-alpine meadows in springtime. Take a drive on the 25-km-long (16-mile) Meadows-In-The-Sky Parkway.

Fort Benton This town on the Missouri was once the center of trade with Canada and is considered the birthplace of Montana.

Calgary The metropolis in the Canadian province of Alberta recently topped the one-million-residents mark. Despite the urban skyline and the Winter Olympics (1988), Calgary is still known as the "City of Cowboys". The annual ten-day "Calgary Stampede" in July is a must.

Waterton Lakes and Glacier National Parks The two mountain parks form the cross-border Waterton-Glacier International Peace Park. The picture shows the small Lizard Island in Saint Mary Lake.

Old Faithful Geyser The first geyser in the Yellowstone National Park to be given a name blasts water 30–55 m (98–180 ft) out of its hole. Upper Geyser Basin has the largest concentration of geysers in the world.

Grand Teton National Park Elk roam the low-lying areas of the Teton Range, one of the most impressive mountain chains in the USA. The highest peak, Grand Teton, is 4,197 m (13,770 ft). Some of the mountains are covered with glaciers while former glaciers have formed deep lakes in the basins.

Salt Lake City The skyline of the Utah capital is dominated by the Capitol building (1915). Salt Lake City, venue for the 2002 Winter Olympics, is the center of the growing global Mormon community.

Grand Canyon The canyon in north-west Arizona was formed by the Colorado River cutting into the Colorado Plateau. The 350-km-long (217-mile) and up to 1.8-km-deep (1-mile) canyon is one of the most impressive natural wonders in the USA.

Phoenix Once an Indian settlement, Phoenix is today an important high-tech center. It boasts buildings from all eras, like this colonial-era mission church. The palms that grow throughout the city are characteristic of Phoenix.

Mission San Xavier del Bac This bright white mission church was completed in 1790 by Franciscans. It is an impressive example of Spanish mission architecture and one of the best-preserved churches in the whole of the United States.

Yellowstone National Park Geysers and hot springs – in this case Morning Glory Prismatic Spring – are the most spectacular attractions in the largest and oldest national park in the USA, situated in the Rocky Mountains at an altitude of 2,400 m (7,874 ft).

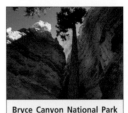

Capitol Reef National Park Rock needles tower over a sandstone cliff 150 km (93 miles) long.

Bryce Canyon National Park The forces of erosion make an impressive display here, especially in the Bryce Amphitheater.

Wupatki National Monument The largest and best-preserved pueblo ruins, built by prehistoric Indians, are to be found north of Sunset Crater in the midst of a desert landscape. In total there are around 2,000 Sinagua and Anasazi dwellings.

Meteor Crater Some 50,000 years ago a meteorite landed in northern Arizona. It left behind a crater with a circumference of 1.3 km (0.81 miles) and a depth of 170 m (558 ft). Because of its geological similarity to the craters on the moon it is used as a NASA training ground for astronauts.

Montezuma Castle National Monument Six hundred years ago the Sinagua Indians built a twenty-room dwelling in a 30-m-high (98-ft) sandstone cliff face, extending over five storeys.

Pima Air and Space Museum There are over 200 planes on display here at the south-eastern edge of Tucson. The collection ranges from Wright Brothers-era models to the most modern of supersonic jets.

Tucson The center of the second-largest city in Arizona, after Phoenix, is dominated by skyscrapers. A colonial-era neighborhood with a number of adobe houses has been preserved in the shadows of the skyscrapers and makes a significant contribution to Tucson's charm.

Map labels:

Bozeman · Mt. Wood ▲ 3859 · Mammoth Hot Springs · Madison Canyon Earthquake Area · West Yellowstone · Lake Village · Cody · Old Faithful Geyser · West Thumb · ⑫ Yellowstone National Park · I d a h o · Butte · Grand Teton N.P. ⑬ · Moran Junction · Casper · Arco · Rexburg · 191 · Idaho Falls · Jackson · Boise · Alpine · Hoback Jct. · ⑭ · Pocatello · McCammon · Thayne · Daniel · Soda Springs · Boise · Downey · W y o m i n g · Montpelier · Garden City · Golden Spike N.H.S. · Bear Lake · Fossil Butte Nat. Mon. · Rock Springs · Tremonton · Logan · Green River · Brigham City · Ogden · Evanston · Ft. Bridger N.H.S. · Cheyenne · Great Salt Lake · Roy · Flaming Gorge Nat. Rec. Area · Reno · West Valley City · SALT LAKE CITY ⑮ · Dutch John · ⑯ Timpanogos Cave Nat. Mon. · Denver · Utah Lake · Provo · Eureka · Spanish Fork · Little Sahara R.A. · Nephi · Fairview · Delta · 15 · U t a h · Gunnison · Grand Junction · Ely · Scipio · Salina · Cove Fort · Loa · Cathedral Valley · Junction · Capitol Reef ⑰ N.P. · Cedar Breaks Nat. Mon. · Cedar City · Las Vegas · ⑳ · Cannonville · Escalante · Grand Staircase Escalante Nat. Mon. · Mt. Carmel Jct. · ⑲ Bryce Canyon N.P. · Hurricane · Kanab · Glen Canyon Dam · Lake Powell · Zion N.P. ㉑ · Pipe Spring Nat. Mon. · ㉒ Marble Canyon · Page · Jacob Lake · Antelope Canyon · White Mesa Natural Bridge · North Rim · Grand Canyon N.P. ㉔ · Cortez · Grand Canyon · Tuba City · Kingman · A r i z o n a · Cameron · Flagstaff · ㉕ · Wupatki Nat. Mon. · Winslow · Ash Fork · Sunset Crater Nat. Mon. · Walnut Canyon Nat. Mon. · Meteor Crater · Tuzigoot Nat. Mon. · ㉖ · Prescott · Cottonwood · Montezuma Castle Nat. Mon. · Albuquerque · Kingman · Congress · 89 · ㉗ · Payson · Aguila · Wickenburg · Show Low · Arizona Pioneer Living Hist. Mus. · 60 · Tonto Nat. Mon. · Sun City · Mesa · Globe · Los Angeles · PHOENIX ㉘ · Florence Junction · ㉙ · Florence · Lordsburg · San Diego · Casa Grande Ruins Nat. Mon. · 10 · Oracle Junction · Biosphere II · Arizona Sonora Desert Museum · ㉚ Tucson · Pima Air and Space Museum · Mission San Xavier del Bac · El Paso · Nogales (MEX)

USA

'The American Way of Life' between the Pacific Coast and the Sierra Nevada

Sun, sea and tanned surfers. It's a popular cliché image that many people have of California and, as with many such clichés, it has an element of truth to it. But the Golden State on the west coast of the USA has myriad other facets as well – majestic mountains, ancient forests with giant redwood trees, superb alpine lakes, breathtaking deserts and one of the most beautiful coastal roads in the country, Highway 1. On top of that there are lively cities such as Los Angeles, San Francisco and San Diego.

"Go West, young man, and grow up with the country!" Since the middle of the 19th century this call has inspired countless people to seek their fortunes in the promised lands of California. Today, millions of tourists from all over the world are also drawn by the magic of this region on the West Coast.

Highway 1, with its magnificent views of the mighty Pacific Ocean, could easily be considered one of the most beautiful roads in the world. Yet the "hinterland" offers equally spectacular natural wonders, from the rock walls and waterfalls of Yosemite National Park and the bizarre limestone formations of

Mono Lake to the glorious giant sequoias (redwood trees) scattered throughout the numerous parks around the state. They flourish wonderfully along the misty Pacific coast as well as in the cool Sierra Nevada mountains. Then there are arid regions such as the Mojave Desert which, at first glance, seem devoid of almost any life. After the brief, irregular showers of rain, however, the desert produces a magical variety of plant life.

Death Valley, somewhat off this tour's path, is surrounded by mountains rising to more than 3,000 m (9,843 ft) and evokes lunar landscapes of spectacular proportions. It also boasts such superlatives as the lowest point in the Western Hemisphere and the highest temperature ever recorded.

European visitors are continually overwhelmed by the diversity and beauty of these magnificent natural landscapes.

The famous Santa Monica Pier has been restored to its former glory.

The awe-inspiring sequoias in Redwood National Park can reach heights of up to 112 m (367 ft).

San Francisco by moonlight. The 2.7 km (1.7-mile) Golden Gate Bridge, at the entrance to San Francisco Bay, was completed in 1937 and links the city with Marin County to the north.

Indeed, Mother Nature has been generous to this Pacific region. Gold discoveries in 1849 brought about the first major wave of settlement.

Hollywood, synonymous with the glamorous world of film, has the sunny Southern California climate to thank for its existence. Yet the same sun that draws tourists to the beaches also makes the hugely important agricultural business here a major challenge, one that is really only possible with the help of sophisticated and far-reaching irrigation systems.

The Californians have artfully mastered their often tough natural environment and do not even seem too distracted by the San Andreas Fault, repeatedly the cause of disastrous earthquakes here.

A tour through California brings to life the many places linked to the region's Spanish and Mexican legacy, like Santa Barbara, San Luis Obispo, or Carmel, all of which play host to mission churches founded by Spanish monks along "El Camino Real", the Royal Road. San Francisco, often considered the most "European" city in the USA and a dream destination for people around the world, originally boomed after the discovery of gold in the foothills of the Sierra Nevada.

It was only in the 20th century that its rival to the south, Los Angeles, grew to its current sprawling size – life without a car is inconceivable here. California's open-mindedness has often promoted important subculture movements that

have even had global influence – the Beat Generation, the Hippies, the Gay Movement, rural communes, ecological movements, and other milieus experimenting with alternative lifestyles. Not to be forgotten is

of course Silicon Valley, the pioneer site of the digital revolution in the 20th century.

As a whole, a trip through California reflects a sort of microcosm of what the "American Dream" is all about.

Yosemite National Park: As the landscape rises, trees become more sparse.

1

In addition to numerous cultural highlights, our tour through California offers a look at some breathtaking natural landscapes. The drive up Highway 1 from Los Angeles to San Francisco is one of the best parts, running high above the spectacular Pacific coast for most of the way.

1 Los Angeles (see pages 108-109). Our route begins in Los Angeles on Highway 101 (the Ventura Highway). From there, the most famous stretch of Highway 1 branches off at Las Cruces (called Cabrillo Highway here), a few miles beyond Santa Barbara. It covers an often breathtaking route over bridges or directly along the steep Pacific coastline, providing continuously spectacular views.

2 Santa Barbara Founded in 1782 as a Spanish garrison, the city's architecture fascinates visitors. After being reduced to rubble in 1925 by a heavy earthquake, the city took the opportunity to rebuild the entire downtown in Spanish colonial style, an example of which is

the County Courthouse built in 1929. From the bell tower you can enjoy a wonderful view of the city. Mission Santa Barbara, officially nicknamed the "Queen of the Missions", also suffered severe damage in the 1925 earthquake and was initially restored before further rebuilding took place in the 1950s. The mission's characteristic combination of Roman, Moorish, and Spanish elements became the archetype of the California mission style. The mission church is the only one of the original California missions that is still being used as a church.

3 San Luis Obispo The heart of this tranquil little town at the base of the Santa Lucia Mountains is the San Luis Obispo de

Travel Information

Route profile
Length: approx. 2,500 km (1,554 miles), excluding detours
Time required: 3–4 weeks
Start and end: Los Angeles
Route (main locations): Los Angeles, Monterey, San Francisco, Eureka, Redwood National Park, Mount Shasta, Lassen Volcanic National Park, Lake Tahoe, Yosemite National Park, Sequoia and Kings Canyon National Park, Mono Lake, Mojave, Los Angeles

Traffic information:
Drive on the right in the USA. In autumn and spring you should enquire as to the condition of the roads in the national parks of the Cascade Range (Mount Shasta, Mount Lassen) and the Sierra Nevada (Yosemite, Sequoia and Kings Canyon) as the roads close in winter. Toll roads along the route: the 17-Mile Drive on the Monterey Peninsula and the Golden Gate Bridge (traveling into San Francisco).

Information:
Detailed information on national parks in California: *www.nps.gov*
Information and departure times for ferries to Santa Cruz Island from Ventura: *www.islandpackers.com* and from Santa Barbara: *www.truthaquatics.com*
Napa Valley information: *www.napavalley.com*

Tolosa Mission, founded in 1772 as the fifth of more than twenty Californian missions. One of the

mission buildings adjoining the church has a museum with interesting art works by the Chu-

mash Indians, once present in the area.

❹ Hearst Castle, San Simeon
Hearst Castle, completed in 1947, is without doubt one of the classic tourist attractions along Highway 1. This bizarre "castle", situated above the town of San Simeon, was built by one of America's legendary newspaper magnates, William Randolph Hearst. Gothic and Renaissance features are combined with Moorish ornaments, while the Neptune Pool bears traces of Ancient Rome. But the 155

rooms of this kitschy, decadent setting also host valuable art treasures, from Ancient Egyptian, Greek, and Roman artefacts, and paintings from the Flemish, Gothic, and Italian Renaissance eras, to baroque pieces and priceless books.

❺ Big Sur The name refers to a 160-km (99-mile) stretch of coastline between San Simeon and Carmel. Sections of this frequently untouched landscape are indeed easy to reach thanks to Highway 1, but there are still remote, deserted bays, a mag-

nificently rocky coast, and backcountry that is easily accessible via the state park. North America's largest kelp forest (a type of seaweed) lies off the coast, as does the Monterey Canyon, which is similar in size to the actual Grand Canyon in Arizona. The unique attraction of this stretch of the highway is the Central Coast Range's sharp descent into the sea.
Architectural attractions include the 80-m (262-ft) Bixby Creek Bridge, an arch bridge dating from 1932.

❻ Carmel This settlement at the southern end of the Monterey Peninsula was established as an artists' colony after the San Francisco earthquake of 1906, taking in the many Bohemians who left the destroyed city. The town retains this character even today. The most original house in the town is the Tor House, carved out of stone blocks and built by the poet

Robinson Jeffers. During the heyday of the missions, the Mission San Carlos Borromeodel Rio Carmelo (Mission Carmel) was established in 1770 and served as a center of religious activities due to its proximity to the then capital of "Alta California", Monterey. The old mission kitchen, garden, and housing have been rebuilt according to the originals.

❼ Monterey During the colonial era this city, with its historically significant center, was the capital of "Alta California" and also the site of another famous mission. The Monterey State Historic Park consists of over thirty

1 Highway 1 joins the 160-km (99-mile) Big Sur Coast between San Simeon and Carmel.

2 Once home to a millionaire eccentric, Hearst Castle, San Simeon is now an impressive museum.

Cypress Point is one of the most popular spots on the California coast between Los Angeles and San Francisco. The gnarled, solitary cypress tree (popularly known as the Lone Cypress) on the tiny rock outcrop has to be one of the most photographed trees in the world.

If you want to see this glorious interplay of land and sea on the Monterey Peninsula, turn off Highway 1 onto 17-Mile Drive. The panorama road includes the tiny outcrop on which the famous tree has stood for over 250 years as well as vast pine and cypress forests.

Los Angeles

The "City of Angels" actually comprises several independent neighborhoods and a multitude of massive freeways. Some traces of the Spanish past can still be seen today in the old town, while Hollywood has become a modern legend. On the periphery are the beaches – Santa Monica, Malibu, and Venice.

Mann's Chinese Theater, a luxurious cinema in the style of a Chinese temple, was built in 1927 by Sid Grauman and was the scene of elaborate premieres during Hollywood's golden years. Legendary stars such as Elizabeth Taylor, Humphrey Bogart, and John Wayne have been immortalized with their hand- and footprints in the cement in front of the entrance. The best view of Los Angeles is from the Griffith Observatory on Mount Hollywood. There are still numerous adobe buildings from the 19th century in the old town. In this "El Pueblo de Los Angeles", Olvera Street is the scene of an annual carnival with street artists and colorful stalls.

Union Station is a magnificent railway station built in 1939 in the style of a Spanish mission. It was once a stop for legendary trains such as the Daylight Special or the City of Los Angeles. In the 1960s Venice Beach was the in-beach for spaced-out Beatniks and Hippies. Today the beach is frequented by countless street performers, skaters, rappers, and bodybuilders. The promenade, "Ocean Front Walk", is full of stalls selling T-shirts and sunglasses.

The J. Paul Getty Museum at the Getty Center is more than just an architectural sensation. On display in the building's five pavilions, the million-aire's legacy includes valuable paintings, graphic arts, furniture, and other exhibitions of note.

The broad, palm-lined Sunset Boulevard takes you through Bel Air and Beverly Hills. Even the smog seems to have disappeared from this artificial luxury oasis with its waving palm trees, blossoming gardens, and magnificent villas. There is hardly a single house without its own swimming pool and tennis court. The rich and famous live behind these walls, and they don't seem to want company.

The 1912 Beverly Hills Hotel on Sunset Boulevard was thoroughly renovated in 2005. Marilyn Monroe was a frequent guest of the famous Polo Lounge. Italian and French designer names dominate the expensive fashion shops on nearby Rodeo Drive.

The famous pier in Santa Monica was built in 1909 and renovated in the 1980s to its former glory. Even the wooden carousel still operates. Three streets away, on the Third Street Promenade between Broadway and Wilshire Boulevard, is a pedestrian zone with the usual chain stores as well as exclusive boutiques. Malibu, located 30 km (17 miles) north of Santa Monica, once a private ranch, has been home to famous film stars and singers since the 1940s. The numerous beaches are especially popular with surfers.

1 Numerous skyscrapers dominate the skyline of downtown Los Angeles.

2 The Boulevard of Broken Dreams – an evening street scene in Hollywood.

3 Rodeo Drive in Beverly Hills, one of the most elegant shopping miles in the world.

The impressive skyline hides the fact that the Downtown of Los Angeles lacks importance although investors have discovered the City anew in recent years. As a result, new high-rise buildings have been constructed, vast parks have been created, and a wave of interesting

restaurants have sprouted all over the place. Even the tramway is back on track. Often known by its initials, L.A., and nicknamed the City of Angels, Los Angeles is a world center of business, entertainment, culture, media, fashion, science, technology, and education.

historic sites including the oldest government building in California, the Customs House, dating back to 1840. The signposted "Path of History" takes you to all the important historic buildings. The Monterey Bay Aquarium presents the flora and fauna of the four large habitats of Monterey Bay – the kelp forest, the reef, the rocky coast, and the outer bay. Our journey then continues to San Francisco via the delightful seaside town of Santa Cruz.

❽ San Francisco (see pages 118–119). You depart San Francisco via its most famous landmark, the Golden Gate Bridge, towards the north, passing through Sausalito with its original houseboats and Victorian houses perched on the slopes above the North Bay. After a short distance on Highway 101 along the waterfront, Highway 1 turns off towards the Pacific at the town of Belvedere. From there it continues through the fabulous Point Reyes National Seashore to Fort Ross, 19 km (12 miles) north of Jenner.

❾ Fort Ross State Historic Park This fortified complex was founded in 1812 by Russian traders sent by the Tsars to supply their fellow fur hunters living in Alaska. Although the fort was abandoned in 1839,

part of the original complex still remains. The Russian Orthodox chapel, dating from 1824, is especially attractive and the cemetery with its Russian crosses is also worth visiting.

❿ Mendocino Fishermen from New England first settled here in 1852. Later adopted by artists as a place of residence, the town has a spectacular location high above the sea and still retains some of its East Coast character. It has often served as a set for Hollywood films.
Highway 1, still offering magnificent views of the Pacific, leaves the coast just north of Westport and joins up with Highway 101 again at Leggett.

⓫ Humboldt Redwoods State Park The 53-km-long (33-mile) Avenue of Giants was originally built as a stagecoach

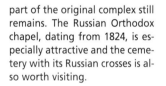

road and runs through the park for about 1 km (0.6 miles) parallel to Highway 101. As the park's name indicates, redwood trees are the main attraction here, and you'll see them in all their colossal glory as they dwarf the humans that marvel at them. Plenty of trails lead deep into the realm of the coastal giants. The trees are often more than 500 years old and they flourish in the mild, misty climate on the coast. Despite extensive deforestation in the past there are still dense clusters in places. One oddity is the almost 100-m (328-ft) Chandelier Tree – it has a passage cut into it that is large enough for cars.

⓬ Eureka Today the most important industrial center on the northern Californian coast, this town was founded by gold diggers in 1850. The examples of

Victorian architecture include the unusual William Carson Mansion, which resembles a haunted castle with numerous towers and gables. Local timber businessman Carson built it in the 1880s. Another must-see is the Clarke Museum with its Victorian age exhibits and its fine collection of Native American artworks.

⓭ Redwood National Park This national park (a UNESCO World Heritage Site), founded in 1968, protects some of the largest redwood forests in the world. It extends over a total of 125 km (78 miles) from Arcata (north of Eureka) to Crescent City (center of the national park). Historic Crescent City was largely destroyed on 28 March 1964 by a tsunami with 6-m-high (20-ft) waves, caused by an earthquake in Alaska.

3

4

In Crescent City you turn onto Highway 99 and travel for about 110 km (68 miles) via Grant's Pass into Oregon where Highway 199 joins Interstate Highway 5. Cave fans can visit the Oregon Caves on the way. The mighty Cascade Range begins with the climb up to the 1,361-m (4,465-ft) Siskiyou Pass beyond Medford.

⑭ **Mount Shasta** This 4,317-m (14,165-ft) volcano towers majestically over the much lower peaks around it. A mountain road with fantastic views climbs up to an altitude of 2,400 m (7,874 ft), but an ascent on foot to the peak of the stratovolcano should only be attempted by experienced mountaineers.
On the south-western side of the mountain is the little village of Mount Shasta City with a remote ranger station.

Highway 89 turns off to the south-east directly after Mount Shasta before making its way through the mountains of the Mount Shasta National Forest past the 40-m (131-ft) Burney Falls in Lassen National Forest. At Subway Cave, a 396-m (1,299-ft) lava pipe, a well-signposted road turns off to the south-west in the direction of Lassen Volcanic National Park, the entrance to which is near Manzanita Lake.

⑮ **Lassen Volcanic National Park** This national park takes its name from the volcano in the Cascade Range. The last dramatic eruption of the 3,187-m (10,457-ft) Mount Lassen took place in 1915 and destroyed some 40,500 ha (100,076 acres) of land. The Bumpass Hell trail is especially impressive, with hot springs, mud pools, and smoke

columns highlighting the undisturbed tectonic activity in the area.
As Lassen Park Road, Highway 89 leads through the national park to Mineral where you turn east onto Highway 36 to Susanville. From there you continue on Highway 395 between the Diamond Mountains in the west and Honey Lake in the east towards the south and over the border to Reno in Nevada. Here, Highway 80 turns off westwards to San Francisco, but you exit the highway after 30 km (19 miles) at Truckee and continue south to Lake Tahoe.

⑯ **Lake Tahoe** At an elevation of 1,920 m (6,300 ft), this alpine lake is 35 km (22 miles) long and 13 km (8 miles) wide. It reaches a depth of more than 500 m (1,641 ft) in parts and is one of the deepest inland lakes in the

world. The majesty of this place is especially apparent from out on the lake itself. The border between California and Nevada actually runs through the middle of it. The 72-Mile Drive that circles the lake includes sightseeing attractions along the shore, and is the access road to the state park there. On the lake's southern shore is South Lake Tahoe, which attracts many visitors with its casinos.
North of the city the replica of a 10th-century Viking fortress stands in Emerald Bay State Park. The backcountry offers perfect conditions for skiers. The 1960 Winter Olympics were held at Squaw Valley on the northwestern side of the lake.
Highway 395 continues through the sparsely populated mountains to the eastern entrance of

1 When it opened in 1937, the almost 3-km (1.9-mile) Golden Gate was the world's longest bridge.

2 A storm on the Pacific coast close to Fort Bragg in Mendocino.

3 Mount Lassen reflected off Manzanita Lake. The volcano erupted often between 1914 and 1921.

4 Emerald Bay, 15 km (9 miles) north of the town of South Lake Tahoe, is in the state park of the same name.

The summit of the impressive Mount Shasta is covered by eternal snow and ice. The giant rises majestically above the rugged mountain landscape in northern California. The permanently snow-capped cone dominates the skyline of southern Oregon and northern California.

for hundreds of miles. Shasta is in fact the most massive stratovolcano in the Cascade chain, rising almost 3600 m (12,000 ft) from the surrounding lowlands, and supports eight glaciers including the largest in California. The deep winter snowpack provides good skiing

The Eagle Falls tumble down the rocks in two foaming cascades into the valley of Lake Tahoe. The picturesque waterfall is a popular destination for day trips at short walking distance from the circuit road around Lake Tahoe. Topping off the whole experience of visiting Eagle

Falls is the fantastic views overlooking Emerald Bay, Lake Tahoe and the surrounding mountains available from the top of the falls. The much more splendid and awe inspiring Lower Eagle Falls drops 42 m (140 ft) and is best viewed during the spring run off.

San Francisco

A unique location overlooking an expansive bay on the Pacific Ocean, historic cable cars, unique neighborhoods like Chinatown and North Beach, bustling Market Street, Fisherman's Wharf, and the Golden Gate Bridge have all made San Francisco, the "Paris of the American West", into a revered travel destination.

The city was founded by the Spanish in 1776 and named Yerba Buena. Only in 1847 was the name changed to San Francisco, when the San Francisco de Asís Mission was founded by Father Junipero Serra.

The city's most turbulent period began in January 1848 when gold was discovered in northern California. San Francisco became a base for many gold diggers heading north. More than 40,000 adventurers and profiteers settled in the city in 1849 alone. It soon grew to become an important trading hub, and has remained so even after the massive earthquake destroyed entire neighborhoods throughout the city in 1906. The famous cable cars were developed by Andrew S. Hallidie in 1869, the first of them rolling through town in 1873. By 1880 there were already eight lines and since 1964 they have been protected as part of the city's heritage. One of the USA's most well-known landmarks, the Golden Gate Bridge, opened for traffic in 1937 following four years of construction. Including its access roads, the bridge is 11 km (9 miles) long, and the pylons extend 228 m (748 ft) out of the water.

1 The characteristic triangular shape of the Transamerica Pyramid is clearly recognizable among the skyscrapers.

2 With their pastel hues and stylish detail, the so-called Painted Ladies are excellent examples of Victorian architecture.

3 Since 1873 cable car lines have been in use throughout San Francisco.

4 Bay Bridge, with tow decks, linking San Francisco to Oakland

Yosemite National Park at Lee Vining. Highway 120 takes you over the Tioga Pass at an elevation of 3,031 m (9,945 ft) and heads west towards Tuolumne Grove, located 56 km (35 miles) away at the north-west entrance of the park.

17 Yosemite National Park

Not only one of the most renowned parks in the USA, but also one of the oldest – the initial areas were first declared a national park in the 1860s. This protected area was extended in around 1890, and it was enlarged to its present size in 1905.

Many of the main attractions here are in the 10-km-long (6-mile) Yosemite Valley, at the epicenter of the park – majestic peaks such as El Capitan or Half Dome, and the glorious Yosemite Falls, over 739 m (2,425 ft) high. Around 500 giant redwoods, some of them over 75 m (246 ft) high, can be found in Mariposa Grove on the park's southern border. The early summer blossoms of sub-alpine plants in the Tuolumne Meadows are a special treat. Glacier Point, at 2,138 m (7,015 ft) , towers almost 1,000 m (3,281 ft) over the valley and offers spectacular panoramic views over large areas of the park. Get there via Glacier Point Road. The visitor center provides background details on the park and the Yosemite Museum gives you an idea of the history of the Miwok and Paiute Indians. The Pioneer Center, another museum made up of blockhouses from various parts of the park, documents the life of the early Wild West settlers.

The approach to the adjoining Sequoia and Kings Canyon National Park is difficult as this is accessible only from the southern side. To reach it you need to leave Yosemite via Highway 41 in the south and head to Fresno. From there Highway 180 leads to the Big Stump Entrance in the west of the park.

18 Sequoia and Kings Canyon National Park

These two national parks, which are administered as one entity, are perhaps less famous than their northern neighbor but they offer breathtaking scenery nonetheless: mountain forests, granite domes, and giant canyons, including Kings Canyon, one of the deepest in America. The Sequoia National Park protects an impressive number of giant redwoods in various sections – Cedar Grove, Grant Grove, and Giant Forest. The "General Sherman" tree in the Giant Forest, standing at 85 m (279 ft), is said to be the largest tree in the world by volume, and five of the world's ten largest trees are in this park. The viewing point at Moro Rock pro-

vides a fantastic panorama of the area and is reached via more than a hundred stone steps. If the 150-km (93-mile) detour is too far for you, then leave Yosemite Park via the same route, return to Highway 395, and then continue to the "most beautiful lake in California".

⑲ **Mono Lake** It has an unusually productive ecosystem, and is a critical nesting habitat. Due to Southern California's need for water since the early 1940s, the tributaries that once fed Mono Lake have been drastically depleted. Until 1994, when the lake was given official protection, evaporation had exceeded inflow rates and the salt content of the lake rose to a level three times greater than that of the Pacific. This cycle turned the lake's islands into peninsulas and exposed the breeding grounds of a number of already endangered waterfowl to pred-

ators and threatened their existence. This problem has been reversed and the lake is recovering. For visitors, however, the lower water level makes the landscape on and around the lake even more attractive because the bizarre tufa pillars that formed under the water over centuries now rise out of the water.

On the southern shores there are a number of hiking trails leading to these extraordinary formations.

The road then continues south through the scenic Owens Valley between the White Mountains and the Sierra Nevada. To the west is Sequoia and Kings Canyon National Park.

On the south-eastern edge of the park stands mighty Mount Whitney, at 4,418 m (14,495 ft) the tallest mountain in the continental United States, towering over the spaghetti-western backdrop town of Lone Pine.

Those heading for the desert can take Highway 190 from here to Death Valley National Park (80 km/50 miles). Death Valley hosts the lowest point in North America, Badwater, and is 193 km (120 miles) long.

If you follow Highway 395 further south, the foothills of the Sierra Nevada are visible to the west, while to the east it becomes increasingly flat and dry. Parts of the Mojave Desert are used for military purposes, in-

1 Yosemite National Park. Even in winter, El Capitan and the 190-m-high (623-ft) Bridal Veil Falls make an impressive picture.

2 The bizarre tufa stone formations in Mono Lake were formed by underwater chemical reactions.

3 The Sequoia and Kings Canyon National Park covers the southern end of the Sierra Nevada Range.

The legendary redwood trees are a must-see when visiting the impressive alpine mountain landscape of Sequoia and Kings Canyon National Parks in the south of the Sierra Nevada. Wheras the trees shown here don't grow as tall as the typical Redwoods in northern

California, their trunk diameter can reach up to 11 m (36 ft). The Kings Canyon park features a number of scenic wonders, including some of the largest trees in the world, one of the deepest canyons in the U.S., and some of the highest mountain peaks in the United States.

The bizarre limestone tufa formations in the waters of Mono Lake have been shaped by an interaction between freshwater and alkali salts. The salinity of the basic lake rises dramatically. The volcanic lake is a temporary habitat for migration birds in spring and fall.

Mono Lake is believed to have formed at least 760,000 years ago, dating back to the Long Valley eruption. Sediments located below the ash layer hint that Mono Lake could be a remnant of a larger and older lake that once covered a large part of Nevada and Utah.

Yosemite National Park

Yosemite National Park is a natural paradise of green valleys, dense forests, mighty waterfalls, and giant rock formations.

The Merced River has left a deep gouge in the ancient landscape of Yosemite National Park, and this long, winding valley is where the lodges and Visitor Center for the park are to be found. Half Dome and El Capitan watch over Yosemite Valley like two colossi, and in particular El Capitan (2,307 m/7,570 ft) is popular with climbers, who can even book courses in the valley below.

The sheer wall of the enormous peak, three times the height of the Empire State Building, is extremely challenging. Rising 2,695 m (8,840 ft) from the valley floor and looking like it has been cut in half with a knife, the Half Dome was formed by massive ice formations about 250,000 years ago, long before there were any humans on the American continent and when Glacier Point was buried under a thick sheet of ice. The first people entered Yosemite Valley during the Ice Age, seeing Tenaya Lake when it was still a glacier. Powerful natural forces formed the valley, shaping the granite rocks. Modern tourists take a shuttle bus or their own car up to Glacier Point, 100 m (330 ft) above the valley, to enjoy one of the most breathtakingly beautiful views in the West.

The mighty cascades of the Yosemite Falls and the Bridal Veil are two waterfalls well worth seeing, and there are giant sequioa trees growing in Mariposa Grove; the Giant Sequoia named Grizzly Giant is between probably 1900–2400 years old: the oldest tree in the grove. It has a circumference of almost 30 m (100 ft). Two of its trees are among the 25 largest Giant Sequoias in the world.

1 El Capitan and the Merced River in a wintry landscape in Yosemite National Park.

cluding the US Naval Weapons Center, for example, which occupies a huge tract of land between the now dry Owens Lake and Ridgecrest.

⑳ Red Rock Canyon State Park This park is located in the Paso Mountains at the far southern foothills of the Sierra Nevada and is a source of fascination with its canyons, its bizarrely eroded rock formations, and its impressive display of colors – red, white, and brown sandstone alternate with the white clay layers and dark lava tones. While the western side of the mountains rise gently, the eastern side dazzles with its steep cliffs. This landscape has been used as the set for so many Hollywood westerns that it evokes a feeling of déjà vu in some visitors. South of the small town of Mojave you pass Edwards Air Force Base, internationally known as the space shuttle landing site. The NASA Dryden Flight Research Center is open to visitors but only by prior appointment. It was from here that Chuck Yeager took off in the aircraft that broke the sound barrier for the first time. The journey then continues via Highway 14 back towards Los Angeles. The San Gabriel Mountains, with peaks rising to nearly

2,000 m (6,562 ft), begin 100 km (62 miles) beyond the town of Mojave and border the greater metropolitan area on its northeast side.
North-west of San Fernando, Highway 14 joins Interstate Highway 5, which you will take back into Los Angeles before exiting at the Hollywood Freeway (170).

㉑ Hollywood The view from Sunset Boulevard of the "Hollywood" sign on the slopes of this Los Angeles district is world famous. The letters originally read "Hollywoodland" and were erected in 1923 as an advertisement for a property scheme. However, they have now long been the symbol of a place synonymous the world over with the film industry, and of course all of its glamor and glitter. Made out to be the main streets

of the city in many a film, Sunset Boulevard and Hollywood Boulevard are in fact relatively unspectacular, but there are a few places to get a feel for the stars of Hollywood's more appealing heyday.
The famous Walk of Fame is part of Hollywood Boulevard. In 1960 golden stars bearing the names of legendary film actors were engraved and set in the pavement. There are now more than 2,000 of them.
Mann's Chinese Theater, where countless noteworthy Hollywood films celebrated their premiers, is also on Hollywood Boulevard (address 6925). The concrete hand- and footprints of many stars, as well as their signatures, can be seen in front of the Chinese-style building.
Today, the majority of the studios have moved to other parts of Los Angeles such as Burbank

or San Fernando Valley. You can visit the final resting places of many stars such as Cecil B. de Mille, Rudolph Valentino, Peter Finch, or Jayne Mansfield in Hollywood Memorial Park.
From Hollywood the route continues via Beverly Hills for a few kilometers to the beaches in Santa Monica or Venice. In nearby Anaheim, Disneyland attracts visitors with its numerous fairground rides and classic comic figures such as Mickey Mouse and Donald Duck.

1 Since many desert tracks and roads, such as this one at Little Lake, run through remote areas, you should make sure the tank is full and you have sufficient water in the car.

2 A thunderstorm approaches over the Mojave Desert.

Redwood National Park Humans are dwarfed by the redwoods (sequoias), which can grow to 112 m (367 ft) – the tallest trees in the world.

San Francisco The imposing Golden Gate Bridge is the landmark of this, the "most European city in the USA". San Francisco is a magnet for many subcultures with the motto "live and let live".

Big Sur Since the 1930s, Highway 1 has run directly along the steep coast, with fantastic views over the mighty Pacific.

Monterey This little town owes its fame to writer John Steinbeck, born in 1902 in neighbouring Salinas, who immortalized it in novels such as *Tortilla Flat* or *Cannery Row*.

Hearst Castle Newspaper tycoon William Randolph Hearst built himself a more than ample residence to house his collection of art treasures.

Los Angeles The "city in search of a center" displays its Mediterranean charm in many of its neighborhoods, be it Malibu or Venice Beach on the coast, the celebrity neighborhood of Beverly Hills, or the slightly more bohemian Westwood.

Oregon Caves National Monument Visit a fascinating underground labyrinth of marble caves with bizarre shapes, created by water over thousands of years, in the Siskiyou Mountains in southern Oregon. The Oregon pine (also called the Douglasie) is one of the tallest trees in the world and grows in this region.

Hollywood The reality of this town on the north side of Los Angeles is not as glamorous as the name might imply, but the Walk of Fame or Mann's Chinese Theater still evoke the golden age of American film.

San Diego A metropolis has arisen around the Old Town, and it radiates a holiday atmosphere thanks to a sunny climate. Balboa Park is certainly worth a visit, with museums and one of the world's most diverse zoos.

Lassen Volcanic National Park The 3,187 m (10,457 ft) high Lassen Peak, the only active volcano left in California, stands within this national park. At the Sulphur Works Thermal Area, foul-smelling sulphur leaks out of the ground in fizzing, stinking plumes.

Yosemite National Park One of the first national parks in the USA boasts many attractions – rock faces like El Capitan with its extreme vertical face, or impressive waterfalls like Yosemite Falls (739 m/2,425 ft).

Kings Canyon Majestic redwoods that reach heights of over 80 m (262 ft) are the main attraction in this wonderful park. Some of the trees have been here for more than 2,000 years.

Mount Whitney California is the state of superlatives – Mount Whitney, at 4,418 m (14,495 ft), is the highest mountain in the USA, excluding Alaska.

Disneyland Mickey Mouse's Empire has been drawing innumerable visitors since 1955 with its various theme parks.

Map labels

Coos Bay
Grants Pass
Eugene
Medford
Cave Junction
199
Klamath Falls
Crescent City
O r e g o n
Oregon Caves Nat. Mon.
Siskiyou Pass (1361)
Klamath
Yreka
Klamath Falls
13 Redwood N.P.
Klamath Mountains
4317 Mt. Shasta
Eureka 12
Mount Shasta 14
89
Burney Falls
Shasta Lake
Humboldt Redwoods S.P. 11
Redding
Subway Cave
Lassen Volcanic N.P.
Leggett
Red Bluff
Mineral
15
Susanville
Fort Bragg
Mendocino 10
Alturas
Honey Lake
Ukiah
Doyle
1
Point Arena
Clear Lake
101
Fort Ross S.H.P. 9
Yuba City
Truckee
Reno
Salt Lake City
Squaw Valley
Carson City
Jenner
Sacramento
South Lake Tahoe
16
Lake Tahoe
Point Reyes Nat. Seashore
Napa
Topaz
395
Golden Gate Bridge 8
Berkeley
Stockton
N e v a d a
SAN FRANCISCO
Oakland
San Mateo
San Jose
Yosemite N.P. 17
19 Mono Lake
Lee Vining
Tonopah
Ano Nuevo
Los Banos
4010
Devils Postpile
Santa Cruz
Monterey 7
4263 Boundary Peak
Bishop
Monterey Peninsula
Pinnacles Nat. Mon.
Kings Canyon N.P.
Carmel 6
Pfeiffer Big Sur S.P.
Fresno
Big Sur 5
18
Julia Pfeiffer S.P.
Mt. Whitney 4418
Lone Pine
4 Hearst San Simeon S.H.M.
Sequoia N.P.
Owens Lake
Death Valley N.P.
Abolones Beach
Paso Robles
Morro Bay
3 San Luis Obispo
Little Lake
Bakersfield
Ridgecrest
Pismo Beach
Santa Maria
20 Red Rock Canyon S.P.
Jalama
Mojave
Lompoc
Mission Santa Barbara
Mt. Pinos 2092
Edwards Air Force Base
Gaviota Beach
Palmdale
Barstow
Santa Barbara
Santa Cruz I.
Ventura
Getty Center
Hollywood
Channel Islands N.P.
Oxnard
21
Pasadena
Santa Monica
LOS ANGELES 1
Anaheim
Phoenix
Long Beach
Disneyland
Huntington Beach
Mission San Juan Capistrano
Oceanside
15
Escondido
SAN DIEGO
Yuma
TIJUANA
Ensenada
M É X I C O

USA

The "Wild West": cowboys, canyons and cactus

"Go West, young man..." – It is no coincidence that tourists in America's South-West still follow the old call made to pioneers and settlers. Virtually nowhere else in the world will you find more bizarre rock formations, wilder mountains, more breathtaking canyons, more remote cactus deserts, more impressive caves, or hotter valleys. The remnants of ancient Native American pueblo culture are also unique, and their adobe buildings and handicrafts still fascinate visitors from all over the world.

The American South-West, which is the legendary "Wild West" of New World pioneers, stretches from the southern Rocky Mountains in the east to the Sierra Nevada in the west, and from the northern edge of the Colorado Plateau in Utah to the Mexican border in the south. Six states make up the region: Arizona, Nevada, Utah, Colorado, New Mexico, and California.

The north is dominated by the Colorado Plateau, which covers an area of roughly 110,000 sq km (2,460 sq mi) at elevations of 1,000 to 3,000 m (3,281 and 9,843 ft). The most impressive and most beautiful national parks are found here, such as the Grand Canyon, Bryce Canyon, Zion, Arches, and Canyonlands. There are a total of eleven national parks in the South-West alone, as well as numerous monuments and state parks. The Organ Pipe Cactus National Monument near Why, Arizona, is even

The authentic "Wild West"

a UNESCO World Nature Heritage Site. Other national monuments are dedicated to ancient and historic Native American settlements.

And if that isn't enough, there are also national historic parks mostly dedicated to the pioneer days, such as the Hubbell Trading Post near Ganado, Arizona. In the south, the plateau stretches out to the Sonora Desert, which extends deep into Mexico. To the north is the Mojave Desert, home of Death Valley with the lowest point in North America. Temperatures of over 50°C (122°F) in the shade are not uncommon here. But anyone driving into the valley before sunrise will experience an unforgettable interplay of hues on the bizarre rock in places like Zabriskie Point.

Monument Valley glowing red in the evening light is for many people the epitome of Wild West romanticism.

Delicate Arch in south-east Utah is the symbol not only of Arches National Park, but also of America's entire South-West. The 13.7-m-high (45-ft) sandstone arch glows in the warm light of the evening sun.

The Colorado River is the dominant feature of the entire South-West and runs for over 2,300 km (1,429 miles).

It originates in the Rocky Mountains, flows through man-made Lake Powell in Utah, continues to whittle away at the Grand Canyon as it has done for millions of years, and finally peters out before reaching the Gulf of California. The spectacular natural beauty of the American South-West was created over 65 million years ago when the pressure of the Pacific Plate formed the mighty Rocky Mountains and the vast Colorado Plateau was pushed up.

Giant fractures allowed stones more than a billion years old to emerge, after which erosion from rivers and the elements created the fantastic worlds of pillars, towers, arches, craters, and gorges.

The rugged, mostly arid land was originally exclusively Native American territory, and the oldest traces of their ancient desert culture are some eight thousand years old. About three thousand years ago, sedentary peoples built multi-storey settlements called pueblos. The arrival of the Spaniards in the mid-16th century, however, marked the beginning of a drastic decline of their civilizations. In the 20th century, cities were built on former Native American lands.

The contrasts in the South-West are therefore remarkable: fascinating remnants of ancient cultures juxtaposed with raucous metropolises, puritan Mormon settlements near the glitz and kitsch of Las Vegas. One journey is really not enough to take it all in, but anyone who follows the dream route laid out before you, starting in Los Angeles, following the Rio Grande northwards through New Mexico, exploring the wonders of Utah, and then making a great arch back towards the City of Angels via Las Vegas and Death Valley, will experience at least a handful of the highlights.

And, don't be surprised, at the end of the trip, you will realize that the only option left is to come back and see more.

This Indian chief only wears his full feathered headdress on festive occasions.

1

This journey from Los Angeles through Arizona, New Mexico, Colorado, Utah, and Nevada back to the Pacific takes you through impressive rock landscapes, deserts, and metropolises, and includes a look into the thousand-year-old history of the Native Americans.

1 Los Angeles Your trip begins in the second-largest metropolis in the United States, Los Angeles. Approximately seventeen million people live in an area that stretches 71 km (44 miles) north to south and 47 km (29 miles) east to west. It is bordered in the West by the Pacific Ocean and in the north and east by high mountains. For some reason, however, the founders of the city, when they established the original Pueblo de Nuestra Señora La Reina de Los Angeles, chose a location 25 km (16 miles) from the coast.

Today, L.A., the most common abbreviation of the city's name, is the most important industrial and services metropolis in the western United States, a status to which the film industry has contributed immensely. The first American film was shot here in 1910, and the first film with sound was made in 1927, bringing world fame to Hollywood and Beverly Hills.

Today, the Hollywood Freeway separates the city's two main centers. El Pueblo in the northeast is the actual Old Town district, and the Civic Center in the south-west is the modern downtown. Chinatown borders the north of the Old Town, while Little Tokyo is located south of the Civic Center. The focal point of the historic center is the Plaza with the old mission church of Nuestra Señora La Reina, built by Spanish Franciscans in 1922. The picturesque Olvera Street unfolds as a Mexican street market and is also home to the city's

oldest house, the Avila Adobe House, dating back to 1818. The focal point of the Civic Center district is the high-rise City Hall

building, erected in 1928. The viewing platform on the 27th floor provides the best views of greater Los Angeles.

The striking Museum of Contemporary Art on Grand Avenue was designed by renowned Japanese architect Arata Isozaki. The section of Wilshire Boulevard between Highland and Fairfax avenues is known as the Miracle Mile and features interesting art deco buildings. Of course, you should not miss Hollywood. Although very little of the former glitz and glamor of the neighborhood remains, Mann's Chinese Theater is still an eye-catcher designed in Chinese pagoda style. The cement blocks in the main courtyard have the footprints, handprints, and signatures of more than two hundred Hollywood personalities. The theater also marks the start of the famous "Walk of Fame" on Hollywood Boulevard, a collection of over two thousand pink marble stars with the names of Hollywood greats embossed on brass plaques.

Not far from the Chinese Theater are a few museums: the Hollywood Wax Museum with famous actors and politicians; the Guinness Book of World Records Museum, dedicated to the world's most bizarre records; and the CBS film and television studios near the Farmers Market. At Paramount Pictures you can get behind the scenes and even watch a live production if you are lucky. Sunset Boulevard begins at the Roosevelt Hotel, which hosted the first Oscars ceremony back in 1929. The point where it turns into Sunset Strip marks the start of Hollywood's nightclub district.

The route then heads south-east along the Hollywood and Santa Ana Freeways towards Anaheim, home of Disneyland.

2 Anaheim The Disneyland amusement park is by far the most significant attraction in Anaheim, a town founded by German immigrants in 1857. The most interesting building in the city is the Crystal Cathedral, a steel pipe edifice built in 1980 with a shell of mirrored glass.

The route now follows Interstate 91 to San Bernardino, where you can make a detour to the surprisingly high San Bernardino Mountains north of the city. The "Rim of the World Drive" heads up to an altitude of 2,200 m (1,367 ft) and provides magnificent views.

You then follow Interstate 10 east before joining Highway 62 and heading north-east towards the town of Twentynine Palms and the magnificent Joshua Tree National Park.

3 Joshua Tree National Park This park is living proof that the desert is alive. Apart from the striking Joshua trees, you will also find palm groves, cactus gardens, and juniper bushes here. After exploring the park, you will come out on the south side where you will get back on Interstate 10 heading east towards Phoenix.

4 Phoenix (see page 136) After visiting Phoenix, Interstate 10 takes you quickly south to the region around Tucson, the second-largest city in Arizona. Anyone looking to spend a bit more time getting to Tucson, however, should travel west on the Interstate 10 back to Buckeye and from there head south on Highway 85 to Why and the Organ Pipe Cactus National Monument. From there you can head east to Tucson on Highway 86 and take a detour through Saguaro National Park-West, just north-west of the city.

5 Saguaro National Park This park owes its name to the candelabra saguaro cactuses.

1 Sunset over the Mormon "Trees of God" in Joshua Tree National Park.

1

Joshua Tree National Park

Joshua Tree National Park in Southern California boasts rare agave plants as well as a great variety of other fascinating plant and animal life.

At first glance, the Joshua Tree National Park, which has only held national park status since 1994, seems a somewhat inhospitable and unattractive place, but journeying further in reveals the true beauty of the land. The rare Joshua trees stand like mute sentries, silhouetted against the mostly clear skies north-east of Palm Springs. The cactus-like plants are related to yuccas and grow to heights of up to 12 m (40 ft). They were given the name "Joshua tree" in the mid 19th century by a group of Mormon settlers, as the angled limbs of the giant succulents reminded the pious community of the outstretched arm of the prophet Joshua, indicating the way to heaven. An asphalt road winds through the park between stands of Joshua trees and Teddy Bear Chollas, which are especially beautiful in the twilight, and there are interesting hiking trails to follow in Hidden Valley and by the Barker Dam. Other plants in the park include the creosote bush, which exudes a poisonous sub-stance to kill other plants, and the palo verde, whose wood is green as photosynthesis takes place on the trunk and branches.

1 The White Tanks in Joshua Tree National Park, seen here illuminated at night, are famously steep rock formations.

2 Cactus-like Joshua trees were named by the Mormons, who thought the trees reminded them of the eponymous prophet pointing the way to heaven.

Phoenix

Phoenix, the capital of Arizona, is a mix of the Old West and unrelenting modernization represented by a series of museums, cultural and recreational facilities, and a booming high-tech industry.

At an altitude of 369 m (1,211 ft), this city in the Valley of the Sun typically has three hundred sunny days a year. However, thanks to countless irrigation systems – which supply water for agriculture as well as golf courses – and despite its desert location, Phoenix is actually quite green. Along with the Piestewa Peak, the Camelback Mountains, which are the city's most famous icon, provide a good view over this urban sprawl in the Sonoran Desert. The suburb of Scottsdale is one of the city's best-known areas and is particularly popular for its luxury atmosphere and pretty Old Town quarter.

Alongside the modern office towers and high-rise buildings, you can still find traces of the past in downtown Phoenix. The famous Heritage Square forms the center of the city and is lined with beautiful Victorian houses. The most famous of these is Rosson House, which dates back to the late 19th century like many of the other Old Town buildings. The square is part of Heritage and Science Park, which also includes the Arizona Science Center (with planetarium) and the Phoenix Museum of History.

The Heard Museum has an extensive collection of prehistoric, traditional, and modern works by Native American artists from the South-West. The Phoenix Art Museum has artwork by international artists from the 15th to the 20th century, as well as modern art from America's western states.

Phoenix Zoo is one of the most famous zoos in the world and breeds many endangered species.

1 St Mary's Basilica among modern high-rise buildings

1

These kings of the desert can live up to 150 years old, grow to a height of 15 m (49 ft), and weigh up to 8 tonnes (8.8 tons). The most beautiful specimens of this cactus can be found in both the East and West sections of the 338-sq-km (130-sq-mi) Sonora Desert park.

On the southern edge of the western section of the park, you should definitely not miss out on a visit to the Arizona Sonora Desert Museum, which has impressive displays of the desert's flora and fauna. You can also see many of the desert animals that most people never get a glimpse of.

6 Tucson The "City of Sunshine", surrounded by the Santa Catalina Mountains, has an av-

erage of 350 sunny days a year. Spanish missionaries built a mission station in 1775, on the site of an old Native American settlement, and it quickly became a Spanish-Mexican colonial town. It is now the second-largest city in Arizona after Phoenix. It has a sizable university and, with military bases in the area, it has also become a high-tech center.

However, there is also an Old Town district in modern Tucson where the Spanish colonial center was located, between Alameda and Washington streets. There are some meticulously restored adobe houses that are representative of the old days. South of the historic Old Town is the Barrio Historico, originally the commercial district of the Spanish quarter. To-

day, many beautiful adobe buildings from the late 19th century are still in use here.

The Pima Air and Space Museum is an absolute must for aerospace enthusiasts. More than two hundred exhibits including airplanes, helicopters, ultralight aircraft, and all kinds of experimental devices are on display.

Fans of westerns will get their money's worth in Tucson as well. They only need to drive about 21 km (13 miles) west of the city to Old Tucson Studios, built in late 19th-century style as the set for some classic western films such as Gunfight at the O.K. Corral and Rio Bravo. Only a few miles further south is the San Xavier del Bac mission.

Leaving Tucson you head east on Interstate 10. In Willcox, you can make a detour on Highway 186 to the Chiricahua National Monument, where innumerable rock pillars stand to attention like soldiers – eroded remains of a volcanic eruption several million years ago. The Apaches held their last stand against US Army troops in the remote gorges of this region.

Back on Interstate 10 heading east, Stein's Ghost Town will appear near the Highway 80 turnoff. It is a typical example of

a stagecoach-era town that was eventually abandoned by its inhabitants.

Today, Stein is basically a tourist attraction. East of Las Cruces, you leave Interstate 10 and head north on Interstate 25, taking Highway 70 to Alamogordo after about 11 km (7 miles).

7 Alamogordo This city has undoubtedly made history. In the nearby San Andreas Mountains, US forces set up the White Sands Missile Range where the world's first atomic bomb, developed and built in Los Alamos, New Mexico, was detonated on 16 July 1945. Alamogordo now offers visitors both a technical and natural experience.

Technology enthusiasts will be drawn to the International Space Hall of Fame, which covers everything from the early Mercury capsule to the Apollo Program, and from the Russian space capsule to the Skylab. If it

1 Dune fields in the White Sands National Monument.

2 The San Xavier del Bac Mission is a perfect example of baroque church architecture in the Spanish colonial style.

was important to the discovery of outer space, it's in this museum. Nature enthusiasts will enjoy an excursion to White Sands National Monument west of the city as it is home to a unique gypsum dune landscape with dunes as high as 18 m (59 ft). To get there, take the 26-km (16-mile) Heart of Sands Drive.

8 **San Antonio** After circling the rocket testing grounds of White Sands, the road reaches the Rio Grande near San Antonio. A vast wetland area straddles the river to the south of this small township.
The Bosque del Apache National Wildlife Refuge is accessible to visitors through the Bosque del Apache Loop. There are viewing towers along the road for observing wild animals. Bosque del Apache has been inhabited for centuries. Over 700 years ago Piro Indians came to the valley for its fertile soil with abundant plant and animal life.

Highways 60, 36, and 117 then take you through the Plains of St Augustin to Grants.

9 **Grants** South of this small town you will find the bizarre rock formations of El Malpais National Monument. Volcanic eruptions roughly four million years ago created the conditions for these fantastic rock structures. Lava covered the existing limestone, and erosion slowly shaped the canyons and uncovered the diverse stone layers. One of the highlights of a visit to the park is the Bandera Crater. It has several ice caves, the most impressive of which is the Candeleria Cave. The Big Tubes are the largest lava tunnels in the United States.
About 48 km (30 miles) southeast of Grants is the most beautiful pueblo far and wide, Acoma, also known as "Sky City". The 1,200-year old village has a picturesque location on a rock plateau 110 m (361 ft) above the

plain. Originally only accessible with ladders, the Spaniards called it "the best fort in the world". You can visit the pueblo as part of a guided tour. About 80 km (50 miles) east on Interstate 40 is Albuquerque.

10 **Albuquerque** After exploring this lovely town on the mighty Rio Grande, travel another 62 km (38 miles) or so north-east along Interstate 25 to Santa Fe.

11 **Santa Fe** Highway 68 takes you to the Native American and artisan town of Taos roughly 112 km (70 miles) away.

12 **Taos** Often referred to as the "Soul of the Southwest", Taos presents itself as an artists' colony dedicated to Native American and Mexican styles with more than sixty galleries. The Artist Society was founded in 1912.

3

The Tiwa tribe had a permanent settlement on the Taos Plateau for some 1,100 years before the Spanish arrived. The city center's picturesque Plaza reflects the colonial style. South of the square on Ledoux Street are the town's oldest and most beautiful adobe buildings.

The Harwood Museum displays works by Taos artists from the last hundred years. Just under 5 km (3 miles) north-east of town is Taos Pueblo where 1,500 members of the Tiwa tribe still live. The village has existed since the 12th century and was always exclusively inhabited by Native Americans. The route now heads west through the southern foothills of the San Juan Mountains towards Farmington. At Bloomfield, a road heads south to the Chaco Culture National Historical Park in Nageezi.

⓭ **Chaco Culture National Historical Park** Chaco Canyon was the spiritual, political, and commercial hub of the Anasazi as early as the 10th century.

The most important sights in the valley can be reached on the circular route. The valley's main attraction is definitely Pueblo Bonito, the largest and best known Great House, which covered an area of 1,200 sq m (12,912 sq ft) and had 700 rooms for about 1,200 people spread over five levels. After returning to Bloomfield, head north on Highway 544 to Aztec.

⓮ **Aztec Ruins National Monument** This is another Anasazi ruin. It was inhabited by up to 1,300 people in 450 rooms arranged in a semi-circle around a kiva (ritual and meeting room). It has now been completely rebuilt, making it the only place in the United States to provide real insight into a major Native American settlement. Take Highway 550 to Durango and then continue on Highway 160 until you reach the next spectacular national park.

⓯ **Mesa Verde National Park** The most beautiful and certainly the most impressive residential complex of the Anasazi is in this park. It is deservedly a UNESCO World Heritage site. Some of the pueblos, which cling impossibly to inaccessible rock overhangs, were built between the 10th and 13th centuries. They have over 100 rooms and many have several kivas. The entire area can be reached from Ruins Road Drive, which provides good views and insights but does not allow direct access. The best cave dwellings are in Cliff Palace, comprising over 200 rooms and twenty-three kivas. The Balcony House is similarly arranged and is only accessible via vertical ladders and a narrow tunnel pipe.

From here, Highways 160 and 191 take you to the Canyon de Chelly National Monument.

1 The cliff settlement of the Anasazi Indians in Mesa Verde National Park was only accessible from above using vertical ladders that could be retracted in the event of danger.

2 The Pueblo Bonito is one of the highlights of the old Anasazi Indian culture.

3 Spider Rock at the base of Chelley Canyon.

The rock houses of Mesa Verde, built in shallow caves and under rock, are located on a 2,500 m-high table mountain in southwestern Colorado. They evoke the heyday of prehistoric Indians, also named "Anasazi" ("the Ancestors") by the Navajos, and they settled on the

Colorado Plateau from 600 to 1400 AD . The oldest and best preserved rock houses are to found in Mesa Verde. Classified as a national monument, they have been under protection since 1906. They are also listed among the UNESCO world heritage sites.

Gunslingers and gorgeous landscapes are essential elements in the romance of the Wild West. It is thus no coincidence that John Ford, one of the most famous directors of Westerns, shot Stagecoach with John Wayne in the leading role against the stunning backdrop of

Monument Valley back in 1939. Location shots for Billy the Kid, Play Me the Song of Death, Fort Apache and The Black Falcon were also filmed here, as well as Walt Disney's legendary nature film The Living Desert, which gives you a fast-motion glimpse of desert flowers

1

⑯ Canyon de Chelly National Monument This canyon is roughly 300 m (984 ft) deep and is carved from red rock faces. From the canyon floor, free-standing formations, such as Spider Rock at 243 m (797 ft) in height, will dazzle any visitor. Over 100 Native American settlements up to 1,500 years old were found in the canyon. As in Mesa Verde National Park, the pueblos here were built into the rock like birds' nests.

The main gorge can be accessed by two roads: North Rim Drive and South Rim Drive. Both offer spectacular views way down into the canyon.

Highlights of the park include the White House Ruin, an Anasazi pueblo made from shiny white limestone; the Mummy Cave, which was once used as a cult and burial site; and Antelope House, which has a rock drawing with an antelope motif.

Highways 191 and 160 will take you to Kayenta and the entrance to Monument Valley.

⑰ Monument Valley Navajo Tribal Park In the middle of the Colorado Plateau, on the border between Arizona and Utah, Monument Valley is home to spectacular rock formations that have been used as the backdrop for countless Westerns. Anyone traveling through here in the early morning or late evening will experience an amazing flush of color as the rocks glow in all shades of red, pink, and purple.

This rugged land was a Native American hunting and settlement region for thousands of years and is now once again a Navajo reserve. The best view of the rock towers, which reach heights of 600 m (1,969 ft), is seen from the 27-km (17 mile) circular route. If you want to learn more about the lifestyle of

2

the Navajo, take a guided tour from the visitor center.

Your journey continues now over Monument Pass to Bluff. From there you take Highway 191 to Moab. The 211 takes you to the southern part of Canyonlands National Park, and the 279 goes into the northern portion from Moab.

⑱ Canyonlands National Park The national park covers

an area of 1,366-sq-km (527-sq-mi) and includes the confluence of the Green and Colorado rivers, which have carved their way into 600-m (1,969-ft) gorges whose walls gleam in red and beige hues. Bizarrely shaped rock towers with chimneys and needles inspire the imagination of visitors. The park is so vast that you have to approach it from two sides. The southern half (Needles) has enchanting

3

rock sculptures and formations. Parts of the Needles district are accessible via two paved roads while other trails requiring four-wheel-drive vehicles lead down to the river.

The northern part of the park (Island in the Sky) comprises the headland between the rivers. The gorges reach depths of up to 600 m (1,969 ft) on both sides and the view is breathtaking in the truest sense of the word. In the dry air, visibility usually reaches 150 km (93 miles). From the Grand View Point at the south end of the park road, you will experience a truly unforgettable canyon landscape. A wide road for four-wheel-drives also runs below the White Rim in the northern part of the park.

⑲ Arches National Park Almost a thousand natural stone arches in all imaginable shapes, as well as giant mushroom rocks, rock towers, pinnacles, and cones, make this 313-sq-km (121-sq-mi) national park something really special. You can enter the park via Arches Scenic Drive, a 29-km (18-mile) panorama road.

Back in Moab, you again follow Highway 191 as far as Interstate 70, which takes you west until the Highway 24 turns off going south at Green River. From there the road heads directly into Capitol Reef National Park.

⑳ Capitol Reef National Park
This park covers an area of roughly 972 sq km (375 sq mi) around the Waterpocket Fold, whose ridges rise out of the desert floor like huge waves that extend over 160 km (99 miles). Their exposed edges have been eroded away into a tangle of bulky domes formed from naked rock, steep cliffs, and canyons. While the north-ern and southern parts of the park are less accessible and mainly prized by hikers, the easy-to-access middle section is home to the more rugged beauty of towering rock formations, among which the green Fruita oasis, created by the Mormons on the Fremont River, looks like an island in a vast ocean.

The most important part of the park is accessed on the 40-km (25-mile) Scenic Drive, which leads to the park's most impressive rock faces, a natural attraction not to be missed.

1 Canyonlands National Park was formed by the Colorado River.

2 Giant sandstone arches dot the rocky, mountainous landscape of Arches National Park.

3 Rock landscapes at Capitol Reef National Park.

1

Canyonlands National Park

The Colorado and Green Rivers have created the magnificent chasms of Canyonlands over the course of millions of years.

Canyonlands National Park in southern Utah boasts some of the most exciting and impressive scenery on earth. The area, accessible only to Native Americans and experienced riders until the second half of the 20th century, was declared a national park in 1964, and has since earned a reputation as a paradise for adventurous hikers. Numerous trails lead deep into canyons and hidden valleys, opening up a fairy-tale world of multi-hued rocks. It takes several days of hiking to really appreciate the park's treasures, and its true beauty only really unfolds many miles from the roads. Motorists are confined to two side roads: one leads to Grandview Point Overlook, a breathtaking vantage point over the Green River and Colorado river valleys, and the other to the Needles Visitor Center, where you can pick up winding trails that will take hikers past the red and white rock pinnacles of southern Canyonlands. The park is divided into three zones. The "Island in the Sky" lies between the Green and Colorado rivers, and here there are the striking depths of Shafer Canyon and the White Rim; Gooseneck Trail will take you down to Colorado. The "Needles", a series of imposing rock towers and other formations shaped by the wind and weathering, run south of the Colorado River.

Confluence Overlook affords a panoramic view of the meeting-point of the Colorado and Green Rivers, but the Maze District in the remote backwoods of the park is for experienced walkers only. Horseshoe Canyon has the most beautiful rock formations and exciting views of canyons up to 600 m (1,970 ft) deep.

1 Magnificent panoramic scenery in Canyonlands National Park.

A 450 m-long (0.5 mi) trail leads up to Mesa Arch in the Canyonland National Park. The trail to Mesa Arch is one of the easiest that you will find in the Island in the Sky district. It has only 3.5 m (100 ft) of altitude difference. The elevation gain is a series of small rises and

drops. The arch provides a natural frame for the La Sal Mountains and Washer Woman Arch. Numerous movies have been filmed in the
Windows Section of Arches National Park, such as "Indiana Jones and the Last Crusade" (1988) and "Thelma and Louise" (1991).

Arches National Park

Dozens of stone arches, domes, and pinnacles can be found in Arches National Park.

Eroded out of the rocks by wind and weather over a period of 150 million years, more than a hundred stone arches near Moab in Utah were placed under government protection in 1929, and since 1971 they have formed part of the Arches National Park. Arches Scenic Drive will take you past the mighty Courthouse Towers, a gleaming rock formation. Several interesting and diverting paths will then take you through Park Avenue, a thoroughfare lined with steep stone walls and rock formations with evocative names like the Organ, the Tower of Babel, and Sheep Rock. The path continues to Balanced Rock, an enormous boulder weighing some 3,556 tonnes (3,500 tons), balanced on a narrow stone plinth. A rocky trail continues on to Eye of the Whale Arch and the jagged Klondike Bluffs. The Windows section of the national park has several other natural wonders in stone, such as the Garden of Eden and the Double Arch, and other attractions include the Delicate Arch, lying at the end of a 3-km (2-mile) path and the height of a seven-storey house, and Landscape Arch, whose 90-m (295-ft) span has earned it a place in the record books. The Devil's Garden boasts over 60 stone arches. The origins of this magical rocky landscape are to be found in a giant lake which covered the local canyons about 300 million years ago. The lake evaporated, leaving a salty crust, and rock strata laid down on top of this were shaped into strange formations. The winds on the uplands of what was to become the national park also helped to erode such seemingly planned formations as Balanced Rock out of the living rock.

1 Landscape Arch: about 300 millions of years ago the area was covered by a giant lake, which was turned into weird formations.

In the evening light, the red rocks in Arches National Park look as if they were on fire: Frost and desert winds generated more than 200 natural stone arches such as the Delicate Arch here. It is the most widely-recognized landmark in Arches National Park and is depicted on

Utah license plates and on a postage stamp commemorating Utah's centennial anniversary of statehood in 1996. Delicate Arch is located at the end of a moderately strenuous 2.4 km (1.5 mi) hiking trail from the parking area at Wolfe Ranch.

1

The trip then follows Highways 24, 12, and 89 to Bryce Canyon National Park.

㉑ **Bryce Canyon National Park** This park extends over an area of 145 sq km (56 sq mi) on the fringe of the Paunsaugunt Plateau, whose cornices drop away 600 m (1,969 ft) over the delicately divided escarpments. At the bottom is the Paria Valley with a natural amphitheater shaped like a horseshoe. Erosion has carved deep ditches and furrows into the soft sandstone slopes, resulting in finely engraved heads, needles, and arches. In the early morning, this magical world glows in a spectrum of hues from pale yellow to dark orange. The rock amphitheater can be accessed via the 27-km-long (17-mile) scenic drive around the upper rim. East of Bryce Canyon, it's worth visiting the Kodachrome Basin State Park, which you can reach via Highway 12. It is home to splendid rock faces of red-and-white striped sandstone, towering rock chimneys, and spindly rock needles that glow in all shades of red, especially at sunrise and sunset. A panorama trail takes you to the most beau-

tiful formations whose rich colors can hardly be surpassed.
Back on Highway 12 and Interstate 89 you will head to nearby Zion National Park.

㉒ **Zion National Park** The vertical walls of the Virgin River Canyon break away steeply here at heights of more than 1,000 m (3,281 ft), forming solid pillars and deep recesses. The Mormons saw this as a "natural temple of God" back in the 19th century. Visitors feel like tiny ants but you can walk along the base of the canyon in areas where even the rays of the sun hardly ever shine. Only the southern part of the park (593 sq km/229 sq ft) is open to vehicles along the 29-km-long (18-mile) Scenic Drive. The rest of the park is accessible on more than 160 km (99 miles) of hiking trails. An absolute must is the Gateway to the Narrows Trail. Along the Weeping Rock Trail, you will pass so-called "Hanging Gardens", a rock overhang covered in ferns.
The best panoramic view over the entire canyon can be seen from Angels Landing, a cliff that drops away to a depth of 450 m (1,476 ft) on three sides. Your

2

route follows Highway 89 past Marble Canyon to Wupatki National Monument back in Cameron, Arizona.

㉓ **Wupatki National Monument** Roughly 40 km (25 miles) south of Cameron, you come

1 The giant craggy rocks and table mountains in Zion National Park impress visitors with their different bands of color.

2 In Zion National Park, gorges are only 4 m (13 ft) wide, as here in Antelope Canyon.

The rock needles in Bryce Canyon National Park, whose colors range from rusty red to yellowish-white, are often reminiscent of human or animal shapes. Over a stretch of around 30 km (19 miles), a giant amphitheater unfolds with unbelievably diverse rock formations

Bryce Canyon National Park

Bryce Canyon is the striking main attraction in the eponymous national park in southern Utah.

The red towers of Bryce Canyon rise up out of the rocky ground like organ pipes. These eye-catching limestone formations, shaped over millennia by wind and weathering, have been given imaginative names such as Thor's Hammer, Queen's Castle, Gulliver's Castle, Hindu Temples, and Wall Street. Nature has never been as wilful as here, not even in the Grand Canyon. John Wesley Powell was the first white man to explore the canyon in around 1870, but it was named after Ebenezer Bryce, a settler who built a ranch here before soon moving on to Arizona, as searching for his cattle was toohard. Bryce Canyon has been a National Park since 1924. The Native American name for the area means "red rocks that stand like men in a bowl-shaped canyon" – legend has it that they were disobedient warriors, turned to stone by the Great Spirit.

There is an asphalt road leading to viewpoints such as Sunset Point and Rainbow Point, but a hike along Under-The-Rim Trail, beneath the lip of the canyon, is much more rewarding, revealing the various shades of rock strata from many different geological periods dating back some 60 million years; the rock formations have been shaped over the years by frost and heat, rock falls, meltwater, and great floods of rainwater. The botany is just as varied as the geology: the lower levels have juniper bushes and pines, and further up there are hardy Ponderosa pines, spruce, and aspens. Even the rare bristlecone pine grows here, reaching an age of up to 1,700 years. Lynxes, foxes, and coyotes roam the beautiful landscape at night.

1 The rocks in Bryce Canyon were formed over the course of millions of years.

Zion National Park

Zion National Park, located in south-western Utah, is an ancient landscape of shimmering rocks.

Zion National Park in southern Utah is a fascinating mixture of high plateaus, deep canyons, and giant mesas. The Virgin River has dug a deep channel in the stone, stretching out to form Zion Canyon, whose biblical name was chosen by the Mormons, the first whites to settle in the area. They had been looking for fertile farming land and believed they had found heaven on earth. Even the strange rock formations were given biblical appellations: East Temple, West Temple, and Great White Throne. Zion has been a national park since 1919.

The asphalted Scenic Drive follows the Virgin River (a tributary of the Colorado River) through the canyon and on to the Temple of Sinawava, 13 km (8 miles) further along. Here you can pick up a trail to Weeping Rock, a rocky cliff covered in undergrowth, and Angel's Landing. The Emerald Pools are surrounded by shady pine forests and rushing waterfalls, and a single road winds through Kolob Canyons in the isolated north-west of the park.

Cottonwood trees, wind-blasted juniper bushes, and the mighty Ponderosa pine are all to be found growing in the canyons in Zion National Park, along with ash and birch trees. In the fall, their yellow leaves provide a nice contrast to the red-brown of the rocks that jut up on either side to touch the sky. Hardy cactuses flourish among the boulders.

The arduous trek further into the wilderness here is rewarded with sightings of bighorn sheep and red deer, and the fortunate may even spot the odd puma or coyote that roam through the park at night.

1 One of the many aspects of the Checkerboard Mesa to be found in Zion National Park.

The South Rim is an excellent vantage point for looking down into the massive gorges of the Grand Canyon. Although the Scenic Drive has, over time, been closed off to individual traffic for ecological reasons, shuttle buses provide easy access to all of the viewpoints.

Anyone really wanting to experience the canyon, however, should do the hike 1,800 m (5,906 ft) down into the gorge. Mules facilitate this adventure to an extent, but even then it is a strenuous undertaking simply because of the high temperatures in the canyon.

across the ancient pueblo of Wupatki on Highway 89. More than 2,000 Sinagua dwellings dating back to between the 9th and 14th centuries can be found in this arid desert landscape on the western edge of the Painted Desert.

A few miles further south of the pueblo ruins is Sunset Crater National Monument. The focal point here is the 305-m-high (1,001-ft) cinder cone of the Sunset Crater, the result of eruptions in 1065 and 1250. The region can be accessed on the Scenic Drive with spectacular views over the volcanic landscape. Highways 89 and 64 take you to the Grand Canyon.

㉔ Grand Canyon National Park This park covers an area of 4,933 sq km (1,904 sq mi) and includes approximately 445 km (277 miles) of the mighty Colorado River, which has carved out a canyon up to 1,800 m (5,906 ft) deep, with spectacular walls. At its farthest point, the canyon is 30 km (19 miles) wide. You can enter the Grand Canyon from both the northern and southern sides, but by far the most spectacular views can be seen from the southern side, which is also where the most important tourist facilities are located. Due to the crush of visitors, the entire South Rim has been closed off to individual vehicle traffic and instead there are free shuttle buses.

Back on Highway 64 and Interstate 40, you continue on to Kingman, where you take the turnoff to Highway 93 and head towards Hoover Dam.

㉕ Hoover Dam Just east of Las Vegas is the world's largest dam – until the Three Gorges project in China is completed. The Hoover Dam is 221 m (725 ft) high, 379 m (1,243 ft) wide, and roughly 200 m (659 ft) thick at the base. A feat of engineering in any era, the dam was completed in 1935. Lake Mead, which is 170 km (106 miles) long and up to 150 m (492 ft) deep, was the result of holding back the Colorado River here. After about 56 km (35 miles) on Highway 93 you will arrive in Las Vegas.

㉖ Las Vegas (see page 163) East of the city is the Valley of Fire State Park. Death Valley, which is 230 km (143 miles) long and 26 km (16 miles) wide, begins just 80 m (50 miles) west of the gaming paradise.

㉗ Death Valley National Park At 86 m (282 ft) below sea level, Badwater, in the middle of the park, is the lowest point in North America. It is the hottest and driest place in the United States. It recorded the hottest ever temperature in the Western Hemisphere, and the second-hottest in the world. In summer it can reach 57°C (135°F). In 2005, an unusually wet winter created a 'lake' in the Badwater Basin and led to the greatest wildflower season in the park's history.

Highlights include: Dante's View, the splendid Zabriskie Point, Artist's Drive, Mosaic Canyon, the vast sand dunes, and the Rhyolite Ghost Town.

By contrast, Sequoia National Park to the west of Death Valley is a completely different world comprising impressive granite peaks, redwood forests, and Alpine rivers.

㉘ Sequoia National Park Giant sequoias are the largest redwood trees by volume and only exist on the western slopes of the Sierra Nevada. Some specimens have a circumference of up to 30 m (98 ft) and live to be over 3,000 years old.

㉙ Mojave Highway 14 runs along the western edge of the Mojave Desert back to Los Angeles. Dry lakebeds, dunes, and precipices accompany you here before you finally reach the Pacific in Santa Monica.

1 The mighty walls of the Grand Canyon gleam magically in the soft light of the setting sun.

2 Sand ridges cover the windswept dunes of Death Valley.

Las Vegas

This glitzy city in Nevada has an almost magic appeal. Bugsy Siegel, an underworld king from the east coast, opened the first casino palace here, the Flamingo Hotel, almost single-handedly making Las Vegas a gambling Mecca.

Gambling was legalized in Nevada as early as 1931, in order to create additional sources of income for the state. Special offers throughout the city now lure visitors inside as they stumble from one slot machine to the next. Life starts in the evening, when the neon lights begin flashing on the Strip and the gambling hordes in tour buses head for the tables. Colorful billboards glint in front of the mega hotels while quarters, dimes, nickels, and silver dollars jingle in the gaming halls.

Since the legendary appearances of Frank Sinatra and Elvis Presley, the stages of Las Vegas have become a make-or-break setting for many artists, at least in the USA. The extravagant shows feature lavish production and are aimed at a wide audience. On the Strip, hotels and casinos vie for visitors while the gaudy palaces flash one after another, showing off ideas borrowed from amusement parks like Disneyland. Of the twenty largest hotels in the world, fourteen are in Las Vegas. Fantasy is the clincher here, designed to enchant visitors and lure them inside the casinos. Las Vegas is still growing rapidly, from a purely gambling city into what is more or less a -gigantic theme park.

An extra service in Tinseltown: You can be married in any of the numerous wedding chapels for cheap!

1 The New York New York Hotel is based on the Manhattan skyline.

2 Fremont Street demonstrates how appearance and reality have been interwoven in the glittering metropolis.

Las Vegas, the capital of gambling, is in the middle of the desert and has daytime temperatures of well over 40°C (104°F) in summertime. But it is a city that never sleeps. At night it is almost brighter than during the day, and fourteen of the world's twenty largest hotels are

downtown and on the Strip. The temple of luck attracts over forty million visitors a year, all of whom are lured by the teetering neon leg of the famous cowgirl, "Vegas Vicky", on Fremont Street (top) or the Sphinx in front of the Luxor Hotel on the Strip (bottom).

Death Valley

Death Valley, stretching out along the border between California and Nevada, is in many respects a place of extremes.

Death valley is considered one of the hottest places on earth – temperatures of over 50°C (122°F) have been recorded in this arid desert – and it is also one of the driest areas in North America, with less than 5 cm (2 in) of annual precipitation. Badwater is also home to the lowest point in the western hemisphere, 86 m (282 ft) below sea level. Settlers attempting to reach the Golden West via a supposed short-cut during the 1849 California gold rush soon gave this valley its ominous name. Winding up in this isolated depression, they survived only thanks to the bravery of a few of their young men and are said to have cried "good-bye, Death Valley!" after their rescue. Borax was mined in Death Valley around 1880, with twenty-strong mule teams dragging the heavy wagons to Mojave.

The valley has been protected since 1933, and in 1994, it was expanded by 5,300 km2 (1.3 million acres) and redesignated a national park. This made it the largest national park in the United States. Its austere beauty can be appreciated in the multi-hued badlands at Zabriskie Point, the sand dunes at Stovepipe Wells, and the bright wildflowers in the mountain meadows above Harmony Borax. Furnace Creek Ranch is a green oasis located in the middle of the magnificent, endless, unforgiving desert.

1 The rocky landscape of Zabriskie Point was made famous in the eponymous film by Michelangelo Antonioni.

2 Even the rattlesnakes hardly move in such heat.

3 Large portions of Death Valley lie below sea level, and here the heat is at its greatest.

Las Vegas This has been the USA's gambling haven since 1931. The countless casinos give their all to outdo each other in an effort to lure more money from gamblers' pockets. Lavish hotel complexes, theaters, and erotic shows provide entertainment and luxury around the clock.

Rhyolite Ghost Town This town on the edge of Death Valley reminds us of the Gold Rush. Its main attractions are a house made of beer bottles and a collection of gold-digger utensils.

Grand Canyon The Colorado River has carved a gorge through the Colorado Plateau up to 1,800 m (5,906 ft) deep, 30 km (19 miles) wide, and 445 km (277 miles) long. The view from the edge of the canyon sweeps over solid yellow-brown and milky white rock outcrops, pinnacles, and towers. The layers in the canyon represent 1.7 billion years of the earth's history.

Death Valley This national park is a desert with impressive rocks, vast sand dunes, and temperatures reaching 57°C (135°F). However, springs also allow for extensive flora and fauna. Rock drawings prove that the valley was already settled thousands of years ago.

Sequoia National Park The southern Sierra Nevada is home to a remote high Alpine region with majestic granite peaks, deep gorges, silent mountain lakes, small rivers, and impressive forests. The highest peaks are over 4,000 m (13,134 ft) high.

Los Angeles Freeways are the lifeline of Los Angeles, which covers 1,200 sq km (463 sq mi) and comprises many individual towns that have grown together. Stretching from Malibu to Santa Ana, and from Pasa-dena to Long Beach, the city's highlights include a visit to the film studios in Hollywood.

Joshua Tree National Park This park south of Twentynine Palms is part of the Mojave Desert and is home to dried-up salt lakes and sparse vegetation with cactuses, junipers, and yucca palms.

Organ Pipe Cactus National Monument Many species of cactus bloom in April and May in the habitat of the rare "organ pipe cactus".

Sonora Desert This desert is full of surprises. The giant saguaro cactuses, for example, are up to 150 years old and up to 15 m (49 ft) high. They flower in May. Everything else the desert has to offer is displayed in the Arizona Sonora Desert Museum in Saguaro National Park.

Phoenix The capital of Arizona is in the hottest and driest part of the Sonora Desert, and its warm winter climate has made it one of the most popular holiday destinations in the USA. Retirement communities such as Sun City have been established on its outskirts.

Marble Canyon Formed by the Colorado River, the color of the walls ranges from white to red depending on the position of the sun.

Bryce Canyon National Park This national park in Utah impresses visitors with a tangle of surreal-looking pinnacles and peaks. Here, the rock needles are bathed in the soft yellow and orange hues of the morning sun.

Arches National Park About one thousand freestanding stone arches are clustered here – more than anywhere else in the world – along with mushroom rocks, rock towers, pinnacles, and domes of smooth sandstone. In the evening light, the red rocks look as if they are on fire.

Canyonlands National Park The fantastic rock landscape in this national park includes the confluence of the Green River and the Colorado River. The two have carved their way down to depths of 600 m (1,969 ft).

Mesa Verde National Park These historic residential settlements of the Anasazi Indians are set into rock niches and caves. Though protected, many of the rock dwellings and pueblos can be visited.

Monument Valley The table mountains and rock pillars formed by the wind are popular film sets. The valley is part of a Navajo reserve, and you can buy handmade Navajo silver jewelry at the Visitor Center.

Taos Pueblo The Pueblo Indians lived in these multistorey flat-roofed houses more than one thousand years ago.

Acoma Pueblo This beautiful settlement, with historic clay-brick buildings and winding alleys, sits gracefully atop a plateau.

Albuquerque This city, founded in 1716, has plenty of Spanish character, with adobe houses and baroque churches in the Old Town. Pictured here is the San Felipe de Neri Church dating from the early 18th century.

White Sands National Monument This 600-sq-km (232-sq-mi) dune landscape is made of white gypsum sand that glistens like newly fallen snow. Dunes rise to 18 m (59 ft) here. The US Army set off the world's first atomic bomb in the northern part of the desert on 16 July 1945. Victoria Island Canada's third largest island is an ideal place to see musk oxen. The island was named in 1839 after the United Kingdom's Queen Victoria.

Mission San Xavier del Bac Founded by Spanish priests near Tucson, this church is located on the Tohono O'odham San Xavier Indian Reservation.

Chiricahua National Monument These charming rock landscapes near the Mexican border were once part of Apache hunting grounds.

USA

Route 66: the American Myth

The first continuous road link between Chicago and Los Angeles still evokes nostalgia today. It is synonymous with freedom and wide open country, cruisers and 'Easy Rider', neon signs and diners – in short, the symbol of a nation whose identity is characterized by being on the road. The West was all about promises and aspirations, a paradise on earth. 'Go California' was the motto – Route 66 was the way there.

The first link between the Great Lakes and the Pacific Ocean has been a continuing legend and the symbol of the American dream ever since Bobby Troup's "Get your kicks on Route 66". It was Horace Greely who popularized the phrase "Go West, young man, and grow up with the country" in the New York Herald Tribune, and with it created the creed of an entire na-

tion. What came of this creed and the people who later followed it through the Depression and droughts of the 1930s has nowhere been described as tellingly as in John Steinbeck's The Grapes of Wrath, in which the Joad family heads out on what later became known as the "Mother Road" to the West. The clash between dreams and reality remains part of the

Route 66 legend today. What has become a long forgotten chapter in the history of fast-moving America began less than 100 years ago as cars began to make a show of competition for

Route 66 in Arizona.

the railways. The "National Old Trails Highway" developed from the first "highways" in the individual states and thus became the predecessor of Route 66. But the nice name still did not stand for much more than sand, gravel, and strip roads. It was only on 11 November 1926 that the eight Federal states of Illinois, Missouri, Kansas, Oklahoma, Texas, New Mexico, Arizona, and California completed the uniform 4,000-km (2,486-mile) route between Chicago and Los Angeles, and the highway was officially opened as Route 66.

The start of Route 66 is marked by a signpost at the Michigan Avenue/Jackson Drive intersection in Chicago. The idyllic countryside of Illinois begins directly after the suburban neighborhoods to the west of town. Re-

View of the Chicago skyline by night from Sears Tower. Left in the background is the tapered 344-m-high (1,129-ft) John Hancock Center adorned with two antennae.

In the state of New Mexico, Route 66 passes through a stark landscape of bizarre rock formations.

mote farms and tranquil villages characterize Abraham Lincoln's home country, while the Amish people's rejection of the technological age takes the visitor back into a bygone era. You finally reach the "Gateway to the West" in St Louis where the road crosses the expanse of the Mississippi and through the 192-m-high (630-ft) steel archway designed by Eero Saarinen.
The gentle hills of the Ozark Mountains and the "glitter world" of the Meramec Caverns are hard to resist. Upon reaching Oklahoma, the "Native American State", you are finally in the land of cowboys and Indians with its seemingly never-ending plains. The cowboys are still in charge on the giant cattle ranches in the area, and this applies to the 290 km (180 miles)

where Route 66 crosses the narrow panhandle in northern Texas.
In New Mexico there is a whole new world waiting to greet the visitor. The special light in the valleys and canyons glows mysteriously on the red and brown cliffs and gentle mountains. Between Santa Fe and Taos you will experience an enchanted landscape with a harmonious combination of Spanish charm and Native American culture.
Next comes Arizona, which is not only the state with the largest Indian reservations, but also an area of spectacular rock formations in Red Rock Country, Oak Creek Canyon, and of course the Grand Canyon. Intoxicated by the beauty of the landscape, you enter California, crossing the daunting Mojave

Desert with its cacti as the last obstacle before heading down towards the Pacific.
San Bernardino marks the start of the fertile "Orange Empire"

as Los Angeles' endless sea of buildings slowly swallows up Route 66. It all finally comes to an end in Palisades Park near Santa Monica.

Mexican children pose in traditional costume in Santa Fe, New Mexico.

1

The first continuous East-West connection in the USA from Chicago to Los Angeles remains something of a legend today. Even though during the course of the 20th century large parts of the original Route 66 gave way to more modern Interstate highways, there are still many original stretches where the legend lives on.

① Chicago (see pages 175–175). Before starting off, it is worth taking a detour to the town of Holland 110 km (68 miles) away. This reconstructed village is a memorial to the region's Dutch immigrants.

The journey along the legendary Route 66 begins at the Michigan Avenue/Jackson Drive intersection in Chicago and from there Interstate Highway 55 takes you to Springfield. North of Springfield is the Chautauqua National Wildlife Reserve.

② Springfield The capital of Illinois still has the aura of an idyllic country town today. A little further north, New Salem was the home of the famous president (Lincoln) who lived here in humble circumstances from 1831 to 1837. The village has now been reconstructed as an open-air museum with staff in period costume who demonstrate how hard life was here 200 years ago.

In Springfield itself the focus is also on President Lincoln and his carefully restored house on Jackson Street is open to visitors, as is his law office on Adams Street where he practised as a lawyer from 1843 to 1853. He found his final resting place in Oak Ridge Cemetery. Lincoln was a parliamentarian in the Old State Capitol in the Downtown Mall; however, since 1877 state business has been conducted in the opulent new

Travel Information

Route profile
Length: approx. 4,000 km (2,486 miles), excluding detours
Time required: 3 weeks
Start: Chicago
Destination: Santa Monica
Route (main locations):
Chicago, St Louis, Tulsa, Oklahoma City, Santa Fe, Albuquerque, Flagstaff, Barstow, Santa Monica, San Diego

Traffic information:
Drive on the right in the USA. Maximum speed limits in built-up areas are 25 to 30 mph (40–48 km/h); on the highways 55–70 mph (88–115 km/h). Speed checks (with tough penalties) are also conducted from the air. Drink-driving is strictly prohibited in all of the states here, with heavy fines. It is prohibited to carry open or even empty bottles or cans of alcoholic beverages in the car (not even in the boot).

Information:
Detailed information on the historical Route 66 as well as the most important sightseeing attractions can be found at:
www.historic66.com or
www.theroadwanderer.net

Illinois State Capitol. Shea's Gas Station Museum imparts true Route 66 feeling.

The journey continues southwards via Interstate Highway 55 toward St Louis.

③ St Louis The largest city in the state of Missouri lies on the western bank of the Mississippi just before the confluence with the Missouri River. The Mark Twain National Wildlife Reserve

was established on the river north of the city. The city was founded in 1764 by a French fur trader, Pierre Liguest, and it was fur traders who first brought wealth to the new settlement. Large parts of the American west were then settled from here. It was from here that the endless wagon trains began their journey across the prairies and it was to here that the riches of the grasslands and the Rocky Mountains were brought back and traded.

The 192-m-high (630-ft) Gateway Arch designed by the Finn Eero Saarinen is St Louis' primary landmark and is purposely visible from great distances. As a symbolic "Gateway to the West", the arch is a reminder that this is where the great tide of settlers heading for the coast began the often perilous expedition.

A short distance south of the Gateway Arch is the Old Cathedral, dating from 1834, which has attractive mosaics as well as a museum of the city's history in the basement. Market Street begins on the Gateway Arch axis and its notable attractions include the dome of the Old Court House from 1864, the magnificent round building that is the Busch Memorial Stadium, and the City Hall, which is based on its counterpart in Paris.

On Lindell Boulevard is the splendid St Louis Cathedral, built in 1907 in Byzantine style. It has a spectacular mosaic dome. You leave St Louis via Interstate Highway 44 and make your way towards Stanton.

4 Meramec Caverns A visit to the Meramec Caverns about 5 km (3 miles) south of Stanton is not to be missed. They are among the largest stalactite caves in the USA and include some fascinating formations. Some doubt that the famous bandit Jesse James and his gang used the caves as a hideout, but legends certainly tell of their presence here.

For the onward journey you continue down Interstate 44 to Springfield, Missouri.

5 Branson South of Springfield, the third-largest city in Missouri, are the Ozark Mountains, which attract a great number of visitors, particularly in the fall months.

The small town of Branson is your specific destination reached via Highway 65. It is known as "America's Biggest Little Town" and the new Mecca of American country music. As such, it has outdone legendary Nashville, Tennessee.

Traditional handicrafts and nostalgic events are staged in "Silver Dollar City". Highway 13 takes you to the Talking Rock Caverns, considered the most scenic of the 5,000 caves in Missouri. Those interested in history can make a detour to the Pea Ridge National Monument.

Back in Springfield continue along Interstate 44 westwards to Joplin.

1 The port and skyline of Chicago. The Sears Tower (second from the left) was the tallest building in the world until 1998.

2 At the height of summer, the St Louis sun sets in the middle of the Gateway Arc.

Chicago

Including its outer suburbs, Chicago sprawls over 100 km (62 miles) along the southern shores of Lake Michigan. The city is a fantastic destination for anyone interested in architecture – downtown Chicago has been highlighted by the works of renowned architects. The city also attracts throngs of visitors with its lively music, museum, and multicultural scenes.

Chicago was already an important transport hub and trading center in the 19th century. Cattle and pigs were unloaded here at the largest livestock station in the country and driven to urban slaughterhouses, of which there are only a few remaining.

In the "Roaring Twenties", the so-called "Windy City" gained the somewhat dubious reputation of being a gangster metropolis, but Al Capone is all but legend now. The skyline of the new Chicago rose up out of the ruins of the old city and is the best proof of the determination and initiative of its residents.

The "Great Chicago Fire" of 9 October 1871 almost completely destroyed the city. Over 200 people died and more than 90,000 lost everything they had. Today, all that remains of the old Chicago is the water tower.

State Street is considered the largest pedestrian zone in the world and attracts crowds with its department stores, boutiques, restaurants, cinemas, and theaters. Passers-by encounter a number of remarkable artworks on the pavements – a 16-m (52-ft) statue left to the citizens of Chicago by Pablo Picasso; "Flamingo", the bright red giant spider by Alexander Calder in front of the Chicago Federal Center; "Universe", a gigantic mobile by the same artist in the lobby of the Sears Tower; or "The Fours Seasons", a 20-m-long (66-ft) mosaic by Marc Chagall in front of the First National Bank.

There is also a series of museums worth visiting – the Museum of Science and Industry houses an underground coal mine and a 5-m-high (16-ft) model of a human heart. A reproduction of the largest saurian (dinosaur lizard) in the world awaits you in the Museum of Natural History. The Art Institute of Chicago is renowned for its collection of modern art. The Adler Planetarium, a star-shaped granite building with a copper dome, has a number of surprising special effects. The attractions in the John G. Shedd Aquarium include a huge coral reef and a shark habitat.

There are numerous restaurants and bars to choose from at the Navy Pier. Chicago continues to be a city of jazz and blues and a live concert in one of the very diverse clubs or bars should not be missed.

1 **2** The city established itself as a center of modern architecture at the start of the 20th century. Whether by day (top) or by night (bottom), the numerous unique skyscrapers are there to be admired on a walk through the streets of Chicago.

3 Chicago shows off its impressive skyline on both sides of the Chicago River.

6 Joplin A part of the original Route 66 turns right from Highway 44 shortly before the small town of Joplin, Missouri.
Continue through Joplin and shortly thereafter you reach the little town of Galena, where time appears to have stood still. The whole town is like an open-air museum.
The next little village is Riverton where the old Marsh Arch Bridge, an arched concrete suspension bridge, was built in 1923 to span Brush Creek. Route 66 passed over this bridge until 1960. The next stop is Baxter Springs where under no circumstances should you miss a visit to Murphey's Restaurant in the Baxter National Bank, which was closed in 1952. Part of the decor comprises former bank furniture, and old cheques from the 1920s lie on the tables under glass.

7 Miami Here too, little appears to have changed on the outside. Miami developed from a trading station set up in 1890.

In 1905 lead and zinc brought a boom to the town. The main attraction is the Coleman Theatre, built in 1929, a cinema with magnificently crafted balconies and a ceiling lined with gold leaf. On the first floor there is a small exhibition about Route 66 and its history.

8 Tulsa The former "Oil Capital of the World", Tulsa has long been stripped of this title, but some of the oil barons' art deco villas are still a sign of the city's former wealth.
Waite Phillips' mansion still houses works of art from the Italian Renaissance. The original Route 66 follows Eleventh Street through downtown. Between Tulsa and Oklahoma City you can also travel along lengthy stretches of the historic Route 66, which maintain their rustic charm.

9 Oklahoma City Founded in 1889 – after Indian territories were opened to whites – the capital of Oklahoma owes its

wealth to oil. There are still a good 2,000 wells within the city limits today, one of which is directly in front of the Capitol. The spirit of the Wild West is still alive and well in the National Cowboy Hall of Fame on Persimmon Hill, which includes the replica of an old western town called "Prosperity Junction". "The American Cowboy Gallery" documents the life of the cowboys, and the "American Rodeo Gallery" is dedicated to that long-standing western tradition. South-west of the city center is the historic neighborhood

Stockyards City, where you can get a feeling for the way things might have been in the heyday of the cattle business here. South of the city are the Wichita Mountains, a hiking area, and to the north-west is the Washita Battlefield where Custer staged an attack on the Cheyenne Indians in the ongoing and tragic clash of cultures that took place in the area. The journey continues via Interstate 40 westwards to Clinton.

10 Clinton The most interesting Route 66 museums on the

whole trip are to be found here. Films, photos, and original exhibition pieces document the route's heyday. Beyond Clinton you stay on Interstate 40. Once you get to Amarillo, a detour on Interstate 27 leads to one of the most interesting canyons in the area.

⑪ **Palo Duro Canyon State Park** This canyon is surrounded by cliffs some 350 m (1,148 ft) high where remote Indian trails lead deep into the canyon to the most spectacular cliff formations. Also called the "Grand Canyon of Texas", Palo Duro is the second-largest canyon in the USA: 195 km (121 miles) long, 32 km (20 miles) wide, and 243 m (797 ft) deep – a good warm-up for the real thing.

⑫ **Amarillo** The city has been a Route 66 city from the very start. Route 66 used to pass along Sixth Avenue in this Texas town, a street lined with some restored buildings from the route's heyday. The American Quarter Horse Heritage Center documents the history of the breeding of the American Quar-

ter Horse. Amarillo is a city where the spirit of the old west still lingers. Cadillac Ranch, 15 km (9 miles) to the west, is a bizarre desert exhibition of old Cadillacs. There is a flint quarry further north, Alibates Flint Quarries National Monument. The route continues on Interstate 40 over the border into New Mexico towards Albuquerque.

⑬ **Fort Sumner** Before reaching the little town of Santa Rosa, it is worth taking a brief detour to the south on Highway 84 to Fort Sumner where 8,000 Navajo and Apache Indians were rounded up in 1864 and forcefully relocated to the fort to survive on their own. Many of them died.

The visitor center and adjacent museum tell the story of this gruesome incident.

The town went down in American history a second time as well, as it was here on 16 July 1881 that Pat Garrett shot the famous Billy the Kid. A small

museum has been erected in his memory.

Back in Santa Rosa, continue to follow Interstate 40. To reach Santa Fe you need to leave the actual Route 66 at Clines Corners, the intersection of Interstate 40 and Highway 285, then head north toward Santa Fe.

⑭ **Santa Fe** The second-oldest city in the USA and the capital

1 They're back: nostalgic diners and the cars to match.

2 Some of the buildings in the Old Town of Muskogee, south-east of Tulsa, are reminiscent of the city's early days.

3 The Oklahoma City National Memorial was erected to commemorate the victims of the attack on the Alfred P. Murrah Federal Building in 1995.

4 Stark cliffs rise 350 m (1,148 ft) in the Palo Duro Canyon.

1

of New Mexico is characterized by both Native American and Spanish culture. There are eight large museums and a multitude of art galleries, jewelry shops, and handicraft stores here. When the Spanish arrived in 1542, there was already a large Pueblo Indian settlement here, which later revolted against the colonials and sent them packing. In the meantime, however, the Spanish made Santa Fe the capital of their new colony. Today the architectural mix of Native American, Spanish, European American, and Mexican influences is the special attraction of Santa Fe's old town.

The famous Santa Fe Trail, a historic trading route running from Independence in the west of Missouri to Santa Fe, ends at the Plaza built in 1610 in the historic heart of the city. This is also the site of the Palace of the Governors, the governor's residence (1614). The oldest buildings are situated south of the Santa Fe River in the Indian settlement of Barrio de Analco, established in the early 17th century by the Tlaxcala Indians.

The Museum of Fine Arts shows the work of regional artists. Those who are especially interested in Native American culture ought not to miss the museums on Camino Lejo. The Museum of Indian Arts and Culture displays artworks from the Indian tribes of New Mexico. The Museum of International Folk Art is one of the largest ethnographic museums in the USA, while the Wheelwright Museum of the American Indian is dedicated to all the Indian cultures of North America.

The numerous interesting Indian pueblos in the area are worth visiting. The Interstate Highway 25 takes you directly to Albuquerque and back to the original Route 66.

⑮ **Albuquerque** The largest city in New Mexico is situated on the Rio Grande at an altitude of 1,600 m (5,250 ft) and is over-

2

shadowed by Sandia Peak. There is a 4-km-long (2.5-mile) cable car ride that takes you up to 3,163 m (10,378 ft) above sea level.

Founded by the Anasazi Indians, who had already been living here between 1100 and 1300, the town was then settled by the Spanish at the beginning of the 18th century; they built what is today known as Old Town. About 170 years later the town was linked to the rail network. There are several museums worth visiting here – the

Albuquerque Museum has a collection of exhibits from the Spanish colonial era; nature fans will enjoy the New Mexico Museum of National History, with exhibits on the natural history of the south-west (such as dinosaurs); and the largest collection of rock paintings is to be found in the Petroglyph National Monument north of the city. The Indian Pueblo Cultural Center north of Interstate 40 is an absolute must-see. It features a brief historical overview of the Pueblo world.

3

4

16 Laguna Pueblo About 10 km (6 miles) west of Albuquerque, north of Interstate 40, is a Keresan pueblo made up of six villages – Encinal, Laguna, Mesita, Paguate, Paraje, and Seama. The site has been in existence since the middle of the 15th century. Colorful local pottery is on sale in every village. The St Joseph Mission on the lake in Old Laguna is also worth a visit.

17 Acoma Pueblo Roughly 48 km (30 miles) south-east of the small town of Grant is Acoma, considered the most attractive pueblo far and wide. The village, which is also known as "Sky City" because of its spectacular location, sits on top of a mesa (table mountain) 10 m (361 ft) above the plain.

The pueblo has been a settlement for over 1,200 years and is considered to be the oldest continually inhabited settlement in the USA. Today, however, there are only about fifty residents, most of the tribe's members having moved to the villages on the plain. As the village is sometimes closed for religious ceremonies, it is best to enquire beforehand whether it is open to visitors. There is a fantastic view of the hinterland from the pueblo. West of Acoma is the El Malpais National Monument, famous for its bizarre rock formations and the more than 150 local bird species.

In the state of Arizona, Interstate 40 continues on more or less the old Route 66. At Thoreau, Highway 371 branches off towards Crownpoint to the Chaco Culture National History Park. Continuing westwards, south of the road is the El Morro National Monument on Highway 53. Both the Indian tribes and the Spanish have left their mark on the 60-m (197-ft) sandstone cliffs.

Sanders, in the "Grand Canyon State" Arizona, is the starting point for a detour to the north.

18 Hubbel Trading Post West of Sanders you should not miss the 50-km (31-mile) detour via Highway 191 to the Hubbel Trading Post. The trading post was founded in 1890 by John Lorenzo Hubbel in the middle of Navajo territory. The buildings date back to the turn of the last century and the Navajo have quality handicrafts on sale here. Back on Interstate 40, the next highlight is only 30 km (19 miles) away to the west.

1 Indian and Spanish cultures characterize the Old Town of Santa Fe. The picture features Canyon Road.

2 Old Town Albuquerque shares Spanish and Indian origins.

3 The El Morro National Monument is a 60-m-high (197-ft) sandstone cliff. The numerous inscriptions have led to the cliff's nickname 'Inscription Rock'.

4 Acoma Pueblo sits on top of a majestic cliff plateau.

"Pueblo Indians" is the name of a group of Indian tribes of related cultures e. g. Keresan, Tiwa, Hopi, Zuni and others in the Wild West, which are descendants of the prehistoric Anasazi desert people. Their name was coined by the Spaniards who referred to early adobe

apartment houses as "pueblos". Such houses were stacked one upon another like terraces. On grounds of safety they were only accessible by ladders that led to portholes in the roof. The Taos Pueblo, a good example for pueblo culture, is located north of Santa Fe.

The Painted Desert stretches out to the east of Flagstaff, a colorful desert landscape with plateaus, rounded mounds, and badlands. The colors come from the minerals embedded in the stone. About 225 million years ago, sediment layers 500 m (1,600 ft) thick settled here

below an inland sea. Then, when the Colorado Plateau rose about sixty million years ago, the top layer eroded, uncovering the myriad tones and sandstone formations. As such, the Painted Desert is a vibrant image of a 200-million-year-old world.

⑲ Petrified Forest National Park This park, spread out over 379 sq km (236 sq mi), offers insight into a geological world that is 200 million years old. Around 100 species of fossilized plants and animals have been identified to date. The most impressive examples are the petrified tree trunks that were infused with quartz around 200 million years ago. Today their fractures glimmer with all the colors of the rainbow. The park, which extends both north and south of Interstate 40, is accessed via the 43-km (27-mile) park road and has two information centers, one of which is located at the north entrance, directly accessible from Interstate 40.

Pintado Point, right at the start of the park road, offers the best overview of the Painted Desert. All the shades of the glowing badlands are seen at their best from here.

Blue Mesa Point, reached by the 4.8-km (3-mile) access road, offers a second spectacular overview. Agate House is an 800-year-old Anasazi pueblo, the walls of which are made of petrified wood that glitters in a myriad of hues. The most beautiful of the petrified trees can be found in the southern part of the park. The Giant Logs Trail leads to Old Faithful, a conifer tree that has a diameter of 2.9 m (9.5 ft).

A visit to the Rainbow Forest Museum ought not to be missed either. The exhibition includes a variety of pre-Columbian Native American artefacts fashioned from petrified wood. At the southern end of the park you will reach Highway 180, which will take you directly back to Holbrook and Interstate 40.

⑳ Winslow About 20,000 years ago, a space "bomb" landed a little further south of the village. The meteorite created a 180-m-deep (591-ft) crater with a circumference of around 1,300 m (4,265 ft). The visitor center has all the details about the meteorite and has pieces of the ce-

lestial body on display. It is now a further 70 km (43 miles) on Interstate 40 to Flagstaff.

㉑ Sunset Crater Before visiting Flagstaff, it is worth making a detour to the north on Highway 89. On the eastern side of the highway is a bizarre volcanic landscape surrounding the Sunset Crater National Monument. The focal point of the volcanic area is the over 300-m-wide (984-ft) cinder cone of the Sunset Crater.

It is the youngest volcano in Arizona and has been active for some 200 years. It first erupted in 1064 and the layer of ash covered an area of over 2,000 sq km (1,243 sq mi).

In 1250 the volcano discharged the red and yellow oxidized lava that today still causes the edge of the crater to glow with the colors of a permanent sunset. The area is accessed via Scenic Drive, with spectacular views of the spooky volcanic landscape. If you take the Sunset Crater National Monument park road a little further north, you soon reach another noteworthy Native American site.

㉒ Wupatki National Monument There used to be more than 2,000 settlements here that were once part of the ancient Sinagua Indian culture. The Indians settled in this region between 500 and 1400.

The Wupatki Pueblo, dating back to the 12th and 13th centuries, is relatively well-preserved. It was once the largest pueblo around. The three-storey pueblo had more than 100 rooms, all ventilated by means of a sophisticated system of wall and floor openings. It could also be heated if necessary.

You can learn anything and everything you want to know about the culture of the Sinagua Indians (Sinagua = sine, aqua = without water) in the visitor center next to the pueblo.

㉓ Flagstaff This city on the southern edge of the San Francisco Mountains was founded in about 1870 when gold diggers followed farmers and ranchers. The railway followed as soon as 1882 and with the completion of Route 66 the transit traffic continued to increase. Flagstaff's sightseeing attractions in-

clude the Museum of Northern Arizona with a range of exhibits from the various cultural strata of the Pueblo Indians. Flagstaff's real attraction, however, is its surrounding natural landscape. North of town are the fantastic San Francisco Mountains with the highest point in Arizona. Take a chair lift up the 3,854-m (12,645-ft) Humphrey's Peak.

South-east of Flagstaff is Walnut Canyon, 36 km (22 miles) long and 12 m (39 ft) deep, definitely worth exploring on foot. The canyon conceals around 300 Zinagua Indian cliff dwellings; they lived here from the 10th century and built their dwellings solely under overhanging cliffs.

From Flagstaff you can travel directly to the Grand Canyon on Highways 89 and 64 or 180 and 64. On Interstate 40 follow the highway as far as Seligman and then take the Highway 66 turn-off.

The most scenic stretch of old Route 66, which is still largely in its original condition, takes you to the next stop, Kingman.

Access roads lead to the Grand Canyon Caverns and to the Havasupai Indian Reservation. You then end up in central Kingman after crossing the Interstate Highway 40.

㉔ Kingman Between the Cerbat Mountains in the north and the over 2,500-m (8,203-ft) Hualapai Mountains in the south is a traffic interchange in the middle of a desert land-

1 Sinagua Indian dwellings used to cover the area that is now the Wupatki National Monument.

2 The Wigwam Hotel in Holbrook. An affordable Native American tradition for modern nomads.

3 The 300-m (984-ft) cinder cone of the Sunset Crater is the product of Arizona's youngest volcano.

4 The Flagstaff railway station, located at 1 East Route 66, dates from the 19th century.

scape. Nowhere else on the entire Route 66 has there been a greater investment in nostalgia than here. Old petrol stations and snack bars have been brought back to life, and road signs and signposts have been saved from obsolescence. The entire town is full of unadulterated Route 66 nostalgia. In the Mohave Museum of History and Arts, with its extensive collection of turquoise jewelry, you learn that the area had already been settled by the Hohokam Indians 1,300 years ago. The museum gives you a history of their work with the precious stones.

After Kingman you need to leave Route 66 and Interstate 40 (which goes towards Barstow), to pay homage to the spectacular Hoover Dam and legendary Las Vegas. Both are easy to reach via Highway 93. If you stay on Route 66 you can also visit Lake Havasu south of Kingman.

㉕ Hoover Dam This dam near Boulder City was once the largest embankment dam in the world. The 221-m-high (725-ft)

and 379-m-wide (1,242-ft) construction, which is an amazing 201 m (659 ft) thick at its base, was completed in 1935. The awe-inspiring structure holds back the waters of Lake Mead, a 170-km-long (106-mile) and 150-m-deep (492-ft) body of water. There is a large visitor center on the dam wall where you learn about the dam's fascinating technical details. You can then take a cruise on Lake Mead with the paddle steamer Desert Princess.

After following Highway 93 for 56 km (35 miles), you then reach Las Vegas.

㉖ Las Vegas The world's gambling capital is located in the middle of the desert and really only consists of hotels and casinos. No less than fourteen of the twenty largest hotels in the world are located here. More than 40 million visitors come to Las Vegas each year to seek their fortune and, more often than not, lose their money to the one-armed bandits and casinos. The big casino hotels stage elab-

orate shows, revues, and circuses in order to provide entertainment for the non-gamblers, or perhaps to raise the spirits of those who do try their hands. The individual casinos each have their own theme and these range from "Stratosphere Tower" to the "Venetian", complete with Doge Palace and Campanile, and the "Luxor", evoking associations with Ancient Egypt with pyramids and pharaohs.

From Las Vegas, Interstate 15 rejoins the old Route 66 at

Barstow. But before you reach Barstow, it is worth paying a brief visit to Calico, a ghost town that was once a very successful mining operation at the end of the 19th century due to the discovery of substantial reserves of silver and borax.

㉗ Barstow This town to the east of the Edwards Air Force Base is situated in the middle of the desert and serves as a supply center for a huge yet sparsely populated hinterland. The California Desert Information Cen

ter is very interesting, providing a plethora of details on the Mojave Desert.
Following Interstate 15 you gradually leave the desert behind and reach the center of the Californian citrus-growing region, San Bernardino County.

28 San Bernardino This city, almost 100 km (62 miles) east of Los Angeles, developed from a Franciscan mission founded in 1810. From here you really must do the "Rim of the World Drive", a panoramic drive through

a spectacular high desert and mountain landscape. It passes scenic lakes, reaches an altitude of 2,200 m (7,218 ft), and offers splendid views of the San Bernardino Mountains.
The Joshua Tree National Park is a worthwhile detour from here, if you haven't done it already, and the entrance at Twentynine Palms can be reached via Interstate 10 and Highway 62.
The historic Route 66 takes you westwards from San Bernardino, just north of Interstate 10, past Pasadena (Pasadena Free-

way) and on towards Los Angeles. Via West Hollywood and Beverly Hills you continue along Santa Monica Boulevard to the famous beach town of Santa Monica. If you want to visit Disneyland, the oldest of Disney's parks, beforehand, take Interstate 15 and Highway 91 over to Anaheim.

29 Anaheim The ending "heim" is indicative of the German origins of this settlement near the Santa "Ana" River, where German immigrants settled in about 1857. Anaheim is in Orange County, around 60 km (37 miles) south-east of Los Angeles. The largest attraction is Disneyland, the leisure park founded by Walt Disney in 1955 and which brought an end to the tranquil atmosphere of this once rustic town.

30 Santa Monica In 1935, Route 66 was extended from Los Angeles to Santa Monica and since then has followed Santa Monica Boulevard, terminating at Ocean Boulevard in Palisades

Park, where a modest signpost indicates the end of the legendary route, the "Mother Road" or "Main Street USA".

31 San Diego If you have plenty of time, it is worth continuing from Anaheim along Interstate 5 to San Diego, 150 km (93 miles) south along the coast.

1 South of Kingman are the Hualapai Mountains, over 2,500 m (8,203 ft) high.

2 In 1885 some 1,200 people lived in Calico and sought their fortunes in one of the 500 silver mines. Calico became a ghost town after 1907 and some of the old buildings, here the old school, have been restored.

3 Santa Monica – here you see the Third Street Promenade – is a popular meeting point for the »Fun People«.

4 Despite high temperatures and irregular rainfall, a great diversity of plant and animal species thrive.

San Diego is located in southern California on the border to Mexico and belongs to the most important harbour cities of the United States. For its average of three hundred sunny days per year the city is especially appreciated by sportsmen; there are joggers and ath-

letes all over the place, and Mission Bay is teeming with boats and sails gleaming in the sunlight. Several museum ships call San Diego Bay home. The "Star of India" and several other boats and ships are the floating collection of the San Diego Maritime Museum.

Clinton, Oklahoma In addition to other exhibits, the Route 66 Museum displays a farming family's original loaded truck.

Tulsa Downtown Tulsa has an impressive number of interesting art deco buildings. The art museums founded and sponsored by some of the oil magnates contain valuable collections and are worth a visit.

Washita Battlefield N.H.S. This site commemorates a battle between the Cheyenne Indians and the US cavalry under Custer.

Muskogee There are numerous historic buildings to be seen in the Old Town at the railway bridge over the Arkansas River.

Wichita Mountains The mountain range south-west of Oklahoma City is a popular recreational area rich in flora and fauna.

Oklahoma City In front of the Capitol, an oil well and the sculpture of an Indian woman evoke the history and identity of the city.

Anadarko The Southern Plains Museum in the "Indian Capital of the Nation" brings the culture of the Plains Indians and the Wild West back to life.

Pea Ridge National Military Park The bloody Civil War battle of 7 and 8 March 1862 in which 26,000 soldiers faced each other is commemorated near Rogers.

Calico Ghost Town This town, abandoned following the "Silver Rush" in 1900, has been restored.

Grand Canyon The largest canyon in the world is about 1,800 m (5,906 ft) deep, up to 30 km (19 miles) wide, and some 450 km (280 miles) long. The view of the giant canyon, with its colorful ridges, turrets, and free-standing outcrops, is overwhelming. At the bottom the Colorado River looks like a tiny little stream.

Los Angeles Palms between the skyscrapers remind passers-by that they are in the "Golden State" and that Malibu and Venice Beach are not far away.

San Bernardino This is where the "Orange Empire" begins, where oranges are grown as far as the eye can see. The California Theater evokes the golden age of Hollywood.

Joshua Tree National Park This park near Palm Springs is dedicated to the cactus-like yucca trees. They were given their name by a group of passing Mormons who were reminded of a biblical story about Joshua pointing to the sky.

Hualapai Mountain Park This park near Peach Springs is located in a side valley of the Grand Canyon.

Sunset Crater This crater is part of a huge lava field in the San Francisco Peaks range and is 300 m (984 ft) deep. The best lava cones, flows, and pipes are accessed from the panoramic drive.

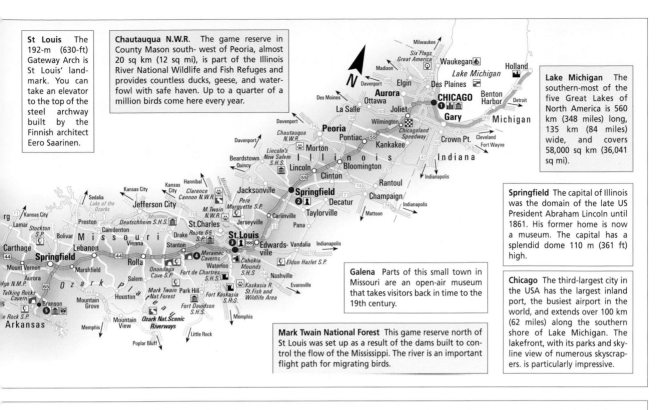

St Louis The 192-m (630-ft) Gateway Arch is St Louis' landmark. You can take an elevator to the top of the steel archway built by the Finnish architect Eero Saarinen.

Chautauqua N.W.R. The game reserve in County Mason south-west of Peoria, almost 20 sq km (12 sq mi), is part of the Illinois River National Wildlife and Fish Refuges and provides countless ducks, geese, and water-fowl with safe haven. Up to a quarter of a million birds come here every year.

Lake Michigan The southern-most of the five Great Lakes of North America is 560 km (348 miles) long, 135 km (84 miles) wide, and covers 58,000 sq km (36,041 sq mi).

Springfield The capital of Illinois was the domain of the late US President Abraham Lincoln until 1861. His former home is now a museum. The capital has a splendid dome 110 m (361 ft) high.

Galena Parts of this small town in Missouri are an open-air museum that takes visitors back in time to the 19th century.

Chicago The third-largest city in the USA has the largest inland port, the busiest airport in the world, and extends over 100 km (62 miles) along the southern shore of Lake Michigan. The lakefront, with its parks and sky-line view of numerous skyscrapers. is particularly impressive.

Mark Twain National Forest This game reserve north of St Louis was set up as a result of the dams built to con-trol the flow of the Mississippi. The river is an important flight path for migrating birds.

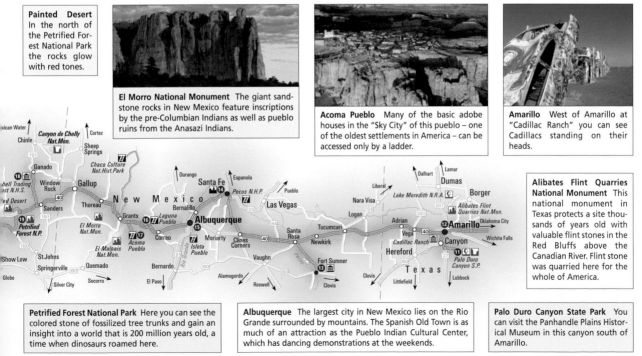

Painted Desert In the north of the Petrified For-est National Park the rocks glow with red tones.

El Morro National Monument The giant sand-stone rocks in New Mexico feature inscriptions by the pre-Columbian Indians as well as pueblo ruins from the Anasazi Indians.

Acoma Pueblo Many of the basic adobe houses in the "Sky City" of this pueblo – one of the oldest settlements in America – can be accessed only by a ladder.

Amarillo West of Amarillo at "Cadillac Ranch" you can see Cadillacs standing on their heads.

Alibates Flint Quarries National Monument This national monument in Texas protects a site thou-sands of years old with valuable flint stones in the Red Bluffs above the Canadian River. Flint stone was quarried here for the whole of America.

Petrified Forest National Park Here you can see the colored stone of fossilized tree trunks and gain an insight into a world that is 200 million years old, a time when dinosaurs roamed here.

Albuquerque The largest city in New Mexico lies on the Rio Grande surrounded by mountains. The Spanish Old Town is as much of an attraction as the Pueblo Indian Cultural Center, which has dancing demonstrations at the weekends.

Palo Duro Canyon State Park You can visit the Panhandle Plains Histor-ical Museum in this canyon south of Amarillo.

USA

From Bass Harbor Lighthouse in Maine to Cape Lookout Lighthouse in Maryland

A fairly narrow coastal plain stretches between the Atlantic Ocean in the East and the Appalachians in the West. Here on the East Coast the cities line up like pearls on a chain forming a massive conurbation that is also referred to as "Boswash" (Boston to Washington). However, despite the high population densities there are still a number of remote natural landscapes to be found.

In 1620, when they disembarked from the Mayflower at Plymouth Rock in present-day Massachusetts, the Pilgrim Fathers could not have dreamt that they were playing "midwife" to what is now the most powerful nation on earth, the United States of America. What they encountered was a largely untouched natural environment only sparsely populated by a number of Native North American tribes. Today the fascination of the US Atlantic coast derives not only from the bustling cities and the centers of political and economic power, but also from the peace and solitude of its idyllic natural setting. The mountain scenery of the Appalachians, which stretch from New England along the East Coast states to the south, can be demanding for hikers on parts of the famous Appalachian Trail. On the coast, beaches close to the metropolitan areas may be crowded, but further afield they are relatively untouched for miles and are a fantastic invitation to simply relax and unwind. Here you can also begin to imagine the courage the first settlers must have needed to set sail across the expansive ocean in

George Washington crossing the Delaware, by Emanuel G. Leutze, 1851.

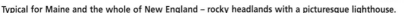

Typical for Maine and the whole of New England – rocky headlands with a picturesque lighthouse.

People all over the world recognize the skyline of New York, the "city that never sleeps". The city has provided a better life for many an immigrant, but is also the scene of many a broken dream.

their none-too-seaworthy sailing ships. The rich history can be seen at a number of places along the Atlantic Coast – from Plymouth Rock, where the Pilgrim Fathers landed, to Salem, where the witch hunts took place (described so exactingly by the writers Nathaniel Hawthorne in The Scarlet Letter, and Arthur Miller in The Crucible), on through to Boston, the starting point of the rebellion against England.

The Declaration of Independence was proclaimed in Philadelphia, Pennsylvania, while Williamsburg presents itself as a historical picture book when actors in traditional costumes take to the streets to relive days of yore.

The eastern USA is also the political nerve center of the USA as a superpower: Washington, with the White House, Capitol Hill, and the Pentagon, has formed the backdrop for the making and implementing of decisions with far-reaching historical impact. And of course there is the city that, for many people, is the very embodiment of the "American dream". It's "the city that never sleeps", the "Big Apple". It's New York.

Nestled between the Hudson and East rivers, New York is a melting pot of folks with an incredible diversity of languages, skin colors, and religions, a shopping paradise with the most exclusive shops for the appropriate wallets, and a cultural center with theaters and museums of international standing. In short, it's a truly cosmopolitan city that captivates nearly every one of its millions of visitors.

The White House, seat of the US President and the nerve center of power.

1

The dream route travels through the forests of New England via Boston and New York to Washington. It returns to the coast via Virginia. All twelve of the East Coast states have one thing in common – a view of the endless ocean.

① Portland The route begins in the largest city in the state of Maine. Henry W. Longfellow, a writer born here in 1807, often extolled Portland's attractive location on Casco Bay. Many parts of the city have been rebuilt after a series of disastrous fires. One of the few historical buildings left is the Wadsworth-Longfellow House, the oldest brick building in the city, dating back to 1786. The Old Port, with its warehouses, new office buildings, and numerous shops and restaurants, is the ideal place for a relaxing stroll.

The route initially heads north via Rockland towards the Acadia National Park. Interstate 95 and Highway 1 run parallel to the coast and always offer wonderful views of the rocky cliffs and islands, scenic bays, and small port villages such as Bath, the "City of Ships".

② Rockland This city at the south-west end of Penobscot Bay calls itself the "Lobster Capital of the World" and attracts visitors en masse at the beginning of August every year for its Maine Seafood Festival.

Two lighthouses ensure a safe approach to Penobscot Bay: Rockland Lighthouse and Owls Head Lighthouse. Information about the lighthouses can be found at the Shore Village Museum. Highway 1 continues via the port town of Camden, especially popular with sailors and windsurfers, before passing

majestically in the ports, or a graceful cruise along the coast at full sail. From Portsmouth, the only port in New Hampshire, it is only 29 km (18 miles) to the next state, Massachusetts.

④ Salem This port town, founded in 1626 about 25 km (16 miles) north of Boston, achieved its tragic claim to fame when the devout Puritans of Salem staged a crazed witch hunt in 1692 where twenty people were brought to "trial" and executed. The town has several museums dedicated to these woeful events – Salem Witch Museum, Salem Witch Village, Witch Dungeon Museum, and

through Belfast and Bucksport on the way to Ellsworth. Highway 3 takes you over a bridge to Mount Desert Island.

❸ Acadia National Park Still outside of the National Park is the fishing village of Bar Harbor, once a popular summer resort among American millionaires. Today, stately mansions reminiscent of this era still line the coast. The National Park, set up in 1916, encompasses half of Mount Desert Island and also in-

cludes the smaller islands of Isle au Haut, Baker, and Little Cranberry. When timber companies began felling timber on the islands at the end of the 19th century, Bar Harbor's "high society" bought the endangered land and donated it to the nation on condition that it be declared a national park.

The 500-m-high (1,640-ft) Cadillac Mountain is located within the park and attracts large numbers of visitors, especially during elusive Indian Summer days. The

stark cliffs of Acadia National Park are constantly pounded by Atlantic surf. The park, which coincidentally lies on a migratory bird route, can be explored on foot, by boat, or by bicycle. Back on the mainland, the return journey to Portland provides the opportunity to stop off at any of the quaint port towns on the coast road, stroll along one of the piers, or take a sailing trip on a windjammer.

It is difficult to resist the fascination of the boats anchored so

1 At the southern end of Mount Desert Island in the Acadia National Park is the Bass Harbor Lighthouse.

2 The Atlantic breakers pound the weather-beaten coast of the Acadia National Park.

Portland Head Lighthouse on Cape Elizabeth in Maine was commissioned by George Washington in 1790, and he personally appointed the first lighthousekeeper in 1791. As the light is now maintained automatically, as with most lighthouses, there is no longer a lighthouse-

keeper and his cottage has been turned into a small museum. The poet Henry Wadsworth Longfellow is said to have visited frequently in

Boston

The capital of Massachusetts resembles a giant open-air museum, a European enclave with historic buildings and winding streets set amid a modern inner city with glazed office towers, world-renowned universities, and leading research establishments.

It was in 1776 that the Declaration of Independence was first read out from the balcony of the Old State House in Boston, a red-brown brick building erected in 1712 as the seat of the English colonial government. Today there is a modern subway station below the historic building, but there is still no avoiding history in Boston. There has been a settlement on the hills around Massachusetts Bay from as far back as the 1720s. The settlement grew into an important port and, with its strategic position, became the economic and intellectual focus of the colony. The conflict with the colonial power exploded onto the public scene in 1770 when a number of citizens rebelled against the harsh tax policies of the British Crown and staged a boycott of all European goods.

On 16 December 1773 the colonists met in the Faneuil Hall, moved on to the Old South Meeting House – both significant points on the present-day Freedom Trail – and gathered in the port where, dressed as Native North Americans, they boarded three British ships and threw the tea bales into the sea. Paul Revere was to become a hero in the war of independence that followed when on the evening of 18 April 1775 he rode from Boston to Lexington to warn citizens that "the British are coming!". The Paul Revere House, the oldest building in the city, has been converted into a museum and is located in North End, a few blocks away from the Old North Church, which housed the two lanterns that gave Paul Revere warning of the approach of the British forces.

The Freedom Trail begins at Boston Common, the first public park in the USA, which in 1634 was originally set aside as pasture for livestock. Today it is the city's green belt and a popular leisure area for people working downtown. North of the park shines the golden dome of the new State House. The King's Chapel, built in 1754, was the first Anglican church in Boston. The Old Corner Bookstore, one of the best bookshops in the city, was already the literary center of Boston in the 19th century.

Other key points on the Freedom Trail are the Benjamin Franklin Statue, erected in memory of the scholars and signatories of the Declaration of Independence; the Old South Meeting House, a former church in which the "Boston Tea Party" was plotted; the Faneuil Hall, another of the colonists' meeting places; and Bunker Hill, scene of an important battle in the American War of Independence.

Apart from the Freedom Trail, the historic area of Beacon Hill is reminiscent of the city's history and its rich tradition. Little has changed here since the 17th century. Romantic patrician houses still stand on both sides of the cobblestone streets.

The country's academic elite are gathered at Harvard University on the other side of the Charles River. The center of Cambridge offers a diverse combination of bookshops, bars, and nightclubs and has become a popular meeting place for foreigners and tourists. The city one of the ten-most-popular tourist locations in the country.

1 Numerous skyscrapers characterize the Boston skyline.

2 One of the covered markets dating back to 1826 at the lively Quincy Market.

3 The narrow Acorn Street in the romantic Beacon Hill area.

the Witch House. The mansions, among the most attractive in the country, bear witness to the former wealth of this trading town. They also include the birthplace of author Nathaniel Hawthorne (1804–1864), and the House of the Seven Gables.

5 Boston (see pp.198–199). Via Interstate 3 it is 65 km (40 miles) to Plymouth which, due to its long coastline and more than 300 lakes and sprawling forests, is a populated commuter area.

6 Plymouth The port town is itself a milestone in American history – it was here that the Mayflower landed on 21 December 1620 after a perilous crossing, and it was here that the Pilgrim Fathers first set foot on American soil. A replica of the ship, the Mayflower II, is anchored in the port. The museum village Plimoth Plantation provides an interesting insight into the world of the first settlers. Not only does it have 17th-century houses and tools on display, but actors also re-enact everyday life at the beginning of that century. The Pilgrim Hall Museum has artefacts from the Pilgrim Fathers on display, and Cole's Hill is the site of the graves of those who died in the

first winter. From Cape Cod Bay the journey continues towards Hyannis on Cape Cod.

7 Hyannis The Steamship Authority ferries set off from Hyannis to Nantucket and Martha's Vineyard all year round.

8 Provincetown This little town at the northernmost end of the Cape Cod headland was founded by artists around 1900. Numerous writers and painters such as Edward Hopper and Jackson Pollock lived there for a time. Today the town still retains its artistic flair. Spectacular whale-watching trips by boat are also on offer in Provincetown.
Cape Cod's elbow shape dates back to the Ice Age. The retreating glaciers left behind some 365 lakes that are ideal for swimming, fishing, and boating. The beautiful Atlantic beaches are extremely popular today, particularly thanks to their warm waters. If you have time you really ought to take a detour to the nearby islands of Martha's Vineyard and Nantucket.
From Falmouth to the south of the peninsula the route initially takes you along Buzzards Bay to Wareham. After crossing the Fall River, it then continues to

Newport in Rhode Island (Highway 24).

9 Newport Founded in 1639, this town, which has 27,000 residents, is among the most beautiful places on the East Coast. Further along there are lovely views of the islands in the bay, with Providence lying at the northern end.

10 Providence The capital and economic center of Rhode Island was founded in 1636 by Roger Williams, whom the Puritans had driven out of Salem because of his reputedly heretical, i.e. cosmopolitan, views. The most impressive building in the town is the State House, built entirely of white marble and with the second-largest self-supporting dome in the world. Once nicknamed the "Beehive of Industry", Provi-

dence began rebranding itself as the "Creative Capital" in 2009 for education and arts.
Coastal Road 1 leads through a series of quaint villages and along the lovely beaches to Mystic Seaport.

11 Mystic Seaport This reconstruction of a port village from the 19th century in the southeast of Connecticut has become an open-air museum. Since the end of the 1920s, around sixty historic buildings have been reconstructed as replicas of the originals. There are up to 430 historic ships anchored in the large museum port. One of the yards specializes in the repair of historical ships. The modern neighboring town of Mystic is a small coastal resort with an aquarium worth seeing. A few kilometers west of Mystic is the

port of New London, where the ferries to Long Island set out. Via Highway 25 along the coast of the Long Island Sound you can reach New York in around two hours.

⑫ New York (see pp. 202–209). If you want to discover the rural charm of the state of New York, then you are best advised to go for an outing to the Hudson River Valley, which stretches north from New York City to the city of Albany.

⑬ Hudson Valley Pine forests sprinkled with lakes, farms, and small villages are what characterize the landscape along the Hudson River. Given the wonderful views, it is not surprising that many of the well-to-do from New York have built themselves stately homes here with well-tended parks. New Paltz, 100 km (62 miles) north of Yonkers, was founded by the Huguenots in 1692.

The next section of the river is lined with historically significant properties.

Springwood (Franklin D. Roosevelt Historic Site), the property where the later US President was born and grew up, is located there. Even more stately is the Vanderbilt National Historic Site, the palace built by the industrialist Frederick W. Vanderbilt in 1890 in the style of the Italian Renaissance. The trip along the Hudson Valley ends in Kingston, the gateway to the Catskills, an important recreational area for New Yorkers.

⑭ Philadelphia From the outskirts of New York the route continues towards Philadelphia,

Pennsylvania. Up until the completion of the various government buildings in Washington, Congress was housed in the Congress Hall of this, the most historically significant city in the USA. The heart of the city is the Independence National Historical Park, with Independence Hall where the representatives of the thirteen colonies signed the Declaration of Independence on 4 July 1776. The Liberty Bell, which was rung to mark the occasion, is housed in the Liberty Bell Pavilion. Numerous significant museums line the Benjamin Franklin Parkway, including the Philadelphia Museum of Art, the Rodin Museum, and the Franklin Institute Science Museum.

From here it is around 100 km (62 miles) along Highway 30 to Atlantic City, the "Las Vegas of the East". Back on Interstate 95, Baltimore in the state of Maryland is the next stop.

⑮ Baltimore This small city has only a few historic buildings left after a large majority of them were destroyed by fire in 1904. Little Italy still gives some impression of how the city must have looked in the past. The renovated port area (Harbor Place) has become attractive again since the 1970s – not to be

missed here are the National Aquarium, the 19th-century Fort Henry, and the Constellation in the docks, a triple-mast sailing ship built in 1854.

The outskirts of Washington extend far into the surrounding states of Maryland and Virginia, and it is therefore not long before you encounter the first suburbs of the capital city 50 km (31 miles) away.

⑯ Washington (see p. 210). In Washington you leave the coast for a short while and travel along the Manassas (Highway 29) and Warrenton (Highway 211) towards Washington, Virginia. Shortly before you enter town, Highway 522 branches off to Front Royal. The broad cave complex, Skyline Caverns, near Front Royal lies at the edge of the Shenandoah National Park.

1 The heart of Providence straddles the Seekonk River.

2 Provincetown became known for its artists' colony from 1900.

3 The Philadelphia skyline along the Delaware River at twilight.

4 The Capitol, built by Pierre Charles L'Enfant, has been the seat of the Senate since 1800.

New York

New York City comprises Manhattan, Brooklyn, Queens, the Bronx, and Staten Island. New York means the Statue of Liberty, the Empire State Building, the Chrysler Building, the Brooklyn Bridge, Broadway, and Fifth Avenue, but also the ghettos of the Bronx.

New York is effectively the "capital of the Western world", a melting pot where immigrants from around the globe have gathered to become an intrinsic part of America's cultural fabric. Of course, many ethnic groups have retained their cultural identity by developing neighborhoods such as Little Italy or Chinatown, just as they would in Palermo or Beijing. Indeed, New York gladly retreats into its "villages", creating its own worlds in neighborhoods such as Tribeca, Soho, Chelsea, and Greenwich Village. Yet the chaos continues in Midtown and on the wide avenues: the wailing of police sirens, the honking horns of taxis, and the pounding of jackhammers. The office towers rise up into the clouds. Be sure to check out Broadway, from the Battery in southern Manhattan as far as Yonkers and Albany in Upstate New York. It is the city's lifeline – in the financial district in the south and especially in the theater neighborhood around Times Square.

One of the most famous buildings in the world, the Empire State Building (1929–1931), was built in art deco style and is 381 m (1,257 ft) high – with the aerial mast, 448 m (1,588 ft.). Central Park, the green oasis in the mega metropolis, stretches from 59th to 110th Street over an area of 340 ha (840 acres). People of all kinds – from ball-playing teenagers and picnicking families – make for interesting encounters.

The Rockefeller Center (1930–1940) is a giant complex with offices, television studios, restaurants, and shops. The neo-Gothic St Patrick's Cathedral (1858–1887) is a replica of Cologne cathedral. The main train station, opened in 1913 as Grand Central Station after several years under construction, was built in the beaux arts style and decorated with baroque and Renaissance elements. An artificial sky sprinkled with 2,500 stars stretches over the somewhat ostentatious main hall.

The Brooklyn Bridge is the most recognizable bridge in the Big Apple. Opened in May 1883 after a sixteen-year construction period, the bridge is 1,052 m long (1,180 yds), excluding the access roads.

The Statue of Liberty stands out on the 4.8-ha (12-acre) Liberty Island (formerly Bedloe's Island), a small rock between Manhattan and Staten

1 The Statue of Liberty, donated by France, has been a New York landmark since 1886.

2 Brooklyn Bridge is one of the oldest suspension bridges in the United States. Completed in 1883, it connects the New York city boroughs of Manhattan and Brooklyn by spanning the East River.

3 Soho is known for its façades and traditional fire-escape stairs.

The East River links Long Island Sound to New York Bay – the tidal rise makes the water fast enough to prevent it from freezing even in winter. This explains the importance of the harbour (here with the historic four-master "Peking") as a berth in times when wooden ships

were in use. By about 1840, more passengers and a greater tonnage of cargo came through the port of New York than all other major
harbors in the country combined and by 1900 it was one of the great international ports.

Island. In her right hand she holds a torch, in the left the Declaration of Independence. The statue became a symbol of freedom for immigrants. The "path to freedom" used to lead through Ellis Island where every immigrant was registered between 1892 and 1917. In the museum you trace the process from the luggage room to the Great Hall.

Once completed, the Chrysler Building (1930) was the highest building in the world for just one year. Some aspects resemble the radiator grilles of the Chrysler cars. The United Nations building (1949–1953) looks over the East River. A number of works of art are on display in the entrance hall.

With its winding, tree-lined streets, the famous artists' neighborhood of Greenwich Village between 12th St, Houston St, Lafayette St, and the Hudson River is reminiscent of the "Old Europe" that early immigrants left behind. The Metropolitan Opera, or the "Met", one of the most well-known opera houses in the world, is part of the Lincoln Center, a giant complex of theaters and concert halls. The Guggenheim Museum, built by architect Frank Lloyd Wright, was disparagingly referred to as the "snail building". The new Museum of Modern Art (MoMa) complex was designed by the Japanese architect, Yoshio Taniguchi, and takes up an entire city block.

1 »Uptown« means towards the north on the city map of Manhattan, »Downtown« means down to the south.

2 Sea of lights every evening on Times Square.

3 For a few months in 1930 the Chrysler Building was the highest building in the world.

4 The magnificent bronze "Atlas with the globe" in the Rockefeller Center.

Manhattan's fascinating skyline is like an architecture museum; the great variety of buildings ranges from ornate, early 19th-century constructions through art deco creations such as the Rockefeller Center, New Objectivity pieces such as Mies van der Rohe's Lever House, and

post-modern office blocks. All these architectural masterpieces stand right next to one of the most extensive municipal parks in the world, Central Park, laid out by Frederick Law Olmsted and Calvert Vaux in 1870. Seen here, the stunning view of the Empire State Building

Washington

Washington, DC is the center of Western democracy and the seat of the US President, a focal point of political power.

The capital of the United States derives its importance from its central geographic location between the northern and southern regions of the original Thirteen Colonies – and also its proximity to Mount Vernon, home of first US President George Washington. Many of the city's buildings, including the Capitol Building, were set on fire during the war of 1812, and the city's present-day appearance is the result of a 'beautification plan' implemented at the end of the 19th century. Today DC is one of the most attractive travel destinations in the USA.

The Capitol sits on top of Capitol Hill opposite the Supreme Court and the Library of Congress. This neoclassical building represents the center point of the city and is one of America's most important political icons. The National Mall, a mile-long boulevard between the Capitol and the Washington Monument, is renowned for its cultural institutions. Numerous first-class museums such as the National Museum of Natural History and the National Air & Space Museum attract visitors all year round. The White House has been the office and residence of the US President since 1800. The Washington Monument, a 170-m-high (560-ft) obelisk made of granite and marble, commemorates the first president of the USA. The extermination of the Jews in World War II is documented in the United States Holocaust Memorial Museum.

1 The White House is the seat and residence of the US president.

2 Abraham Lincoln Memorial to honour the 16th US president (1861–1865).

3 The majestic Capitol dominates the cityscape of Washington, DC.

The George Washingtons statue dominating the rotunda of the Capitol where the US Congress meets. The statue seems to interact with the fresco painted by Greek-Italian artist Constantino Brumidi in 1865 and visible through the oculus of the dome. The Apotheosis of

Washington depicts George Washington becoming a god (apotheosis). Washington, the first U.S. president and commander-in-chief of the Continental Army during the American Revolutionary War, is allegorically represented, surrounded by figures from classical mythology.

Shenandoah National Park

This nature reserve in the Blue Ridge Mountains was established in 1926.

Shenandoah National Park includes much of the picturesque Blue Ridge Mountains, which run out east of the Appalachians between Pennsylvania and Georgia. The much-feted Shenandoah River flows from east to west through the valley. The 19th century saw many European immigrants settle in the mountains, and their descendants still live in tiny villages and on farms outside the protected area, becoming famous for their "hillbilly" lifestyle. One of the most beautiful scenic routes in the USA, the 160-km (100-mile) Skyline Drive, crosses the park from north to south, enjoying fantastic views of picturesque mountain valleys and forests which have hardly changed since the times of the settlers. There are over 800 km (500 miles) of signposted hiking trails in the park, including the famous 160-km (100-mile) Appalachian Trail, which crosses several states.

No less than six waterfalls crash down from the rocks of Whiteoak Canyon, and the Big Meadows have hardly changed in centuries, with the same wildlife to be seen as in the times of the Native Americans; deer, bears, and wild turkeys. There are also old farms, mills, and cemeteries, attesting to the arrival of the settlers. Bear Mountain affords the best views of this green and hilly land, whose slopes are strewn with wildflowers in the summer.

1 **2** A distant view of the chains of peaks, covered in thick vegetation, in the Blue Ridge Mountains.

3 **4** The Shenandoah River flows through the eponymous National Park in Virginia. The park includes the most beautiful parts of the Blue Ridge Mountains, the eastern arm of the Appalachians.

17 Shenandoah National Park You should plan five hours for the 170-km-long (106-mile) Skyline Drive through the national park because it is worth making multiple stops at the viewing points to take a look at the Shenandoah Valley. The park covers a particularly scenic part of the Appalachians with the panoramic route ending in Waynesboro. From there it is another 60 km (37 miles) to Monticello.

18 Monticello This property, which once belonged to Thomas Jefferson (1743–1826), is located to the east of Charlottesville. Jefferson designed the building for the Monticello plantation in Palladian style. Construction began in 1770. After 100 km (62 miles) on Interstate 64 you reach Richmond, the capital of Virginia.

19 Richmond The State Capitol on Capitol Square, designed by Thomas Jefferson, is considered to be the first neoclassical build-

ing in the USA. Here you will find the only statue for which George Washington posed in person. The Canal Walk on the northern bank of the James River is perfect for a leisurely stroll. With its Victorian houses the city has retained the flair of the Old South.

20 Williamsburg During the 18th century the town was the capital of Virginia. "Colonial Williamsburg", as the town calls itself, is home to eighty-eight buildings restored as facsimiles of the originals. Parks in the style of the 18th century complete the scene.
Highway 158 leads you to Point Harbor via Hampton, Norfolk, and Chesapeake (Highway 64). The port town of Albermarle Sound is the gateway to the pristine Cape Hatteras National Seashore with endless beaches. The nearby Wright Brothers National Monument commemorates the Wright Brothers' attempted flights in 1903, turning the pages of aircraft history.

21 Cape Hatteras National Seashore The 210-km-long (130-mile) group of islands off the east coast of North Carolina is known as the Outer Banks. The only road that goes there is the 150-km-long (93-mile) Highway 12, which connects the islands of Hatteras and Roanoke with each other.
The Outer Banks were once frequently targeted by pirates, and countless ships have been wrecked along the rocky coast. Today the often empty beaches, picturesque lighthouses, and other monuments attract nature lovers, recreational sports enthusiasts, and even the odd surfer. The majority of the islands are protected areas within the Cape Hatteras and Cape Lookout National Seashores.
On the return journey to Washington, DC take Highway 13 after leaving Chesapeake. At Salisbury turn off towards Ocean City (Highway 50) via Highway 611 and the bridge over Sinepuxent Bay. There you come to Assateague Island.

22 Assateague Island National Seashore Due to its exposure to wind and waves, this island is constantly changing shape.
A diverse animal and plant world braves the raw climate here. From the only small road on the island you can even see herds of wild horses roaming this narrow spit of windswept dunes and grass.
The return to Washington takes you via Highway 50. A bridge links the eastern side of Chesapeake Bay with quaint Annapolis, Maryland. Picturesque fishing villages, quaint historic towns, and scenic bathing spots line the shores of the bay. The founding of Annapolis, the capital of the state of Maryland, dates back to 1649. From Annapolis you are just a few kilometers away from Washington DC.

1 Not far from the busy American capital there are idyllic spots to be found on Chesapeake Bay.

Boston The colonial revolt against the English hegemony began with the 'Boston Tea Party'. You still encounter traces of history in many of Boston's neighbourhoods. It is also home to important research institutions and universities such as Harvard University and MIT.

New York The heart of this megacity beats loudly in places like Times Square. Every year thousands of people gather here on New Year's Eve to ring in the new year together. Here, in the middle of downtown Manhattan, the impressive skyscrapers rise up into the clouds.

Philadelphia This is where the Declaration of Independence was signed and the constitution drawn up. Today the metropolis is an important commercial center.

Washington The main American political nerve centers are in DC: the White House, the Capitol and the Pentagon, seat of the Dept of Defense.

Shenandoah National Park This beautiful park contains part of the Appalachian Trail, which stretches from Maine to Georgia.

Monticello This classic Palladian mansion was once the home of Thomas Jefferson, the third President of the United States.

Nantucket Island Prosperity here came in the 18th – 19th centuries from whale hunting, as documented in the Whaling Museum.

Acadia National Park Mount Desert Island, with its impressive craggy coast, is home to majestic Cadillac Mountain, also part of this striking national park.

Bath Both the town and its shipyards are rich in tradition. The Maine Maritime Museum and the Bath Iron Works document the history of shipping and shipbuilding in the area.

Martha's Vineyard The 'Vineyard' is a popular getaway among East Coast urbanites and plays host to the summer homes of the elite.

Atlantic City This East Coast counterpart to Las Vegas attracts visitors with the promise of big winnings and glamorous shows. The boardwalk along the Atlantic is especially scenic.

Cape Hatteras Lighthouse The highest lighthouse in theUSA has been warning ships of the shallows off Cape Hatteras for more than 100 years.

Williamsburg The many old buildings in Williamsburg, such as the Governor's Palace (1706–1722), bring the colonial history of this coastal town back to life.

Richmond This defiant granite building was constructed in 1894 and was for a long time the city hall in Virginia's capital.

Cape Lookout The 51-m-high (168-ft) lighthouse at Cape Lookout, built in 1859, rises above the shallows of Core Sound. It is characterized by its unusual decoration – black stripes on a white background.

USA

Florida: between the Atlantic and the Gulf of Mexico

Hardly anywhere else in the land of opportunity offers a chance to experience the American way of life like Florida, the "Sunshine State". Situated at the southern end of the east coast, the 27th US state is an exotic paradise of palm trees; its eventful history and the influx of immigrants, especially from Cuba, mean that in contrast to its northern neighbors it enjoys an exciting mix of cultures.

Juan Ponce de León, the Spanish explorer, called the peninsula "la Florida" – "the land in bloom" when he "discovered" it in 1513 (the Seminole Indians had been there for some time!). This flat peninsula between the Gulf of Mexico and the Atlantic Ocean has something for everyone: hippies and yuppies, the restful and the restless, happy souls and dreamers. Rockets are sent to the moon from here and people go to the ends of the earth for one another, comic-book heroes are brought to life and well-off pensioners enjoy their retirement – welcome to the land of opportunities! It is little wonder that Florida's population has been growing steadily: its 170,000 sq km (65,640 sq mi) are shared by 17.5 million people, and ever more people are flocking to Florida to spend their retirement, a warm winter, or just a holiday.

The Sunshine State is a mass of contradictions; the typically American – malls, highways, and

Ocean Drive in Miami Beach.

snack bars – seems to co-exist quite happily with the Cuban and colonial flair of the cities, the Caribbean atmosphere of the Keys, the Spanish, French, or English customs of the residents, even with the songs and dances which have come from Haiti or Latin America; these contradictions seem to resolve themselves effortlessly into what is most typical and most loved about Florida, and a tour of the 800-km (500-mile) long state will help you experience these contrasting worlds.

Only one thing seems to be missing from Florida – the feeling of being in a Southern state. The American Civil War began in 1861 with the secession of the Southern states from the Union. Florida was one of these eleven breakaway Confederate states,

Opened in 1997, the MacArthur Causeway connects southern Miami Beach to the mainland.

Sunset between the tall cypresses of the Everglades, a unique kind of swampland found only in southern Florida.

but it has lost much of the character of a classic Southern state as it has modernized and become more cosmopolitan. For this reason the route begins in Florida's northern neighbors, passing through selected coastal areas of Georgia and the Carolinas, to give an idea of the spirit of the Grand Old South. The colonial architecture preserved in cities like Wilmington, Charleston, and Savannah attest to the eventful past it has lived through.

History has played only a marginal role in Florida, however, and the State does not seem to pay too much attention to the issues of slavery and the displacement of the Native American; apart from a few forts and museums, most of the historical traces seem to have faded. Instead, Florida has its sights set on the future: it is difficult to miss the rocket launchpad at Cape Canaveral in the east or the skyscrapers of Tampa Convention Center in the west; the self-confidence of Miami in the south is equally apparent. Among all these is the greatest symbol of success and entertainment: Disneyworld in Orlando, the most popular amusement park in the world.

Anyone tiring of the bustle of the coastal cities can withdraw to the islands of the Keys or the amphibian world of the Everglades, but both of these so-called paradises are endangered: the Florida Keys National Marine Sanctuary is the second largest marine nature reserve in the USA, but like its northern neighbor it is threatened by sewage, fertilizer run-off, and the rubbish generated by human civilization. A further serious challenge is presented by the regular devastating hurricanes, which cause much damage and require considerable safety precautions.

The annual Race Week makes Key West a date for international sailors.

1

Visitors to the "Sunshine State" and parts of North Carolina (NC), South Carolina (SC), and Georgia (GA) will be able to get a taste of the deep south, before discovering everything that Florida has to offer on a round tour of the state.

❶ Jacksonville (NC) The route begins at Jacksonville in North Carolina (pop. 70,000) with a visit to the Bellair Plantation and Restorations, a classic example of an antebellum Southern plantation. The city is an ideal place from which to explore the islands and coastline of North Carolina, and an excursion visiting the Outer Banks to the north-east is recommended. Take the US-17 heading east and turn off after 500 m (a third of a mile) onto State Highway NC-24, which takes you to Morehead City and then continues to Cedar Island as the US-70.
After visiting the nature reserve, retrace your steps but continue on past Jacksonville. The south-

bound US-17 runs parallel to Onslow Bay and reaches Wilmington after a journey of 55 km (34 miles).

❷ Wilmington The largest city (pop. 90,000) on the North Carolina coast is a strategic port which played a significant role for the Confederates in the Civil War. The most important tourist attraction in the region lies at anchor in Wilmington port: the North Carolina, a former battleship. Wilmington was founded in 1739, and a stroll through the city's historic downtown area

East Battery Street in Charleston, the first settlement founded by English pioneers in 1670.

Travel Information

Route profile
Route length: 2,400 km (1,500 miles); 3,200 km
Time required: 3–4 weeks
Start: Jacksonville (NC)
Destination: Orlando (FL)
Waypoints: Jacksonville, Charleston, Savannah, Brunswick, Saint Augustine, Tampa, Naples, Miami and Miami Beach, Boca Raton, Cape Canaveral, Orlando

Immigration:
No visa required; immigration is only possible with a machine-readable passport and after giving fingerprints.

Traffic information:
The top speed on highways is 70 mph (112 km/h), in built-up areas often 35 mph (56 km/h).

Best time to travel:
Late summer to mid-December or after Easter.

Health:
Mosquitoes are a real pest in Florida and almost unbearable in the Everglades. Insect repellent is absolutely essential.

Further information:
North Carolina:
www.visitnc.com
South Carolina:
www.discoversouthcarolina.com
Georgia:
www.georgia.org/tourism
Florida: *www.flausa.com*
www.floridastateparks.org
Florida Keys:
www.fla-keys.com
Nationalparks: *www.nps.gov*

and a visit to the Cape Fear Museum, North Carolina's oldest museum, are both a must.

The route leaves Wilmington heading west and crosses the Cape Fear River, which flows into the sea about 40 km (25 miles) south of the city.

The road forks after a further 7 km (4.5 miles), becoming the US-17 and running south-west towards the state line, which lies some 70 km (45 miles) behind Thomasboro. Once across the border into South Carolina, Myrtle Beach is a further 40 km (25 miles).

3 Myrtle Beach "America's Majorca" is the hub of the Grand Strand resort area, the largest and busiest in South Carolina, with fine sandy beaches stretching for 90 km (56 miles). The beach is lined with hotels, theaters, amusement parks, and any number of sport and leisure facilities. There are almost 100 golf and minigolf courses, go-kart circuits, and water parks, and nearly 2,000 restaurants, making Myrtle Beach a tourist infrastructure without compare in South Carolina.

The charming scenery of Brookgreen Gardens, with its sculpture garden, wildlife preserve, and institute for landscape gardening, is in stark contrast to its built-up surroundings; the park is 30 km (19 miles) further south on the US-17. The highway soon heads inland, passing Georgetown and reaching Charleston after 120 km (74 miles).

4 Charleston The birthplace of the eponymous dance was founded by the British on a peninsula in 1670. Despite hurricanes and extensive rebuilding, Charleston has managed to retain its historic cityscape. There are still about 140 houses dating from the 18th century, and more than 600 pre-1840 buildings are still inhabited. Houses, gardens, and plantations are open to the public and can be explored from a horse-drawn coach; this charming town is one of the most beautiful in the USA. Your attention will be drawn to several key dates: in 1670, English pioneers founded their first settlement in Charleston, and the first playhouse in the American colonies was opened in the town in 1736. The city also has a chapter in American history, as the Civil War began here on 12 April 1861. The scenery is reminiscent of Gone With The Wind, with the roads to the city leading through avenues of oaks and walnut trees, and the US-17 has just such surroundings as it leads south across the border to Georgia, reaching Savannah after 177 km (110 miles).

5 Savannah The charm of the South can be felt everywhere here. The city was founded in 1733 as the first English colonial capital of Georgia, with James Oglethorpe, an English seafarer, drawing up the plans for "Charleston's sister city". Modern Savannah can boast that a French newspaper has singled it out as the most beautiful city in North America, and this former cotton port on the banks of the Savannah River has retained much of its 18th- and 19th-century architecture and flair. Savannah's Historic District, with its trees hanging with Spanish moss and its parks with their distinctive treetops, is best visited as part of a guided tour, which will take you into the city's past as the most important exporter of cotton.

1 A merchant's house in East Battery Street in Charleston. Established in 1670, the city was the first lasting settlement to be founded by English pioneers.

The trunks of the high cypresses reflect in the dark, almost still water of Okefenokee National Wildlife Refuge (2,000 sq km/770 sq mi) between Waycross (Georgia) and the northern Florida state line. The Native Americans who first lived here called this region of swamps

one of the largest in the USA, "Trembling Earth" similar to a floating island of turf, a meter (3 ft) thick. The moor is best explored by canoe, but you shouldn't be of a nervous disposition: 30 species of snake live here, along with big cats, bears, and thousands of alligators

Leaving the city via "new" Savannah, the route follows the I-16 for a short while before turning off onto the I-95, heading for Brunswick, which is about 130 km (80 miles) away. The I-95 is lined with brilliant green trees and idyllic rivers can be seen in the distance. At about the halfway point, the road passes Sapelo Island Nature Reserve on the coast to the left, which is famed for its salt marshes. Descendants of slaves still maintain the African culture and customs of their ancestors here.

6 Brunswick Founded in 1771, Brunswick is also known as the "Shrimp Capital of the World" because of its seafood industry. The city is the ideal place from which to explore the idyllic islands along Georgia's coast, and one of the best-known of these is Cumberland Island. Visitors wishing to get an idea of the interior should not miss the Okefenokee Swamp Park, about 50 km (31 miles) to the south-west, near Waycross. Heading north along Egmont Street, the route leaves Brunswick and reaches the I-95S via the US-25 and the US-17, finally arriving in Jacksonville, the first large city we are visiting in Florida, after a journey of some 110 km (68 miles).

7 Jacksonville (FL) An industrial and commercial hub with a population of more than a million, this is the biggest city in the Sunshine State and indeed the biggest conurbation in the USA by area – its city limits enclose more than 2,000 sq km (770 sq mi). Jacksonville was named for General Andrew Jackson (1767–1845), who became the seventh president of the United States in 1828. Known as "Jax" for short, the

city's extensive health infrastructure makes it the educational and commercial hub of Florida. The impressive skyline is dominated by the skyscrapers ranged along the St Johns River, the longest river in Florida; restaurants, beautiful promenades, and countless stores make a stroll along its banks into a real experience. There are several interesting bridges crossing the river downtown. You can leave Jacksonville either via Atlantic Boulevard to the north, heading for Atlantic Beach, or Beach Boulevard to the south, heading for Jacksonville Beach; either way you will hit State Highway A1A after about 25 km (15 miles), where you should head south. This is the beginning of a particularly charming section of the route, with the road gener-

ally following the coast and magnificent sea views.

The route passes through idyllic Guana River State Park at the halfway point, and after a further 50 km (31 miles) you cross the Vilano Bridge into St Augustine.

8 St Augustine The oldest European settlement in North America, St Augustine was the capital of Florida for 235 years. On 8 September 1565, the town's name day, Pedro Menéndez de Avilés founded St Augustine in the name of Philip II, the king of Spain, as a bastion against the growing dominance of France in Florida, which had been discovered in 1513 by Ponce de León, the Spanish explorer. In 1562 the French had built Fort Caroline at Jacksonville and staked their claim to a region that until then the Spanish had neglected. Menéndez and his troops succeeded in driving the French from the colony, and the fort their descendants built at Castillo de San Marcos (1672–1696), which saw action in the war with the British, is now a national monument.

There is still a Spanish feel to the streets of St Augustine; this is particularly true of the Victorian buildings in the Downtown His-

toric District, where St Augustine experienced a second heyday at the end of the 19th century. Two luxurious Flagler hotels were built, one of which is now Flagler College and the other, the Alcazar Hotel, is now the Lightner Museum.

Leaving St Augustine and continuing south across the narrow barrier islands is just as charming a journey; to get back onto the A1A, leave Downtown via King Street, cross the Bridge of Lions over the Matanzas, and take Anastasia Boulevard to St Augustine Beach. This section of the route also follows the coast, crossing several State Parks, and after about 30 km (19 miles) you will reach Marineland of Florida, the oldest oceanarium in the world. There are plenty of opportunities to enjoy a dip in the sea or some sunbathing as you follow the coast road, whether at Flagler Beach, where you can

observe seabirds at the Flagler Recreation Area, or at Ormond-by-the-Sea, on whose beautiful beaches a vintage car rally is held every November.

9 Daytona Beach A seaside resort located on a narrow spit of land – at low tide, the long sandy beach is more than 150 m (500 ft) wide. It is known locally as the "world's most famous beach" and Daytona is principally famous for its long tradition of motor racing (see sidebar on following page). The Cuban Museum, which houses works taken

1 Sapelo Island is divided into the characteristic zones of a barrier island: forested uplands, extensive salt marshes, and a system of dunes.

2 A skyline view of Jacksonville, the biggest city in Florida, from the St Johns River.

in 1959 from the Cuban national museum in Havana by Batista, the exiled dictator, is also well worth a visit.

The I-4 offers the quickest route from Daytona Beach to the next waypoint, the west coast of Florida, turning inland past Orlando and continuing for 215 km (134 miles) to Tampa. To reach it, take the Beville Road from Daytona, which becomes the I-4 after 6 km (4 miles). The 2.5-hour journey begins at sea level, but in Polk County the scenery slowly becomes more hilly. Fans of architecture and fine buildings might want to make a pilgrimage to Lakeland, the largest city in he county, to pay homage to Frank Lloyd Wright's Annie Pfeiffer Chapel (1941).

The hills gradually start to diminish as the road approaches the Gulf of Mexico, and after leaving the I-4 at Exit 2, you take the Crosstown Expressway towards the port town of Tampa, which exudes Caribbean flair.

⑩ Tampa This industrial port is the commercial center of West Florida and it boasts Busch Gardens, an African-themed amusement park, which is the biggest tourist attraction on the west coast. The town's skyline is dominated by the skyscrapers in the business district and the mighty bridges across Tampa Bay, into which the Hillsborough River flows.

The bay was discovered in 1513 by the Spanish, but the area was not settled until Fort Brooke, a military outpost, was estab-lished in 1824. The industrial development of the modern city began in the 1880s with the arrival of Henry B. Plant's railroad and the construction of a cigar factory by a Cuban, Vicente Martinez Ybor. Ybor City, which bears his name, is essentially a separate town, but is still considered Tampa's "old quarter", and has a very Cuban feel.

⑪ St Petersburg This spa town, declared "the healthiest town in America", is in the immediate vicinity of Tampa on the western side of Tampa Bay, with the seaside resort of Clearwater next door. This "pensioner's paradise" is devoted entirely to tourism, and the Salvador Dalí Museum, which opened in 1982, houses more than 1,000 works by the Spanish artist. You should definitely leave St Petersburg via the I-275, as this crosses the phenomenal Sunshine Skyway Bridge, a 21-km (13-mile) long masterpiece of engineering which is a delight to behold. The bridge will take you to Highway 41 which runs parallel

to the I-75; even though you sometimes lose sight of the coast, this road is more interesting for tourists.

After stopping at or passing through little towns like Sarasota and Venice, continue down the Gulf of Mexico for another 150 km (93 miles) to the next city, Fort Myers.

⑫ Fort Myers The inventor Thomas Edison and the car manufacturer Henry Ford both once had their winter homes in this rapidly expanding town. The main attraction in this residential town lies off the coast. Accessible via a toll bridge, Sanibel Island is famed for the variety of mussels that wash up from the Gulf onto its idyllic beaches, and it is no surprise to learn that the largest mussel museum in the USA is located here. Naples is 55 km (34 miles) further along Highway 41.

⑬ Naples Some 10 km (6 miles) north of "Millionaires' Row" you will pass the Delnor–Wiggins State Recreation Area, with its 1 km-long (0.5 mile) beach, considered one of the ten best in America. Naples, the southernmost city on the west coast, is a very smart resort, with art galleries, exclusive boutiques in up-market malls, and more golf courses per capita than anywhere else in the USA. Naples was founded by twelve Kentucky real estate speculators, who bought up the land in 1886 and sold it on in parcels to the wealthy.

Naples is situated on the edge of the Everglades National Park, which can be easily visited from the city; take the Tamiami Trail, a continuation of US-41, which runs south-east for a further 55 km (34 miles) to Carnestown, the turn-off for Everglades City.

⑭ Everglades City This little town is the north-western entrance to the 600,000 ha (2,300 sq. mi) Everglades National Park (see sidebar on following page). Nature trips to the north and boat tours through the Ten Thousand Islands further to the south can be booked here. The park protects one of the largest mangrove estuaries (funnel-like river mouths) in the USA, where seawater and fresh water combine to create unique living conditions for wildlife.

The most involving way to explore this swampy world, a habitat of wood storks, red-tailed hawks, ospreys, and royal terns, is by canoe, and for longer trips you can even hire houseboats in Everglades City to navigate e. g. on Shark River in the southwestern portion of Everglades National Prk.

1 Ancient swamp cypresses create a unique waterscape near Lakeland.

2 The Tampa skyline towers over the Hillsborough River.

3 Delnor–Wiggins State Park, where visitors are met by mile upon mile of white, sandy beaches.

Everglades National Park

The Everglades on the southern tip of Florida form the only protected subtropical region in North America.

The third-largest national park in the USA covers an area of some 6,100 sq km (2,400 sq mi) and encloses a giant region of swampland stretching from the Tamiami Trail in the north to Florida Bay in the south, and from the Keys in the east to the Gulf of Mexico. The Native Americans called the Everglades "Pay-hay-okee" – a "sea of grass" – and when the wind blows the tough Jamaican sawgrass, the marshes look like a stormy ocean. For centuries the grass was nourished by south-flowing flood water from Lake Okeechobee, but now man-made dams channel this water into canals and the Everglades are dependent on rainwater for survival – an intervention in the circle of life which has been condemned by conservationists and others.

Park rangers now maintain constant vigilance to ensure that no further damage is caused: noisy airboats are banned from the park, and long wooden walkways leading deep into the swamps allow visitors to observe the rare wildlife and the many-hued plants. Rare birds such as the anhinga, which swims with only its head above water, scooping fish into its beak, the endangered wood stork, which can swallow its prey in seconds, and the bald eagle, the USA's heraldic animal, have found a home among the hammocks (islands of trees in the sea of grass) and mangroves. Other birds, such as the spoonbill and the purple swamphen, derive benefit from the seasonal changes here and the ideal conditions for breeding and feeding. As a rule, alligators only become dangerous to people after they have been fed by tourists.

1 The Everglades in Florida are an endangered eco-system.

2 Alligators feel at home in the Everglades.

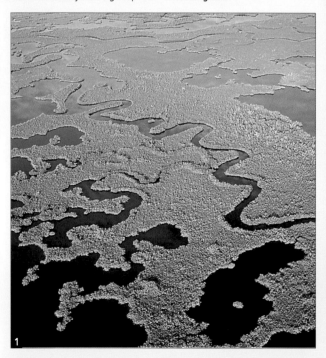

Manatees, a sub-species of the sea cow, live in flat marshlands, where the herbivores are protected from their predators – sharks, alligators, and orcas. These mammals, which can reach 4.5 m (15 ft) in length and weigh up to 700 kg (1,500 lb), are threatened with extinction.

Top: The great blue heron is just one of the 300 bird species native to the Everglades. Middle: Raccoons looking for food scraps often bother tourists.Bottom: The Cuban tree frog is mainly found in Cuba, the Bahamas, and on the Keys in the south of Florida.

1

There are many rewarding views to be enjoyed at stopping-points along the next stretch of the Tamiami Trail, and at many of these you can arrange a trip on an airboat. The road passes through the wet cypress forests, prairies, mangroves, and "hammocks" (stands of hardwood trees on mounds) of the Big Cypress National Preserve, the last remaining preserve of the Florida panther.

The only official road leading into the Everglades National Park is the FL-9336 from Florida City. To reach it, as you reach the western city limits of Miami turn south off the Tamiami Trail onto the Florida Turnpike (FL-821), and Florida City is some 30 km (19 miles) further on. The winding trail through the expanses of the Everglades begins 15 km (9 miles) the other side of the city, at the Visitor Center & Park Headquarters near Homestead. There are severable possible stopping-places at viewing plat-

forms and wooden paths leading through the "sea of grass". The road ends about 80 km (48 miles) further on, at Flamingo.

⑮ Flamingo The "capital of the Everglades, on the southern tip of the Florida peninsula, is a tourist center with some excellent facilities. You can take a tour with a ranger, who will provide you with plenty of information about ecological errors of the past and how they are now slowly being corrected. Follow the same road to return to Florida City, and from there take the US-1, heading north towards Miami.

⑯ Miami and Miami Beach (see following pages)
Four more or less parallel roads connect Miami to Fort Lauderdale, some 35 km (22 miles) away to the north: the turnpike (toll road), the I-95, the US-1, and the A1A, the narrow coast road. The best route probably

2

3

swaps between the two last-mentioned, starting on the US-1.

⑰ Fort Lauderdale Fort Lauderdale is named after a wooden fort built here by Major William Lauderdale in 1837, during the Seminole Wars. Today, only the name remains of the fort. The first drainage ditches were dug in 1906 and a 300-km (186-mile) system of waterways soon developed from these. Lined with palm trees, the countless canals are now filled with a flotilla of smart yachts belonging to the locals and water-taxis for the less well-off tourists, earning Fort Lauderdale the soubriquet of "the Venice of America". Sun-seekers from all over the world come to Fort Lauderdale to play, relax, and sometimes even to work. The city is an important cruise ship port, and many ocean liners stop off at Port Everglades on their way to the Caribbean. The US-1 passes numerous white sandy beaches during the 30-km (19-mile) journey to Boca Raton.

⑱ Boca Raton Built on reclaimed Everglades swampland, this modern resort with 170,000 inhabitants was a notorious haunt of pirates in the 17th century. Plans for an Italian quarter with exclusively Mediterranean architecture were drawn up by the society architect Addison Mizner in 1925, but were subsequently shelved during the Great Depression. Mizner's unmistakable style has, however,

1 A view of the Downtown Miami skyline from Biscayne Bay.

2 A holiday paradise under the palm trees: Miami Beach.

3 Art deco hotels line Ocean Drive in Miami Beach.

4 Exclusive yachts at anchor in Fort Lauderdale marina.

233

Miami and Miami Beach

Miami is situated on Biscayne Bay on Florida's south-eastern coast. The second-largest city in the state has a population of 370,000 and has expanded massively since 1896. The separate city of Miami Beach, one of the busiest and most extravagant holiday resorts in the USA, lies on a 20-sq-km (8-sq-mi) island just off the coast.

Called "Mayami" – "sweet water" – by the Native Americans, this spot at the mouth of the river was settled by the Spanish in the middle of the 16th century, but after a while they found the oppressive location with its dangerous predators and clouds of mosquitoes too much to bear. The first American settlers arrived at the beginning of the 19th century, growing cotton and fruit; Fort Dallas was built in 1836, and was followed by a trading station in 1871.

Connection to the railroad network proved to be the turning point for Miami. Henry Flagler, a speculator and rail pioneer, extended his East Coast Railroad from St Augustine in the north to Miami and built the first hotel here. The railroad and the hotel provided the initial spark for Miami's subsequent rapid development. By 1925, there were more than 85,000 residents and more than 500 hotels had been built.

The development of the city was strongly influenced by the gigantic wave of immigration from Cuba: many hundreds of thousands of Cubans fled to Miami from Fidel Castro's revolution and, with other immigrants from Latin America and Haiti, these make up over half the current population; as many people speak Spanish as English in Miami. The Cuban quarter, "Little Havana", has grown up along the Calle Ocho, with everything you would expect to find on the island, including some cigar factories.

The city's central business district is home to the largest concentration of international banks in the United States as well as home to several corporate headquarters and television studios. Additionally, the metropolis' namesake port, the Port of Miami, is the busiest cruise ship passenger port in the world. Since 2001, Miami has been undergoing a large building boom with more than 50 skyscrapers rising over 122 m (400 ft). Miami's skyline is ranked third most impressive in the U.S., behind New York City and Chicago.

Miami boasts several museums that are well worth a visit, including the Historical Museum of Southern Florida, the Gusman Center for the Performing Arts, and the Rubell Family Collection. The Vizcaya museum and Gardens in the Coconut Grove district is a fine example of the Mediterranean Revival style, which is especially common in Miami; planned completely in this style, Coral Gables is the most beautiful district in the city. Its Caribbean flair, multicultural society, and not least its mild winter climate have made this commercial and financial center a popular holiday destination, and more than ten million tourists make the journey every year, despite the soaring rates of criminality and the ever-present threat of hurricanes.

Miami Beach covers only 4 sq km (1.5 sq mi) but always draws large crowds of visitors. South Beach, although actually a separate city, is generally treated as a suburb of Miami. The two cities are linked by five bridges, the first of which was built in 1912. Miami Beach's 14-km (8-mile) stretch of sand is a playground for the rich and famous and anyone who enjoys people-watching and all the hustle and bustle of the area. Ferraris, Lamborghinis, and stretched Lincoln limousines routinely pull up outside the pastel art deco façades of the buildings to bring actors, models, and fashionistas to all-night parties.

1 Lit up at night: Miami marina and skyline.

Top and bottom: Miami Beach's palm-lined Ocean Drive is a popular spot for a stroll, and the promenade has featured as a backdrop in countless stills and movies. Many artists and celebrities have bought houses or run restaurants here. Miami Beach life really begins to hot

up in the evening, as the lights go on in the pastel art deco palaces and extravagant parties are held in the neon glare of the bars and

1

left its mark on the skyline of Palm Beach, some 40 km (25 miles) away.

19 Palm Beach This smart Gold Coast resort – home to superstars and the super-rich – lies on a long, narrow island off the Atlantic coast. The success story of this small but urbane city (pop. 10,000) began in 1894, when the oil magnate Henry M. Flagler extended his railroad line to Palm Beach and built the first luxury hotel. Wealthy hotel guests from the north soon learnt to appreciate the mild climate and the idyllic white beaches, and returned in droves. A wave of winter retreats for millionaires was built soon after – with Flagler's being among the first – and these days Ocean Boulevard, which runs parallel to the beach, is lined with villas the size of palaces.

The coast north of Palm Beach is less built-up and more attractive, and it is worth taking the narrower A1A, which follows

the coastline and the barrier islands. After 100 km (62 miles) of dunes and unspoilt beaches you will reach Fort Pierce.

20 Fort Pierce Just like Fort Lauderdale, this town (pop. 45,000) bears the name of a fort constructed during the Seminole Wars. The US Army arrived here in 1838 to forcibly relocate the local tribes, but were met with resistance. Fort Pierce on the Indian River is the county seat of rural St Lucie County, whose inhabitants live from cattle ranching and cultivating citrus fruits. Fort Pierce market is consequently one of the largest in the USA.

Crowds of divers come here too; many richly laden merchant ships came to grief on the coral reefs of the "Treasure Coast" and their wrecks are popular diving sites. A trip to the Manatee Observation and Education Center a little to the north of the city is recommended, where visitors can observe the endan-

2

gered manatee, a sub-species of the sea cow.

The Indian River, which runs between the coast and the island groups, follows the A1A towards Melbourne (90 km/56 miles away), and the view from the road is of many plantations and small towns; there are even places to stop off for a swim along the way.

At Melbourne, the A1A becomes a four-lane highway and continues for 40 km (25 miles) to Cape Canaveral.

21 Cape Canaveral The name is world-famous, and a synonym for one of mankind's greatest technical feats – space travel. NASA's Space Port, the scene of the most spectacular rocket launches, is located here (see sidebar far left), but very few people would also associate the name of Cape Canaveral with an extraordinary nature reserve where there are more endangered species than in many parks across the whole United States. The Canaveral National

Seashore and Merritt Island National Wildlife Refuge together cover a total surface area of 56,000 ha (216 sq mi) and are both situated on the same barrier island as the launchpad, with the protected area beginning to the north of the actual cape.

Some 300 species of birds live here, many of which are quite rare, as well as creatures such as bobcats, alligators, snakes, manatees, and armadillos, as well as leatherback and hawksbill turtles. The aptly named Mosquito Lagoon, east of Merritt Island, is an eco-system composed of swamps, mudflats, and marshes, rounded off with some 40 km (25 miles) of idyllic, white sandy beaches on the barrier islands.

The only access to many parts of this protected area is provided by small, dead-end spur roads, and the Kennedy Space Center is reached via the NASA Parkway, from which you can turn straight onto the Beeline Expressway (FL-528W, toll road), the quickest route to reach Orlando, some 85 km (53 miles) away.

22 Orlando The history of the city dates back to 1838; at some point during the turmoil of the Seminole Wars a fort was built here, and by 1840 was occupied by a troop of soldiers. Orlando was officially recognized as a settlement in 1875, with a population of just 85. That there are now around 1.4 million residents is almost entirely due to a cartoon figure: Mickey Mouse.

Since the opening of Disneyworld in 1971, this sleepy little town of ranchers and fruitgrowers has become the fourth-largest city in Florida and the most popular tourist attraction in the world.

There are also many delightful lakes and a number of notable museums, including the Orlando Science Center, the Orlando Museum of Art (19th- and 20th-century American art), the Albin Polasek Museum with its sculpture garden, and the Charles Hosmer Morse Museum of American Art, which has a considerable Tiffany collection.

1 A space shuttle launch at Cape Canaveral spaceport.

2 Sunset along the Canaveral National Seashore.

3 A view of the skyline at Orlando, famed for Disneyworld.

There are some fifty amusement and leisure parks around Orlando, all of which benefit from the pulling power of Disneyworld. The walls of Cinderella's Palace on Main Street in the Magic Kingdom are lit up every evening in summer with a magnificent firework display.

Brookgreen Gardens The scenic park was founded on Myrtle Beach in 1931 to protect wildlife and plants and to provide a forum for sculptors.

Charleston The Caribbean feel of this historic city in South Carolina has made it one of North America's most popular tourist destinations. The 17th-century port has transformed itself into a city almost out of a picture book, in whose bars the "Charleston" was invented in 1925.

Savannah The city was established as an English colony in 1733. Once a significant port for the cotton trade, it has retained much of the architecture and flair of its past.

Jacksonville This industrial and commercial city on the St Johns River has a modern skyline and at over 2,000 sq km (770 sq mi) has the largest area of any city in the USA.

Tampa The office blocks in the business district define the look of this city on Tampa Bay. There is also Busch Gardens amusement park and zoo, the biggest tourist attraction on the west coast of Florida.

Everglades This swampy, sub-tropical wilderness is the largest marshland in the USA. The "River of Grass" is a globally unique eco-system ideally suited to alligators.

Key West Tourists and hippies alike from all over the world are drawn to this small island at the far western tip of the Keys by the surroundings and the memory of its most famous resident, Ernest Hemingway (1899–1961).

Cape Lookout The lighthouse on the isolated Core Banks is part of the National Seashore conservation area.

Cumberland Island One of the largest unspoilt chains of barrier islands in the world, the national park authorities took over ownership of the island in 1960, saving this natural idyll from industrial development.

Cape Canaveral The NASA spaceport is a byword for mankind's technical achievements. Neil Armstrong, Buzz Aldrin, and Michael Collins left here in 1969 on their way to the first moon-landing.

Disneyworld Since opening in 1971, the "Magic Kingdom" near Orlando has become the most popular amusement park in the world. The inspiration behind it all was the cartoon pioneer, Walt Disney.

Miami Beach The smart resort of Miami Beach has over 800 art deco buildings and one of the highest concentrations of up-market sports cars.

Miami An international banking hub located on the shores of Biscayne Bay. Life in the city has a strong Cuban influence thanks to the presence of the largest Cuban community outside Cuba.

Norfolk
Whalebone
Columbia
Waves
Swanquarter
Cape Hatteras Nat. Seashore
Cape Hatteras Lighthouse
Ocracoke Lighthouse
Cedar Island
North Carolina
Raleigh
New Bern
Morehead City
Cape Lookout Nat. Seashore
Jacksonville ❶
Hubert
North Carolina Aquarium at Pine Knoll Shores
Cape Lookout Lighthouse
Folkstone
Surf City
Burgaw
Wilmington ❷
Bolton
Supply
Florence
Carolina Beach
North Carolina Aquarium at Ft. Fisher
Conway
Southport
Bald Head Island Lighthouse
Brookgreen Gardens
❸ Myrtle Beach
Andrews
Huntington Beach S.P.
South Carolina
Columbia
Georgetown
Moncks Corner
Tom Yawkey Wildlife Center
Boone Hall Plantation
McClellanville
Charleston ❹
Cape Romain N.W.R.
Mt. Pleasant
Yemassee
Garnett
Osborn
Folly Beach
Springfield
Atlanta
Edisto Beach
Pinckney Island N.W.R.
Beaufort
Hilton Head Island
Richmond Hill
Wassaw N.W.R.
Hinesville
Sapelo Island
Georgia
Jesup
Eulonia
Blackbeard Island Nat. Seashore
Darien
Waycross
Fort Frederica Nat. Mon.
Tifton
Nahunta
❻ Brunswick
Kingsland
Okefenokee N.W.R.
St. Marys
Cumberland Island Nat. Seashore
Folkston
Fernandina Beach
Callahan
Atlantic Beach
JACKSONVILLE ❼
Jacksonville Beach
Orange Park
Tallahassee
❽ St. Augustine
Starke
Gainesville
Palatka
Marineland of Florida
Ormond-by-the-Sea
Bunnell
Daytona Beach ❾
Barberville
De Land
Ocala
Sanford
Deltona
Titusville
Apopka
Cape Canaveral ㉑
Clermont
Disney World
Merritt Island
Orlando
Melbourne
㉒ Cypress Gardens
Tallahassee
❿ **Tampa**
Lakeland
Yeehaw Junction
Sebastian Inlet
Palm Harbor
❹ Lake Wales
Vero Beach
Clearwater
St. Petersburg
Brandon
Florida
㉒ Fort Pierce
⑪
Port St. Lucie
Okeechobee
Stuart Rocks
Bradenton
Sarasota
Arcadia
Port Mayaca
Royal Palm Beach
Jupiter
Palm Beach
Venice
Port Charlotte
La Belle
⑲ ❶
Punta Gorda
Coral Springs
⑱ Boca Raton
Fort Myers
San Carlos Park
⑰ **Fort Lauderdale**
⑫
Golden Gate
Carol City
Hollywood
Sanibel
Miami Beach
Naples ⑬
The Everglades
⑯ **MIAMI**
Everglades City ⑭
Ochopee
Homestead
Biscayne N.P.
Everglades National Park
John Pennekamp Coral Reef S.P.
Key Largo
⑮ Flamingo
Islamorada
Florida Bay
Great White Heron N.W.R.
Marathon
Fort Jefferson Nat. Memorial
Key West
Big Pine Key
Florida Keys
Dry Tortugas National Park

USA

Mississippi: in the footsteps of Mark Twain

The evocative name of the river is said to originate from the language of the Algonquin tribe, who called it "misi sipi". Translated literally, "misi" means "big" and "sipi" means "water", but for the Algonquins it came to mean "Father of Rivers" or "Great River", and it is easy to see how – the Mississippi is the second-longest river in North America, flowing through ten states for some 3,778 km (2,348 miles). Counting its major tributary, the Missouri, the total river system reaches a length of 6,021 km (3,741 miles).

The word "Mississippi" conjures up splendid images of a broad, majestic river, plied by grand old paddle steamers and accompanied by the gentle, melodic strains of "Ol' Man River"; the song, from Jerome Kern's hit musical Showboat, entrancingly captures the spirit of the river and has now almost become a folk song in the South. However, while these images might be very beguiling in the mind's eye, they ignore the reality of life on the water for the boat crews, for whom river travel was anything but a holiday. Their story can be read in the works of the most famous chronicler of the Mississippi, Mark Twain, whose memoir Life on the Mississippi, published in 1883, records much of the detail of his time as a steamboat pilot.

The banks of the Mississippi, especially the lands along the river's middle course, had been settled long before white settlers arrived in in America. Some of the most important archeological sites in the USA, such as the Cahokia Mounds and the Effigy Mounds, attest to an ancient Native American culture that

Alligators: at home in the Mississippi.

flourished many centuries before the arrival of the Europeans, and many a local farmer ploughing his fields has come across arrowheads and other relics from these times. The Mississippi river also played an important role in the opening up of the west; initially forming an impassable barrier, it later marked the last outpost of civilization before the difficult journey across the prairie began. Originally founded by pioneers keen to explore the vast, uncharted land to the west, the metropolis of St Louis prospered as hardy settlers stopped here to provision their wagon trains.

The romance of river travel on the Mississippi begins only after St Louis, far from the perilous rapids that hinder navigation on the northern part of the river;

The carriage drive to the old house on Oak Alley Plantation leads through an avenue of mighty oaks.

The West Bank Expressway crosses the Mississippi via the Greater New Orleans Bridge. The first bridge was built in 1958 and an identical, parallel bridge was constructed in 1988.

nonetheless, riverboats on the southern stretch still require pilots (or suitable technical equipment) where the river enters shallows.

By the time you get to Memphis, lying south of the confluence of the Wolf River with the Mississippi, the river has truly entered the world of the Old South.

Even today, for many here time still falls into only two periods, pre- and post-war; the war they mean is the American Civil War (1861–1865), the most significant in the nation's history. Most of the war was fought in the South, which suffered greatly as a result, but fortunately some magnificent mansions set in spectacular grounds – with more than a whiff of the epic tale Gone With The Wind about them – still survive from the an-

tebellum golden age of the South.

Life was turned well and truly upside down in New Orleans on the Mississippi Delta when Hurricane Katrina struck in August 2005, almost submerging the town and forcing most of the population to flee. Since then, a comprehensive clean-up program has been undertaken, and the repair work begun by the returning inhabitants is slowly restoring the city to its former glory. The extravagant procession on Mardi Gras and the jazz clubs on Bourbon Street, whose roots date back to 18th-century French settlers and the Afro-American community respectively, have regained some of their traditional liveliness.

The silty river drifts along lazily on the last part of its journey to

the sea, slowly depositing material and extending the land out into the water. Until the ravages of Hurricane Katrina, it was possible to round off a journey along the Mississippi with a beach holiday on the Gulf of

Mexico, but the extent of the devastation, which especially affected the coastal resorts (in Biloxi, some 90 percent of the housing stock was destroyed), means that it may be some years yet until normality returns.

The French Quarter in New Orleans is taken over by jazz music at night.

1

Marked out with a green sign in the form of a paddle steamer steering-wheel, the Great River Road runs parallel with the Mississippi to the sea. Mostly following the US-61, the route is often some distance away from the river, because of the danger of flooding; when it does happen to get near, the view is often blocked by a levee.

1 Minneapolis The departure point for the Mississippi route is the largest city in the state of Minnesota, which lost its capital city status to its twin city, Saint Paul, in 1858.

Minneapolis is situated near St Anthony's Falls, the Mississippi's only waterfall, most of which was lost during the canalization of the river. Culture vultures should take in the modern art in the Walker Arts Center and the delights of its extraordinary sculpture garden. The city has the second-highest per capita theater attendance in the USA, so a visit to the Guthrie Theater is recommended.

If you want to escape the exertions of culture for a while, take a shopping trip to Bloomington and visit the Mall of America, one of the country's largest shopping centers.

You can relax beside the many lakes in the surrounding area, including Lake Cedar, Lake Calhoun, and Lake Nokomis, or beside Minnehaha Creek, a waterway that links some of the lakes. The route now leads through the towns of Red Wing, Winona, and La Crescent and on to the next waypoint, La Crosse.

2 La Crosse La Crosse is located at the confluence of the La Crosse and Black Rivers with the Mississippi. Founded in the 18th century as a trading post for trappers to sell furs, this modern city in the state of Wisconsin is an important economic center

with a population of just under 100,000. There are many heights overlooking the river in the area; one well-known rocky outcrop, Grandad's Bluff, even gets a mention in Mark Twain's Life

244

on the Mississippi. La Crosse is also widely renowned as a brewing town; beer is made here in accordance with German purity laws and a big "Oktoberfest" is celebrated every year.
Side roads on the far shore of the Mississippi will take you to the Effigy Mounds National Monument.

❸ Effigy Mounds National Monument The prehistoric mounds date back to 500 bc and are relics of eastern Native American forest culture. Of the 206 mounds, 31 are shaped to resemble animals, such as bears or eagles; the others are oblong or cone-shaped, and many of these conical mounds once contained tombs. The Effigy Mounds are one of the largest and most important prehistoric sites in the country. The route continues on the other side of the river.

❹ Prairie Du Chien This, the second-oldest city in Wisconsin, grew out of a 17th-century trading post at the confluence of the Wisconsin and Mississippi rivers. The days of making a fortune in furs live on In The Villa Louise, which was built by an agent of Jacob Astor's furtrading company. The Fur Trade Museum next door recounts the history and significance of the fur trade, and Fort Crawford Medical Museum has an exhibition of traditional Native American medicine; there is also a completely reconstructed drugstore from about 1900.
A detour to Madison via Highway 18 is possible from here (see right sidebar). To get back to the Mississippi and the next waypoint, take Highway 18 as far as Dodgeville, turn off onto Highway 151, and then take Highway 61.

❺ Dubuque This Iowa town, founded by Frenchman Julien Dubuque, is now a traffic hub where several highways and railway lines converge. One of the oldest European settlements in modern-day Iowa, Dubuque lies at the junction of three states: Iowa, Wisconsin, and Illinois, a region locally known as the Tri-State Area. The National Mississippi River Museum & Aquarium is not to be missed; one section of the museum deals with the local people who relied on the river for their livelihood and nourishment, and the other explores the history of steamers. The aquarium is dedicated to the wildlife living in the Mississippi, such as catfish, sturgeon, stingrays, and alligators. If you want a panoramic view of the river, take a ride up the hill on the Fourth Street Elevator, supposedly the steepest cable railway in the world. To reach Quincy,

❶ Minneapolis and its sister city, Saint Paul, together form the first big riverside conurbation on this route.

❷ Building bridges across the mighty river, like this one at Dubuque, presented engineers with quite a challenge.

you can either take the shorter route via the US-61 or drive along the river.

6 Quincy The westernmost city in Illinois, also known a the "Gem City", was founded in 1818 and renamed in 1825 for John Quincy Adams, the sixth president of the USA, who was born here. On Quinsippi Isle, an island located in the middle of the Mississippi, there is an open-air museum whose authentically recreated log cabins demonstrate the living conditions with which settlers had to cope in the early 18th century. It also sheltered hundreds of Mormons during their exile from Missouri. A stroll along Maine Street will take you past beautiful houses from Quincy's heyday in the second half of the 19th century, when the town was one of the largest in Illinois. After having visited the town of Quincy on the east bank, the route returns to the western side of the river.

7 Hannibal This city in Missouri would have remained an inconsequential little town on the banks of the river if Mark Twain had not spent his youth here and later set his stories about Tom Sawyer and Huckleberry Finn in a fictionalized version of the town. Following in the footsteps of the writer and his heroes is like stepping back into the 19th century. Next door to the house where Mark Twain lived from 1844 to 1853 is a small museum illustrating the author's life and works. The house where Twain's father sat as a justice of the peace is also open to the public. Another stop on the walk through Hannibal is the house where the girl who inspired Tom Sawyer's sweetheart, Becky Thatcher, once lived. Grant's Drugstore presents a snapshot of life in Hannibal at the time.
To learn more about the life, work, and times of Mark Twain, visit the Interpretive Center and

the Museum Gallery. Before the route reaches the city of St Louis, there is one more archeological site on the eastern bank to visit.

8 Cahokia Mounds State Historic Site These prehistoric mounds mark the site of what was once the largest pre-Columbian American city north of the Aztec settlements in Mexico. Founded around ad 650, the city was at the height of its importance and development at the turn of the millennium but was abandoned between 1250 and 1400; archeologists are still uncertain as to whether the inhabitants deserted the city because of disease or political unrest. The Native Americans who built the city flattened the land and raised up mounds of earth on which to erect dwellings or to bury their dead. There are approximately one hundred mounds and the chief's residence was built on the highest,

which is also the largest man-made earthen mound in North America. The modern town of Cahokia is located near the archeological site. After crossing the Mississippi once more, you reach the Gateway to the West.

9 St Louis St Louis was founded in 1703 as a missionary base, expanding as a French settlement until the Louisiana Purchase of 1803. The town grew prosperous on the basis of its geographical location as the Gateway to the West – ever more settlers were setting off from here to conquer the still Wild West – and also on the popularity of steamboat travel on the Mississippi. The high point of its rise was probably reached in the year 1904, which saw the town hosting both a world's fair and the Summer Olympic games.
The town's significance as the Gateway to the West is also celebrated in its most striking

building – Eero Saarinen's Gateway Arch, a slender 192-m (630-ft) steel arch. Eads Bridge over the Mississippi was the longest arch bridge in the world at its completion in 1874. It is still used today by cars and trains crossing the river. St Louis also has some large churches, such as the Old Cathedral of St Louis, constructed in 1834 and the oldest cathedral west of the Mississippi. The modern diocesan Cathedral Basilica of Saint Louis, which, like the old building, is

dedicated to St Louis, the French king, is also a bishop's see. Constructed in 1910 in a mixed Romanesque and Byzantine style, it has the world's largest collection of mosaics.

Beyond St Louis, the river begins to wind through the countryside in a series of sharp bends, but the road follows a straight path.

⑩ New Madrid The town has a fantastic location where the river makes a turn of more than 180 degrees, the so-called New

Madrid Bend; the city fathers have constructed the Mississippi River Observation Deck at a convenient point to enjoy the view over 12 km (7.5 miles) of local landscape. The municipal New Madrid Historical Museum features displays of Native American artefacts and many exhibits that record life in the town from the days of the early settlers and the Civil War. The documentation relating to the devastating earthquakes of 1811/12 is particularly interesting. The route to the next destination once again takes you across the Mississippi.

⑪ Memphis Founded in 1819, this town in Tennessee is known to millions of music fans across the world. A host of performers either grew up in this region or began their careers here, including Elvis Presley, Johnny Cash, B.B. King, Aretha Franklin, and "the father of the blues", as W.C. Handy came to be known. He was the composer of the fa-

mous "Beale Street Blues", and fans can still stroll down this street which is so important in the history of the blues. However, the main attraction in terms of visitor numbers remains Graceland, Elvis Presley's home and estate. An altogether different kind of memorial is to be found at the National Civil Rights Museum in the former Lorraine Motel; it was here that the 39-year-old civil rights activist, Martin Luther King Jr, was assassinated in 1968.

The next interesting city on the route is 120 km (75 miles) to the south and a little way from the river, visit the White River National Wildlife Refuge, famed for its varied wildlife.

1 The impressive Gateway Arch, by Eero Saarinen, on the banks of the Mississippi at St Louis.

2 Elvis Presley's Graceland has turned into a site of pilgrimage for fans from all over the world.

After the invention of paddle steamers, the Mississippi became increasingly important as a transportation route – until trains and cars took over. There are still a few steamers left offering river cruises, and these are very popular with American tourists and visitors from all

over the world. The multiple decks and luxurious interior décor of paddle steamers such as the Mississippi Queen, the American Queen, and the Delta Queen transport passengers back into the world of the Old South as they travel along the mighty river.

Beale street is one of the top Memphis attractions. In the home of the blues and the birthplace of rock and roll. In the early 1900s, Beale Street was filled with clubs, restaurants and shops, many of them owned by African-Americans. Everyone knows about the terrific

nightlife on Beale Street, one of the nation's premier entertainment districts with great music, dancing, food and drinks. But Beale Street is also a family-friendly and group tour-friendly destination offering history, arts, music, and culture.

12 Clarksdale As befits the official birthplace of the blues, the genre has its own dedicated museum in the town: The Delta Blues Museum is located in a restored railway depot.

A collection of photographs, musical instruments, and writings can be viewed to the strains of Muddy Waters or John Lee Hooker, and visitors will learn many fascinating facts about the creation and history of the blues, the inspiration for so many later styles of music.

The Spanish conquistador Hernando de Soto is said to have been the first European to lay eyes on the Mississippi, at a spot not far from Clarksdale; 250 km (155 miles) further on, Vicksburg comes into view.

13 Vicksburg American Civil War enthusiasts will not want to miss the opportunity of visiting this small town.

The Northern states finally gained control of the Mississippi region in the Battle of Vicksburg on 4 July 1863. Nonetheless,

Vicksburg is still highly regarded today among the Southern states, as it surrendered to General Ulysses S. Grant's troops only after a 47-day siege.

The Vicksburg National Military Park, established in 1899 on the site of the battle, is a memorial to the events of 1863. Other military attractions include an ironclad Union gunboat, the USS Cairo.

Vicksburg has one more claim to fame, unrelated to the Civil War: it was here, in 1894, that a local entrepreneur, Joe Biedenharn, first bottled the popular soft drink, Coca-Cola, which became a world-famous label.

Keep to this side of the river and follow Highway 61 to Natchez, located in the heart of the Old South.

14 Natchez One of the Mississippi's oldest cities, Natchez is famous for its spectacular antebellum houses. In the South's heyday, Natchez was one of the richest towns in the USA. Its modern importance is now somewhat diminished, but Mississippi steamboats still make landfall here and it boasts a row of pleasant restaurants with terraces and river views.

You can make a detour to visit the Rosemount Plantation in

Woodsville (see sidebar, right) before arriving in Baton Rouge.

15 Baton Rouge The second-largest city in Louisiana briefly became the largest when so many of New Orleans' citizens fled from the havoc wreaked by Hurricane Katrina.

1 The view from the port of Baton Rouge, where large tankers dock to reach the oil refineries.

2 The Mississippi Trace Bridge from Natchez to Arkansas is a work of art in steel.

Oak Alley Plantation: A glimpse into the bedroom of one of the most sumptuous and best preserved mansions shows how luxurious and comfortable the life of the plantation owners was in the heyday of the southern states during the cotton boom era.

Plantation houses exude just the romanticism that most people associate with the Southern states. The old oaks of Oak Alley Plantation appear to form a guard of honor to welcome arriving guests. They served as a unique backdrop for successful movies such as "Gone

with the Wind" adapted from a novel by Margaret Mitchell. The mansions are rather referred to as Antebellum Houses, which means pre-war houses. The glory of Oak Alley Plantation (1841) in Louisiana is partly due to its impressive setting at the end of an old oak alley,

Louisiana's capital city has two capitol buildings: the old state capitol, now a museum, built in 1849 in a rather flighty neo-Gothic style, and a 34-storey sky-scraper, constructed in 1932 by the controversial Governor Huey Pierce Long, who was assassinated there in 1935.

The main employers in Baton Rouge are the huge oil refineries that unfortunately dominate large sections of the cityscape, especially along the banks of the Mississippi.

Following Interstate 10 west takes the route deep into Cajun country.

⑯ **Lafayette** Founded in 1821 by the Acadian (Franco-Canadian) Jean Mouton, who called the town Vermilionville, the modern name was chosen in recognition of the French aristocrat the Marquis de Lafayette, a military officer and hero of the American War of Independence. Lafayette and its surrounding area is a cultural stronghold of the Cajuns, descendants of Franco-Canadians driven out by the British in the 19th century, who

settled in Louisiana. Their famous cuisine as well as their music, which is celebrated at festivals such as the annaul Festival de Musique Acadienne, attract many tourists. Before continuing on the route to New Orleans, it is worth making a detour to visit the Rosemont Plantation, Houmas House Plantation, and Oak Alley Plantation estates (see detours on previous page).

⑰ **New Orleans** Until 29 August 2005 and the Hurricane Katrina disaster, New Orleans was the most highly populated city in Louisiana. No population figures are currently available, as no one knows exactly how many of the former residents will return to the city once it has been rebuilt. Life goes on, however: Mardi Gras is once celebrated every year to show that the city's spirit remains unbowed. Jean-Baptiste de Bienville, a Frenchman, founded the city in 1718 as Nouvelle Orléans, named for Philippe II, the Regent of France. Since then, the city has changed hands several

times: the Spanish took over from the French under the 1763 Treaty of Paris, then in 1801 the French returned, and it finally passed to the USA in 1803 as part of the Louisiana Purchase. In 1884, a world's fair, the World Cotton Centennial, was held in New Orleans.

In the early 20th century, further stretches of land lying between the Mississippi and Lake Pontchartrain were drained and surrounded with levees. Subsequent subsidence resulted in parts of the city lying below sea level, leaving them vulnerable

to flooding when the levee breaks, as happened after Katrina. Reconstruction and restoration are in full swing to revive the former glory.

1 The Mississippi flows out in every direction in the Delta, its deposited silt gradually extending the land.

2 Large ships still find their way into the port of New Orleans, which was the USA's second-most important port before Hurricane Katrina struck.

Minneapolis Lying on the west bank of the Mississippi across from Saint Paul, the city is a lively commercial and industrial center with a skyline dominated by skyscrapers.

St Louis The town can look back on a long history as the gateway to the once wild west, as symbolized by the Gateway Arch, designed by the Finnish architect Eero Saarinen and built between 1961 and 1966 on the shores of the Mississippi.

White River The National Wildlife Refuge was established in 1935, mainly for the protection of migratory birds. Endangered species of birds and a large variety of mammals, reptiles, and fish inhabit this region of lakes, rivers, and bayous.

Mardi Gras "Fat Tuesday" is celebrated in wild style in New Orleans, with spectacular parades, dazzling costumes, and plenty of music. How could it be otherwise, in the birthplace of jazz? The celebrations last for two weeks.

Natchez The city's name has Native American origins. However, European settlers also have a long history here, closely interwoven with that of the Old South. "Antebellum" tours take you to the splendid old mansions that survived the Civil War in the 19th century.

New Orleans This city on the banks of the Mississippi was founded by the French in 1718, and French influence is still in evidence today, both in the houses of the French Quarter and in crossover Creole-Cajun culture. The motto here is: Laissez les bons temps rouler, let the good times roll!

Saint Paul The Minnesota State Capitol is in this half of the Twin Cities of Minneapolis/St Paul.

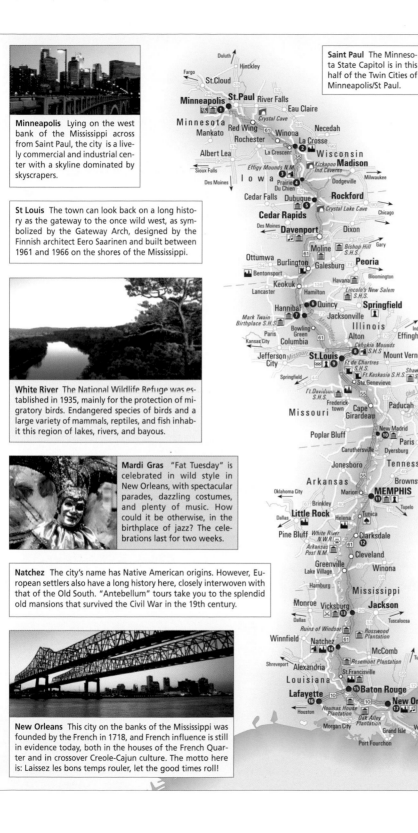

La Crosse The Mississippi viewed from above at La Crosse. Even at the headwaters, the Mississippi is a formidable river, large enough for steamboats.

Dubuque A Mississippi town with a museum that will tell you everything you could want to know about the river, from its role as a natural habitat to its navigation and regulation. The nearby lock has an excellent view across the river.

Memphis This city has Elvis Presley to thank for its fame, with the nearby Graceland estate drawing millions of visitors every year. Many soul and blues stars began their careers in the clubs that line the city's streets.

Vicksburg The decisive battle of the Civil War, during which the Southern states were finally defeated, took place here in 1863. Guided tours of the museum and the historic battlefield site are available in the National Military Park.

Oak Alley Plantation One glance at a bedroom in one of the most spectacular and well-preserved mansions will show how luxuriously and comfortably the masters of large plantations once lived.

The Bahamas

A Caribbean paradise

Tropical sun, white sandy beaches, rustling palms, and the blue ocean make the Bahamas one of the most popular vacation destinations in the world. In Nassau and Freeport, you can enjoy both fun activities and relaxing luxury, while the Family Islands offer seclusion and peace.

"It's better in the Bahamas" was the advertising slogan that was used by the islands' tourist board for many years. The islands are still the perfect place to leave everyday life behind on white sandy beaches beneath rustling palms, and to wash your troubles away in the warmth of the ocean. Pastel houses in brilliant sunshine, bright coral, and turquoise water... it really is a tropical paradise.

The Bahamas are made up of around 700 islands and have been independent since 1973. They are also part of the British Commonwealth and the British influence is still in evidence everywhere. The best known islands are New Providence Island with the capital city of Nassau, Paradise Island, and Grand Bahama with Freeport, the economic center of the islands and the home of numerous casinos. The Family or Out Islands, as the Bahamas excluding New Providence, Grand Bahama, and Paradise Island are known, are also a magnet for tourists in search of seclusion and a place to chill out. The people are warm and friendly, the water is crystal clear, and the coral reefs are some of the most beautiful in the world. The original inhabitants, known as the Lucayans, lived undisturbed on the islands until the 15th century. On Octo-

Young girl from Cat Island in the south-east of the Bahamas.

A fantastic sunset on Andros, the largest island of the archipelago and still largely untouched.

A yacht anchors near the Abacos Islands. Out at sea it is still possible to enjoy peaceful isolation, unlike on those islands overrun by large numbers of tourists.

ber 12, 1492, Columbus anchored off the shore of the island now known as San Salvador, and is said to have uttered the words baja mar (shallow sea), which eventually became the name Bahamas. Over the next century, the Lucayans who lived there were either killed or enslaved by the Europeans. The first permanent settlers were Puritans from Bermuda who had been religiously persecuted and so took up residence on one of the larger islands, naming it Eleuthera after the Greek word for freedom.

During the 18th century, Nassau developed into an important refuge for pirates. The infamous Blackbeard and over a thousand of his compatriots hid in the many coves and caves and at-tacked European trading ships as they sailed the Caribbean Sea. Some of the galleons that were sunk here still lie on the ocean floor today and treasure hunters search for valuable hoards of gold in the wrecks. The British crown finally brought the reign of the pirates to an end when it gained control of the Bahamas in 1717. The statue that stands outside the Hilton Hotel in Nassau is a monument to the most successful bounty hunter, Captain Woodes Rogers.

Until slavery was abolished in 1834, the islands formed an important hub for the slave trade. In the Bahamas themselves, however, plantation owners had little success farming the dry ground and so set most of their slaves free. During the American Civil War, the English set up a base in the Bahamas to provide the Southern States with war supplies, and during the 1920s , with the event of the Prohibition era rum-runners smuggled illicit alcohol from the Bahamas into the USA.

Intelligent dolphins are sometimes seen in the waters around the Bahamas.

1

Nassau in New Providence is both the starting point and destination of the Bahamas round trip. Many islands lie on the route in between, such as Grand Bahama, Bimini, Harbour Island, and Andros.

❶ Nassau (New Providence)
The round trip begins in Nassau, the administrative capital of the Bahamas on New Providence Island. Over half of the population in the Bahamas lives on this island, although it is significantly smaller than Andros and Grand Bahama.

Nassau was founded in 1656 by English settlers, who named it Charlestown; it was renamed in 1689 for the English king William III from the Dutch house of Orange-Nassau. The legendary Cable Beach was first named in 1907 after the transatlantic cable that was laid under the sea at the turn of the century between Jupiter, Florida, and Nassau.

The city center of Nassau has a fascinating Caribbean charm and contains reminders of the eventful colonial era in its hous-

es, Victorian villas, and fortifications. Trade is brisk at the numerous markets and in the boutiques and shops selling crafts and expensive jewelry. Luxurious hotels, huge casinos, and the marinas make Nassau an upmarket, fashionable destination for tourists.

A relic of British colonial times is Parliament Square, situated in the middle of the town with imposing governmental buildings. The Houses of Parliament, the

1 A typical scene: Fishing boats are moored next to cruise ships in the port of Nassau.

2 The Columbus statue outside the seat of government in Nassau is a reminder that the explorer first set foot in the New World on one of the Bahamian Islands in 1492.

Travel Information

Route profile
Length: approx. 1,600 km (1,000 miles)
Duration: 14 days
Start and end: Nassau
Itinerary (main locations):
Nassau (New Providence), Paradise Island (New Providence), Abaco, Freeport (Grand Bahama), West End (Grand Bahama), Bimini, Eleuthera, Harbour Island, Cat Island, Long Island, Great Exuma, Andros Town (Andros), Nichol's Town (Andros)

Travel tips
Major travel agents offer attractive package tours in the Bahamas. Once you are there, it's possible to arrange interesting excursions at short notice, such as to Harbour Island.

Tourist information
Bahamas Ministry of Tourism, P.O. Box N-3701, Nassau, Bahamas
Tel. 242-302-2000
Fax. 242-302-2098
www.bahamas.com

2

Dinghies jostle for position along the coast of New Providence, where radiant sunshine and stiff breezes offer ideal conditions for off-shore sailors. Many yachts sailed past Nassau during the World Championship Regatta 2001.

1

old Colonial Secretary's Office, the Supreme Court, and buildings in soft, pastel shades surround the imposing marble statue of Queen Victoria. The Public Library in Shirley Street was once a prison. Opposite stand the ruins of the Royal Victoria Hotel, the first hotel in Nassau, surrounded by gloriously blooming gardens.

The 66 steps of the Queen's Staircase connect Fort Fincastle to the Princess Margaret Hospital. They are thought to have been carved out of the hard limestone by slaves between 1793 and 1794 and were named for Queen Victoria. The view of the city is stunning from Fort Fincastle on Bennet Hill; it was designed in the shape of a ship's bow and built in 1793. Fort Montagu was completed in July 1742 and is famous for its terrace-shaped cistern, which collects the rain that falls in the fort and drains off the excess. Fort Charlotte, the largest fort in Nassau, was built between 1787 and 1789 and was named after the wife of King George III. However, no shot has ever been fired from the fort, which is protected by a moat, high walls, and a drawbridge.

The pink Government House is located in Parliament Street and was constructed in 1801. The Royal Bahamian Police Force Band plays in front of the statue of Columbus every Saturday to mark the changing of the guard. The late 18th-century Pompey Museum building was a trans-shipment center for slaves and goods before being converted into a museum. The exhibitions show what life used to be like for African slaves in the Bahamas.

The straw market on Bay Street, which has been held since the 1940s and has become a tradition in New Providence, is rather more cheerful.

It arose when the sponge industry collapsed, and many women started to weave baskets, bags, hats, dolls, and other souvenirs from palm fronds and sisal leaves and would sell them at the markets in Nassau, on Cable Beach, and on Paradise Island. Today the straw market is one of the most popular attractions in the Bahamas.

Worthwhile excursions lead to quiet locations such as Coral Harbour and Adelaide and to Lynford Cay with its idyllic residential areas. All of the beaches have enticing white sand.

② **Paradise Island (New Providence)** Walk across the bridge from Nassau and you'll find yourself on the luxury resort of Paradise Island, with its casinos, bars, and vibrant nightlife. Until tourism develop- ers rediscovered it, the former Hog Island was for the most part unknown. However, once the first hotels and casinos had been set up, the island grew into a tourist playground and its character gradually began to change. Since millionaires such as Howard Hughes and the Shah of Persia moved here in the 1950s, it has become a very exclusive place in which to live (see panel, left).

③ **Abaco** The first European settlers on the Abaco Islands were supporters of the English King George III. They arrived in 1783, having fled to the Caribbean during the American War of Independence when they realized they were on the losing side. They were farmers originally but soon realized that they would only be able to survive on the Abaco Islands as fishermen. A number of tiny islands

and the third-largest barrier reef in the world are located off the coast of the main island. Today the inhabitants of Abaco still live off the sea, their tiny villages clustered along the craggy shores, but tourism has now become an important source of income in addition to fishing. The wonderful water attracts the tourists, who enjoy swimming and exploring underwater, fishing, and sailing in the surrounding ocean. There are more boat mooring points than hotel rooms on the island.

Abaco Island is particularly popular among sailors and yacht owners because of its proximity to other islands. The same is true for divers, who can explore the phenomenal "blue holes" off the coast. These are underwater cave systems entered via what, when viewed from above, appear to be "holes" in the ocean surrounded by rocks or reefs. Wreck divers can search for sunken treasure in more than five hundred galleons on the ocean floor. Equally exciting are the underwater caves and coral reefs at the Pelican Cays Land & Sea Park near Great Abaco. Abaco National Park was founded in 1994 in order to protect the endangered Bahama parrot, a subspecies of the Cuban Amazon parrot that is native to this region. The major attractions on this island are the villages founded by the loyalists, which are similar to those of New England.

Marsh Harbour is the island's commercial center. Half of the 15,000 inhabitants live in the small town, which has only one traffic light. There are a number of banks, insurance companies, supermarkets, and offices in the quite drab town center. The Marina District is rather more romantic, with restaurants and boutiques largely suitable for the more wealthy tourists. Many boats and yachts bob on the water. North of Marsh Harbour is Treasure Cay, a tourist paradise with luxury hotels, villas, 18-hole golf courses, and a huge marina. Before Captain Leonard Thompson recognized the potential of the peninsula and built the first hotels here with US backing, Treasure Cay was known as Sand Bank Cay. South of Treasure Cay lies the Leisure Lee, a quiet community of residential property and protected canals. The inhabitants of Ca-

1 The lighthouse at Hope Town on Abaco.

2 Treasure Cay, an exclusive tourist resort on the Abaco Islands.

Sunken wrecks are common in the waters off the coast of the Bahama Islands, and attract huge schools of fish. These are welcome prey for predators such as sharks and barracudas. White sharks are only dangerous to humans if they panic or are injured and bleeding. Sharks

do not actually like the taste of human flesh. Many only attack when provoked or when they confuse a diver, surfer, or swimmer with their prey, particularly in those areas of the sea where they hunt for seals. But even in those places, attacks are rare.

suarina Point and Bahama Palm Shores to the south are less affluent. Hundreds of coconut palms border the long sandy beach. Nearby is the Cherokee Sound, a sleepy fishing village that provided protection for the fleeing supporters of George III after the American War of Independence was over, which is in stark contrast to the Abaco Club and its luxurious golf course. Crossing Rock in the south of the island is a popular fishing spot.

The capital city Hope Town, one of the most famous tourist destinations in Abaco, is located in the Outer Cays.

Hope Town's protected port is set in a picturesque cove. Its red and white striped lighthouse is the island's landmark and offers great views over the port. Ironically, the inhabitants of Hope Town protested loudly against the construction of the lighthouse when the English were drawing up their plans in 1860. Today they are proud of the dis-

tinctive landmark. Since Elbow Cay, the smaller island, was opened up for tourism, the area around the port has been booming. New hotels and apartment blocks appear nearly every day. The nearby Lubber's Quarters, with its tangled thick mangroves, and the large boatbuilding yard in Man-O-War Cay offer a nicely contrasting atmosphere.

Great Guana Cay ("the sleeping giant") is an island 11 km (7 miles) long, which really came to life when tourists discovered the lively Nippers Beach Bar and made it their meeting point. Increasing numbers of visitors took the ferry to the island for the weekly pig roast. Small hotels and villas started appearing. The spectacular Nippers Beach used to be an insiders' secret. Green Turtle Cay, a tiny island also populated by loyalist settlers, has met the same fate. The island's name comes from the turtle trading that once took place on its shores. Nowadays, lobster-

catching is the island's most important source of income.

❹ Freeport (Grand Bahama)
From Abaco, the journey continues toward Freeport, the legendary entertainment center on Grand Bahama. The Spanish explorer Ponce de León anchored on the shores of the island back in 1513. However, it was not well known until the 1950s when Wallace Groves, a financier from Virginia, invested in tree-felling on the island and founded the town of

Freeport/Lucaya. As a free trade area and popular cruise port, the town has developed into a world-famous entertainment destination with huge casinos, restaurants, boutiques, and bars. Freeport is particularly popular among American cruise ship passengers because of its

1 An exclusive sports car outside a jeweler's boutique in Freeport.

2 The red and white striped lighthouse on Grand Bahama.

Hot sauces and herbs, such as this selection from the Captain's Charthouse Restaurant (top), are part of the Caribbean cuisine common in the Bahamas. Fresh vegetables are sold by the local farmers at markets like this one (bottom).

1

duty-free shopping. The cash tills ring constantly in the town's large casinos, meanwhile guests are entertained by internationally renowned performers.

Tropical plants grow in the Hydroflora Gardens on East Beach Drive. You can marvel at the exotic flowers and birds in The Garden of Groves, the town's botanical gardens. The Grand Bahama Museum is located in the center of the gardens and has interesting exhibitions about the eventful history of the Bahamas. Shopping is highly recommended at the International Bazaar, a shopping center with over ninety stores from many countries, and the marketplace at Port Lucaya.

From Freeport, you can continue along the costal highway through Hawksbill, a quiet residential area, to Eight Mile Rock, the largest community on the island. The town is made up of a series of individual districts, which have merged together over the years.

Holmes Rock and Seagrape are famous for their unique cave, which fills with fresh water at low tide and with seawater when the tide rises.

Paradise Cove at Deadman's Reef is one of the best locations for underwater exploration. It is possible to swim out to the brightly colored reef. Nearby, numerous artifacts left behind by 13th-century Lucayans, mainly bones and shards of pottery, have been discovered at one of the most important archeological sites in the Bahamas.

⑤ **West End (Grand Bahama)**
West End is located at the westernmost point of the island, a peaceful fishing village that played an important role during the 1920s Prohibition in America. At that time it was a busy trans-shipment center for European whisky, which was smuggled into the USA through the Bahamas. The so-called rumrunners built large beer halls and bars where the tough guys

2

could relax after their work. Even Al Capone is believed to have once visited one of the gin palaces on Waterfront Road. However, these times have long since passed. West End now thrives on tourism and is home to the oldest hotel on the island, the Star Hotel, which was built in 1946. It belongs to the successors of a certain Austin H. Grant, who came from Eight Mile Rock and built the inn for Americans who journeyed over to the Caribbean on boat trips. The ho-

tel was forced to close in 1988, although the restaurant and bar still remain popular among visitors to the island today. The new Old Bahama Resort has provided some much needed stimulation for the town, which had grown sleepy since the old rumrunning days. Other worthwhile sightseeing opportunities on Grand Bahama are the small town of Freetown, where the first slaves were liberated in 1834, the fishing village Sweeting's Cay, which offers first-class

3

lobster and fresh conches, and the quiet Lightbourne Cay, an ideal place to get away from the hustle and bustle of the cruise metropolis Freeport and enjoy a leisurely picnic.

6 Bimini Since Ernest Hemingway became famous, the romantic islands of North and South Bimini are no longer an insiders' secret. The writer lived at Blue Martin Cottage between 1931 and 1937 and his last novel, Islands in the Stream, is also set here. Visitors arrive at Alice Town, the largest town in North Bimini, which is a collection of stores, restaurants, and bars along King's Highway. South Bimini is barely populated and has just one landing strip for small airplanes and a few hotels.

The Bimini Islands are a paradise for sea-anglers and divers. There are many shipwrecks on the ocean floor off the island's coast, but it is thought that something much more interesting is hidden beneath the deep

waters: the lost city of Atlantis. In September 1968 divers found blocks of stone under the water off Paradise Point, the so-called Bimini Road. Some archeologists are convinced that the stones form an ancient road or some other manmade structure left behind by a lost civilization. Another legend associated with the island is the Fountain of Youth, which Spanish explorer Ponce de León claimed was in Florida, but some parascientists actually believe is located on Bimini.

7 Harbour Island Dunmore Island, the peaceful main city on Harbour Island, can be reached on a small airplane or by boat. The town was named after Lord Dunmore, the island's former governor (1786–1797) and is one of the oldest settlements in the Bahamas. Pastel houses with white picket fences around tiny gardens give the place a contemplative atmosphere. The Hill Steps were carved out of the hill

by prisoners and a tunnel leads to Rock House, a nearby resort hotel. Titus Hole, a cave above the port, was used as a prison by the first settlers.

The main attraction on this island is, however, the hue of the sand on the Atlantic shore. The pink sand stretches for miles along the beaches here, the pinkness comes from the ground coral it contains. There are many coral reefs near the island, which provide excellent conditions for divers and underwater explorers.

8 Eleuthera This beach paradise is only 1.5 km (1 mile) wide but 180 km (112 miles) long, and one of the most popular destinations among the Family Islands. Airplanes land in Governor's Harbour, the administrative center of the small island. Before the journey continues to Cat Island, which lies to the south-east of Eleuthera, it is worth stopping over here.

The Arawak Indians who once inhabited this island were either killed or sold as slaves by Spanish conquerors in the 16th century. Puritan settlers arrived at Eleuthera in 1648. Between 1950 and 1980 a number of US industrialists and Hollywood stars such as Robert de Niro stayed here. However, most hotels were closed down when the island was made independent and tourism has only started to pick up again over the past few years.

Among the island's attractions are the Glass Window Bridge,

1 The Bahamas are a divers' paradise. Encounters with sharks are very rare.

2 Harbour Island settlers were some of the earliest to arrive in the Bahamas.

3 The pink sands of Harbour Island are some of the most beautiful in the Bahamas.

which connects the Atlantic Ocean to the quieter waters of the Exuma Sound and offers a spectacular view of the gloriously blue sea; and Preachers Cave, used as a natural chapel by the first settlers. The huge cave in Hatchet Bay, however, seems more like a cathedral.

The shipwreck in Yankee channel, which is around three hundred years old, and a sunken train (that was being transported on a barge) at Devil's Backbone are exciting places for divers to explore.

9 Cat Island The next stop is Arthur's Town on Cat Island. The famous actor Sidney Poitier (born in 1924) spent his childhood in this small community before heading for Hollywood, where be became one of the first black superstars, starring in such classic movies as The Defiant Ones and In the Heat of the Night.

Some believe that the island is named after the English pirate Arthur Catt, who used a cave here as a hideout. Another version of the story is that the island was named after the many feral cats that made life difficult for the first settlers from America. These are descendents of the tame housecats that were brought to the island by the Spanish conquerors. For 400 years, Cat Island was actually known as San Salvador as it was thought to be the San Salvador where, in 1492, Christopher Columbus first set foot in the New World. In 1926 Watlings Island was renamed San Salvador and Cat Island was given back its original name. A reminder of the loyalists who settled on the island in 1783 is the plantation in Port Howe, a small community founded by Colonel Andrew Deveaux, the man who reconquered Nassau from the Spanish.

Cat Island is only slightly over 60 km (37 miles) long and just over 1.5 km (1 mile) wide, and is one of the most fertile islands in the Bahamas. The first settlers planted mainly cotton and pineapples here and raised cattle. Tropical flowers thrive in the thick grass and bushes. The tranquility of the island and the bright hues of its flora make it the ideal place to escape from civilization and get back to nature. This is what Father Jerome Hawkes was probably thinking when he built a medieval-style monastery on Mount Alvernia, the highest point on the island (63 m/207 ft). The architect and priest came to the Bahamas to repair Anglican churches on Long Island. There is a breathtaking view of Fine Beach, a 16-km (10-mile) dream beach with pink sand, from his monastery, which is known as The Hermitage.

10 Long Island Just a stone's throw away is Clarence Town on Long Island, one of the most charming of the Bahamian islands with grass-green hills, fertile pineapple and banana plantations, and flat salt lakes. On the gulf side perfect white beaches are lined with palm trees, while on the bleaker Atlantic side, the surf crashes against craggy rocks. Long Island is particularly popular among divers due to the thrill of shark-feeding trips offered by local organizers.

A white cross at the northernmost point of the island forms a memorial to Christopher Columbus, the first European visitor. He named the island Fernandina in recognition of his sponsor in Spain. Supporters of the English king George III based in North America followed his footsteps in the late 18th century, and grew cotton on large plantations. Some of their houses are still standing today. Clarence Town and other communities lie along a former coach road built for the farmers.

1 Conch snail shells on the coast of Cat Island.

Before 1900 there were thought to be over 100,000 flamingoes in the Bahamas. Early settlers hunted them for their meat and their numbers fell to 3,000. Today, over 80,000 Caribbean flamingos once again thrive in the Bahamas, in particular on Great Inagua.

One of the major events held on the island is the Long Island Sailing Regatta, which takes place in early summer each year. Swimmers and sunseekers can relax at Cape Santa Maria, one of the most beautiful beaches in the world.

From Clarence Town you can enjoy an excursion to Gran Inagua.

⓫ Great Exuma The journey continues to Georgetown on Great Exuma, the largest of over 360 mainly tiny islands referred to collectively on maps as Exuma or Exuma Cays.

The Tropic of Cancer runs right through the town, which reflects the character of the entire island. There are no mooring points for cruise ships, no tourist traps, and just small hotels. The only concession to tourism is the famous Club Peace and Plenty Hotel in Georgetown. Endless sunshine, turquoise water, and fantastic beaches make Exuma the perfect Caribbean island paradise.

Worth seeing in Georgetown are the St Andrew's Anglican Church and Elizabeth Harbour, where the National Family Island Regatta starts each year. Another highlight is the Bahamian Music and Heritage Festival, which also takes place annually.

Exuma was settled in 1783 by royalists from North America, who set up a cotton plantation on the island.

Some settlements on the Exumas are named after Lord John Rolle, one of the most prominent royalists. A section of the beach and a number of caves and coral reefs are contained within the Exuma National Land and Sea Park and are protected sites. Thunderball Grotto was used as a filming location for the 1965 James Bond film Thunderball.

⓬ Andros Town (Andros) Covering an area of around 6,000 sq km (2,316 sq miles), Andros Island is one of the largest

but least developed of the Bahama islands in terms of tourism. When you disembark in Andros Town, the commercial center of the island, you will see only a small town with a few hundred inhabitants and two hotels, mainly used by sea-anglers. Andros Island is one of the best fishing locations in the Caribbean, along with the Bimini Islands. It is said to be the bonefish (a premier game fish) capital of the world.

Off the coast of this island is the largest reef in the Bahamas, around 225 km (140 miles) long,

an immense habitat for fish, not to mention a paradise for divers and underwater explorers, as most of the coral is only 4 m (13 ft) below the surface of the water. Behind the reef the water depth plunges to 2,000 m (6,562 ft).

The Spanish landed on Andros Island in 1550 and enslaved the local Indians. The contagious diseases the Spanish brought with them wiped out the remaining inhabitants. The Spanish named the island Espiritu Santo (Holy Ghost), but the name appears to have been

changed later. According to a map made in 1782, it was called San Andreas. It is believed that its modern name was chosen to commemorate Sir Edmund Andros, who led the English forces in Barbados at the end of the 17th century and later made a name for himself as the governor of New York, New England, Maryland, and Guernsey. The name may, however, also come from the inhabitants of St Andro Island (Columbia), who settled on the island in 1787. In the 18th century, many pirates (including the infamous Welsh buccaneer Henry Morgan) took over control of Andros Island, and in the 19th century US settlers arrived on the island, as they did in many places in the Bahamas, and set up plantations worked by slaves.

Andros Island has been able to contain its tourism and preserve the beauty of its landscape. Light pine forests stretch out to the north of the island and over fifty types of orchid grow in the mangrove marshes and rainforests. Wild pigs roam through the scrubland. Two hundred types of bird are native to this island, including the Bahama Yellowthroat, but also two mythical creatures: Lusca is a sea monster said to pull careless divers exploring "blue holes" down into the depths, while the Chickcharnie, a large owl that used to live on Andros but is now extinct, which also gave its name to a mythical bird-like dwarf creature with glowing red eyes, is believed still to be seeking revenge many years after a British famer cut down the trees in which the bird nested.

The island is also blessed with plenty of fresh water, which collects in the many caves and grottos. Even the capital city Nassau lives off water shipped from Andros to New Providence.

As fresh water is lighter than salt water, it is possible to separate it from sea- water without a large amount of technical equipment.

Andros has seen its share of celebrity visitors. In the 1960s the Rat Pack (Peter Lawford, Sammy Davis Jnr, Frank Sinatra, and Dean Martin), hung out at Fresh Creek, and thanks to its excellent diving conditions, French diver and scientist Jacques Cousteau spent some time exploring its waters

⑬ Nicholl's Town, Andros

Along the coast of the turquoise ocean is Nicholl's Town at the northern point of Andros Island, one of the largest settlements on the island with a population of around six hundred. Most visitors staying at the hotels in Nicholl's Town are anglers looking for bonefish and tarpon off the coast. However, Andros is also famous for its crafts. Wood carvings and imaginative products made from straw are some of the most attractive souvenirs you can buy here. Many of the craftspeople are descendants of Seminole Indians from Florida. Androsia, the bright material used for clothing in the Bahamas, also comes from Andros Island, where it is manufactured at the Androsia Batik Factory.

This round cruise through the Bahamian islands ends with the return journey to Nassau.

1 The quiet coves of the Exuma Islands are the perfect place to sail and relax.

2 Exuma has wide sandy beaches and the gentle surf provides excellent conditions for swimmers.

A large reef shark makes its way through the banks of coral, searching for prey. A huge school of fish swims past, but this shark is not a threat to them. There are, however, other kinds of shark that would attack schools of fish like this one with their tail fins.

Bimini Islands The small islands of North and South Bimini are top destinations for divers and underwater explorers. There are several shipwrecks along their coasts and on the ocean floor.

Abaco There are more places to moor than hotel rooms to stay in on this island. Sailors and fishermen will find excellent facilities in Marsh Harbour and Hope Town (illustrated).

Harbour Island Coral reefs have made the island popular. The capital city Dunmore Town has charming houses in pastel shades and attractive beaches.

Grand Bahama Tourism is the most important source of income for the northernmost island in the Bahamas, some 9 km (5 miles) off the coast of Florida. Shown here is the High Rock Lighthouse.

Cat Island The island impresses guests with its pink sand and cornucopia of tropical fruits and flowers. It is not clear whether the island is named after cats (our feline friends) or a pirate called Catt.

Walker's Cay
Green Turtle Cay
Great Sale Cay
Cedar Harbour
Grand Bahama
Treasure Cay
Marsh Harbour
West End
Hope Town
McLean's Town
Cherokee Sound
Pelican Cays Land and Sea Park
Lucayan National Park
Freeport
Abaco
Crossing Rock
Sandy Point
Abaco National Park
Cornwall
Harbour Island
Great Isaac
Dunmore Town
Eleuthera
Bullrock's Harbour
Current
Governor's Harbour
Bimini
Berry Islands
Glass Window Bridge
Alice Town
Paradise Island
Tarpum Bay
Savannah Sound
Cat Cays
Nicholl's Town
New Providence
Rock Sound
Arthur's Town
Brown's Cay
Nassau
Bannerman Town
Cat Island
Cockburn Town
Dixons
Mastic Point
Andros
New Bight
The Hermitage
Port Howe
San Salvador
Fresh Creek
Exuma Cays Land and Sea Park
Landfall Park
Andros Town
Exuma Cays
Devil's Point
Rum Cay
Port Nelson
Behring Point
Black Point
Burnt Ground
Simms
Mangrove Cay
Long Island
Samana Cay
Underwater Caves
Congo Town
Rolleville
Kemps Bay
Green Cay
Great Exuma
George Town
William's Town
Deadman's Cay
Crooked Island
Mars Bay
Clarence Town
Pitts Town
Pinefield
Mortimers
Colonel Hill
Snug Corner
Ragged
Acklins
Island
Salina Point
Range
Little Inagua Island
Great Inagua Island
Inagua N.P.
Matthew Town

Andros The largest of the Bahamian islands has retained its original beauty. Offshore is the longest coral reef of the islands, 225 km (140 miles) in length.

Nicholl's Town The small town at the northern point of Andros attracts many fishermen and anglers. The local crafts with their Indian influence are also popular.

Exuma Cays The tiny islands along the Tropic of Cancer, of which there are around 360, are an isolated Caribbean paradise.

Long Island Dream beaches, banana and pineapple plantations, good diving spots, and salt lakes are key features of this island. Cape Santa Maria is said to have one of the finest beaches in the world. The shark feeding that takes place at some locations along the shore is a spectacular sight.

Nassau (New Providence) The capital city of the Bahamas, founded in 1656, was renamed Nassau in 1689. Shown here is the seat of government.

Paradise Island This luxury resort has the largest open-air ocean aquarium in the world, the largest casino in the Caribbean, and many other theme park attractions.

Hawaii

Dream beaches, tropical flowers and volcanoes: from Big Island to Kauai

Fantastic pure-white beaches, the gentle murmur of palm trees, hula dancers, and bright garlands of flowers, together with tropical rainforests, cascading waterfalls, active and dormant volcanoes, Honolulu city life, and the magic of the indigenous people: these are just some of the many faces of Hawaii. The largest island in the archipelago, and its namesake, trumps almost any other island on the planet with its magnificent and extraordinary lava landscape.

"Aloha komo mai" ("Welcome to Hawaii") will greet you on arrival at the airport. Wherever you go in these dreamlike Pacific islands, you'll discover the "aloha spirit" and enjoy the islanders' infectious friendliness. The sky is a deeper blue here, the beaches wider and cleaner than anywhere else, and the

The Silversword grows only on Maui.

wind rustles gently in the palms and along the magical cliffs on Na Pali Coast. In the language of the Polynesians, who came to Hawaii around ad 500, the island's name means heaven or paradise. Every visitor is greeted with a traditional "lei" (Polynesian garland of flowers), and the warm air seems to echo with the romantic chants that rang out over the islands when kings still reigned and before Western people arrived.

The Hawaiian Islands extend some 2,436 km (1,513 miles) across the northern Pacific, meaning that travel between them is possible only by plane or boat. Island-hopping is certainly the right term for it, since the best-known islands in the archipelago are within hopping distance of each other: Kauai,

Oahu, Molokai, Lanai, Maui, and Hawaii (Big Island). The islands are as varied as their names: Kauai is a surprising mix of tropical rainforests, beautiful gardens, the Waimea Canyon, and the stunning Na Pali Coast, the backdrop to films like King Kong and Jurassic Park. On Oahu, the most developed of the islands, the main attractions are Honolulu, the legendary Waikiki Beach and the high breakers in the surfers' paradise on the North Coast. The history of Molokai is both moving and interesting, with Father Damien at its center: in the late 19th century, he cared for those suffering from leprosy on the Kalaupapa Peninsula. Lanai, one of the smallest Hawaiian Islands, is a paradise for golfers and has the most isolated beaches.

At the Akaka Falls west of Hilo on Big Island, the water pours 130 m (426 ft) down the green rock face.

A jewel of nature on Kauai: the legendary Na Pali Coast was the setting for Steven Spielberg's film Jurassic Park.

Maui, the most popular haunt of American holiday-makers, boasts luxurious hotels, a tropical wilderness on both sides of the legendary Hana Road, and Haleakala, one of the largest volcanoes on earth. Big Island, the main island in the south, also has its fair share of active volcanoes and tropical flowers.

The turbulent past of the islands lives on in Pu'uhonua o Honaunau and a series of other villages. Before the arrival of European settlers, the larger islands were ruled by kings who reigned with absolute power over their subjects. They paraded before their people in dazzling robes, surrounded themselves with pomp and ceremony, and lived in awe of supernatural beings. Hula dance, originally reserved exclusively for men,

was a Hawaiian way of worshipping the gods. Kahunas, the priests of the people, were responsible for enforcing kapus or rigid taboos; death was the penalty for anyone who transgressed them. Professional storytellers still tell of these turbulent times and in the cities statues are a reminder of powerful kings like Kamehameha I.

In 1778, Captain Cook discovered the islands for the Western world. A monument to him at Kealakekua Bay bears the inscription, "In memory of the great circumnavigator, Captian James Cook, RN, who discovered the islands on the 10th January, ad 1778 and fell near this spot on the 14th February, ad 1779". Settlers and missionaries followed and there has been a recent influx of Asian migrants.

The mix of peoples on the islands has resulted in a particularly tolerant society. Hawaii became the fiftieth US state in 1959, and tourism has helped it develop into a popular and flourishing destination.

In spite of everything, the language of the islands has been

preserved in Hawaii, and if there was a prize for the friendliest and most beautiful state in the USA, Hawaii would undoubtedly be up there among the top contenders. Even the relentless spread of commercialism on some islands is no match for that aloha spirit.

Mauna Loa, one of the world's largest active volcanoes, last erupted in 1984.

From Hilo, Hawaii's main port, our island journey initially crosses barren terrain, where lava still spills out of the earth. The winding roads pass through thick forests and along steep coasts, while the snow-capped peak of Mauna Kea shines like a beacon in the distance. Our route heads north-west along the curve of the islands to Kauai.

1 Hilo, Hawaii Planes land on the east coast of Big Island in Hilo, the island's largest settlement (population: 40,000) and the southernmost city in the USA. In the mid-19th century, missionaries arrived in Hilo Bay and built churches. In 1929, a tsunami devastated the area around Hilo Bay. The town owed its expansion to the sugar plantations. When the sugar plantations closed down in the 1990s, Hilo became known as a cultural center.

2 Hawaii Volcanoes National Park, Hawaii This National Park in the south of Big Island is a UNESCO World Heritage Site. It includes part of Mauna Loa, the active crater of Kilauea and

parts of the rugged coastline. For an eye-opener of a drive, take the 16-km (10-mile) Crater Rim Drive on Kilauea and the Chain of Craters Road, past lavascapes and fern thickets to the coast, where lava flows occur every few years. Here you can get a view of the fires of Halemaumau, a crater cone on Kilauea. In the rainforest, lava has solidified into what is known as the Thurston Lava Tube.

3 Kailua-Kona, Hawaii This small and bustling city, full of hotels and restaurants, lies on a sunlit coast, complete with black lava cliffs and white sand beaches. The highways lead you through a lunar landscape.

Travel Information

Route profile
Length: approx. 2,500 km/ 1,554 miles (excluding detours)
Time needed: approx. 14 days

Start and end: Hilo (Hawaii)
Itinerary (main locations): Hawaii, Maui, Lanai, Molokai, Oahu, Kauai

Travel tips
Travel between islands is simpler by air than by boat. Aloha Airlines and Hawaiian Airlines fly most days. On the islands, it is advisable to hire a car for touring.

When to go
The best time to travel to

the islands is in late spring, when you will encounter pleasantly warm temperatures, flowers in bloom and fewer tourists, since it is also before US school holidays begin (mid-June to early September). Prices rise in summer and over Christmas and the New Year.

Accommodation
Many hotels are cheaper than you might imagine; affordable accommodation is available on all the islands.

Tourist information
www.hawaii-tourism.co.uk
www.hawaiitourism.com.au

Head back to Hilo via Waimea in the north. The beautiful Scenic Drive passes through the jungle along the steep coast; rising

1 The peak of Mauna Kea (4,205 m/13,796 ft) is snow-clad, sometimes even in the summer months.

Nature at its most spectacular: what seems to be an endless flow of bubbling molten lava spurts out into the Pacific Ocean from Kilauea on Big Island. This crater next to Mauna Loa is one of the world's most active volcanoes and covers an area of around 10 sq km (4 sq miles).

1

above it all is Mauna Kea, a dormant volcano.

4 Kahului, Maui The commercial center of the island of Maui has all the conveniences (and excesses) of America, including several shopping centers and the island's only movie house. Just a few miles away, in the Iao Valley State Park, the Iao Needle juts sharply out of the lush vegetation to a height of 675 m (2,214 ft) above sea level. Legend has it that the demigod Maui turned an unwanted suitor of the beautiful Iao into this stone pinnacle.

5 Lahaina, Maui This is where history and commerce come together, where business flourishes in the shade of historic buildings that date back to the whaling era. Things were much the same centuries ago, when the Hawaiian kings and

nobility frequented the west coast as a retreat. In the 19th century, Lahaina became a major whaling port. Over five hundred ships were moored in the town's bay over the winter. Post-1850, crude oil took over from whale oil and the demise of whaling hit Lahaina hard. It became a sleepy plantation town once more and did not reawaken until 1966. Part of historic Front Street was declared a National Historic Landmark and luxurious hotels and leisure centers sprang up north of Lahaina. The whales swimming offshore, once a much sought-after commodity, became a star attraction, and whale-watching is now an important feature of every visitor's itinerary. The actors Errol Flynn and Spencer Tracy both enjoyed the fabulous view from the legendary Pioneer Inn, which dates back to 1901. The massive banyan tree,

2

planted in memory of the missionaries, goes back even further. Just behind it you will spot the old court building and jail. From Lahaina our route leads back to Kahului.

6 Haleakala, Maui Drive up to the crater of Haleakala before sunrise and you will be rewarded for your efforts with a spectacular view of the natural world. The journey up follows Routes 37 (Haleakala Highway),

377 (Upper Kula Road) and 378 (Haleakala Crater Road), a winding road popular with mountain-bikers. The islanders of Maui call Haleakala the "house of the sun" and watch with reverence as the fiery star seems to rise out of the crater in the morning and sink back into it at the close of day. The crater covers an area of just under 52 sq km (20 sq miles) with a perimeter of 34 km (20 miles). Add the 7,000 m (22,966 ft) lying below

3

sea level and you have before you one of the world's biggest mountains. The volcano last erupted 200 years ago.

7 **Nahiku, Maui** Nahiku has the dubious distinction of being one of the wettest places on earth. Fewer than a hundred people live in this tropical little nest where ex-Beatle George Harrison once made his home. Near Wailua, Hana Road takes you to the Waikani Falls on the

Puaa Kaa State Wayside and the Waianapanapa State Park, one of nature's gems, with tropical hala trees, temples, and a wide beach of black lava sand.
The route returns to Hana and from there along the north coast and back to Kahului for the plane trip to Lanai.

8 **Lanai** This exclusive island is the preserve of multimillionaires on holiday. The Lodge at Koele, located in an idyllic spot

in the mountains, and the Manele Bay Hotel, a luxurious beach resort boasting one of the best golf courses in the world, are two of the top hotels on the islands.
Sights worth seeing on Lanai include the Kaunolu, a huge rock massif that rises out of the ocean around a natural port, and the Munro Trail, a steep track that is often shrouded in mist and winds its way for around 10 km (6 miles) through the tropical rainforest.

9 **Hoolehua, Molokai** This sleepy little place on the island of Molokai is the gateway to another world. Aloha spirit is very much alive and kicking here. The fifth-largest island in the archipelago has remained virtually untouched by tourism. There are no skyscrapers, no gourmet restaurants, and not even a set of traffic lights. Instead, the is-

land boasts wide expanses of beach and is imbued with the essence of Hawaii as it once was.

10 **Kalaupapa, Molokai** Visitors can only reach this infamous peninsula by helicopter or on the back of a mule. Kalaupapa is isolated from the outside world by high cliffs and rough seas. For almost a century it served as a detention center for more than eight thousand lepers.

1 Nature's drama: sunrise over Haleakala on Maui.

2 The only place in the world where the Silversword grows is on Suu Kukui and the crater of Haleakala on Maui.

3 Craters in Haleakala National Park.

Windsurfing originated in New Zealand and the USA and is more akin to sailing than surfing. Hookipa Beach on Maui is a popular meeting place for windsurfers, who traverse the waves on their sailboards at speeds of up to 40 km/h (25 mph).

The next stop on our route is Honolulu on the island of Oahu.

⑪ **Honolulu, Oahu** Honolulu, a busy metropolis (around 380,000 inhabitants) in the Pacific, is the only big city on the islands. Formerly the seat of the Hawaiian kings, it is now the center of government and the hub of all social and political life. Honolulu was once a major port and an important supply base for the American troops during World War II. Nowadays the city makes its living from trade with Asia and from tourism.

The very heart of the city can be found on King Street, a bustling area right in the middle of Honolulu. A statue commemorating King Kamehameha I stands here.

⑫ **Pearl Harbor, Oahu** On December 7, 1941, Japanese bombers, torpedo jets, and fighter-planes attacked the US naval base of Pearl Harbor. It was one of the great defining moments in world history. The Americans were taken utterly by surprise, even though intelligence services had cracked the Japanese secret code months before. Some people still maintain that the US President withheld his knowledge of the forthcoming attack to pave the way for his country's entry into war following the catastrophe. The US Pacific Fleet was unprepared: seven of its battleships lay anchored like open targets in Battleship Row. Japanese planes appeared over Pearl Harbor at 7.55am and launched their deadly attack. At 8.10am the USS Arizona was hit by a huge bomb. The massive vessel sank in less than nine minutes, with 1,177 crew on board. The USS Oklahoma was hit in the side and rolled over, trapping 400 men inside. The USS Utah also keeled over in the water and other ships were seriously damaged.

The Japanese ceasefire came at 10am, leaving a scene of devastation and destruction in its wake. In total, 2,395 soldiers were lost, 164 planes destroyed, and the proud ships of the Pacific Fleet lay sunk or severely damaged.

The USS Arizona Memorial marks the spot where the battleship went down and is a reminder of this horrific event in history. The white, open-air shrine displays the names of all the men lost on the Arizona and

1 Waikiki beach.

2 The Arizona Memorial was erected in remembrance of the dead.

1

remains one of Hawaii's most visited historic sites.

⑬ **Haleiwa, Oahu** Haleiwa, the former mission station at the mouth of the Anahulu River, has become a mecca for aging hippies, New Age followers, North Coast surfers, and others in search of an alternative lifestyle. The surfing beaches along the legendary North Shore are less than 100 m (109 yds) from the two-lane road that leads to the ocean in Haleiwa and ends on the surfers' beaches.

Just a few miles further up the road is Banzai Pipeline, which ranks among the most famous surfing beaches in the world. It was the location for the 1950s film Surf Safari, which attained cult status and brought worldwide fame to the tunnel-shaped breakers on the North Coast. Only the most experienced surfers brave the "Pipeline" wave that is thrown up by a flat tabletop reef.

Next door is Sunset Beach with its long (3 km/2 mile) stretch of sand, packed with surfers' cars during the winter. According to surfing pros, this is where you'll find the best waves. Beginners should look for calmer waters before trying their hand at the sport, however. The breakers here are extremely dangerous and should be braved only by skilled surfers with years of experience.

⑭ **Polynesian Cultural Center, Oahu** Students admitted to the Mormon Brigham Young University in Laie swear that they will never grow a beard and promise to lead a wholly moral life, free of alcohol and drugs. They earn their pocket money in the nearby Polynesian Cultural Center, an informative pleasure park with a touch of Disneyland about it in the early evening. Later in the evening the park explodes into a kitschy but spectacular and opulent show, in which Polynesian musi-

2

cians, singers, and dancers perform the history and myths of the South Seas. Volcanoes spewing fire, rushing waterfalls and palm-roofed huts are the backdrop to a spectacle that not even the IMAX Polynesia Theater's big screen can rival.

The Polynesian Cultural Center was built in 1963 and many people expected it to flop. Few believed that tourists would travel from Waikiki to Laie to visit a cultural park. They thought that

people visiting Hawaii would want to do little else but lie on the sand and swim in the sea. How wrong they were. The "PCC" as most locals call it, has become a real tourist magnet. Profits go to Brigham Young University and the Latter-day Saints.

The Center's seven villages represent the cultures of Samoa, New Zealand, Fiji, Hawaii, the Marquesas, Tahiti, and Tonga. Polynesian students, mainly

from the same islands, sing traditional songs, play historical instruments, cook their native dishes, and relate the stories and legends of their home. Their houses are situated on the banks of a man-made river and lectures and concerts are held in the public square.

⑮ Valley of the Temples, Oahu The Valley of the Temples, a non-denominational place of worship, is set against

the dramatic backdrop of the verdant mountain slopes of Oahu's Windward Coast, which are usually covered in cloud. It offers magnificent views over the coastline.

The Byodo-In Temple is a faithful replica of the 900-year-old Byodo-In in Uji, Japan. It was built in 1968 to commemorate the centenary of the arrival of the first Japanese immigrants to Hawaii. Kiichi Sano, a famous landscape architect from Kyoto,

designed the tranquil garden refuge at a distance from the hustle and bustle of Honolulu. The sound of a 3-ton brass bell spreads the word of Amidha Buddha and calls people to meditation while peacocks fan out their bright tail feathers along the pathways.

⑯ Kailua, Oahu The journey along the Windward Coast heads south and through the old part of Kailua, past the beach homes of the rich and famous. Kailua Beach Park, a wide expanse of sandy beach with perfect conditions for surfing, is the meeting place for Hawaii's bravest and most experienced surfers. The only place you will see brighter sails is on the North Coast of Maui. Windsurfing is relatively rare on the islands, since any surfer worth his salt would prefer to take to the waves aboard a "proper" surfboard.

Sparse woodland separates the white strip of sand from the in-

land area and provides some extremely welcome shade during the midday heat. The beach is relatively quiet, in fact by Oahu's standards it is virtually deserted, and particularly popular with families. Kailua Beach is one of the safest beaches on Oahu, since it shelves further out to sea and there is no strong current; the only danger is at the weekend, when the bay is packed with surfers and you might get hit by the sharp end of a surfboard.

Further south is Lanikai Beach, which slopes even more gently into the sea and is not widely

1 Stormy weather on Oahu's Windward Coast.

2 A young Hawaiian woman greets the sunrise.

3 Lush nature and a dramatic crater in the Oahu interior.

known. The place has managed to hold out against the spread of commercialism. Its key attractions include soft sand and clear blue water, perfect for a picnic. As you head back to Honolulu, just some 20 minutes away on the Pali Highway, it is worth making a slight detour along the coast via Kahala. This is Honolulu's smart suburb, filled with luxurious villas.

⑰ Lihue, Kauai Our tour of Kauai begins in Lihue, the island's capital, and as a result of the impassable cliffs on the north-west coast the route is best described as fork-shaped. Lihue has a busy shopping area and many commercial outlets. Ninini Point Lighthouse provides a spectacular setting overlooking the Pacific Ocean. The Kauai Museum provides information on the island's past. Kalapaki Beach and the palm-flanked Kauai Lagoon are just a few miles away.

⑱ Kapaa, Kauai The route to Na Pali Coast takes us via Kapaa, a small town with an attractive shopping area. The "Sleeping Giant" is a gigantic rock in the mountains that lies just inland. Legend has it that the giant once helped to build a temple and ate so much during the ensuing festivities that he fell asleep, never to wake again.
One of the must-dos in this region is a boat trip on the Wailua River to Fern Grotto, a romantic cavern covered in ferns. The Wailua Falls are not far from here.

⑲ Hanalei, Kauai This sleepy fishing village serves as a base camp for trips to Na Pali Coast. Several artists have settled here and there's a lively nightlife in the few local pubs and bars.
A luxury hotel is situated on nearby Hanalei Bay, and Hanalei Lookout offers fantastic views over the ocean and the lush tropical landscape.

⑳ Na Pali Coast, Kauai The rugged mountain slopes on this legendary coast are one of the world's most amazing natural wonders. The sun creates bizarre images on the furrowed rock face that rises high above the ocean and casts a long shadow. Most of Na Pali Coast is a conservation area. Above the coastline, the Kalalau Trail passes through forests and over ridges to the Kalalau Valley. The trail ends at Kalalau Beach.

㉑ Poipu Beach, Kauai The route initially heads south via Lihue and then west to the most popular beach on Kauai. A massive reef protects the sandy beach against the raging waves. This is where half of the island's inhabitants meet at the weekend. A bumpy sand track leads to nearby Mahaulepu, the collective name given to Gillin's Beach, Kawailoa Bay, and Haula Beach, all of which are usually peaceful and deserted.

㉒ Waimea Canyon, Kauai Waimea means "red water" and the glistening red river of the same name lies embedded here in the volcanic earth.
Above the river, the winding Waimea Canyon Drive heads up into the mountains. With its luscious vegetation and emerald-green forests, highlighted oasis-like against the red, brown, and purple rock, the Waimea Canyon is the largest in the Pacific and is a dramatic, awe-inspiring sight. It is the Pacific's answer to the Grand Canyon and, although smaller, it is just as spectacular.
There are numerous lookouts offering fabulous panoramic views overlooking gorgeuous landscapes. The canyon brings our journey to a spectacular close.

1 The wildly romantic Na Pali Coast in the north of Kauai.

Na Pali Coast (Kauai) Fabulous sandy beaches line the rugged slopes, most of which are conservation areas, in the north of Kauai.

Molokai Just 8,000 people live on the fifth-largest Hawaiian island. The absence of tourist facilities has helped to keep the whole island relatively unspoilt.

Maui The north of the island features excellent conditions for surfers. Winter months are best for stunning views of huge breakers rolling onto the shore.

Pearl Harbor (Oahu) Since December 7, 1941, Pearl Harbor on the island of Oahu has been remembered for a traumatic event in modern US history. Japanese planes bombarded the battleships anchored there, leaving a scene of devastation behind them. Today the port is still a US deep-water naval base and includes a memorial to those who died.

Haleakala National Park (Maui) A walking trail winds up the side of the crater of Haleakala, a massive volcano that covers three-quarters of Maui.

Waikiki Beach (Oahu) The world-famous city shoreline in the south of Oahu is a suburb of Honolulu. Many restaurants, hotels, boutiques, and bars vie for tourist trade.

Mauna Kea (Hawaii) Few views can beat the one over Hawaii from this peak, named "white mountain" in Hawaiian for the snow that usually covers its summit.

Pu'uhonua o Honaunau Historical Park (Hawaii) The Ku-Kaili and Ku-Ki'i-Akua statues belong to the temple gardens in the park where breakers of kapu once sought sanctuary.

Hilo (Hawaii) This bustling city lies at the most southerly point of the USA and is the main settlement on Big Island, as the largest island in the archipelago is also known. The sugar-cane industry that made Hilo its fortune has now all but vanished, but with its Caribbean ambience and houses of bright hues, the city is now a center for arts and culture. It also has a number of dockyards and tourists come here to enjoy its great variety of tropical flowers.

Hawaii Volcanoes National Park This park, located in the south of Hawaii, has been designated a UNESCO World Heritage Site, as are parts of Mauna Loa, Kilauea, and the coast. Molten lava can often be found flowing through the dark and primeval-looking scree landscape. A journey along the 16-km (10-mile) Crater Rim Drive on Kilauea is an extraordinary experience.

Mexico

The Route of the Conquistadors

Beginning in Mexico City (Ciudad de México), the Route of the Conquistadors crosses the Mexican highlands and reaches the Pacific Ocean. Its cultural highlights include the cities founded in what is now Mexico by the Spanish conquistadors and associated religious orders during 300 years of colonial rule; yet the ruined cities built by pre-Columbian peoples who established great civilizations with their own cities, calendar, and writing system are just as fascinating.

Post-colonial Mexico is on the cusp of becoming an industrial nation, presenting a contradictory mixture of unimaginable poverty, modest prosperity, and ostentatious wealth. Mexico City, one of the greatest cities in the world, is both repellent and fascinating – almost nowhere else on earth is the air so polluted, and yet it can offer world-class tourist attractions like the Museo Nacional de Antropología (National Anthropological Museum). The surrounding area is no less spectacular: two of the country's most beautiful volcanoes, Popocatépetl and Iztaccíhuatl, can be seen from the capital. Until the arrival of the Spanish in the 16th century, the indige-

Indian heritage in Guadalajara.

nous peoples of Mexico maintained their own interconnected cultures, developing a calendar, using the same building techniques and venerating the same gods. The cultural legacies of the Maya, Olmec, Zapotec, Mix-

tec, Toltec, and Aztec civilizations, and of other Mesoamerican peoples, have been preserved in museums across the country. Ruined cities such as Teotihuacán and Xochicalco, which are not far from Mexico City, or Monte Albán near Oaxaca, which is a UNESCO World Heritage Site, are proof of the high level of development achieved by pre-Columbian societies. Despite the destruction that some of them have suffered, the size and spectacular location of such cities – and the craftsmanship necessary to construct them – is still impressive today.

Even though some of the Mesoamerican civilizations could boast more than 3,000 years of history when the Europeans arrived, they had no

The impressive backdrop of mighty colonlal buildıngs on the Plaza de Armas in Guadalajara, the second-largest city in Mexico.

Mariachi bands often play in Mexican public squares; their traditional costume includes a broad-brimmed sombrero.

chance of resisting the Spanish conquerors. Hernán Cortez's defeat of Montezuma's empire in 1520 and the conquest of Tenochtitlán marked the end of the Aztec empire. Military conquest was followed by Christian missionary expeditions led by Jesuit and Franciscan monks, who built magnificent monasteries such as those at Cuilapan de Guerro near Oaxaca or others on the slopes of Popocatépetl. The Spaniards' search for precious metals brought them to northern central Mexico, where abundant deposits of silver led to the foundation of cities displaying distinct Iberian influences, with magnificent baroque palaces, churches, and monasteries. In later years, many of these cities were to become the cradle of the inde-

pendence movement: the first resistance began in Querétaro and Guanajuato, and Morelia later witnessed decisive battles. In 1921 the Mexican muralists Diego Rivera, José Clemente Orozco, and David Alfara Siqueiros began to treat themes from Mexican history in their paintings. They were encouraged by education minister José Vasconcelos, who wished to create a specifically Mexican art form that was intended both to foster a sense of identity and to educate the public.

Mexico's scenery is as diverse and contrasting as its culture: two-thirds of the country lies at elevations above 1,000 m (3,300 feet), and some 120 Mexican mountains and volcanoes reach heights greater than 3,000 to 5,000 m (10,000 to 16,400 feet).

The route will take you to the best-known and most beautiful volcanoes in the country, and you will also see the Pacific twice; at the Lagunas deChac-

ahua National Park and at the sophisticated seaside resort of Acapulco with its legendary rock jumpers. Both are equally recommended.

The monastery of Nuestra Señora de los Remidos with Popocatépetl.

The meandering dream route of the Conquistadors leads to the core region northwest of the capital for a start, and then it continues towards the mountain ranges of the Sierra Madre del Sur in southern Mexico. Besides the cultural sights on the way, the variety of landscapes throughout central Mexico is impressive again and again.

❶ Mexico City (see pages 292-295). Built on the ruins of Tenochtitlán in 1521, in a fertile highland valley, the present-day capital was still quite a tranquil place a little more than 50 years ago, but its population of more than 20 million now makes this metropolis one of the largest on earth. A wealth of tourist attractions can be seen in the city center or are easily reached on public transport or by taxi; these include a day-trip to Teotihuacán, which lies about 50 km (31 miles) to the north-east of the capital.

❷ Teotihuacán Until being overtaken by Tenochtitlán, this now ruined city in the central highlands with its mighty pyra-

mids was the largest in the western hemisphere (see sidebar). Having returned to the capital, take the Mex 75 highway to Tula, 85 km (53 miles) away, which lies on a broad plain dotted with agave plantations and cactuses.

❸ Tula Between 968 and 1168, Tula was the capital of the Toltecs, a people said to have paved the city's streets with gold. The center is dominated by serried ranks of temple pyramids, while the ruined city has achieved special fame for its four atlantes, intricately carved 4.6-m (15-foot) high basalt statues of warriors standing on a 10-m (33-foot) ziggurat. They were once pillars supporting the

roof of the Temple of Quetzalcóatl. Tula's other sights include a court for a ball-game and a 40-m (132-foot) serpent wall. Heading north-west toward Querétaro, the Mex 57 is the quickest route.

❹ San Juan del Río This commercial center is a popular desti-

Travel Information

Route profile
Route length:
about 2,500 km (1,550 miles)
Time required:
 four to five weeks
Start and destination:
Mexico City
Route (main locations):
Mexico City, Tula, Querétaro, San Miguel de Allende, Guadalajara, Colima, Playa Azul, Uruapan de Progreso, Morelia, Toluca, Taxco, Acapulco, Puerto Escondido, Oaxaca, Tehuacán, Pueblo, Mexico City

Traffic Information:
Driving in darkness should be avoided if possible, because

of the poor road conditions, wild animals on the carriageway and tendency of other motorists to drive without lights. The Mexican capital has a system whereby automobiles (selected according to the last figure of their registration plates) are banned from using the roads on certain days, and this applies to hired vehicles too.

Information:
Mexican embassy in the USA:
portal.sre.gob.mx/usa
Mexican embassy in London:
mexico.embassy-uk.co.uk
Mexican tourist board:
www.visitmexico.com

2

3

nation for excursions by the capital's residents, who have learnt to prize the attractive range of wines, provisions, craft objects, and gemstones on offer here. The Museo de la Muerte (Museum of Death) is a local peculiarity exploring the somewhat macabre-seeming Mexican traditions surrounding death and burial. Querétaro is the next stop. Gemstones, usually cut as jewels, are sold all along the highway, but not all of these semi-precious stones (such as opals and topaz) are actually products of the region.

⑤ Querétaro This industrial city with its university lies in the fertile Bajíro lowlands on the eastern rim of Mexico's colonial heartland. It was founded in 1446, is the capital of Querétaro state and its largely traffic-free Old Town is now protected as a UNESCO World Heritage Site. The city is closely connected with several historical events of great importance to Mexico: Querétaro was the starting-point of the independence struggle about 1810, briefly served as the Mexican capital in the mid-19th century, and with-

in its walls were signed the treaties forcing Mexico to concede half its territory to the USA. Mexico's last monarch, the Emperor Maximilian, was executed here. These and many other events are explained in the Museo Regional in the Convento de San Francisco. There is an 8-km (5-mile) aqueduct of 74 arches built 250 years ago, the city end of which is to be found behind the Convento de la Santa Cruz. The route follows the Mex 57 through "Mexico's breadbasket" to idyllic San Miguel de Allende.

⑥ San Miguel de Allende This historic and protected city nestles picturesquely around a hill, so that steep alleys and steps connect its different quarters. The pleasant climate and special quality of light here have always attracted painters, writers, pensioners, and the leisured classes from all over the world, and it is almost impossible to tire of strolling through its cob-

bled streets, past the patrician houses and atmospheric churches. The city was once a hub for wagon trains, which went on through the Rio de la Laja valley to Dolores Hidalgo before taking a road to the south-west to Guanajuato, once the wealthiest city in Mexico.

⑦ Guanajuato Capital of the state of the same name, seat of a university and the birthplace of the muralist Diego Rivera, Guanajuato is thought to be the most attractive mining city in Mexico.

1 The façade of the church of La Parroquia in San Miguel de Allende was designed by a Native American sculptor.

2 The Cathedral of San Juan de los Lagos is one of the most sacred places in Mexican Catholicism.

3 The atlantes of Tula once supported a mighty roof.

Above: The Catedral Metropolitana in Mexico City is the largest ecclesiastical building in America. It was begun in 1573 but the neoclassical roof and towers were completed only 240 years later. The cathedral towers over the Zócalo, the second largest municipal square in the world.

Below: El Ángel, the golden angel on the Monumento a la Independencia looks down on the Paseo de la Reforma from a 40-m (132-foot) column. Mexico City's main traffic artery was once lined with colonial buildings but mundane office buildings now dominate the skyline.

Mexico City

The capital is located at an elevation of 2,250 m (7,380 feet) in Mexico's central highlands. The historic center of the capital was built on the ruins on the old Aztec city of Tenochtitlán and the Reforma quarter further west combines colonial period buildings with more modern structures.

The twin focal points of the historic center are the Zócalo and the Catedral Metropolitana which towers above it. Built between 1525 and 1813, this the largest ecclesiastical building in Latin America has begun to sink under its own weight into the soft ground of what was once Lake Texcoco. The Sagrario Metropolitano, the 18th-century archbishop's palace, is to be found next to the cathedral. The eastern side of the Zócalo is dominated by the Palacio Nacional, the official residence of the president of Mexico. The steps and the main courtyard are decorated with murals by Diego Rivera, while the Suprema Corte de Justicia courthouse (1941) on the south side of the square is decorated with frescoes by José Clemente Orozco. The remains of the Templo Mayor, an Aztec temple discovered by chance in 1978, and once the central point of Tenochtitlán, lie to the north of the Palacio Nacional. The Museo de la Ciudad de México and the ornate façade of the Iglesia de la Santísima Trinidad (c. 1760) are both within easy reach of the Zócalo. The Escuela Nacional Preparatoria (National Preparatory School) boasts a series of bright murals, including Rivera's first completed fresco, The Creation. Early murals by famous Mexican muralists also grace the walls of the Secretaria de Educación Pública.

The 182-m (597-foot) Torre Latinoamericana (1954) near Alameda Central, a park to the west of the Zócalo, is one of the tallest buildings in Latin America. Although it is an office block, there is an observation deck at the top where visitors will get a real sense of the size and location of this mega-city – on smog-free days at least. The Casa de los Azulejos (House of Tiles, 1596) near the tower is certainly worth a visit for the beautiful Spanish-Moorish tiles used on its main façade. The Palacio de las Bellas Artes (fine arts complex, 1934) beside the Alameda Central is renowned for its glass theatrical stage curtain. The Franciscan monastery of San Diego is now a museum of 16th to 18th-century religious art and also houses another mural by Rivero, depicting caricatures of the most important figures in Mexican history.

The Paseo de la Reforma, the city's 15-km (9-mile) main traffic artery, connects the historic center with the Bosque de Chapultepec leisure park. The Castillo de Chapultepec (1785), the summer palace of the viceroys and emperors of Mexico and now a national museum, lies in the eastern corner of the park. The Museo de Arte Contemporáneo Internacional Rufino Tamayo exhibits the private collection of modern art amassed by the painter, who died in 1991, as well as his own work. The Museo Nacional de Antropología (National Anthropological Museum) is one of the best and architecturally most striking museums in the world. The district of Coyoacán to the south of the city center was once the home of colonialists and artists and the main objects of interest here are the Museo Frida Kahlo and the Casa León Trotzky. The Ciudad Universitaria, with its world-famous murals in the university library, lies to the south.

1 The painter Diego Rivera (1886–1957) depicted scenes from the history of his country in giant murals. His masterpiece is the famous mural in the Palacio Nacional which looks back on the golden age of Quetzalcóatl. Begun in 1929, the work was never quite completed.

An evening in the Teatro Degollado on Plaza de la Liberación in Guadalajara becomes a feast for the eyes and ears when the proud dancers of the Folclórico de la Universidad de Guadalajara dance company take the stage. Their performances present an insight into various

Mexican folk dances while the Jarabe Tapatio – a dance from Guadalajara where the dancers spin around the stage, swishing their skirts to the intoxicating melodies of the mariachis – has become world-famous, and many would regard it as the essence of Mexican folk dance.

Lying in a narrow mountain valley, it made its fortune from the local deposits of gold and silver. Some of the winding streets of the cramped Old Town with its many churches are too steep for cars, and the city authorities have been obliged to build an underground road network. The Old Town was added to the list of UNESCO World Heritage Sites in 1988.

The Carretera Panorámiche (Panoramic Road) and the monument to Pípila, a local freedom fighter, afford a wonderful view of the city and of the unusual Museo Iconográfico de Quijote (Don Quixote Iconographic Museum), devoted to depictions of Cervantes' hero. On the mountain slopes themselves, the Museo de las Momias (Museum of Mummies), which contains the exhumed and mummified bodies of many of the town's citizens, is also worth a visit. There are two recommended excursions in the area surrounding Guanajuato: the town of La Valenciana, 5 km (3miles) beyond the city, boasts the Templo de San Cayetano, perhaps the most beautiful church in the country,

built by a mine-owner named Valenciano in the 18th century. The Cerro del Cubilete, the geographical center of Mexico, is marked with a 20-m (66-foot) figure of Christ, the second-largest of its kind after the Corcovado statue in Rio de Janeiro. The Mex 45 will take you through Silao to León.

8 León This center of the Mexican shoe-making industry has an elegant Old Town with several colonial churches and a cathedral that betrays art deco influences. The vaults beneath the Templo Expiatorio (an unfinished church) are also recommended. Take the Mex 45 toward Aguascalientes as far as Lagos de Moreno, an 18th and 19th-century city which is rarely visited, despite its many attractive buildings. A short stretch of the Mex 80 will take you on to San Juan de los Lagos.

9 San Juan de los Lagos The inner city has lost most of its colonial charm, but you will find one of the most popular shrines in Mexico here: the imposing Cathedral of San Juan de los La-

gos, visited by some nine million pilgrims a year. A miraculous icon of the Virgin Mary originally intended for an altar in Rome is kept here. Follow the Mex 80 to the lakes and volcanoes surrounding the city of Tlaquepaque.

10 Tlaquepaque This southern satellite of Guadalajara has retained an almost rural feel, despite its 300,000 inhabitants. Pottery-making is very popular here and the city's name translates as "town on the high clay hill."
The Museo Regional de la Cerámica (Regional Ceramics Museum) has a collection of especially beautiful traditional

and modern ceramics, as well as the original kitchen fittings and utensils from a 16th-century aristocratic house.

1 An agave plantation near Tequila to the west of Guadalajara. The town, which has given its name to Mexico's national drink, is surrounded by countless plantations. Tours are available at several tequila distilleries.

2 The Teatro Degollado in Guadalajara is the pride of the city. The most precious feature of the interior is the ceiling painting on the cupola, which features motifs from Dante's Divine Comedy.

The Mercado Libertad in the historic center of Guadalajara is generally acknowledged to be the largest covered market in the world; it is certainly one of the most impressive markets in Mexico, with four levels of stalls selling every kind of everyday products.

1

⑪ Guadalajara The capital of the state of Jalisco lies in a fertile highland valley at an elevation of about 1,600 m (5,250 feet). Mexico's second-largest city has a pleasant climate and seems leafy and verdant, despite its four million inhabitants. The city was founded at the very end of the Spanish colonial period and its main tourist sight is the intricately decorated, 16th-century cathedral, flanked on each of its four sides by a square; the 1,400-seater neoclassical Teatro Degollado adjoins the largest of these. The Museo Regional or Museo del Estado Jalisco (Jalisco Regional Museum) has a range of exhibits from the peoples living in the state. The Palacio de Gobierno (Governor's Palace), is where the abolition of slavery in Mexico was proclaimed in 1810, and its stairs and assembly rooms are decorated with murals painted by José Clemente Orozco (1883–1949) to celebrate the freedom fighter Miguel Hidalgo. The baroque Augustinian monastery church of Templo de Santa Mónica (1720) is also worth a visit, as is the main hall of the university, which is decorated with a large Orozco mu-

ral. Orozco's frescoes in what used to be the chapel of the Instituto Cultural de Cabañas, one of the most beautiful colonial buildings in the Americas, are more famous still. The spectacular journey across the plain along the Mex 54 to the provincial capital of Colima affords excellent views of the active Volcán de Colima and the extinct Volcán Nevado de Colima.

⑫ Colima The capital of the small, picturesque state of Colima is located in a tropical valley nestling at the foot of several volcanoes. Many of the old colonial buildings were unfortunately destroyed in a severe earthquake, but the museums, parks, and the pre-Columbian passage graves at the La Campaña archeological site are still worth seeing. A toll highway offers a quick and comfortable route back to the Pacific coast and the next stop is Manzanillo, a bathing resort popular with the inhabitants of Colima.

⑬ Manzanillo The Gold Coast (Riviera d'Oro) at Manzanillo is one of the most attractive stretches of the Mexican Riviera.

Manzanillo itself is the most important port on the west coast and the headquarters of the Mexican navy (see sidebar, page left). Hernán Cortez built warships in the New World's first shipyards at Bahía de Manzanillo. Manzanillo lies on the Panamericana (Carretera 200) highway, which runs the entire length of Mexico's west coast. Do plan to stop for a swim somewhere as you follow the spectacular scenic highway between the lagoons of the Pacific coast and the coastal rainforest on the slopes of the Sierra de Coalcomán – most of the seaside resorts on the road to Playa Azul are clean, friendly, and tourist-orientated: the Laguna Cuyutlán, not far from Manzanillo, is lined with 32 km (20 miles) of coconut palms and is also home to the Centro Ecológico el Tortugario, a research center dedicated to the conservation and breeding of sea turtles. The little town of Paraíso has an excellent beach with bars right beside the sea, while Boca de Pascuales is very popular with campers. The last chance for a dip in the surf is to be found at the resort of Playa Azul, where

the route leaves the humid heat of the Pacific coast and crosses the Sierra Madre de Coalcomán on its way to Uruapán.

⑭ Uruapán del Progreso The city lies at an elevation of 1,610 m (5,280 feet) in the cooler highlands of the Sierra de Uruapán, where the lush, sub-tropical lanscape is covered with extensive avocado plantations. The two main sights are the Parque Nacional Eduardo Ruíz on the edge of town and the Museo Regional Huatápera. The museum exhibits typical craft pieces from the region and is housed in an old hospital. The Río Cupatitzio rises near Uruapán and falls 25 m (82 feet) into a chasm at the Cascadas de Tzaráracua a little beyond the town. Explorer and naturalist Alexander von Humboldt called it the most beautiful river in the world.

To the west of town there is a good view of Paricutín (2,775 m/9,104 feet), the country's newest volcano.

⑮ Parque Nacional Paricutín When the earth began to quiver on the plains to the north-west

2

of Urapan del Progreso on the 20 February 1943, no one could have guessed that within eight years a completely new volcanic cone would have arisen, eventually towering 442 m (1,450 feet) over the upland plains. Not a single human life was lost in the process, but some 4,000 people were forced to relocate. All the houses in San Juan Parangaricutiro and some 20 sq. km (8 sq. miles) of arable land were destroyed by the spectacle. Only the church was miraculously preserved from the streams of lava and still pokes out of the bizarre lunar landscape today. Expect to take a whole day for an ascent to the crater's edge, as climbing the pumice scree is a slow and arduous undertaking. The route continues through more sub-tropical scenery to the lakes of Pátzcuaro at an elevation of more than 2,000 m (6,600 feet).

16 Pátzcuaro The popular resort of Pátzcuaro (2,170 m/7,120 feet) is renowned for its tree-lined plazas and arcaded houses, and has a unique backdrop formed by the forested slopes of the surrounding volcanoes and

the Pátzcuaro lake. The town has few exceptional tourist sights, yet it is one of the most agreeable in the country, with a wealth of fine colonial era buildings. One undoubted cultural highlight is provided by the murals painted in the Biblioteca Gertrudis Bocanegra (the library) by Juan O'Gorman (1905–1982), acclaimed by many as the legitimate heir to the mantle of Rivera and Orozco. The scenic highpoint is reached during the 90-km (56-mile) drive around Lago de Pátzcuaro, a lake where the old traditional technique of butterfly-net fishing is still used, and which has six islands. A popular – but for many, quite disappointing – boat trip will take you to the island of Janitzío in the southwestern corner of the lake, which is dominated by a monument to the freedom fighter José María Morelos y Pavón.

17 Tzintzuntzan The old capital of the Tarascans, once famous for their metalworking skills, lies about 15 km (9 miles) north of Pátzcuaro on the eastern shores of the lake. At the time of the Spanish conquest

the "place of hummingbirds" was inhabited by about 40,000 people, but now there are neither people nor hummingbirds; the latter may even have been wiped out by the Tarascans, who were fond of adorning themselves with feathers. Their religious center can still just about be made out – there is a reconstructed platform and several pyramid-like structures with T-shaped bases (the so-called yácatas). There is an impressive Franciscan monastery (1530) where the indigenous population is said to have been Christianized in huge numbers. It is also worth dropping into the craft fair before moving on to Morelia.

18 Morelia The capital of the state of Michoacán is one of the most astonishing cities in Mexico, filled with magnificent churches and monasteries built by the first settlers – monks and aristocrats from the Spanish motherland. It was originally known as Valladolid, but in 1828 was renamed Morelia in memory of its greatest son, the freedom fighter José María Morelos y Pavón. The colonial Old Town,

with its grid-like network of streets, has since been listed as a UNESCO World Heritage Site. The façades of new buildings have been dressed with typical local pink limestone to blend harmoniously into the historic town center. The town's emblem is a 2-km (1,2-mile) 18th-century aqueduct with 250 arches which once brought water to private households and the municipal well from a spring 8 km (5 miles) away. The arcades of the Plaza de los Mártires (named for martyrs of the war of independence) adjoin a baroque cathedral of remarkable stylistic purity. The exhibits in the Museo Regional Michoacano illustrate Tarascan culture and the history of the state. The approach to Toluca, the next stop, is an experience in itself, with its spectacular location at the foot of Nevado de Toluca, a

1 Morning mist covering Lago de Pátzcuaro and its six islands.

2 The indigenous population knew the Nevado de Toluca (4,690 m/15,390 feet) as Xinatécatl – the "naked man."

The Templo de la Santa Veracruz is reflected by pavements wet with rain. The foundation of the church was laid in 1753, and it features a Baroque façade typical at that time. The main attraction inside ist the "Black Christ" which dates from the 16th century. The Carmen

Convent and the La Merced Monastery were also built in colonial or Baroque style. The city's face, however, was mainly shaped in the 19th century, when numerous buildings were created in French-influenced neoclassical style.

1

4,690-m (15,387-foot) volcano, which is Mexico's fourth-highest mountain.

⑲ Toluca This is the capital of Mexico State (sometimes called Edomex) and is also the country of Mexico's highest city. Besides the colonial-period churches it is worth looking into the market held on Fridays by the Otomi and Matlatzinca peoples, which is popular with visitors from the capital. Although the space allotted to it has been reduced by half, it is still Mexico's largest open air market. In the Jardín Botánico Cosmovitral gardens there is an art deco stained-glass mosaic roof of almost unparalleled beauty. Two detours from Toluca are recommended: the village of Calixtlahuaca to the north-west has a round pyramid built by the Matlatzinca people, and in the village of Metepec world-famous and many-hued ceramic "trees of life" are made by hand.

This round trip follows Highway 15 through the colonial heartland of Mexico back to the capital and the Paseo de la Reforma

boulevard. To continue, leave Mexico City heading south via the Mex 95 and passing the volcano of Ajusco (3,937 m/12,917 feet), and you will soon reach the Xochicalco archeological site near Cuernavaca. There is a beautiful view of the surrounding hills from this ruined fortified town, which is considered the missing link between Teotihuacán, whose star was rapidly waning by 700, and the Toltecs, whose rise began in the 10th century. Take the back roads leading from Xochicalco to Malinalco on the Mex 55.

㉑ Malinalco This sleepy village, a sight in itself, is surrounded by one of the most important Aztec religious sites. Follow the 400 steps up from the village to the excavated site and enjoy the fantastic view of the surrounding area. Archeologists have uncovered a sacred precinct with rotunda temples where initiation rites and sacrifices were carried out. Parts of the structure (the main building and the steps) have been carved out of the living rock and or-

nately decorated. The Cerro de los Idolos ("Hill of the Idols") was still being built at the time of the Conquista.

㉒ Taxco The location of this city on an upland slope surrounded by spectacular mountains is a little reminiscent of Tuscany or Andalusia. The usually whitewashed cottages, no more than three floors high and topped with a red tiled roof, are protected monuments. The Native American tribe which once lived here used to pay tribute to the Aztecs in the form of silver and gold; when the Spanish heard of the mines they confiscated them and systematically exhausted them. Even so, precious metals are still very important to Taxco, as 80 percent of the population subsists on the silverware manufactured here and offered for sale on every street corner.

The pink baroque church of Santa Prisca with its roof of vivid tiles towers over the sea of houses. It was donated by a mine-owner and has been decorated in the most lavish style.

The interior, which has a separate side chapel for the indigenous population, is decorated with 23-carat gold.

The square in front of the church, the beautiful market, and the road leading up to the church are full of people throughout the day, but the little side streets offer plenty of quiet spots far from the tourists and honking taxis.

The Moorish-looking Casa Humboldt, where the naturalist and explorer once stayed, houses the Museo de Arte Sacro Virreinal (Museum of Sacred Viceregal Art), a collection of exquisite artworks and liturgical apparatus.

On the road to the coast (Mex 95), a stop is recommended at Chilpancingo de los Bravos, tucked away at the end of a valley in the Sierra Madre Occidental. Few tourists venture here, but the Museo Regional de Guerrero (Guerrero Regional Museum) has a number of excellent exhibits illustrating local culture. Acapulco, one of the most famous resorts on the Pacific, lies 130 km (80 miles) further on.

㉓ Acapulco Over the last few decades this once sleepy town spread along the Bahía de Acapulco has become a ghetto of hotel rooms with a population of well over one and a half million. Two-thirds of Mexico's total tourism receipts are taken here, and for a good reason. It is worth climbing to the top of one of the surrounding hills, which offer a breathtaking view of the city and the countless beaches along the bay. Acapulco's main tourist sight is provided by the world-famous clavadistas, divers who plunge 38 m (125 feet) into a desperately narrow rocky gorge. Join the remarkably few automo-

bilesheading south along the coast on the Panamericana.

㉔ Parque Nacional Lagunas de Chacahua This 14,187-ha (35,057-acre) national park with its eight large lagoons was established to help conserve the tropical and sub-tropical dry forests and mangrove swamps of the Pacific coast. Nevertheless, the danger to the plants and animals in the park from irrigation and reclamation of the mangroves for agriculture is still increasing.

㉕ Puerto Escondido This "Hidden Port" and former hippy hangout 25 km (16 miles) south-

east of the national park did not remain an insider tip for long; it is now one of the most popular tourist destinations on the Pacific coast of Mexico. Not far from the port and the town there is a chain of bays separated by headlands – take a taxi or a boat and you will find the perfect beach for every taste there somewhere, although the surf can be quite rough in places.

Puerto Ángel, a charming, peaceful, and inexpensive little fishing village with tropical beaches and sheltered rocky bays, lies 70 km (44 miles) further on. Cross the Sierra de Miahuatlán, the southern spur of the Sierra Madre del Sur, and you will reach a fertile upland valley revealing one of the most beautiful colonial cities in the country.

㉖ Oaxaca The town has a wealth of colonial grandeur and indigenous culture, and despite crowds of people it has retained a little of its provincial essence. Many Native Americans live here, flocking to the Plaza de Armas with its cathedral, rebuilt

in a less than harmonious style in 1730 after an earthquake. The Iglesia de Santo Domingo is smaller and rather unassuming from the outside, but the ornate décor of the interior will take visitors' breath away. Decorating the church has consumed an unimaginable 12 million gold pesos over the course of 200 years.

The equally impressive Museo de las Culturas de Oaxaca in the Centro Cultural Santo Domingo houses fascinating pre-Columbian finds from nearby Monte Albán, including the fabled Mixtec treasure. The Museo de Arte Prehispánico exhibits Rufino Tamayo's exquisite private col-

1 The white houses of the "silver town" of Taxco nestle on a hillside.

2 Dusk in Acapulco, renowned as the "Pearl of the Pacific."

3 The ruins of the abandoned monastery of Cuilaopan de Guerro, south-west of Oaxaca, which was built on the foundations of a Zapotec pyramid.

The baroque façade of the Iglesia de Santo Domingo in Oaxaca gives it a rather squat and unprepossessing air, making the magnificent interior all the more of a surprise. Construction of the church began in 1575 and every interior surface is decorated with lavish stucco.

work, paintings, and gilded carvings, including a representation of St Dominic's family tree. The image shows the Chapel of the Rosary.
The ornately decorated altar with its icon of the Mother of God is considered a gem of Mexican rococo work.

lection of finds from the pre-Hispanic period. The town's markets, selling a selection of typical regional handicrafts, are also worth a visit; the comical, brightly painted carved animals and black or green-glazed ceramics made in Oaxaca have become popular all over the world.

The churchyard of the nearby village of Santa María el Tule conceals a remarkable natural phenomenon: a Ahuehuete tree that is more than 2,000 years old, making it one of the oldest trees in the world, standing 48 m (157 feet) high and with a girth of almost 60 m (165 feet). The largest sight in the area is the ruined Monte Albán, 400 m (1,300 feet) above the town.

㉗ Monte Albán The area surrounding the town of Oaxaca has been populated since at least the 6th century, and the Olmec people were the first to work the mountain above the Oaxaca valley. The plateau they created was named Monte Albán and later became the religious center of the Zapotec culture, who were masters of

mathematics and possessed their own system of writing. As Monte Albán fell under Teotihuacán's sway the shrine's importance declined, with its 20,000 inhabitants gradually abandoning it after about 800. It was briefly used by the Mixtec as a necropolis in about 1250 but fell into ruins with the advent of the Aztec civilization (1490). This cultural treasure of world standing boasts such features as depictions of contorted human figures on the "Building of the Dancers," tunnels connecting the various temples, and a structure which is thought to have been an observatory. Carretera 190 will take you through the barren Mixteca Baja to Yanhuitlán in the arid Mixteca Alta region, some 2,500 m (8,250 feet) above sea level.

㉘ Yanhuitlán The Dominican monastery here looks like a fortress, but its interior reveals a magnificent wooden altar and many other precious carvings. The complex was built in the 16th century on a large, pre-Columbian terrace that had been used by the Mixtec culture

for religious purposes, and is now one of three Dominican monasteries in the area where mass baptisms and sermons are conducted.

㉙ Tehuacán Located in a semi-arid valley on the Mex 150, this spa is famous throughout Mexico for "Agua de Tehuacán," its mineral water, while its architecture rather resembles that of a French spa town. The Balneario (spa) Ejidal San Lorenzo on the edge of town includes natural pools fed by springs. The Museo del Valle de Tehuacán is an exhibition in a Carmelite monastery and offers fascinating insights into the history of the cultivation of maize in Central America.

The oldest known specimens of cultivated maize are about 5,500 years old and were found in the San Marcos Caves near Tehuacán, while the settlements in the valley are thought to be some of the oldest in Central America. From the spa, there are a further 110 km (69 miles) to cover before reaching Puebla, one of the high points of Central Mexico.

㉚ Puebla Situated in a fertile valley, the city of Puebla is surrounded by the three highest volcanoes in the country: Pico de Orizaba (5,747 m/18,855 feet), Popocatépetl (5,465 m/17,930 feet), and Iztaccíhuatl (5,286 m/17,343 feet).

Founded in 1532, the city has expanded in a grid pattern to become the fourth-largest in Mexico. Puebla's cathedral was built during the 16th and 17th centuries and is the second-largest in Mexico, while the university is the oldest in the country.

The brightly-hued talavera tiles adorning the houses are typical of Puebla, as are the many churches, which have earned it the nickname "the Rome of Mexico." The Old Town, with its many colonial buildings, is listed as a UNESCO World Heritage Site.

Follow the Mex 150 for a further 130 km (81 miles) to reach Mexico City.

1 Baroque ceiling frescoes in Puebla Cathedral.

Guadalajara The second-largest city in Mexico with a population of four million, situated in a highland valley. The city boasts a number of magnificent 16th- to 20th-century buildings, such as the cathedral on the Plaza de Armas.

San Miguel de Allende Cobblestones, ornate palaces, and churches of all ages: this old colonial town is justly considered one of the most beautiful in Mexico.

Mexico City The capital is an equal mix of the old and the new. The Bosque de Chapultepec, the only park of any size, is located next to the independence memorial, and the Museo Nacional de Antropología now stands where Aztec princes once strolled.

Guanajuato This former silver-mining town and the birthplace of painter Diego Rivera is now one of the most beautiful colonial style cities in Mexico.

Teotihuacán Little is known of the original builders, inhabitants, or even the destroyers of this 20-sq. km (8-sq. mile) religious site; its pyramids and mighty boulevards were already deserted when the Aztec arrived. Modern research suggests a heyday between about 150 BC and 750 AD, with some 200,000 inhabitants. The Pyramids of the Sun (65 m/215 feet) and of the Moon (45 m/148 feet), and the 43-m (140-foot) wide Avenue of the Dead are simply breathtaking.

Popocatépetl There are still 14 magnificent monasteries on the slopes of this 5,465-m (17,930-foot) volcano to remind visitors of the age of the Christianization of Mexico; some were built on indigenous religious sites.

Tula The Toltec capital, famed for its giant stone atlantes, was razed to the ground by invaders from the north in 1116.

Puebla The Old Town of Puebla, the "Rome of Mexico," has been declared a UNESCO World Heritage Site and the Renaissance cathedral is the second-largest in the country. The greatest treasure of the Iglesia Santo Domingo is its Capilla del Rosario (Rosary Chapel).

Morelia The town has taken as its emblem a 1,000-m (half-mile) aqueduct. The arcades of the Plaza de los Mártires are especially attractive at night.

The Pacific coast of South Mexico boasts sophisticated resorts like Acapulco and sleepy little villages like Puerto Ángel. Several sections are still largely unspoiled.

Xochicalco This pre-Columbian religious site boasts an impressive location, some fine reliefs, and a mixture of architectural styles. The Pyramid of Quetzalcóatl is one of the finest in Mexico.

Acapulco "The Pearl of the Pacific" is now Mexico's premier seaside resort and a city of millions, but was once just a village. Don't miss the cliff-jumpers in La Quebrada bay.

Oaxaca The main attractions in this provincial capital are the churches, such as the Monastery of Santo Domingo. Stroll round the stalls on the Zócalo.

Monte Albán The Zapotec cleared a whole mountain summit to build this temple complex 400 m (1,260 feet) above Oaxaca.

Mexico, Guatemala and Belize

Through the Kingdom of the Maya

Culture and beaches all in one – a journey through the Yucatán Peninsula. In the heartland of the Mayan region you can marvel at both ancient pyramids and Spanish-colonial-style baroque towns, while the white sand beaches of the Caribbean offer idyllic relaxation after your adventures.

The name of the peninsula separating the Caribbean Sea from the Gulf of Mexico originally arose from a misunderstanding. When the Spanish conquistadors first set foot on the peninsula at the start of the 16th century they addressed the indigenous people in Spanish. The Maya answered in their language: 'Ma c'ubab than', meaning 'We do not understand your words'. It is also claimed to be an Aztek word meaning 'place

of richness'. Three countries lay claim to the Yucatán Peninsula: the north and west belong to Mexico, the south-east coast and Barrier Reef to Belize, and the mountainous south-east to Guatemala. Detours from the route also take you to the most significant ruins in Honduras – Copán.

When the conquistadors arrived in Mexico they discovered a uniquely advanced civilization. The Maya had both a precise

calendar and their own alphabet. Their massive constructions – pyramids, palaces, places of worship – are all the more astounding given that the Maya had neither the wheel as a means of transport nor iron, metal implements, winches, pul-

Mexico: a well-earned siesta.

leys, ploughs, or pack or draught animals. Mayan ruins are often located in the midst of tropical rainforests, are often overgrown and have only been partly uncovered. Sites that are easily accessible for tourists along the route we suggest here are Chichén Itzá, Tulum, Tikal, Edzná and Uxmal. The city of San Cristóbal de las Casas and the surrounding Indian villages in the south-west of the peninsula, Chiapas (Mexico), provide wonderful insight into the present-day life of the descendants of the Maya.

The Indian population of Mexico and Belize makes up around one-tenth of the overall population of each country. In Guatemala, however, half of all citizens are of Indian origin. In Mexico and Guatemala numer-

San Miguel is the largest town on the holiday island of Cozumel off the coast of Cancún.

High above the Caribbean Sea sits Tulum, meaning 'fortress', a mighty wall that once encircled the Mayan town. The original Mayan name was Zama, meaning 'City of Dawn'.

ous Mayan languages are also still spoken. The Spanish who first landed on the Yucatán Peninsula in 1517 greatly underestimated the scale of Mayan civilization and unfortunately destroyed a large part of their physical culture and records. In their place rose a series of colonial cities from the ruins of older Mayan settlements.

The Spanish legacy includes baroque monasteries, cathedrals, palaces and large town plazas in true colonial style. The oldest cathedral in the Americas is in Mérida (1560), Campeche was once the most important port on the Yucatán Peninsula for goods headed to Europe, and there are important monasteries dating back to the 17th and 18th centuries in Antigua, Guatemala.

The route we recommend includes some of the most scenic nature reserves in Central America. On the north-east coast is the Sian Ka'an biosphere reserve (a UNESCO World Heritage Site) covering 4,500 ha (11,120 acres) of jungle and swamp as well as a 100-km-long (62-mile) coral reef. Belize is home to the Blue Hole National Park and the 300-km-long (186-mile) Belize Barrier Reef (also a UNESCO World Heritage Site).

Guatemala is home to the Sierra de Las Minas biosphere reserve. Wild cocoa trees can still be found in the north-east of the peninsula and also in the mountainous regions of the south. Today the east coast, known as the 'Mayan Riviera', is a popular holiday destination – white sand beaches and the splendid reef

between Cancún in the north and Tulum Playa in the south provide ideal conditions for both snorkelling and diving. Yet swimming, diving, snorkelling and relaxing on the 'Mayan Riviera' are just some of the many options for an active holiday on

the Yucatán Peninsula. If you go for a hike through the often still pristine tropical rainforests of the national parks and nature reserves in the interior of the peninsula, you will discover an unparalleled wealth of flora and fauna.

'The Old Man from Copán' a Mayan sculpture in the Honduran forest.

1

The Yucatán tour goes through Mexico, Guatemala and Belize, with a detour to the ruins of Copán in Honduras. From the idyllic Caribbean beaches you head to the mountainous regions of Guatemala before visiting the Petén rainforest and the magnificent coast of Belize then heading back to the start.

1 **Cancún** The journey across the Yucatán Peninsula begins in Cancún on the north-east coast. The town's name derives from the name of the former Mayan settlement 'Can-Cune' ('End of the Rainbow'). Until the beginning of the 1960s Cancún was a tiny fishing village with barely 100 residents. The Mexican government then decided to create an international seaside resort, a project that met with massive success.

Today more than 2.5 million tourists visit this town of 300,000 residents. South of the town the MEX 180 highway turns towards Mérida. The turn-off to the most architecturally significant Mayan site on the peninsula, Chichén Itzá, is well

signposted, 40 km (25 miles) beyond Valladolid.

2 **Chichén Itzá** The largest and best preserved pre-Columbian ruins on the Yucatán Peninsula represented an important economic, political and religious center between the years 400 and 1260, with a population of about 35,000 people. The best-known building at the site is El Castillo, a 24-m-high (79-ft) pyramid. Other buildings worth seeing are the Templo de los Guerreros, the observatory (Caracol) and the Cenote de los Sacrificios, as well as the 168-m-long (180-yd) playing field, the largest of its kind in the whole of Mesoamerica. Four 45° angle steps lead up to the El Castillo

Travel Information

Route profile
Length: approx. 2,800 km (1,740 miles)
Time required: min. 4 weeks
Start and end: Cancún
Route (main locations): Mérida, Campeche, San Cristóbal de las Casas, Antigua, Ciudad de Guatemala, Quiriguá, Tikal, Belmopan, Belize City, Chetumal, Tulum

Traffic information:
Drive on the right on this trip. Most of the roads in Mexico are decent. In Guatemala expect bad roads, apart from the Pan-American Highway and the main roads – best to travel by day. The roads in Belize are in relatively good condition. Caution during flooding in the rainy season!

Information:
Mexico:
www.mexicotravel101.com
Guatemala:
www.enjoyguatemala.com
Belize:
www.travelbelize.org

platform from where you will have a breathtaking view of the entire site.

3 **Mérida** At the turn of the 19th century, the capital of the Federal state of Yucatán was a center for the cultivation and production of sisal, a type of

hemp. Magnificent town villas, spacious plazas and lovely parks are reminiscent of the town's heyday. Today it is an important industrial and commercial center and a hub for tourism on Yucatán Península. At Uman, 20 km (12 miles) south of the town, a road branches off from the

MEX 180 to the Parque Natural Rio Celestún.

④ Parque Natural Rio Celestún Nature Park It is about 70 km (43 miles) to the small fishing village of Celestún on the Bahia de Campeche coast. In addition to the white, sandy beaches, the waterfowl living here are the main attraction. Fishermen offer boat trips through the mangroves and to a petrified forest on the Isla de Pájaros. The same route takes you back towards the MEX 180. In Uman the MEX 261 branches off towards Muna and Uxmal (60 km/37 miles).

⑤ Uxmal Archaeologists presume that the first stages of construction took place in the year AD 1. The majority of the buildings, however, date back to between the 7th and 10th centuries when parts of the peninsula were ruled from Uxmal. Uxmal is the best-known example of the Puuc civilization, represented by elongated buildings with attractive courtyards, facades decorated with stone mosaics and the conspicuous lack of cenotes (natural limestone pools) typical of this style. Indeed, it was the ability to build artificial cisterns that enabled the Mayans to settle in this arid region.

Opposite the entrance to Uxmal stands the 35-m (115-ft) 'Fortune Teller's Pyramid', with its oval foundation, dating from the 6th–10th centuries. The steep, 60° staircase up the pyramid has a safety chain for visitors to hold when climbing.

From Muna it is then around 40 km (25 miles) to the MEX 180.

1 Uxmal: The Palacio del Gobernador from the 9th–10th century is considered a highlight of Puuc architecture.

2 Chichén Itzá: The Warriors' Temple with Chac Mool in the foreground.

Top: The imposing 25-m-high (82-ft) pyramid Temple of Kukulcán in Chichén Itzá is often referred to as "El Castillo". On the summer and winter solstice, the sun shines on the pyramid in such a way that a shadow in the form of a snake falls on the steps, winding down to

meet a chiseled snake head at the bottom. Bottom: The most famous observatory of the Mayans, Caracol, is also in Chichén Itzá. The Mayans charted the exact path of the sun for agriculture. The observatory is also called "Las Monjas", or "The Snail", for its shell shape.

1

2

6 Campeche During the colonial era Campeche became an important port from which the Spanish shipped wood and other valuable raw materials back to Old Europe. The mighty city wall was reinforced with eight bastions (baluartes) to protect it from constant pirate attacks, a major risk at that time.

From this significant port town on the peninsula we then follow the MEX 180S to Champotón, where we turn onto the MEX 261 towards Francisco Escárcega further south.

7 Calakmul The detour to Calakmul in the Reserva de la Biósfera Calakmul is around 150 km (93 miles). The reserve protects the largest continuous tropical rainforest area in Mexico and is also host to a number of important Mayan sites – Balamkú, Becán, Xpujil and Calakmul. After around 110 km (68 miles), at Conhuas, a road turns off the two-lane MEX 186 south towards Calakmul. During the rainy season the 60-km (37-mile)

surfaced road, first built in 1993, is often passable only with four-wheel-drive vehicles.

Although it has not been extensively researched to date, this sprawling settlement, which was continuously inhabited from 500 to 1521, is one of the most important examples of a classic Mayan town and was declared a UNESCO World Heritage Site in 2002. Until the year 1000 Calakmul was the capital of a former kingdom. Thereafter it served merely as a ceremonial center. The 50-m (164-ft) pyramid is the highest in Mexico and from the top is a breathtaking view of these overgrown rainforest ruins. There are around 100 pillars spread around the site, but more valuable archaeological treasures such as the priceless jade masks have been moved to the museum in Campeche.

Back in Francisco Escárcega take the MEX 186 to Palenque.

8 Palenque These ruins, covering an area of 6 sq km (4 sq

mi), are about 12 km (7.5 miles) outside of town and surrounded by the last sicable area of rainforest on the peninsula. The town, which must have been an important trading center in the region, experienced its heyday between 600 and 800.

One important Mayan ruler is still known by name – Pacal the Great, whose reign coincided with one of the most splendid eras in Mayan history. Today only part of the site is accessible to visitors. Try to plan a whole day for it. Inside the most famous temple, the 20-m (66-ft) Templo de las Inscripciones (Temple of

the Inscriptions), sixty steps lead 25 m (83 ft) down into the crypt. Similar to the Egyptian pyramids, the step pyramids of Palenque were also the tombs of rulers. The most valuable possessions are now on display in the Museo Nacional de Antropologica in Ciudad de Mexico. Opposite the Temple of the Inscriptions is the El Palacio, where the royal family lived, while other accessible temples are located on the other side of the Otulum River.

One of the most important discoverers of ancient Mexican culture was the American John

Lloyd Stephens, who visited the Yucatán between 1839 and 1841. According to his report, when Stephens first visited Palenque, 'a single Indian foot-path' led to the archaeological site. He travelled all over the Yucatán with English draughts-man and architect Frederick Catherwood. Stephens recorded his impressions in travel journals while Catherwood captured his in drawings.

On the way from Palenque to San Cristóbal de las Casas it is worth making a stop at the Agua Azul National Park. The more than 500 waterfalls are es-pecially worthy of their name, 'blue water', during the dry pe-riod between April and May. They vary in height from 3 m (10 ft) to an impressive 50 m (164 ft).

Beyond Palenque the road climbs gradually into the moun-tainous area of Montañas del Norte de Chiapas.

⑨ San Cristóbal de las Casas

This lovely little town at an alti-tude of 2,100 m (6,890 ft) carries the name of the Spanish Bishop of Chiapas, who was especially committed to the interests of the indigenous peoples. Particu-larly noticeable are the low-slung buildings in the town, a result of constant fear of earth-quakes.

San Cristóbal is the center of one of Mexico's important co-coa-growing areas. The Mayans were already growing the wild plant as a monocrop before the arrival of the Europeans, and even used slave labour to work on their plantations. The strik-ing terrace-like fields on these steep slopes (sometimes at an angle of 45°) date all the way back to the Mayans who built rows of stones running diago-nally over the slope in order to fashion fields of up to 50 by 70 m (164 by 230 ft). The fields were enclosed by walls measur-ing over 1.5 m (5 ft) high.

Many visitors take trips from San Cristóbal into the outlying villages of the Chamula Indians, for example to San Júan Chamu-la (11 km/7 miles), or to Zinacan-tán, where the Tzotzil Indians live (8 km/5 miles).

Another worthwhile excursion from San Cristóbal is to Cañon El Sumidero, with fantastic views of gloriously coloured craggy cliffs that tower to heights of 1,000 m (3,281 ft). With a bit of luck you might even see crocodiles during a boat trip on the river.

From San Cristóbal to Ciudad de Guatemala the route follows the Pan-American Highway, known as the CA1 after the bor-der. Around 85 km (53 miles) south-east of San Cristóbal is Comitán de Dominguez. From there you can take an excursion to the Mayan site of Chinkultic. You will reach the border at Pa-so Hondo after another 80 km (50 miles). On the Guatemalan side a mountain road leads via

1 Cleared ruins in the north of the Palenque archaeological site.

2 In Palenque, nine terraces lead up to the Temple of the Inscriptions.

3 One of the many waterfalls in the Agua Azul National Park.

1

La Mesilla through the Sierra de los Cuchumatanes to Huehuetenango. The roads in the rugged mountainous regions of Guatemala are generally in bad condition and are often full of potholes. Turning off at Los Encuentros, Lago de Atitlan is one of the featured sights in these highlands.

🔟 **Lago de Atitlan** Three volcanoes – San Pedro (3,029 m/9,938 ft), Atitlan (3,535 m/11,598) and Toliman (3,158 m/10,361 ft) – are reflected in the water of this alpine lake, which lies at 1,560 m (5,118 ft). Alexander von Humboldt wrote of the beauty of this 130-sq-km (81-sq-mi) azure blue lake, describing it as 'the most beautiful lake in the world'. There are fourteen Indian villages located around the lake, some of which already existed prior to the arrival of the Spanish conquistadors.
Today the residents are farmers or make a living from selling traditional handicrafts. The famous Friday market in Sololá, high above the lake on the northern shore, is even frequented by

hordes of Indians from the surrounding areas. The largest settlement is Santiago Atitlan at the southern end of the lake. In 1955 the government declared the lake and surrounding mountains a national park.
At Los Encuentros a narrow road turns off towards Chichicastenango, 20 km (12 miles) further north.

🔟 **Chichicastenango** This town, lying at an altitude of 1,965 m (6,447 ft) is characterized by its classic white colonial architecture. In the pre-colonial era the town was an important Mayan trading center. Markets are the main attraction and draw residents from the surrounding areas in their colourful traditional costumes, who come to sell their textiles and carvings.
In 1540 a Spaniard erected the oldest building in the town on the ruins of a Mayan temple, the Santo-Tomás church. Each of the eighteen roads leading to it represents a month in the Mayan calendar, which comprised 18 months each with 20 days.

2

🔟 **Antigua** This village in Panchoytal is situated in a tectonically active region at the foot of three live volcanoes – Agua (3,766 m/12,356 ft), Fuego (3,763 m/12,346 ft) and Acatenango (3,975 m/13,042 ft). In 1541, mud-slides from Agua destroyed the town of Ciudad de Santiago de los Caballeros founded by the Spanish in 1527, but it was rebuilt further north in 1543. Numerous religious orders settled in this Central American capital where monasteries, schools and churches were erected. However, only parts of the Catedral de Santiago (1545) with its five naves have survived the earthquakes

of the subsequent centuries. Nuestra Señora la Merced is one of the most attractive examples of the Churrigueresque style. Together with the Palacio de los Capitanes Generales and the Palacio del Ayuntamiento, the Capuchin monastery Las Capuchinas is an impressive example of Spanish colonial architecture.
The town was destroyed by strong earthquakes in 1717 and 1773, but the Spanish rebuilt it as La Nueva Guatemala and it later became present-day Ciudad de Guatemala. The previous capital was then simply called Antigua. In 1979 the old city, which in the 18th century was

one of the most beautiful baroque ensembles of the Spanish colonial era, and which still retains a great deal of flair today, was declared a UNESCO World Heritage Site.

⑬ Ciudad de Guatemala The rebuilding of the residential town for the Spanish governor took place at a safer distance of 45 km (30 miles). Today, La Nueva Guatemala de la Asunción is still the economic and political center of Guatemala. It lies at 1,480 m (4,856 ft) and is the seat of several universities. The main sightseeing attractions include the cathedral (1782–1809), the National Palace (1939–1943) and

the Archaeological Museum. Another important Mayan site is located in Tazumal, not far from Santa Ana in El Salvador, roughly 200 km (124 miles) away.

From the capital it is about 150 km (93 miles) on the CA9 to Rio Hondo where the asphalt CA10 takes you via Zacapa, Chiguimula and Vado Hondo to the border post at El Florido.

About 12 km (7.5 miles) beyond the Guatemala-Honduras border is Copán. On the return journey along the same road, about 70 km (43 miles) beyond Rio Hondo, you reach another UNESCO World Heritage Site – the Mayan ruins of Quiriguá in the valley of the Motagua River.

⑭ Quiriguá This Mayan town on the lower Rio Motagua saw its heyday between 500 and 800. Its layout is very similar to that of Copá, only 50 km (31 miles) away. Explorer John Lloyd Stephens discovered Quiriguá in 1840.

Today the archaeological site at the edge of the Sierra del Espiritu Santo is still surrounded by thick jungle, and this is a major part of its attraction. The large mythical creatures carved in stone and the pillars measuring over 10 m (33 ft) in height, which constitute a high point of Mayan sculpture, are among the special attractions here. The highest pillar, E, is 10.5 m (34 ft) high and weighs 65 tonnes (71.5 tons).

Approximately 45 km (28 miles) beyond Quiriguá you leave the CA9 and turn to the north-west towards Lago de Izabal. The lake, 590 sq km (367 sq mi) in size, is surrounded by dense rainforest. Between the largest lake in Guatemala and the Rio Dulce, lined by rainforest, is the Spanish Fort Castillo de San Felipe. The fortress was originally

constructed in 1595 to defend the arsenals on the eastern shore of the lake from the repeated attacks of determined pirates plying the broad river.

The national road CA13 now crosses the foothills of the Sierra de Santa Cruz and continues via Semox into the lowlands of Petén. The small town of Flores on an island in Lago Petén Itzá is a good starting point for a visit to Tikal.

⑮ Tikal National Park This 576-sq-km (358-sq-mi) national park is surrounded by dense forest and includes one of the most important Mayan sites on the

1 The Toliman and San Pedro volcanoes form an impressive backdrop to Lago de Atitlan in the Guatemalan highlands.

2 Universidad de San Carlos (1763) in Antigua.

3 Relief of a high priest in the Quiriguá Archaeological Park, also home to the tallest Mayan pillars.

The god kings who ruled Mayan cities were honored with ornate columns. Even during their lifetime they took on not only the status of worldly rulers, but also the status of gods. The columns, which often recorded the date of birth, death and ascension to the throne, made

it possible for researchers to follow precisely the dynastic orders of the many city states, including here in Copán. The weaving motif was a popular one in Mayan art. It symbolized the woven mats on which the rulers sat.

peninsula. Together, the park and rainforest, one of the largest continuous forests in Central America with over 2,000 plant varieties, has been declared a UNESCO World Heritage Site. Between 600 BC and AD 900 as many as 55,000 people lived in Tikal. Today, many of the 4,000 temples, palaces, houses and playing fields are buried under the encroaching forest.

A climb up one of the pyramids, the most important of which are on the Gran Plaza, gives visitors an impressive view of the 16-sq-km (10-sq-mi) Tikal National Park. The Jaguar Temple, some 45 m (148 ft) high, houses a burial chamber where the ruler Ah Cacao lies at rest.

From Flores it is about 100 km (62 miles) to the border with Belize, and from there it is another 50 km (31 miles) to Belmopan, which has been the capital of Belize since 1970.

16 Guanacaste National Park
3 km (2 miles) north of Belmopan is the 20-ha (49-acre) national park named after the

large Guanacaste tree (Tubroos). It grows in the south of the park and is one of the largest tree types in Central America. The many tree species in the park also include mahogany, the national tree of Belize. South of Belmopan is the Blue Hole National Park, on the road to Dangriga.

17 Blue Hole National Park
This 2.3-ha (5.7-acre) national park is a popular leisure area for the residents of Belmopan. Large areas of the park contain cave formations and are covered by dense rainforest.

Sightseeing attractions include the 33-m (108-ft) collapsed crater that feeds a tributary of the Sibun River. It flows briefly above ground before disappearing into an extensive underground cave system. The 7.5-m (25-ft) 'blue hole' takes its name from its sapphire blue colour.

Also within the park is St Herman's Cave, used by the Mayans as evidenced by the ceramics, spears and torches that have been found inside. The next stop brings us back to the coast.

18 Belize City Until 1970, Belize City was the capital of the former British Honduras. Today it is still the largest city in the country as well as an important seaport. St John Cathedral, the oldest Anglican cathedral in Central America, was built in 1812 from bricks that sailing ships from Europe had used as ballast. The British Governor lived at Government House starting in 1814 (today it is the House of Culture museum). The city is an ideal base for excursions to the Belize Barrier Reef, a renowned diving paradise.

18 Belize Barrier Reef System
The 300-km (186-mile) Barrier

Reef is one of the longest in the northern hemisphere. The many islands and cays off the coast are covered with mangroves and palms. The cays that are within

1 Guanacaste National Park: The jaguar is the most well-known wild cat on the Yucatán Peninsula.

2 Tikal: Temple 1 is one of the most attractive pyramid tombs of the late classic Mayan period. It rises about 45 m (148 ft) above the central square. Around 55,000 people lived here in the town's heyday. It was abandoned in the 10th or 11th century.

Spectacular diving territory: the Blue Hole in Belize's Barrier Reef is 80 km (50 miles) east of Belize City. About 10,000 years ago a cave collapsed here as land sank into the sea. The hole has a diameter of 300 m (984 ft) and is 125 m (410 ft) deep.

Hidden in the lowland mist is the mysterious outline of a Mayan temple pyramid in Petén. Located in the evergreen rainforests of what is now north-eastern Guatemala, Petén was one of the most important cities in pre-Columbian (before Columbus) Mayan culture. Of the rough

ly 4,000 buildings that once filled this metropolis, only a few have been preserved, or even found – the tropical forests have covered most of it in centuries of dense vegetation. The so-called Temple II with its high roof ridge sits atop a pyramid out on the Gran Plaza (above).

reach include Ambergris Cay some 58 km (36 miles) north of Belize City as well as the Turneffe Islands. The reef's main attraction is its underwater world, with visibility of up to 30 m (98 ft), the bird reserve, Half Moon Cay and the Blue Hole, a massive collapsed cave.

20 Altun Ha The ruins of Altun Ha are close to the village of Rockstone Pond. It is postulated that this Mayan ceremonial center was originally settled over 2,000 years ago. The Mayans built up much of their trading around Altun Ha. The most valuable finds from Altun Ha include a jade head of the Mayan Sun god that weighs 4.5 kg (9.9 lbs). Via Orange Walk the road continues through the lowlands of Belize to the Mexican port town of Chetumal and along the second largest lake in Mexico, Laguna de Bacalar (MEX 307), to Felipe Carrillo Puerto. Here an access road branches off to the Sian Ka'an biosphere reserve.

21 Tulum This ancient Mayan town is a popular destination on the peninsula, primarily due to its spectacular location on a cliff overlooking the sea. The conquistadors were impressed by its imposing and protective walls. Five narrow gates opened the way into town. Outside the walls there were two ancient Mayan temple sites north of town.

Tulum has always had a safe port from which pilgrims in the pre-Columbian era once travelled to the island of Cozumel to honour the Moon god Ixchel with sacrifices.

After 1540 Tulum was engulfed by tropical vegetation and forgotten until 1840. From Tulum there is a road leading to the small fishing village of Punta Allen in the Reserva de la Biósfera Sian Ka'an. In the forest 48 km (30 miles) north-west of Tulum you can visit another ruins complex – Cobá.

22 Cobá You can reach the site of the ruins on the well-made road in half an hour. US archaeologists began the first excavations of the complex (210 sq km/130 sq mi) in the 1920s, and further excavation projects that are still going on today began in the 1970s. Cobá also has a pyramid. From the top you can see smaller pyramids, temples, a series of procession streets, a playing field, pillars with life-size images of kings and queens, and of course dense forest. In Cobá you can see peccaris (wild pigs), iguanas, tortoises and the colourful toucan.

The 130-km (81-mile) stretch of coast between Tulum and Cancún is also known as the 'Mayan Riviera'. Small villages and bays such as Puerto Morelos provide swimming and diving opportunities for water enthusiasts. The seaside resort of Playa del Carmen is only a few kilometers south of the more upmarket and touristy Cancún, which is the start and end point of this round trip through the Yucatán Peninsula.

1 Belize's main attraction is the Barrier Reef. At just less than 300 km (186 miles) in length, it is the longest barrier reef in the western hemisphere. Divers will find unique coral, good visibility and more than 350 types of fish. Hundreds of small islands (cays) are scattered along the length of the reef.

2 Never-ending white Caribbean beaches with crystal-clear water characterize the north-east coast of the Yucatán Peninsula, also known as the 'Mayan Riviera'.

Mérida The 'white town' was founded in the 16th century. At its center are the Montejo Palast and the cathedral, one of the first sacral buildings in Mexico.

Chichén Itzá The highlights of the complex in the northern part of the Yucatán Peninsula are the Kukulcán and El Castillo pyramids, probably constructed by the Mayas and the Tolteken. Close by is a deep cenote, an underground limestone well from which water rises and forms a pool.

Cancún With its magnificent beaches and tropical climate the former fishing village in the north-east of the Yucatán has become Mexico's most popular holiday destination. With 20,000 beds and all-night entertainment options, more than 2.5 million tourists visit the giant hotel town each year.

Uxmal The 'Fortune Teller's Pyramid' is a highlight of Mayan architecture. The name dates back to the Spanish era but does not have anything to do with the actual purpose of the construction.

Tulum Situated on a cliff over the Caribbean Sea south of Cancún, the ruins of this Mayan town are easily accessible for even the laziest of beachcombers.

Palenque This archaeological site in the middle of the rainforest is among the most attractive in Mexico. Many of the buildings date from the reign of King Pacal and his son, Chan Balum.

Lago de Atitlan This lake in the highlands of Guatemala (1,560 m/5,118 ft) is tucked between the San Pedro, Atitlan and Toliman volcanoes.

Altun Ha The largest archaeological site in Belize is made up of two plazas with temple and residential complexes. Important jade artefacts have been found here, including a magnificent axe.

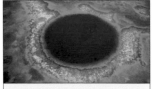

The Blue Hole In the Lighthouse Reef Atoll off the coast of Belize is one of the most beautiful coral reefs in the world. The Blue Hole has a diameter of 300 m (984 ft) and a depth of 125 m (410 ft).

Antigua The Spanish Governor used to rule Central America from this Guatemalan town. A number of baroque churches and palaces from the Spanish colonial era survived the earthquakes of 1717 and 1773, and are definitely worth seeing.

Tazumal Close to Santa Ana in El Salvador is the country's oldest Mayan settlement. The ruins of the 10-sq-km (6-sq-mi) complex with five temples were first cleared only 40 years ago.

Quiriguá The tallest and most artistic Mayan pillars can be found here. Their multitude of shapes evokes associations with the surrounding rainforest.

Tikal These ruins, buried in the jungle in the heart of the Mayan lowlands in present-day Guatemala, have inspired awe in many a visitor. Gustav Bernoulli discovered the ruins in 1877.

Mexico and Central America

The Panamericana from Mexico to Panama

Deserts, tropical forests, volcanoes, and high peaks, sites cleared by ancient cultures, modern buildings and the legacy of colonialism – the route from Mexico to Panama has pretty much the full palette of highlights that Central America has to offer.

From its starting-point in the US American/Mexican border town of Mexicali to its final destination at the Panama Canal, our route follows the course of the Panamericana for long stretches through Central America. It crosses seven countries – Mexico, Guatemala, El Salvador, Honduras, Nicaragua, Costa Rica, and Panama – whose scenery and culture exhibit as many contrasts as they have points in common.

All were influenced by the great Central American civilizations of the Maya, Zapotec, Toltec, and Aztec peoples and the imposing buildings which they left behind, but also by their Spanish conquerors and the missionaries who Christianized the continent. These, too, created extraordinary buildings in their newly founded colonial cities, and all have been influenced to a greater or lesser degree by the United States, whose lifestyle is admired, adored, and hated in equal measure; tourists from America are greeted with open arms, but its political influence

in the region, which has been steadily increasing since the turn of the 19th century, is often viewed with suspicion.

Northern Mexico is a semi-desert. The Baja California peninsula is hot, dry, and inhospitable, like much of the Pacific coast of northern Mexico, and things only really change at the Tropic of Cancer; south of here, the coast is greener and the

A folk dance performance in the city of Oaxaca in southern Mexico.

A remote island with an idyllic beach: the desert island of Los Grillos, on the Archipiélago de San Blas.

A hotel terrace on Acapulco Bay. The magnificent location, miles of sandy beaches, and permanent good weather have made this Mexican coastal resort a dream leisure destination.

mountains closer to the sea, increasing the precipitation levels. This is the most beautiful stretch of the Mexican Pacific coast, with resorts such as Acapulco and Puerto Ángel. Here we leave the coast to thread our way through the Sierra Madre del Sur and explore the southern highlands of the Guatamalan border. Guatamala is a country of volcanoes, with more than 30 peaks, some of which reach heights of 4,000 m (13,200 feet). Many towns have been destroyed in eruptions and earthquakes, but the lava is so fertile that the highlands often resemble a sea of flowers.

We pass through El Salvador quickly; Central America's smallest country is also the only one with no access to the Pacific or the Caribbean. Nicaragua follows, unique in Central America in being the only country to be named after a Native American chieftain: Nicarao was the leader of the Niquirians when the Spanish landed here in 1522. Costa Rica is an exceptional case in Central America; after the last civil war in 1948, the Costa Ricans voted to abolish the army and the country has since been able to develop in peace. The tourist industry has kept pace, as the land is not short of natural beauty.

Panama lies at the end of the route. Best-known for the canal, it was a department of Colombia for many years and has long since fallen under US influence. The country can boast a number of islands and islets in the Pacific and the Caribbean, and an impressive range of mountains.

The colonial era cathedral in Antigua, the former capital of Guatamala.

329

This contrasting route through seven Central American countries begins in northern Mexico, and a choice must soon be made between the deserts of the Baja California peninsula or the west coast of Mexico on the Gulf of California. The later journey toward Panama will take visitors through the cities of many ancient cultures and impressive scenery.

1 Mexicali This faceless city of 800,000 inhabitants is the capital of the Mexican state of Baja California Norte. The only original feature is the name, a combination of Mexico and California, much like the corresponding US city of Calexico just over the border. US day trippers who cross into Mexico for shopping or business provide most of the city's income. A detour to the Baja California peninsula is possible at this point before moving on (see right-hand page).
The route heads east from Mexicali following the Mexican highway 2 through to the edge of the Desierto Altar and the junction with highway 15. Follow this south to Hermosillo,

near Guaymas on the Gulf of California, before journeying on to Ciudad Obregón, Los Mochis, and finally San Ignacio. To continue south, a choice must be made: is it better to take the faster autopista past endless fields or the old road with its dense forests, mesas, and bizarre rock formations? The latter route will take you through the town of Culiacan before hugging the Sierra Madre Occidental with its idyllic views.

2 Mazatlán The best view of this big city and its miles of beaches, in a beautiful location on a little peninsula in the north, is from a 160-m (525-

foot) lighthouse which also serves as a viewing tower. Mazatlán is a popular destination for package visitors from both Mexico and the USA. There are excellent water sports facilities and it has also become a

rendezvous for game anglers, who pursue a range of fish, including orcas.

1 Estuary near San Ignacio on the Baja California Peninsula.

The largely unexplored Baja California peninsula runs 1,150 km (715 miles) from north to south parallel to the Mexican coast and divides the Gulf of California from the Pacific. Cactuses shrouded in coastal fog - an atmospheric image of the barren desert.

The rocky cliffs of Cabo San Lucas at the southern tip of Baja California rise up steeply from the sea. The southern half of the peninsula is composed of spectacular mountain scenery whose loftiest peak, the Picacho de la Laguna, reaches a height of 2,163 m (7,097 feet).

Surrounded by the Pacific and the Gulf of California, Baja California's coastline varies greatly. The climate is hot and despite its proximity to the sea, the vegetation consists largely of desert plants. Politically, Baja California is divided into two thinly populated states.

3 Puerto Vallarta Although Puerto Vallarta subsists entirely from tourism, it has retained some of its old charm. The high-rise buildings are restricted to the beaches to the north and the Old Town offers narrow, winding streets, lots of palm trees, and a nice promenade on the beach. Between mid-December and early March, the town is popular with nature fans who makes trips from here to Banderas Bay to watch humpback whales mating and giving birth. The road to the immediate south of here is not especially exciting, although a detour from the coast to the little town of Colima to see the twin peaks of the Colima volcano (3,960 m/12,992 feet and 4,330 m.14,206 feet) is recommended.

4 Acapulco Acapulco's fame rests on its unique location, with two peninsulas encircling the wide sweep of a bay and a host of islands, the largest of which is the uninhabited Isla La Roqueta.

The white beaches and azure-blue waters made Acapulco one of Mexico's most idyllic destinations in the early 20th century. By the time Hollywood stars and starlets had arrived in the 1930s and 1940s – Tarzan actor Johnny Weissmüller spent the later part of his life here – the town was ready for the systematic development as a destination for mass tourism carried out especially under president Míguel Alemán from 1946 onward. The city's 700,000 inhabitants now live principally from tourism and the seafront promenade is lined with hotel complexes and apartment blocks.

The city center is spared the attentions and impact of international tourism, however – the Zócalo, the central square upon which the most important municipal buildings such as City Hall are located, is a peaceful, traffic-free island of cafés and restaurants. Enjoy the views of the cathedral and the bustle of everyday life, and only a few

paces away you will find the Fuerte de San Diego, a fort built in 1615 and restored after an 18th-century earthquake. It is the only remnant of Acapulco's colonial past, when the town became one of the hubs of world trade – the Spanish had been using the bay as an anchorage since before the mid-16th century as part of the trade routes with East Asia. Spices, silks, and porcelain were brought ashore here before being transported by pack mule to

Veracruz on the Gulf of Mexico and on to Europe. The city and its trade routes flourished in equal measure until the early 19th century and the collapse of the Spanish empire, at which point other routes to East Asia became more attractive. Built during Acapulco's heyday, the fort has a magnificent view of the bay and it houses an interesting museum with ample information about local history. Acapulco is most famous for its daredevil divers, however – sev-

eral times a day, the clavadistas, the world-famous cliff-jumpers, will hurl themselves from cliffs more than 40 m (130 feet) high into a narrow Pacific gorge. South of Acapulco, the route threads it way though verdant, sub-tropical scenery (running parallel to the Pacific without offering any particularly good sea views) before reaching a series of beach and leisure resorts of various sizes – Puerto Escondido is typical of these – with no large hotel complexes but a good tourist infrastructure and a selection of smaller hotels and B&Bs. Puerto Angel is considerably quieter and on some beaches you can still find places where you have a sense of privacy. None of these are international tourist centers, but rather the places where Mexicans go for a break. The route branches off into the highlands at Puerto Angel, snaking through 235 km (146 miles) of endless hairpin bends among the wild scenery of the Sierra Miahuatlán before reaching Oaxaca (see sidebar, page right). Here, the route squeezes through the narrow Istmo de Tehuantepec to Tuxtla Gutiérrez.

⑤ Cañón del Sumidero One of Mexico's great natural spectacles is to be found not far from Tuxtla Gutiérrez; the Rio Grijalva has carved a canyon almost 1,000 m (3,280 feet) deep into the mountains here and you can see it either from above – there is a road leading to various observation points, of which the most spectacular is El Robar – or from below, from a boat on the river (beware of the crocodiles!). Leaving Tuxtla Gutiérrez, the route climbs into the mountains in a series of hairpin bends. The long trip – it will take two hours to cover just 60 km (37 miles) – is compensated for by the magnificent views, and at an elevation of 2,200 m (7,220 feet) you will eventually reach San Cristóbal de las Casas, whose tranquil streets and cathedral make it one of the most romantic and beautiful little towns in Mexico. Head briefly toward Palenque to make a flying visit to Cascadas de Agua Azul (Blue-water Falls).

⑥ San Cristóbal de las Casas Surrounded by dense forest on the Guatemalan border, this colonial-era city has become a rendezvous for backpackers from all over the world and yet

1 Acapulco Bay: still an idyllic leisure destination despite all the apartment blocks.

2 Organized chaos: a bustling market stall in San Cristóbal de las Casas.

3 A colonial jewel: the pretty town center of San Cristóbal de las Casas.

4 The Cascadas de Agua Azul are just one of the water features in the national park.

1

has lost none of its charm. Many come here for the mild, but rainy climate at this altitude, or for the vibrant local dress of the ubiquitous indigenous population; intrusive photography is frowned upon here, and those determined to find a bright subject for their pictures should visit the collection of costumes from the local culture at the Casa Sergio Castro.

San Cristóbal's skyline is a mixture of squat, whitewashed houses with red-tiled roofs, colonial townhouses, and baroque churches. There is a particularly picturesque group of houses on the Zócalo and the lavish gilt interior of the 16th-century church of Santo Domingo is recommended, as is the nearby market. Interesting museums in the area include the Museo de la Medicina Maya, which offers an insight into the mysterious world of traditional local medicine, and the Museo Na-Bolom ("House of the Jaguar") founded by two Danish researchers who specialize in

the archeology of the Chiapas region.

❼ **Chinkultic** Near Comitán, a little side road branching off north toward Tziscao will bring you to the small excavation site of the Maya ruins of Chinkultic. The particular charm of this tranquil place lies in how few visitors it attracts. Several typical 6th- to 8th-century Maya pyramids have been discovered here, although most are smothered in undergrowth, and from the tops of those that can be climbed you will enjoy a broad, panoramic view of the mountains and the nearby little National Park of Lagos de Montebello with its forests and 58 lakes of various sizes.

You will reach the border about 80 km (50 miles) beyond Comitán at the little village of Cuauhtémoc. There is not much to see here apart from the border post, and this is also true of La Mesilla, the first town you reach in Guatemala. Following a winding road past the moun-

2

tains and volcanoes of the Sierra de los Cuchumatanes you will pass through Quezaltenango, Guatemala's second-largest conurbation, which was destroyed in an earthquake in 1902 and has since been rebuilt as a modern city, before reaching the country's first city of real interest.

❽ **Lago de Atitlán** Lago de Atitlán is located south of Chichicastenango at an elevation of about 1,500 m (4,920 feet). The lake is about 30 km

(19 miles) long and 16 km (10 miles) across, and is one of the most beautiful in Central America, being ringed by three volcanoes with peaks over 3,000 m (9,800 feet).

❾ **Chichicastenango** This town was once a religious site and a trade hub for the local indigenous population.

The town market continues to be influential today: people come from the surrounding towns to sell products such as beautiful woven woolen fabrics

and leather, clay, and wooden craft objects.

⑩ Antigua Guatemala's old capital was one of the richest cities in the world in the 17th century and some sense of this still remains, even though Antigua was destroyed in an earthquake in 1717 and again in 1773. Several beautiful colonial buildings from its heyday nonetheless survive, including parts of the cathedral, the church of La Merced, and the parliament building on the

Plaza de Armas, which was only built in the 18th century; Antigua ceased to be the capital shortly afterward.

⑪ Guatemala City (Ciudad de Guatemala) Guatemala was established as the new capital in 1776 and has been the hub of the country ever since. It is home to about one and a half million people and is growing fast – all the country's universities and governmental departments are based here, as well as the most important companies.

The five-naved cathedral, a squat building dating back to the city's foundation, was completed in the classic colonial style with two spires flanking its façade and a dome above the central nave. The classical National Palace is of a similar age and both buildings were intended to emphasize the importance of the new capital. The collection of Mayan cultural objects in the National Archeology and Ethnology Museum is worth a visit, but nothing else should detain you – apart from perhaps the border guards – from proceeding to the next city.

⑫ San Salvador El Salvador's capital is the political and commercial hub of the whole country. A fertile valley with a mild climate prompted the Spanish to found the city here in 1525, but there is not much else going for the location: earthquakes and volcanic eruptions have ravaged the area and destroyed the city on several occasions. Little remains of the colonial-era

architecture and the major tourist attraction is the bustling market district.

The next country on this route through Central America is Honduras, but we pass through this narrow strip of coastland without stopping on our way to Nicaragua.

⑬ Managua About a third of Nicaragua's population lives in the capital and although all the major businesses and public institutions are based here, the cultural heart of the country lies to the north at León, the birth-

1 The waters of Lago de Atitlán, with the Atitlán volcano in the background.

2 The yellow façade of the 18th-century church of La Merced in Antigua (Guatemala) is decorated with lavish white stucco work.

3 A riot of hues and aromas: the market hall at Chichicastenango.

A chain of volcanic mountains crosses Costa Rica from the north-west to the south-east. The surrounding soil is extremely fertile and the slopes are overgrown with dense vegetation. The twin craters of Poás, a 2,704-m (8,871-foot) volcano, are both filled with water; one lake

is clear and cold, the other (see above) is lower-lying with a diameter of 1,300 m (4,260 feet), and its acidic waters can reach depths of 300 m (1,000 feet). Sulphurous gases rise continuously from the bowels of the volcano, occasionally shooting water into the air like a geyser.

1

place of the poet Rubén Darío. Managua has been badly damaged in earthquakes at several points in its history, most recently in 1972. The twin towers and the façade are all that remain of the colonial-style cathedral – the nave behind them has collapsed completely. The restored National Palace is now used as a museum. Managua is situated on the shores of Lake Managua, the second-largest lake in the country (1,042 sq. km/402 sq. miles).

⑭ Lake Nicaragua Lying further to the south, Lake Nicaragua is 148 km (92 miles) long, 55 km (34 miles) wide and about eight times the area of Lake Managua – its size makes what is the largest lake in Central America look more like the sea.. There are more than 300 islands on the lake, including the Islas de Solentiname, idyllic islets where numerous artists have taken up residence. Nicaragua's renowned naïve art flourished here in the 1980s and the poet and priest Ernesto Cardenal also

founded a Christian community. The lake's largest island is the Isla de Ometepe with its perfectly formed volcano peak, the 1,610-m (5,282-foot) Concepción. Lake Nicaragua flows into the Caribbean through the Río San Juan.

The southern shore of Lake Nicaragua is close the border with Costa Rica, a nation which has invested massively in tourism in recent decades, becoming one of the most popular destinations in Central America. Being increasingly concerned with promoting ecological tourism, the government has designated large areas of the country as nature reserves. The first national park was established in 1969 and there are now about 20, accounting for more than a quarter of the country's total surface area; the Panamericana passes the first of them shortly after crossing the border.

⑮ Rincón de la Vieja Volcano National Park The Rincón de la Vieja volcano (1,916 m/6,286

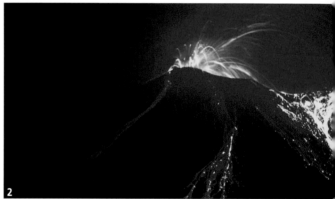

2

feet) lies to the east of our route, surrounded by national park it is named for. Its acidic crater lake is about 250 m (820 feet) across and the volcano is still extremely active, erupting most recently in 1995 and 1998. The national park covers about 14,000 ha (54 sq. miles) of varying vegetation zones from tropical rainforest to dry areas at elevations above 700 m (2,300 feet).

⑯ Arenal Volcano A short distance later at Las Cañas, the

road forks to the east via Tilarán to reveal the perfectly formed cone of the Arenal Volcano. The volcano, one of the most active in the world, is about 1,633 m (5,358 feet) high, although constant eruptions in recent years have added to this figure – lava regularly flows down its slopes into the valley and glowing rocks are thrown into the air. The best time to see this impressive spectacle is at night, and tours with expert guides can be booked in the village of La Fortuna de San Carlos.

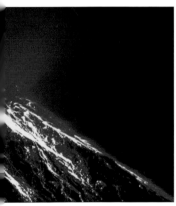

17 **Puntarenas** If you enjoy swimming, this is the place for you. The beaches of Puntarenas ("sandy point") are especially popular with the residents of nearby San José, the capital, who frequently spend their weekends here. They also know the most beautiful spot: the Gulf of Nicoya with its islands and islets of spectacular natural beauty is a haven for swimmers.

18 **Parque Nacional Manuel Antonio** Puntarenas is a good place from which to explore the Manuel Antonio National Park. With an area of only 7 sq. km (3 sq. miles) it is the smallest in the country, but the fine white sand of its beaches and the turquoise water of its picturesque bays, perfect for swimming, have made it one of the most popular. As many as 350 plant species, 109 mammals, and 184 different kinds of bird have been recorded here, but besides the dense vegetation the species you are most likely to see are waterfowl such as brown pelicans and yellow-crowned night herons, or smaller songbirds, lizards, and black iguanas. The best view of the whole park is to be had from a vantage point known as the Mirador which is reached by marked paths.

19 **San José** Everything is close together in Costa Rica and you will soon reach San José, the capital. The largest city in the country is home to about 350,000 people, with about the same number again living in the satellite suburbs. Founded as "Villa Nueva" by the Spanish in 1755, it remained an insignificant village for many years until 1824, when president Juan Mora Fernández moved the seat of government here from the old capital Cartago. Subsequent growth was boosted still further by the success of the local coffee plantations after 1840. As San José was only really developed in the 19th century it is missing the usual Spanish colonial-era buildings – the cathedral is classical and the Teatro Nacional, the finest building in the city, was built in 1897 in homage to the Grand Opera in Paris, financed with a surtax on coffee exports. Visitors should not miss the Gold Museum in the Banco Central, whose exhibits include small models of reptiles made by the indigenous peoples in solid gold, or the National Museum with its comprehensive collection of historical and archeological exhibits illustrating the country's history.

A longish detour takes us from San José to the Caribbean coast: head south-east out of town on the Ruta 10 and you will soon reach Cartago. Founded in 1563, the town is one of Costa Rica's oldest and was the capital until 1823. It is now the nation's most famous pilgrimage site (see sidebar, page right). The Basílica de Nuestra Señora de los Angeles (Basilica of Our Lady of the Angels) was built in 1926 when its predecessor was destroyed in an earthquake. Follow Ruta 10 for another 165 km (103 miles) through the mountains to Puerto Limón ("Port Lemon") and the Caribbean.

20 **Puerto Limón** The dock area here is one of the most important in the country, exporting mainly coffee and bananas (but not many lemons!); this is the best place from which to ex-

1 The most popular bathing spot in Costa Rica: the idyllic beaches of the Manuel Antonio National Park.

2 The Arenal volcano is one of the most active in the world, with an almost constant lava flow.

The many hues and varieties of Costa Rica's tropical vegetation. Dense cloud forest covers the mountain slopes of the Reserva Santa Elena (top), but the lush and seemingly impenetrable rainforest on the flanks of the Poas volcano reveals the occasional clearing (bottom).

There is a huge variety of Caribbean and Pacific fauna in Costa Rica's rainforests, and some five percent of all the species on earth are represented here such as keel-billed toucans, red-eyed tree frogs, green iguanas, tree boas, coatis, and three-toed sloths (top to bottom).

plore the local beaches or the Tortuguero National Park further up the coast to the north. The name of the park is derived from tortuga, the Spanish word for turtle, and translated literally, it means "the place where the turtles come from." These 25 km (15.5 miles) of Caribbean beach form one of the most famous hatching grounds for the green turtle in the western Caribbean. The females dig a hole in the sand in which to lay their eggs and the hatchlings emerge a few months later. Their sex is determined partly by the depth at which the eggs are buried and partly by the weather – at certain temperatures, most or all will develop as females. Returning to San José, the road continues in a southeasterly direction through Costa Rica's central highlands. After entering Panama you will gradually be approaching the narrowest point of the isthmus between North and South America. At David, the first town of any note, there is a

road branching off to the north which will take you to the cross-border La Amistad ("friendship") National Park, run in conjunction with Costa Rica.

The little town of Boquete, about three hours by automobile from David, is the best base for excursions into the mountains of north-western Panama, not least to see the volcanic cone of Chiriquí (3477 m/11,407 feet), the country's highest mountain. About halfway to the capital, the Panamericana passes the Azuero peninsula; the south-western portion of this tongue of land is the driest area in Panama and the location of the semi-arid Parque Nacional Sarigua (about 8,000 ha/31 sq. miles).

㉑ Panama City Thanks to the canal, Panama's capital is also its largest commercial hub – four out of every ten businesses in the country are based here and 60 percent of the workforce is employed here. The city continues to grow, spreading along

some 10 km (6? miles) of the Pacific coast, and nearly one in three of Panama's population of three million lives in the outlying suburbs. Panama City was originally founded in 1519 on a site about 10 km (6? miles) to the east of the modern city center (Casco), but after this settlement was destroyed by the British pirate Henry Morgan, the city was rebuilt on its current site. Preserved as a ruin, the old town was listed as a UNESCO World Heritage Site in 2003.

Besides the central plaza with its cathedral, town hall, and episcopal palace, there are also several monasteries to admire; Panama City offers a palette of the most varied cultural, ethnic, and architectural influences, while the skyline of its modern districts are dominated by high-rise buildings. A detour to Archipiélago de San Blas is recommended from Panama City.

㉒ Archipiélago de San Blas The Archipiélago de San Blas, a chain of some 365 islands and

islets in the Caribbean, can be reached by boat or by plane – a 30-minute flight will take you to coral islands with magnificent white sandy beaches.

There is a community of about 25,000 indigenous Kuna people living on the islands, barely a tenth of which have any permanent population at all. The Kuna have declared their region semi-autonomous and some of the islands are closed to visitors. Apart from tourism, they still live on hunting and fishing. The best-known of the San Blas Islands, the Isla El Porvenir, has been developed for tourism, as have Sapibenega, Wichub Wala, and Okuptupu.

Visiting the southern province of Daríen is not recommended at all – the areas of jungle near the Colombian border are a hotbed of drug dealers and smugglers.

1 Fishing boats against the Panama City skyline.

Hermosillo Highlights of the state capital of Sonora include the neoclassical cathedral and the 19th-century parliament building.

Baja California The sparsely populated Baja California peninsula is some 1,150 km (715 miles) long. Its charming landscape includes such features as the El Vizcaino Biosphere Reserve (image).

Mazatlán Located on a peninsula, this resort is extremely popular with water sports enthusiasts and game fishermen. The sights include the El Faro lighthouse and the historic Teatro Angela Peralta.

Puerto Vallarta The church of Nuestra Señora de Guadelupe is situated on the main square of the charming Old Town of Puerto Vallarta.

San Cristóbal de las Casas This Mexican town near the Guatemalan border has a picturesque skyline and should not be missed by anyone wishing to see authentic indigenous culture.

San Salvador San Salvador's capital is located in a fertile region ringed by mighty volcanoes. The main attraction is the market area.

Chichicastenango What was once a religious site for the indigenous people is now a mercantile center of national importance. The image shows the market hall.

Acapulco Wonderfully located in the sweep of a wide bay, this Mexican city became a dream leisure destination for the international jet set in the early 20th century.

Antigua The old capital of Guatemala grew very rich before being destroyed by an earthquake in the 18th century. The image shows the cathedral.

Managua Nicaragua's capital has been plagued by earthquakes and in places can look a little battered – many of the buildings, including recent constructions, have been badly damaged. Murals brighten up the streets.

Parque Nacional Manuel Antonio The glorious beaches in this tiny (7 sq. km/2? sq. miles) Costa Rican national park, where the rainforest reaches almost to the ocean, are extremely popular.

Panama City The capital of Panama has a rather American-looking skyline (image). The Old Town has been a UNESCO World Heritage Site since 2003.

Cuba

Cigars, Rum, and Revolution

Miles of gleaming white beaches, a treasure trove of underwater riches for divers, tropical rainforests, colonial-era cities, and mercurial, honest people who approach the shortcomings of their socialist economy with a creative spirit of improvisation – these are just some of the attractions of the largest island in the Caribbean.

Our circumnavigation of the island begins in Havana, the much-lauded capital of Cuba, vibrating day and night to the rhythms of son and the rumba. Restored baroque palaces compete to catch the eye of the tourists in the city center, pensioners and young couples watch patient anglers on the Malecón, and the imperious Castillo El Morro looks down over the narrow port entrance. The route heads east through the sleepy little town of Matanzas and the sugar cane and tobacco plantations of Santa Clara, a town of great importance during the revolution. It was here that Che Guevara (1928–1967) won a decisive victory over the dictator Batista, and the mortal remains of this great revolutionary, who is still passionately revered in Cuba, were buried here in 1997. Eastern Cuba is famed not just for its heroic past – truly idyllic beaches such as Cayo Coco, Cayo Sabinal, and Guardalavaca also lie

only a few miles to the north of our main route. Beach tourists will find most hotels on peninsulas or little islands (cayos) just off the coast. Cuba's tropical coast and the little colonial

Tobacco plantation in Viñalestal.

town of Baracoa are surrounded by the mountains of the Sierra del Cristal and the Alturas de Baracoa, while the jungle in the Parque Nacional Alejandro Humboldt is dense and lush, thanks to the heavy rainfall there. The furthest south-eastern reaches of the island are a complete contrast; cactuses and agave plants are often the only vegetation in this sterile promontory.

Santiago de Cuba is considered the island's musical capital and also its dark heart. The proportion of the black population is particularly high here and the son is melancholy and atmospheric as nowhere else. Fidel Castro and Che Guevara both sought refuge in the mountains of the Sierra Maestra to the south-east and from here

The center of Havana is a mixture of colonial gems and the buildings of a socialist capital.

Cuba sways to the thrilling rhythms of son, as here on the Plaza Central in the heart of Trinidad beside Casa de la Trova, a traditional music bar.

guerilleros drove the dictatorial Batista out of the country. The route passes through Bayamo, Camagüey, and Sancti Spiritus, three pretty little colonial-era towns, before looping back to the west. As the coast is very marshy here, the route runs deep inland, only approaching the sea again at Trinidad.

Trinidad has retained its historic charm like no other Cuban city, and its narrow streets, lined with houses painted in pastel shades, echo to the strumming of guitars and the chatter of claves. Cienfuegos, nestling in a deep, sheltered bay, exudes colonial flair even though it is a modern industrial port city; the Castillo de Jagua watches over it and its fairytale Palacio Valle. The Playa Girón, the Bay of Pigs, the scene of a failed invasion by

Cuban exiles in 1961, lies to the west. The adjoining marshy Peninsula de Zapata is criss-crossed with channels which are home to numerous crocodiles, both wild and farmed. The beaches and diving areas on the Isla de Juventud are reached most quickly and easily by plane from Havana.

The last section of our round trip takes us to the picturesque Valle de Viñales at the western end of Cuba, where the finest varieties of tobacco on the island grow. Densely overgrown karst hills (of limestone eaten away by water, and known here as mogotes) lend the scenery a particular charm. The fields around the tobacco town of Pinar del Río are thickly planted with lush green tobacco plants; tobacco leaves hang on drying

racks in the blistering sun before eventually being hand-rolled into valuable puros in cigar factories. The trip round the island comes to an end as we return to Havana.

Pinar del Río: Che lives – the revolutionary is revered like a saint in Cuba.

347

Vintage cars on parade in the heart of Havanna: The cars here, which are ripe for museum, are prettily spruced up with much care and still serve as taxis. On the streets you can find cars from the first half of the 20th century in magnificent conditions, which takes you back in history and feel

the old atmosphere of the cities. More than 60,000 American cars made in the 1940s and 1950s are still in full use and for many people are their only way of transport in this Caribbean island. In any other country they would be on show in a museum or belong to a millionaire's collection

1

Cuba from west to east and back again: this 2,600-km (1,610-mile) trip round the island will take you past the idyllic beaches of the north and the greenery of the north-east, and from bustling Santiago de Cuba on the south coast through little colonial towns like Trinidad to the Valle de Viñales in the west, as a final scenic high-point before returning to the capital.

1 **Havana (La Habana)** See pages above.

Cuba's capital is a varied city of fascinating colonial-era architecture and has been listed as a UNESCO World Heritage Site. The Old Town with its predominantly Spanish baroque buildings and the sophisticated suburb of Vedado are just two of the city's many faces.

Follow the coast road past the Playa del Este, a beach popular with the locals, and head east toward Matanzas. The golden sandy beaches are a good opportunity to experience how Cubans relax, and they are especially crowded at the weekend when sun-seekers pour in.

2 **Matanzas** Matanzas is known as a "city of bridges" because of the two rivers which flow into the sea here. The Museo Farmacéutico's herbarium in the historic Old Town's romantic Parque Libertad should not be missed; a married couple called Triolet, both doctors, opened a drugstore here in 1882, augmenting the knowledge they had brought from Europe with the wisdom and experience of healers from Africa. The recently restored Teatro Sauto, also built in 1882, is one of the most beautiful theater buildings on the island and can seat an audience of 700. Matanzas is a good base for an excur-

Travel Information

Route profile
Route length: about 2,600 km (1,610 miles)
Time required: 18–21 days
Start and destination: Havana
Route (main locations):
Havana, Matanzas, Santa Clara, Holguín, Guantánamo, Baracoa, Santiago de Cuba, Bayamo, Camagüey, Sancti Spiritus, Trinidad, Cienfuegos, Pinar del Río, Valle de Viñales, Havana

Traffic Information:
The speed limit on highways is 140 km/h (87 mph) and 60 km/h (37 mph) in built-up areas. The roads are sometimes in extremely bad condition and riddled with potholes, and speed should be adjusted accordingly. Vehicles are generally old and often in a poor state of repair.

Journeying at dusk or at night is not recommended as many unlit vehicles, carts, and pedestrians are to be found on the roads. A national driving permit is required to hire a car, for which the driver must be at least 21 years old. Hire charges are exceptionally expensive.

Weather:
The best time to travel is between November and April. Temperatures during the dry season can average 25 °C (January is the coolest month) and water temperatures are a balmy 24–27 °C.

Further Information:
www.infotur.cu
www.travel2cuba.co.uk

sion to the miles of palm-lined beaches at Varadero. The scenic coast road has been converted into a highway and after 37 km (23 miles) there is a turning which will take you to a little peninsula with countless hotels and restaurants. The Carretera Central (CC) leaves Matanzas and crosses the island's interior, passing through the major sugar cane regions. Tobacco is also cultivated here.

❸ Santa Clara The industrial heart of central Cuba is a busy modern city of 200,000 inhabitants. The majority of the sights here are of relatively recent date. In 1958, Che Guevara – an Argentinian doctor and Fidel Castro's brother in arms – derailed a train laden with soldiers and weapons here, dealing Fulgencio Batista, Cuba's dictator, a decisive blow and aiding the revolution's eventual victory. The event is commemorated with the Monumento al Tren Blindado (Monument to the Armored Train), and Cuba's most popular hero is further remembered with a monumental memorial on the Plaza de la Revolución which is adorned with scenes from the revolutionary's life and quotations from his diary. His remains, rediscovered in Bolivia as recently as 1997, now lie nearby in the Mausoleo del Che.

The route leaves Santa Clara on Highway 321 and heads northeast to Caibarién and the sea before following the Circuito Norte past varied coastal scenery to Morón. The quickest route from here to the idyllic beaches of the Caya Coco will take you through San Rafael; to reach the Cayo Sabinal and the Playa Santa Lucía further to the south-east you should turn off at the industrial town of Nuevitas. After taking this detour to the beach (see sidebar, page right) the route heads south to the Carretera Central and from there proceeds directly to Holguín.

❹ Holguín Its location as a traffic hub and its international airport make this industrial city a major point of entry for incoming visitors. The La Periquera building in Holguín's small colonial center houses the Museo Provincial de Historía, with its collection of tools and weapons that once belonged to the island's indigenous inhabitants. The pilgrimage site of Loma de la Cruz lies high above the city at the top of a flight of 450 steps, and here St Lazarus, known in the Afro-Cuban pantheon as Babalu Ayé, patron saint of the sick and of healers, is petitioned for support and help. For an excursion to idyllic beaches, take the local Highway 241 to the north-east as far as Fafael Freyre before continuing to Guardalavaca (55 km/34 miles). The surrounding hillsides are covered with plantations and thatched farmhouses and the local farmers still till their fields with archaic, horse-drawn equipment.

Head east on the local Highway 123 from Holguín, passing through Mayarí, and after leaving Sagua de Tánamo the route climbs south through the mountains toward Guantánamo.

❺ Guantánamo A poem by the Cuban national poet José Martí describing a girl from Guantánamo has found worldwide fame set to music as Guantanamera. The US military base to the south of the town has also achieved a more melancholy notoriety as a detention center.

1 From Havana's Parque Central there is a view past the 60-m (197-foot) Capitolio building to the sea.

2 The Spanish fortress of El Morro guards the narrow entrance to Havana port.

Havana – Queen of the Caribbean

Pastel shades surround the city with the romance of son, and peeling plaster and ramshackle walls play the bolero of decay – Havana is one of the oldest and most fascinating cities in the New World.

Founded in the 16th century, Havana soon became the central hub of trade between the Old and the New Worlds. Impressive Spanish baroque palaces and churches soon lined the Plaza de Armas and the Plaza de la Catedral in Habana Vieja, the oldest part of town, and after exemplary restoration they now give a sense of the former wealth of the city. The pretty colonial cottages on the Calle Obispo are a charming backdrop for a stroll, and don't miss the Bodeguita del Medio on the Calle Empredado – this was Ernest Hemingway's best-loved bar. The best view of the Castillo del Morro and the Fortaleza de la Cabaña fortifications can be obtained from the parking garage on the Avenida del Puerto. These two forts, the largest Spanish military installations of the time, were built to protect the entrance to Havana port. The Prado leads from the sea to the shade

of the Parque Central and the Capitolio, built by the dictator Machado in 1929.

The most popular promenade in Havana is the Malecón between Castillo de San Salvador and La Rampa, and in good weather it is filled with couples, tourists, anglers, pensioners, and young rappers. The historic façades of the houses on the Malecón are in every state of repair from recent restoration to dilapidation.

Known officially as Calle 23, la Rampa is the main traffic artery of the suburb of Vedado, and in the "golden age" from the 1930s to the 1950s this was where the millionaires and mafiosi lived and partied. The gingerbread façade of the Hotel Nacional and the tower of the Habana Libre Hotel, which Fidel Castro made his headquarters after the guerillas had marched into Havana, are also to be found on this street. The Coppelia ice cream parlor next door is

an institution, and is still a popular place for young people to meet. Wrought-iron gates and overgrown gardens often conceal imposing colonial villas, and the old haunts of the rich and famous are now home to embassies, global companies, and the Cuban nouveau riche. The Cementerio Colón in the far south-west of Vedado is a surreal world of the dead, with marble angels, putti, wreaths, and flowers. The Finca Vigía in south-eastern Havana is a place of pilgrimage for all Hemingway enthusiasts: the American writer lived in this 19th-century residence from 1940 until 1960 and it is now open to the public as a museum, in its original state.

1 On stormy days, the surf washes over the sea wall along the Malecón promenade, submerging it.

2 A flea market on the Plaza de Armas; Che memorabilia is always popular.

3 Have a break in one of the cafés on the Plaza de la Catedral.

The Castillo de los Tres Santos Reyes Magos del Morro – the Castle of the Three Wise Moorish Holy Men – known simply as El Morro, was built between 1589 and 1630 on a spit of land, and several trenches were carved out of the rock to protect it. Along with the fortress of

La Punta, lying opposite, El Morro was intended to command the narrow entrance to the port, and at night a chain used to be strung between the two forts as a barrier to ships. Trips to the fort are now a popular leisure activity for Habaneros, who enjoy the view.

Take the Carretera Central from Guantánamo to Cajobabo before exiting onto the spectacularly scenic La Farola mountain road, heading north-east to Baracoa. The route crosses a barren landscape strewn with conifers and cactuses before plunging into a tropical world of luxuriant, dark-green rainforest vegetation. The city extends over a series of hills surrounding the Bahía de Miel beneath the El Yunque cliffs.

6 Baracoa The city was founded in 1512 as the first Spanish settlement on the island, becoming Cuba's capital a few years later. Baracoa's greatest treasure is a crucifix made of seagrape wood and kept in the parish church of Iglesia de la Asunción; Christopher Columbus is said to have raised this cross personally when he landed in 1492. Three fortresses were built in the 18th century to protect Baracoa: one is now used as a hotel and another is a muse-

um. North-Eastern Cuba is very rainy and Baracoa is surrounded by dense forests and dominated by the dramatic peak of El Yunque (598 m/1,962 feet). The Parque Nacional Alejandro Humboldt Biosphere Reserve to the south-west is a UNESCO World Heritage Site. Visitors can choose between a boat trip on the Río Toa, trekking on the El Yunque, or a walking tour through the rainforest.

From Guantánamo, follow the A1 to the south coast and Santiago de Cuba.

7 Santiago de Cuba Cuba's second-largest city (population about 440,000) lies in a sheltered bay flanked by the foothills of the Sierra Maestra, and the heart of its Old Town is formed by the enchanting Parque Céspedes, a park named for the leader of the 1868 rebellion. The Casa Diego Velázquez, the oldest surviving building in Cuba, was built here in 1516. The attractive Casa Grande Hotel,

which is now an interesting museum of the colonial period, the blue-and-white Ayuntamiento (town hall), and the Catedral de Nuestra Señora de la Asunción all date back to the late 19th or early 20th century. In the next street concerts are held in the Casa de la Trova (18th century) almost every evening, featuring both well-known performers and budding stars. The Museo del Carnaval in the Calle Heredia is certainly worth a visit, and Santiago's carnival is considered one of the most lively and authentic in Cuba.

The Moncada barracks to the north-east of the town center have become a pilgrimage site, especially for revolutionaries – it was here that Fidel Castro and a handful of friends made their first attempt to topple the Batista regime in 1953; the assault on the barracks failed and the attackers were imprisoned or shot. Just as in Havana, the grid-like Santa Ifigenia cemetery here is particularly worth see-

ing; this city of the dead has become the final resting place of the poet José Martí and several members of the Bacardi rum dynasty. The mouth of the bay is guarded by the El Morro (Castillo de San Pedro de la Roca) fortress, built to the south of Santiago in the 17th century, and this Cuban World Heritage Site now houses the Museo de la Piratería (Museum of Piracy).

The pilgrimage church of El Cobre lies on a hill about 27 km (17 miles) north of Santiago (heading toward Bayamo on the CC). The Virgen de la Caridad is Cuba's patron saint and is worshipped both in her Christian incarnation and also as an avatar of the Afro-Caribbean goddess Ochún. From El Cobre, the CC will take you through the mountains of the Sierra Maestra and the sugar plantations of the plains surrounding Bayamo.

8 Bayamo Originally a Native American settlement, this town was conquered by the Spanish

in 1513 and is now the coachwork capital of Cuba: the carriages built here are to be found all over the island. The main attraction, the Parque Carlos Manuel de Céspedes, is surrounded by elegant 19th-century townhouses. Bayamo is a good base for expeditions to the Sierra Maestra. Follow the local expressway 152 and the CC further west to Camagüey

🔟 **Camagüey** The Zona Vieja (Old Town) of the city is a surprising and confusing jumble of streets and squares – the city's unusual design was intended to cause assailants to lose their bearings during the frequent pirate attacks. The colonial-era Old Town has hardly been restored at all and the charming tiled cottages on the wonderful Plaza San Juan de Dios have lost none of their charm. Head west out of Camagüey on the CC toward Sancti Spíritus.

🔟 **Sancti Spíritus** This little town, one of the oldest settlements in Cuba, once grew rich on the sugar and slave trades. Lying at its heart, the parish church of Espíritu Santo was one of the first places of Christian worship on the island; the foundation stone was laid in 1522. From Sancti, head south-west along the Carretera Sur to the Valle de San Luís.

🔟 **Valle de San Luís** During the heyday of the plantations and the slave trade, this idyllic valley of palm trees and sugar cane 12 km (7? miles) beyond Trinidad was the site of 50 sugar mills (ingenios). Because of this cultural and historical significance, the site, like the rest of Trinidad, has been declared a UNESCO World Heritage Site. The Iznaga family's hacienda, from whose 50-m (164-foot) Torre de Iznaga the work of slaves was once monitored, is now a restaurant.

🔟 **Trinidad** The wealth once brought to this little town by slavery and sugar plantations is reflected in the imposing colonial-era buildings and the Plaza Mayor. Now housed in the Brunet y Muñoz plantation residence, the collections of Meissen porcelain and antique furniture in the Museo Romántico (1808) give a sense of the elegance of life here in the 18th century. The premises of the Museo de Arquitectura Trinitaria date back to 1738 and its exhibits are devoted to the finer points of local architecture, which can also be appreciated as you stroll through the cobbled streets: the ornately deco-

1 The Catedral de Nuestra Señora de la Asunción towers over the Parque Céspedes in Santiago de Cuba.

2 The Plaza Mayor is the colonial heart of Trinidad.

3 The church of San Francisco in Trinidad, with the Sierra d'Escambray in the background.

357

Large parts of Cuba display features of classic karst scenery, and the domed hills, known here as mogotes, are an ever-impressive sight. They are especially prevalent in the enchanting landscape of the Valle de Viñales in western Cuba. Mogotes are all that remain of a sys-

tem of karst caves whose roofs have collapsed, and numerous other caves are to be found still intact. These include the Gran Caverna Santo Tomás, which can be explored with a helmet and a headlamp. UNESCO has listed the entire valley as a World Heritage Site.

rated wrought-iron railings adorning the doors and windows of the single-storey houses are a fine example. Most of the old houses possess an inner courtyard, from which you will often hear melodies drifting, and the musicians of Trinidad transform the entire Old Town into an open air concert hall. The Carretera Sur will take you on through charming coastal scenery to Cienfuegos.

⓭ Cienfuegos Its population of 140,000 makes Cienfuegos one of Cuba's smaller cities, but its economic significance is not to be underestimated: the Bahía de Cienfuegos, a bay 20 km (13 miles) deep, shelters a major industrial port and gigantic quays for sugar transporters, surrounded by oil refineries and a power station.
The grid pattern of the town center (Pueblo Nuevo) around

the Parque Martí, which has been a UNESCO World Heritage Site since 2005, features surprisingly modern-looking colonial architecture. Famous artists such as Enrico Caruso have performed in its luxuriously appointed Tomás Terry theater, but the city's centerpiece is the Moorish Revival-style Palacio del Valle château on the Punta Gorda peninsula, which was built in 1913–17 for a Spanish millionaire.
Follow the Carretera Sur northwest to Aguada de Pasajeros and the A1 freeway to Havana. For the detour to the Zapata peninsula (see sidebar page left), turn south onto Route 116 at Jagüey Grande, or return to the capital and continue on to western Cuba – the A4 is the fastest route to Pinar del Río.

⓮ Pinar del Río The capital of Pinar del Río Province is indeed

provincial, in fact almost rural. Founded in 1571, it was the site of the first tobacco factory in 1760, but most of the colonial-era buildings here date back only to the late 19th century and the turn of the 20th. The houses here are noteworthy for their

shaded arcades and a partiality for the use of columns. Built in 1914 in a mixture of styles from all over the world, the Palacio Gausch is evidence of the travels of its original owner, who wanted things that he had seen abroad to be reflected in its

Havana The contrasts of its colonial-era architecture have earned the Cuban capital UNESCO World Heritage status. Havana is one of the most fascinating cities in the Americas, despite its incipient decay.

North coast beaches The leisure infrastructure of the Varadero peninsula justifies its status as Cuba's principal tourist site. The hundreds of islets of the Jardines del Rey archipelago are also magnificent.

Matanzas Situated at the confluence of two rivers, the "city of bridges" has one of the most beautiful theaters in Cuba. The image shows the cathedral with its statue of Columbus.

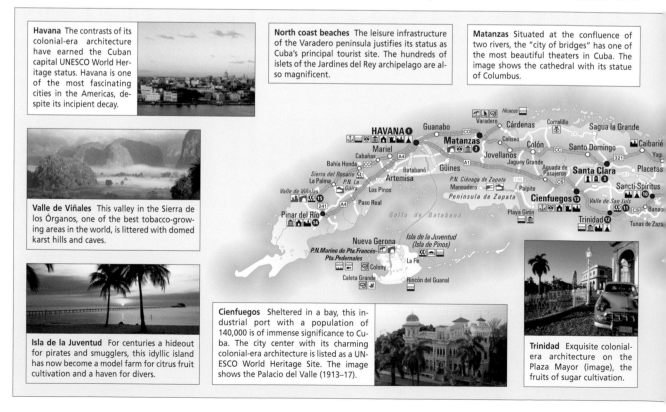

Valle de Viñales This valley in the Sierra de los Órganos, one of the best tobacco-growing areas in the world, is littered with domed karst hills and caves.

Isla de la Juventud For centuries a hideout for pirates and smugglers, this idyllic island has now become a model farm for citrus fruit cultivation and a haven for divers.

Cienfuegos Sheltered in a bay, this industrial port with a population of 140,000 is of immense significance to Cuba. The city center with its charming colonial-era architecture is listed as a UNESCO World Heritage Site. The image shows the Palacio del Valle (1913–17).

Trinidad Exquisite colonial-era architecture on the Plaza Mayor (image), the fruits of sugar cultivation.

façade and detailing; there are Egyptian hieroglyphs next to Gothic windows and neo-Moorish crenellations atop Corinthian columns.

The Fábrica de Tabacos Francisco Donatién cigar factory is definitely worth a visit. The leaves are first sorted by size and quality before the puros are rolled and the banderole label attached, and while the work proceeds it is the job of one employee to read out newspaper reports or literature to entertain the other workers. The cigars manufactured in Pinar are reserved for the Cuban market.

Local expressway 241 meanders north through a charming landscape of tobacco fields and king palm groves to the sleepy and traditional Valle de Viñales.

⑮ Valle de Viñales This valley in the Sierra de los Órganos is part of the Vuelta Abajo, one of the world's prime tobacco-growing areas. No other scenery in Cuba can compete with the picturesque mogotes and densely vegetated hillsides of this unique and magical landscape; its dark-green tobacco fields, gabled drying barns, and palm-thatched farmhouses, known as bohíos, make the area around Viñales one of the most beautiful and authentic in Cuba.

Cave finds and rock paintings are evidence of settlements in the valley dating back some 6,000 years; the original population fled to the cayos and islands along the coast when the Spanish arrived.

The tobacco farmers in the Valle de Viñales still cultivate their crops according to rules laid down centuries ago, and in 1999 UNESCO recognized this cultural legacy as a World Heritage Site. The valley takes its name from the little village of Viñales lying at its heart, where a little church, pretty wooden cottages, and shady verandas provide a backdrop for the surprising number of amateur artists whose work is exhibited here.

The Mural de la Prehistoria, commissioned by Fidel Castro and executed by the Cuban painter Lovigildo González, is one of socialist Cuba's greatest achievements; following in the footsteps of Mexican muralists, the artist has decorated the rock walls of the Mogote Dos Hermanas with motifs depicting human development. There are two routes back into town: either return to Pinar del Río and take the A4 or follow the Circuito Norte.

Diving enthusiasts should take a detour just before the capital to the Isla de la Juventud in the Caribbean Sea (see sidebar page right - check). The quickest way to reach the island is by plane.

1 Every cigar-roller is allowed a certain number of puros for her own consumption.

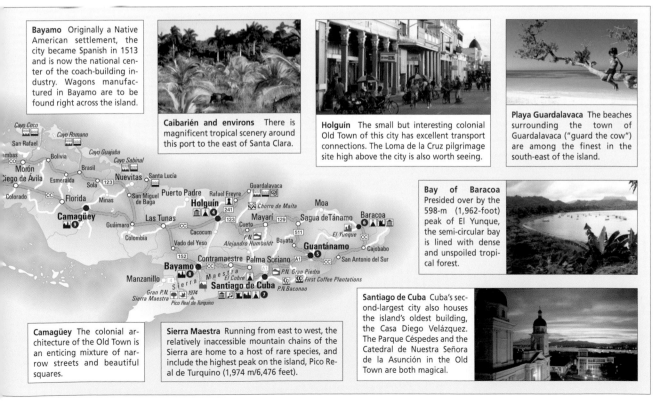

Bayamo Originally a Native American settlement, the city became Spanish in 1513 and is now the national center of the coach-building industry. Wagons manufactured in Bayamo are to be found right across the island.

Caibarién and environs There is magnificent tropical scenery around this port to the east of Santa Clara.

Holguín The small but interesting colonial Old Town of this city has excellent transport connections. The Loma de la Cruz pilgrimage site high above the city is also worth seeing.

Playa Guardalavaca The beaches surrounding the town of Guardalavaca ("guard the cow") are among the finest in the south-east of the island.

Bay of Baracoa Presided over by the 598-m (1,962-foot) peak of El Yunque, the semi-circular bay is lined with dense and unspoiled tropical forest.

Camagüey The colonial architecture of the Old Town is an enticing mixture of narrow streets and beautiful squares.

Sierra Maestra Running from east to west, the relatively inaccessible mountain chains of the Sierra are home to a host of rare species, and include the highest peak on the island, Pico Real de Turquino (1,974 m/6,476 feet).

Santiago de Cuba Cuba's second-largest city also houses the island's oldest building, the Casa Diego Velázquez. The Parque Céspedes and the Catedral de Nuestra Señora de la Asunción in the Old Town are both magical.

Lesser Antilles

Caribbean cruise: from Puerto Rico to Grenada

Just the name "Caribbean" makes you think of paradise and the sun-blessed islands of the Lesser Antilles don't disappoint with their dazzling sandy beaches, palm trees swaying in the trade winds, lush rainforests, mighty volcanoes, crystal-clear waters, coral reefs, and rich mix of cultures. The music, art, cuisine, and religions of Europe, Africa, America, and Asia all come together here in a heady combination.

On 15th-century maps predating the voyages of Christopher Columbus the long chain of islands to the north of Colombia and Venezuela are called the Antilia Insula. Situated between the South and North American continents and dividing the Caribbean Sea and the Atlantic Ocean, the islands include both the Lesser and Greater Antilles, covering a total area of 236,507 km (146,965 miles). Heading from west to east, the Greater Antilles includes Cuba, Jamaica, Haiti, the Dominican Republic, and Puerto Rico, where our cruise begins. There are over a hundred populated Lesser Antilles islands, ranging from the Virgin Islands in the north to the ABC Islands (Aruba, Bonaire,

Tobago: Fresh crayfish in the grill.

and Curaçao) near the South American mainland. Depending on their location in relation to the prevailing trade winds that blow east to west, the islands are subdivided into the Windward Islands and Leeward Islands near the South American mainland.

The Windward Islands were so called because they were situated more windward in relation to ships arriving from the American continent (the prevailing wind came from the side), while the Leeward Islands were in the lee, or downwind, of the prevailing wind.

The Lesser Antilles region is a tropical paradise. The climate remains the same all year round, with average temperatures of 26–30°C (79–86°F) on the coasts. The peak season for the many cruises around this part of the world is from December to April, when the weather is a little cooler and drier. Tourists also avoid the dangerous hurricane season. The shape of the islands and their volcanoes, many of

Cruise ships are a familiar sight in the port of Fort-de-France in Martinique.

British Virgin Islands: One of the most beautiful coves in the world is Deadman's Bay on Peter Island, with its long stretch of snow-white sandy beach lined with palm trees.

which are still active, is indicative of their position along the boundary of the Caribbean and American tectonic plates.

But what would the Caribbean be without the appeal and openness of its hospitable inhabitants? The lively mix of people who now live on the islands has developed over many years. The original inhabitants, Carib Amerindians, died out long ago. The European colonizers brought Africans to work on the plantations as slaves. When slavery was abolished at the beginning of the 19th century, workers from Asia also arrived.

This created a combination of cultural influences that has nowadays also succumbed to the both the cultural and economic influence of the nearby USA. The islands' languages and dialects, music, art, regional cuisine, and religious beliefs are very diverse.

The gorgeous tropical backdrop, with sun and sea, and the islands' unique atmosphere have all made the Caribbean a top location for the best and most beautiful cruises in the world. A new day means a new island. Cruise passengers aren't limited to life on board, they can also take excursions to the island towns for shopping or sightseeing, or book a tour of the island, go swimming or diving, or can stopover on land (usually in an exclusive hotel).

Or they can head for shore independently and find a taxi or one of the local tour guides that are to be found in every port, or plan their own individal round trip by hiring a car, and explore the islands off the beaten tracks.

The eight sovereign states of Lesser Antilles are: Antigua and Barbuda (Leeward Islands in the north), St Kitts and Nevis, Dominica, St Lucia, Barbados, St Vincent and the Grenadines, Grenada, and Trinidad and Tobago (in the south near Venezuela).

Everyday life in Grenada shows the contrasts in Caribbean culture.

1

Many Caribbean tours begin in Miami or Lauderdale. An ideal starting point for island-hopping around the Lesser Antilles is the port of San Juan in Puerto Rico, where pelicans fly overhead and luxury sea liners berth. The final destination for the cruise is Grenada.

Travel Information

Route profile
Length: 750 nautical miles (1,389 km/863 miles)
Duration: 10–14 days
Start: San Juan/Puerto Rico
End: St George's/Grenada
Itinerary (main locations):
San Juan, Charlotte Amalie, Basseterre, St John's, Point-à-Pitre, Roseau, Fort-de-France, Castries, Bridgetown, St George's

Cruises
There are a number of cruise companies including:
Royal Caribbean Cruises
Tel: 1-888-313-8883 (toll free)
1-727-906-0444 (international)
www.royalcarib.com

Tourist information
www.geographia.com
www.caribbean-on-line.com
www.islandcruises.com
www.onecaribbean.org

① Puerto Rico The easternmost island of the Greater Antilles was the final bastion of the Spanish in the Caribbean before it was taken over by the USA in 1989. In 1950, the island's inhabitants took part in a referendum to establish whether they would prefer to remain an American colony or become an autonomous US territory. Three-quarters of the population voted for autonomy.
Despite the fact that Spanish is the main language, the economy is strongly influenced by the USA. San Juan is one of the largest metropolises in the Caribbean, with over three million inhabitants. Broad streets and high-rise buildings in the new part of town are reminiscent of American skylines.

Before the cruise departs from the port, the picturesque old town of San Juan, with its narrow alleyways and old houses with beautiful wooden balconies, is a must-see. The huge defense fortifications, including the Castillo de San Felipe del Morro, the Fuerte San Cristóbal, and La Fortaleza, are all under the protection of UNESCO. They typify the character of the city and port. Since 1822, La Fortaleza has been used as the headquarters for the Governor of Puerto Rico and is therefore the oldest government building in the western hemisphere to have been in constant use.
If you do not wish to explore the old Spanish colonial town, you may like to visit Luquillo, a mile of golden beach at the eastern-

most point of the island, or the Bacardi Rum Distillery and adjoining museum right by the gates to the city.

② American Virgin Islands To the east of Puerto Rico and the adjacent Virgin Passage is the series of islands that make up the Virgin Islands. You will head for St Thomas and the port of Charlotte Amalie, landing at

the West Indian Company Dock with other cruise ships. The island began to flourish in the 17th century when the Danish West India Company operated a commercial settlement here. It offers excellent views of Margins Bay and the port. The ample shopping for tourists on Main Street, together with a visit to Fort Christian, which also houses the Virgin Island Muse-

um, are both highly recommended.

The adjacent island St John, of which two thirds forms a national park, and the former sugar cane island of Saint Croix can be seen from a distance. Farther to the east are the British Virgin Islands.

❸ British Virgin Islands The islands jut out of the turquoise-blue Caribbean Sea in a series of green forested peaks, the tops of an underwater chain of volcanoes. The two largest islands are Tortola and Virgin Gorda, where only medium-sized cruise ships can dock. Tortola is named after the turtles, of which there are almost 15,000 on this island. The British Virgin Islands are considerably more peaceful than the lively US islands. People spending their vacation here will stay in one of the attractive beach hotels. The conditions for diving are excellent. The islands are best explored by ferry, or chartered yacht if you can sail. The route now heads for Anguilla.

❹ Anguilla It was the Spanish who first discovered the group of small islands in the English-speaking Leeward Islands, including the main island of Anguilla that gives its name to this small group. They did not stay long however, as they found the landscape too flat and dry, but

1 The fortress of Castillo de San Felipe del Morro, located at the entrance to the port of Puerto Rico's capital city San Juan and surrounded by the sea, was built when the Spanish settled on the island.

2 Luquillo Beach in Puerto Rico is considered to be one of the most beautiful in the world.

3 An historic sugar mill is a reminder of the "white gold" era in the Virgin Islands.

Sheltered bays with crystal-clear water, offshore coral reefs, white sandy beaches with coconut palms, and mountainous inland areas with dense tropical forests characterize the Virgin Islands east of Puerto Rico. The island of St John is part of the American Virgin Islands.

Together with Hassel Island, the majority of these volcanic islands, form the Virgin Islands National Park, which was established in 1956, and provides a habitat for over 100 species of bird, six types of bat, and over 800 different plants. The marine life is fascinating, too.

1

the islands kept their original Spanish name (meaning "eel") referring to the shape of the islands.

⑤ St Kitts and Nevis Nevis Peak (985 m/3,232 ft) is a dormant volcano (the last eruption was in prehistoric times) often enveloped in fog, assumed to be neive (snow) by Columbus during his voyage, hence the origin of the island's name. Covered in tropical rainforest, the main island, St Kitts, is made up of three mountain ranges. A circular road provides access around the island. The central town of Basseterre, originally founded by the French, was built in the British style. The main square, featuring a photogenic Victorian clock tower, has an easygoing atmosphere.

The route passes through sugar cane fields to Old Road Town, the former capital city of the island, and to the Brimstone Hill Fort with its excellent views. It

then follows the shoreline with its numerous hotels. You can reach nearby Nevis, with its mighty lava cone, by boat through The Narrows, a canal about 3 km (2 miles) wide.

⑥ Antigua It is only a short journey to tropical Antigua and the adjacent island of Barbuda. Most of the sugar cane fields have now been abandoned, but the sugar mills, of which there are over two hundred, are a reminder of the past when African slaves worked the fields here in terrible conditions.

Due to its sheltered port and suitable position, the British developed Antigua into one of their most important bases in the Lesser Antilles. The numerous forts and military bases, including Fort James and Fort Barrington, are a reminder of the former economic and strategic significance of the island. At the pier, you find yourself in the typical Caribbean port town of St

John's, dominated by its beautiful cathedral with twin towers. You can walk to the many little stores, businesses, bars, and restaurants at Heritage Quay and Redcliffe Quay, eventually arriving at the Museum of Antigua and Barbuda, which explores the history of the island. There are excursions around the island, to Nelson's Dockyard National Park or Betty's Hope, the oldest plantation on the island, which, for the past fifty years, has been open to tourists. The visitor center explains how sugar was processed and gives an interesting insight into the life and work of the slaves.

Visitors who have the time to stop at Barbuda around 45 km (28 miles) away, will find a large coral atoll and a true paradise for nature lovers with many rare species, including types of lizard, turtles, and birds. A large colony of frigate birds, one of the most interesting species of tropical bird, nest in Codrington

Laguna (see panel, right). Passing by Montserrat, the cruise moves on to the next destination, Guadeloupe.

⑦ Guadeloupe The ship sails overnight and by dawn the largest island of the Lesser Antilles should be looming on the horizon, just as Columbus perhaps once first saw it. He named it Santa María de Guadalupe de Extremadura, after an icon of the Virgin Mary worshipped at a Spanish monastery in Guadalupe, in Extremadura, Spain.

The French took possession of the island in 1635, but it was subsequently seized by the British several times during the ensuing centuries, passing back and forth between the two countries. In 1815 it was acknowledged to be under French control in the Treaty of Vienna and is now an overseas department of France (départements d'outre-mer). As part of France,

Guadaloupe is also part of the European Union and the currency is the Euro.

Evidence of its French history and cultural influence are everywhere. French cars dominate the streets, the tricoleur waves in the gentle breeze, the police are typical gendarmes, and people chat nonchalantly in cafés and shop in boutiques with a French ambience selling international products. However, the islanders do add a touch of their own lively Caribbean-Creole culture too.

When sugar cane was introduced to the area in the late 17th century, it marked the beginning of the islands' great "white gold" era in vast plantations worked by slaves. Slavery was eventually abolished in 1848 and day-wage workers from India were hired. They left behind a Hindu temple.

But things are changing. The distillation plants are now antiquated and rum production is declining. Sugar cane is gradually being replaced by other crops: bananas are now the most important, along with other tropical fruit, vegetables, and flowers.

Guadaloupe comprises five islands, including the two main islands of Basse Terre and Grande-Terre, which are connected by a bridge crossing the Rivière Salée. The butterfly shape of the island's outline is striking. Grande-Terre is smaller and flatter, while Basse Terre has more mountainous terrain, including

1 St Kitts and Nevis: A trip to the volcano Nevis Peak on the island of Nevis.

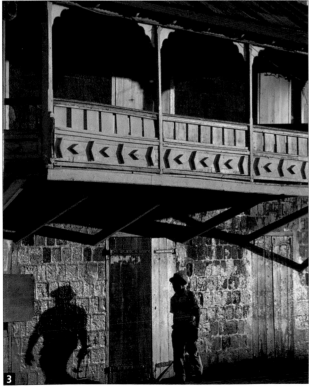

2 Guadeloupe: View of the densely overgrown mountains Les Mamelles on Basse-Terre.

3 An alleyway in Basseterre, the main city on the island of St Kitts.

369

the 1,467-m (4,813-ft) volcano La Soufrière.

Cruise ships dock at Point-à-Pitre. If you go ashore, you can explore the lively capital city of the island and its Creole markets, such as the Marché Couvert, and the shops along Rue Frébault and in the port area. Don't miss the opportunity to sample some Creole dishes before taking an excursion on the well-constructed N1 to the rainforest, with its unique vegetation and beautiful waterfalls, finally arriving at La Soufrière, known affectionately as the Old Lady.

In 1975, people had to be evacuated from the surrounding area when La Soufrière became active. There is not normally enough time on a cruise to make it to the top of the volcano, and the peak is often encased in mist so views are not guaranteed.

In the recent past catastrophic hurricanes have had a more devastating effect on the island than the volcano, including Hurricane Ines in 1966, David in 1979, and the tail ends of Frederic and Hugo in 1989.

8 Dominica The third-largest island in Lesser Antigua is a short journey away. Cruise ships anchor in the port of the island's capital city Roseau to enable their passengers to disembark and explore the island. The island is full of unspoiled natural beauty: mountainous terrain covered with untouched rainforest, and hot springs with their sulfurous vapor, and the "Boiling Lake" are evidence of the geo-thermal activity taking place just below ground. Farther on is the Morne Trois Pitons National Park (see panel, right), covering around 6,800 ha (16,803 acres), and then the

Northern Forest Reserve, home of endangered Sisserou and Jacquot parrots. The diverse flora of the rainforest includes a rare display of over fifty types of orchid and a variety of ferns. Over three hundred waterfalls and rivers are fed by heavy downpours of rain in late summer, brought about by the incessant north-east trade wind. The island's economy depends

on mainly agriculture and sund & beach tourism.

9 Martinique Like Guadaloupe, Martinique is a French island. It combines magical tropical scenery with a Creole atmosphere, and the je ne sais quoi of the French way of life. The island's previously peaceful volcano giant, Mont Pelée, erupted on May 8, 1902, killing the entire popula-

tion of 30,000 people living in the island's former capital St Pierre, except for a single survivor who was serving time in prison. Today, Fort-de-France is the lively capital of the island. Taking a stroll through the streets of the town, you will see colonial-style houses decorated with ornate wrought-iron work. A short excursion will take you through the capital city's sub-urbs, past the Sacré-C?ur church, built in the style of the original in Paris, to enjoy fine views over the town and the bay. Farther on you can see the volcanic mountain range and the town of St Pierre. Once known as the Paris of the Antilles, it is now little more than a tourist destination. A charming way to visit it is the by the Cyparis-Express tourist train, which takes in all the main sights; the small Musée Vulcanologique is also worth visiting. The painter Paul Gauguin lived nearby in Anse Turin for several months. You can learn more about his stay here in the Musée Gauguin. The best beach on the island, Grande Anse des Salines, is also here.

On your way out, via the Baie de Fort-de-France and the Baie des Flamands, you can tour the grounds of the 17th-century Fort-St-Louis.

⑩ St Lucia "The Helen of the West Indies" is how both the French and the British affectionately refer to the island of St Lucia. Both countries have contributed significantly to the island's history, as its control has passed back and forth between them least fourteen times, until the island was finally handed over to Great Britain in 1815 in the Treaty of Paris. Since 1979, St Lucia has been independent but remains a member of the Commonwealth. Bright red British telephone boxes and French place names, the Creole language, also spoken on Martinique, and of course the Creole cuisine and French architectural influences all reflect the island's cosmopolitan past.

When approaching the island and port, two prominent landmarks, the volcanoes Gros Piton

1 Surf at Pointe des Chateaux in Guadeloupe.

2 Guadeloupe: The small colonial museum in the old town of Point-à-Pitre displays exhibits from the time when plantations formed a major part of the economy here.

3 St Pierre in Martinique was a lively colonial town until Mont Pelée erupted in 1902

1

and Petit Piton, surrounded by tropical green mountain forests, dominate the landscape. The island's capital city Castries contains little else of real interest other than the usual souvenir stores, so a trip around the island is far more worthwhile. Not far from the town of Soufrière are the two Piton volcanoes and the rainforest. If you are interested in seeing the beautiful beaches and hotel district, you can take a taxi to the north-west side of the island and visit Choc Bay and Rodney Bay.

⑪ Barbados The next stop on your journey, Barbados, is the easternmost Caribbean island, around 4,500 km (2,796 miles) from the African coast.

It was discovered by a Portuguese sea captain, Pedro a Campos, who was caught up in a storm in 1536 and became stranded on the island. The relatively flat and sparse landscape (at least three-quarters of the land consists of a plateau of coral-reef limestone) was of little interest to the Portuguese, who moved on and left the island to be taken over by the British in 1625.

Barbados was made independent in 1966, although many reminders of the island's colonial history still remain. Except for the climate and landscape, you could easily think you were in Britain: cars drive on the left, the government and constitution are based on the British model, people play cricket and golf, and many take tea at five in the afternoon. The origins of the island's name are unclear. It is possible, however, that the

2

imposing bearded fig trees, with aerial roots hanging down like beards, have something to do with it. The lively island capital, Bridgetown, with a population of over 100,000, is one of the Caribbean's major economic centers. Fishing boats and pleasurecraft are moored at the Careenage, a small, lively port with

a shipyard, a variety of stores, restaurants, bars, and cafés. Only a short walk away is the National Heroes Square, which was known as Trafalgar Square until only a few years ago. The parliamentary buildings constructed of coral stone are located here, as well as the statue of Lord Nelson, who was stationed on the

challenging those surfers who dare to ride the terrifying waves that can reach heights of 12 meters (39 ft). Make sure you include a stop at the beautiful gardens and mansions of the former plantation owners. Many island tours include the present-day luxury hotel Sam Lord's Castle, a typical mansion. Britain's Queen Elizabeth II stays here when she visits the island. It is a good spot to take a break and enjoy a refreshing rum punch.

If the experts are to be believed, the beaches on the western and southern coasts of the island are the most beautiful in the Caribbean. The nickname "Garden of Eden" does indeed suit this place: perfect sandy beaches and a turquoiseemerald green Caribbean sea glittering in the sunlight tick all the right boxes.

After splashing around in the ocean, head back to the quay to begin the final part of the journey through the vibrant Lesser Antilles.

w St Vincent and the Grenadines The small island nation of St Vincent and the Grenadines comprising over 700 islands, coral atolls, and flat sandbanks provides a real paradise for sailors. Winds sweep steadily and constantly across these sun-

island in his younger years. The memorial was erected here some thirty years after its famous counterpart in London.

After shopping in Broad Street, take a trip around the island in a Mini Moke, an open-top vehicle similar to a jeep, but smaller. Barbados is incidentally one of the most densely populated parts of the world with over 620 inhabitants per square kilometer (239 per square mile).

The excursion will take you past sugar cane plantations and miles of banana plantations before finally arriving at the stormy east coast of the island. The Atlantic Ocean batters the coast here with huge waves,

1 The well-known landmarks of the mighty twin peaks of the Pitons on the south-west coast of St Lucia.

2 A dark volcano beach at Soufrière Bay, St Lucia.

3 A dramatic sunset framed by the palms on the west coast of Barbados.

ny Caribbean islands. Life on St Vincent, the largest island in the group, is overshadowed by the volcano Soufrière (which should not be confused with La Soufrière in Guadaloupe), which last erupted in 1979 and threatened to envelop the island inhabitants and adjacent islands in a huge cloud of ash. Fortunately due to the advance warning there were no casualties.

Those wishing to spend their vacation in the Grenadines will find a variety of luxury hotels providing all creature comforts and excellent conditions for diving. There are excursions available between the islands on the island-hopper airplanes and on various boats, or you can charter a yacht yourself.

⑬ Mustique The ultra-stylish island of Mustique is also part of the Grenadines. Mosquitoes gave the island its name at a time long before the jet-set arrived and built their luxury villas and the small, exclusive hotel here. It has seen its fair share of rich and famous visitors, from

Mick Jagger to Princess Margaret.

⑭ Grenada The city of St George's has a picturesque setting wrapped around a fine natural anchorage. The inner part of the port, the Carenage, is the backdrop for most of the boating activity here and small fishing boats and elegant yachts bob up and down side-by-side. Grenada is the southernmost of the Leeward Islands and only 150 km (93 miles) from the South American continent. The British colony of Grenada is known as Spice Island and the island state's flag has nutmeg at its center. Spices sold in baskets of palm leaves are on on offer everywhere around the island, and in the lively local markets too of course.

With its many small alleyways, traditional houses with red-tiled roofs, and mix of 18th-century French colonial style and British influences, including examples of Georgian architecture, St George's is one of the most attractive of all the Caribbean

cities. A tour of the town leads along Young Street to the national museum, and then to Fort George, today used as a police station, which offers fine views over the sea, then on to the Anglican and Catholic churches across from the Supreme Court.

If you have enough time, it is worth going inland to see the Grand Etang National Park in the island's volcanic mountain range. It contains ancient crater basins, one of which holds the Grand Etang lake.

Also not to be missed on this part of the cruise is a visit to the

Grand Anse beach, a few miles from St George's. Its long stretch of fine white sand is world famous.

Sadly, however, this marks the end of our cruise through the beautiful Lesser Antilles.

1 The long chain of Grenadine islands runs all the way from St Vincent to Grenada offering excellent conditions for sailors. Yachts at Union Island are shown here.

2 Cruise liner in the port of Grenada's capital city St George's.

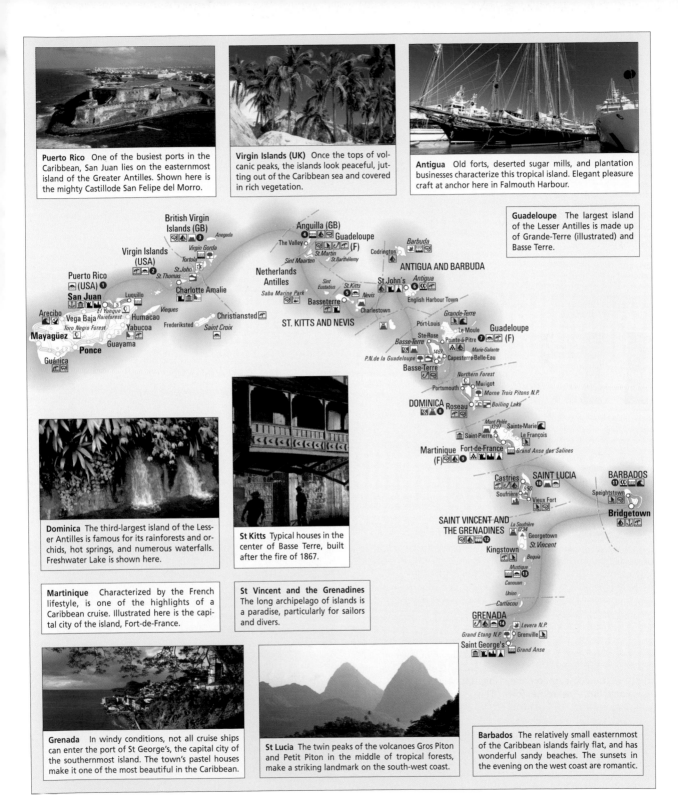

Puerto Rico One of the busiest ports in the Caribbean, San Juan lies on the easternmost island of the Greater Antilles. Shown here is the mighty Castillode San Felipe del Morro.

Virgin Islands (UK) Once the tops of volcanic peaks, the islands look peaceful, jutting out of the Caribbean sea and covered in rich vegetation.

Antigua Old forts, deserted sugar mills, and plantation businesses characterize this tropical island. Elegant pleasure craft at anchor here in Falmouth Harbour.

Guadeloupe The largest island of the Lesser Antilles is made up of Grande-Terre (illustrated) and Basse Terre.

Dominica The third-largest island of the Lesser Antilles is famous for its rainforests and orchids, hot springs, and numerous waterfalls. Freshwater Lake is shown here.

St Kitts Typical houses in the center of Basse Terre, built after the fire of 1867.

Martinique Characterized by the French lifestyle, is one of the highlights of a Caribbean cruise. Illustrated here is the capital city of the island, Fort-de-France.

St Vincent and the Grenadines The long archipelago of islands is a paradise, particularly for sailors and divers.

Grenada In windy conditions, not all cruise ships can enter the port of St George's, the capital city of the southernmost island. The town's pastel houses make it one of the most beautiful in the Caribbean.

St Lucia The twin peaks of the volcanoes Gros Piton and Petit Piton in the middle of tropical forests, make a striking landmark on the south-west coast.

Barbados The relatively small easternmost of the Caribbean islands fairly flat, and has wonderful sandy beaches. The sunsets in the evening on the west coast are romantic.

Colombia and Venezuela

Pearls of the Caribbean

Lonely beaches of fine sand and well-preserved colonial towns, tropical joie de vivre and lively cities, with amazing animal and plant life – the Caribbean coasts of Colombia and Venezuela are a great introduction to the exploration of South America.

Colombia, Venezuela and the islands of the Lesser Antilles just off the coast were among the first areas of the New World to be conquered by the Spanish. The tour begins in Cartagena, one of the first colonial settlements to be founded on the new continent. The route follows Colombian roads between the Caribbean Sea and the delta of the Río Magdalena, the longest river in the country at 1,538 (1,406 miles), before crossing the river close to its estuary at Barranquillla and passing be-

tween the Caribbean and the Sierra Nevada de Santa Marta. This chain of mountains is the steepest coastal range in the world and its tallest peak, the Pico Cristóbal Cólon, is at 5,775 m (18,947 feet) also Colombia's highest point.

The route crosses into Venezuela at the Golfo de Venezuela. In 1499, sailing near what is now the city of Maracaibo and its lake, the Spanish sighted a settlement that had been built out into the sea on piles. The new arrivals immedi-

ately named it Venezuela ("little Venice"). Making landfall, they built their capital city at Coro and called the entire region

Venezuela. Passing Lago de Maracaibo and Coro, the road continues east. The islands of the Lesser Antilles lie just off the

Many of the inhabitants of Tobago have African roots.

The wooded hills of the island of Trinidad have a magnificent view of the Caribbean Sea.

coast: Aruba, the first island, is Dutch sovereign territory, as are the two islands of the Dutch Antilles, Bonaire and Curaçao, and these are followed by countless islets belonging to Venezuela, strung out like a chain of pearls in the sea, with fine beaches, shady coconut palms, and lapped by warm waters that are home to sea turtles and corals.

Caracas, Venezuela's hectic capital, also lies along the route, which continues east to the Isla de Margarita, the best-known tourist resort in the country, before a further excursion to Trinidad, the largest island in the Lesser Antilles, and the island state of Trinidad and Tobago as part of the British Commonwealth.

To reach one of the greatest natural phenomena in Venezuela and indeed all South America, the route has to penetrate further into the interior, and a combination of automobile and plane will take you first to Ciudad Bolívar and then on to the Parque Nacional Canaima in the middle of the Guayana highlands. Not far from the town of Canaima, the Salto Angel, the highest waterfalls in the world, plunge 1,000 m (3,300 feet) into the depths from a flat-topped mountain, feeding the Río Churún below.

Such mountains are known as tepuis and are typical of southern Venezuela and the surrounding area. Isolated for centuries, each tepui is a world of its own and there are more than a few animal and plant species which occur on one island plateau only.

A hawksbill turtle on a coral reef off the coast of Curaçao.

1

Our route follows properly developed roads running mostly a short distance inland from the Caribbean; only a few stretches run directly along the coast. The route ends in Ciudad Bolívar, about 300 km (186 miles) into the interior, and the last leg to Salto Angel has to be covered by plane.

① **Cartagena** This city was founded by Pedro de Heredia in 1533 and it did not take long for it to flourish, becoming one of the major trading ports connecting the northern Spanish colonies in South America with the motherland. Ships from Cadiz and Seville put in here, bringing produce from Spain and returning with gold and silver. The wealth of the town attracted envious interest and Cartagena was subject to repeated pirate attacks. English freebooters in particular were the terror of the Caribbean and Cartagena was assaulted and taken by a succession of feared privateers, including Francis Drake in 1586, who "magnanimously" refrained from razing

the city to the ground upon payment of a colossal ransom. The city's fortifications were subsequently improved when the Spanish surrounded it with some 11 km (7 miles) of curtain wall and built the giant fortress of San Felipe. The entrance to the bay and the port was guarded by the two forts of San José and San Fernando. These two strongpoints are unique in South America and ensured that Cartagena remained unconquered until the end of the colonial period, assuring its place as the most important Spanish port in the New World, especially after the construction of the canal to the Río Magdalena.

The city center features numerous magnificent buildings dat-

Travel Information

Route profile
Route length: about 3,100 km (1,930 miles)
Time required: at least six weeks
Start: Cartagena
Destination: Parque Nacional Canaima
Route (main locations):
Cartagena, Santa Marta, Coro, Caracas, Barcelona, Isla de Margarita, Ciudad Bolívar, Parque Nacional Canaima

Security:
Colombia leads the world in

kidnapping. Before going, consult the recommendations of your country's foreign service.

Information online:
Colombia:
www.colombia.travel/en/
Venezuela:
www.visit-venezuela.com
Aruba: *www.aruba.com*
Bonaire:
www.infobonaire.com
Curaçao: *www.curacao.com*
Trinidad and Tobago:
www.gov.tt

ing back to the colonial period: the cathedral of 1575, the monastery of Santo Domingo, founded in 1570, and a 17th-century Jesuit monastery. Built in 1770, the Palace of the Inquisition now houses the History Museum, and there are numerous townhouses that once be-

longed to aristocrats and dignitaries.

② **Barranquilla** The capital of the Departemento Atlántico has grown to become the fourth-largest city in the country with a population of one million, and the most important industrial

and commercial conurbation on the coast. Founded in 1629, the port was overshadowed by Cartagena for many years as the Río Magdalena estuary delta was navigable only with great difficulty. Everything changed at the end of the 19th century with the canalization of the river and the dredging and development of the port, since which times Barranquilla has been Colombia's foremost port. The city center around the Plaza de Bolívar, a lively market quarter not far from the modern cathedral and

completed in 1982, is especially recommended. The more elegant suburb of El Prado contains the city's two best museums: the Museo Romántico, devoted to the history of Barranquilla, and the Museo de Antropología, whose exhibits principally date back to the pre-Columbian period.

Crossing the Río Magdalena beyond Barraquillla, the route continues toward Santa Marta and passes the Isla Salamanca, which has been declared a national park. The principal vegetation

here is provided by the mangroves whose buttress roots allow them to live in the brackish water. The swamps offer marine animals such as shrimp, sea turtles, rays, and sharks ideal breeding and living conditions, and the Parque Nacional Isla de Salamanca has the greatest mangrove reserves in Colombia.

③ Santa Marta Colombia's oldest city was founded in 1525, but has unfortunately been subjected to countless attempts at modernization, so that very little colonial architecture can now be found. The cathedral has survived, as has the Quinta de San Pedro Alejandrino, where Simón Bolívar spent his final days. Beyond the city there are several tempting beaches and beautiful fishing villages, such as Taganga. Continuing beyond Ríohacha and Maicao, the route crosses the Venezuelan border in the Sierra de Perija and soon reaches Lake Maracaibo (see sidebar, page right).

The Venezuelan National Freeway 3 stretches away to the east from Lake Maracaibo, although unfortunately it does not follow the coast directly, instead running parallel about 20 km (13 miles) inland. Just before Coro, it reaches the Paraguaná, a peninsula connected to the mainland by a narrow strip of land known as the Istmo de los Médanos, which is mainly covered with sparse vegetation: plants other than cactuses and dry thornbushes are to be found in only a very few places here.

④ Parque Nacional Médanos de Coro The entrance to the

1 Impressive fortifications: Cartagena's city wall.

2 Much of Cartagena's population is descended from African slaves.

3 Quiet and peaceful: the fishing village of Taganga near Santa Marta.

1

Paraguaná peninsula is guarded by the Parque Nacional Médanos de Coro, an area of rolling dunes whose location and formation are constantly changing and forever blocking the roads. The park is not big, but even a short hike through the dunes will give a sense of this expansive desert scenery.

❺ **Coro** Founded in 1527 by Juan de Ampiés, Coro is Venezuela's second-oldest city and another colonial gem; its town center has been designated as a UNESCO World Heritage Site. In 1529, two years after its foundation, the town changed ownership, with Germans taking over from the Spanish. These were Welser representatives under the leadership of Ambrosius Dalfinger, who was relieved by Philipp von Hutten in 1535. The Welser bankers of Augsburg had lent King Charles V generous financial aid and supported his election as emperor. In return they had received

the rights to the colony of Little Venice for three decades and Coro was the entrance to this new asset. The Welsers were also feverishly obsessed with finding El Dorado, the realm of the legendary golden king said to exist somewhere in the Colombian highlands. Setting off from Coro into the interior, they plundered village after village, but El Dorado remained elusive. After 18 years of terror, the territory was taken back from the Welsers in 1546, no doubt to the relief of the local population. Coro, which had remained the capital and the seat of the bishopric, sank into oblivion, and only flourished again in the 17th and 18th centuries as trade with the Dutch Antilles picked up.

Most of the surviving colonial architecture dates back to this period, and only the Cruz de San Clemente remains from the city's earliest days; it is rumored to have been built on the square of the same name by the city

2

founder himself, and here the first mass on South American soil is said to have been celebrated.

As the other buildings are all of a later date, they are not so Spanish-influenced, and thanks to the long trading relationship with the Netherlands, there are many which suit Dutch colonial tastes: instead of flat roofs there are red tiles, and wrought-iron railings have been replaced by delicate wooden ones. The colourful houses are painted

predominantly yellow, blue, green and red.

Head east from Coro and you will soon reach La Vela de Coro, Coro's port, from which there are regular ferries to Curaçao. There are further regular ferry connections from Willemstad on Curaçao to Aruba and Bonaire (see excursion on following pages).

The road follows the coast for another 30 km (19 miles) before heading briefly inland, returning to the sea at Tucacas, a

3

4

sleepy fishing village enlivened by tourists only at the weekend. Tucacas is the best base for trips to the Parque Nacional Morrocoy to the north, which offers mainly mangrove forest, but also coral reefs, little lagoons, and wonderful, palm-fringed beaches. Passing industrial and port towns such as Puerto Cabello, Valencia, Maracay, and Los Teques, we soon reach Caracas.

6 Caracas Venezuela's capital is the undisputed focal point of the country. The city's limits are constantly expanding, it suffers from traffic noise and pollution, and its extremes of poverty and wealth are like no other anywhere else in the country: it is a short hop from the elegant, air-conditioned office blocks owned by global companies to the shanty towns along the freeway approach roads. Such rapid growth and the unplanned mushrooming of more and more poor suburbs make the population difficult to esti-

mate. About two and a half million people live around the city center, with anything between five and eight million living in the whole agglomeration.

Caracas is situated in a long valley about 1,000 m (3,300 feet) above sea level, and this elevation affords the city a relatively pleasant climate. After his visit here, Alexander von Humboldt wrote: "you often hear the Caracas climate compared to an eternal spring. What could be more delightful than a temperature that remains at a constant 20 to 26 °C during the day and 16 to 18 °C at night, and where banana, orange, coffee, apple, and apricot trees can happily grow alongside wheat?"

These days you would be delighted to discover any tree at all in the hectic city center – only on the Plaza Bolívar, the absolute focal point of the city, will you find a few shady trees under which to draw breath. The monument to Simón Bolívar in the middle of the Plaza was

erected in 1874. The cathedral, which was largely built in the 19th century, lies on the eastern side of the square, and its interior conceals a magnificent main altar gilded with Mexican gold. Simón Bolívar's family vault is also recommended. The remains of the liberator himself are buried in the Panteón Nacional, the old Trinity Church which was rededicated as a national monu-

1 A lone hiker in the desert-like dunes of the Parque Nacional Médanos de Coro.

2 The Casa de las Ventanas de Hierro in Coro is named after the gratings on the windows, which were specially imported from Spain.

3 Capitolio, the Parliament of Caracas, where politics are made.

4 The reconstructed house of Simón Bolívar, the national hero, is now a museum.

Venezuela's politics are controversial bother at home and abroad. Failing to complete a putsch against the elected government in 1992, the current president, Hugo Chávez won the election of 1999 and took office in 2000. His supporters consider him a modernizer with left-lean-

ing, democratic ideals; his opponents decry him as an undemocratic authoritarian and a left-wing populist, and this ideological war is prosecuted in Caracas in murales, giant wall-paintings. Chávez supporters are pointed in their criticism of the policies of the US Government.

ment and memorial in 1874. Bolívar's supposed birthplace is situated a block to the south of the Plaza, but this typical colonial-era dwelling was built to old plans on the site of the original house only at the turn of the 20th century.

Caracas was founded by the Spanish in 1567 as Santiago de León de los Caracas, and destroyed by earthquakes several times during the 16th and 17th centuries. Oil profits have financed its greatest boom in the second half of the 20th century and now Caracas is predominantly a modern city, with architecture such as the Torres, twin 32-storey office blocks marking the western end of the Avenida Bolívar, which was built as the main traffic artery through the city center in 1953.

It will take a little while to drive clear of the suburbs of Caracas, but Ruta 1 and then Ruta 9 will soon take you to Barcelona, 280 km (174 miles) away, a city with Catalunyan roots.

❼ Barcelona The state capital of Anzoátegui was founded in 1671 when the governor of the time decided to incorporate two existing settlements into one. As most of the settlers were from Catalunya, they named the resulting city San Cristóbal de la Nueva Barcelona.

Only a few structures have survived from the colonial period. The most important are the ruins of a former Franciscan monastery – which had a brief career as a fortress called La Casa Fuerte during the war of independence, before being destroyed – the cathedral of San Cristóbal (1773), and two recently restored colonial buildings which now house museums: the Casa de la Cultura, which exhibits modern art, and the Museo de la Tradición, which has an informative collection illustrating municipal and regional history. Beyond Barcelona the route passes the port town of Puerto la Cruz before reaching the Parque Nacional Mochima.

❽ Parque Nacional Mochima This 95,000 ha (366-sq. mile) national park is considered one of the most beautiful in Venezuela. Established to protect the mangrove forests and coral reefs of the area, it also boasts enchanting beaches that might well tempt you to stop for a while to swim. Many of these are only accessible by sea, perhaps from a hired fishing boat, although others, such as the Playa Colorada, named for the reddish tint of its sand, can

be reached directly from the coast road. There are a few camping sites in the national park where visitors can spend the night, otherwise there are

1 Dusk in the Parque Nacional Mochima. Many of the beaches are accessible only by boat.

2 Brightly painted fishing boats on the sandy beaches of the Isla de Margarita. The constant winds here make it popular with surfers.

A kaleidoscope of tropical fruit on the market stalls run by the Isla de Margarita's greengrocers. Bananas, pineapples, limes, papayas, mangos, melons, and many other varieties look equally tempting.

The underwater world of the Caribbean is one of the region's principal attractions for tourists from all over the world. Free diving will let you explore coral reefs and great schools of tropical fish, and scuba diving will open up the whole palette of undersea life. White, red,

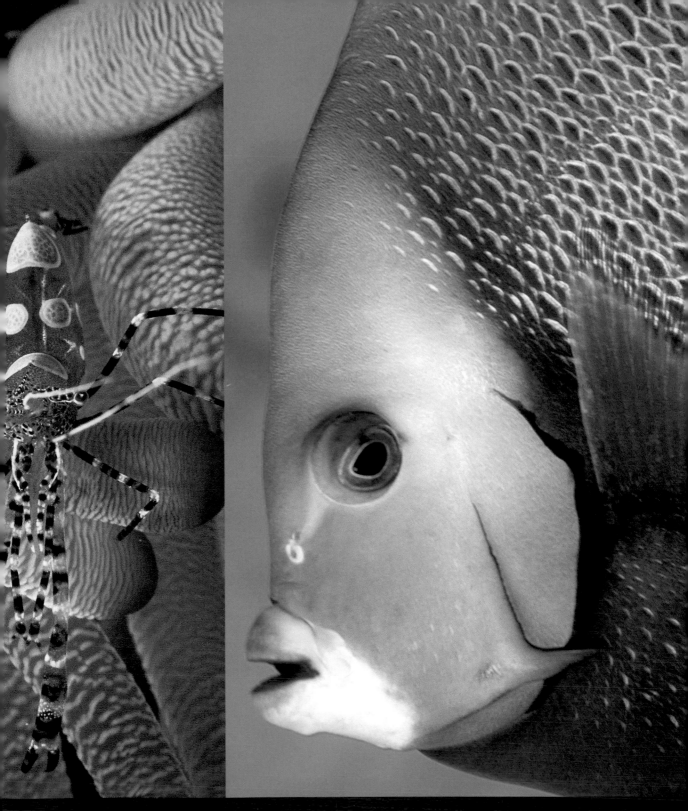

and yellow corals, brightly patterned shrimp, and angelfish, whose hues continually change, are just a few of the Caribbean's wealth of species. On the mainland coast, well developed coral reefs are only found the west, in the Morrocoy and San Esteban National Park

The mountains of Guyana, and particularly those of the Parque Nacional Canaima, consist of gigantic mesas, and from the top of one of these mesas, the Auyán tepui, plunges the world's highest waterfall, the Salto Angel (left). The water falls almost 1,000 m (3,300 feet)

over the two sections of the cascades, and daring souls can climb the lower of these to leap into the plunge pool at the base of the falls (right). The Salto Angel has become a magnet for tourists, just bear in mind that during the dry season the water slows to a trickle.

small hotels in the area. The next stop is Cumaná, where ferries to the Isla de Margarita put in. Before boarding, it is worth taking a stroll through the oldest continually inhabited town on the South American subcontinent: Cumaná was founded in 1521 and fortified by the Spanish, first being called Nueva Toledo before being rechristened as Nueva Córdoba de Cumaná in 1569.

The major attraction in the bustling town center is the fortress, which has been extensively rebuilt since 1660.

9 Isla de Margarita The tropical swimming paradise of Isla de Margarita derives its name from "Garitas del mar," the Spanish for oyster beds; it was the presence of oysters that led to the settlement of the island in 1499. The beds were soon exhausted, however, and the

sleeping beauty of the island was only awakened again in the mid-1970s when it was discovered by tourists; people come here especially for the beaches and the palm-fringed bays in the north-east of the island in particular. La Asunción, the capital, can still boast a few colonial-era buildings, such as the Castillo de Santa Rosa and the Iglesia Nuestra Señora de La Asunción, which was built in the late 16th century.

Returning to Cumaná, take the Ruta 9 the short distance east to Carúpano and then continue east to the furthest reaches of the Península de Paría.

10 Península de Paría The Paría peninsula has some of the finest beaches in Venezuela, including the Playa Medina near the village of Río Caribe and the nearby Playa Puipui: shallow turquoise water, gleaming

white sand, palm trees leaning out over the sea – the perfect place to relax.

It is possible to take a trip from Güirá to Trinidad and Tobago (see previous pages), but to continue the tour you should return to Barcelona and take the Ruta 16 heading south, which has been widened to resemble a freeway. This stretch of road passes through some rather monotonous scenery before reach-

ing the Orinoco River at Soledad, the site of the only bridge along the entire course of the river.

The Puente Angostura, a 1,678-m (5,505-foot) suspension bridge was built between 1963 and 1967 and now carries traffic 50 m (164 feet) above the river's narrowest stretch. Ciudad Bolívar lies on the southern bank named after the liberator of five South American Republics.

⑪ Ciudad Bolívar After earlier settlements in the region had failed, owing to attacks from pirates sailing up the Orinoco, in 1764 the Spanish founded the township of Santo Tomé de la Nueva Guayana de la Angostura del Orinoco, located at a strategic point on the mighty river where the water traffic could easily be controlled. The town initially attracted little interest, but at the turn of the 19th century it played an important role in South American history: Simón Bolívar gave an important speech here in 1819, calling for a united Gran Colombia, and the republic was proclaimed here after the Spanish had been driven out. The city changed its name in 1846 to Ciudad Bolívar to commemorate these events, and the square where Bolívar addressed the crowds also bears his name. There is a monument to the liberator which depicts him surrounded by the figures of five women, representing Bolivia, Colombia, Peru, Ecuador, and Venezuela.

The square is flanked by the baroque cathedral (1771) and several other beautiful classical buildings now used by the municipal and regional government. The Paseo Orinoco on the banks of the river is a good place to stroll through the town's old warehouses.

Ciudad Bolívar marks the end of the route than can be covered by automobile – to reach the Canaima National Park you will have to take a plane, as Canaima, the best base from which to explore the park, is accessible only by air.

⑫ Parque Nacional Canaima Established in 1962, the national park is one of the largest nature reserves on earth, with an area of about 30,000 sq. km (11,580 sq. miles), and it encloses a mountainous region of Guyana composed of mighty sandstone mesas reaching heights of up to 2,000 m (6,600 feet).

The isolated location of these upland plateaus has led to the evolution of unique plant and animal varieties and many prevalent species. The jaguar, the giant armadillo (on open ground), and the anteater are a few of the larger mammals which roam free here.

In 1936, the American bush pilot Jimmy Angel chanced upon an amazing natural spectacle in the middle of this inhospitable landscape: the Salto Angel, the highest waterfall on earth, which has been named after him. The water plunges a distance of about 1,000 m (3,300 feet) – estimates vary between 965 m (3,166 feet) and 985 m (3,232 feet) – from the edge of the Auyán tepui.

The water is not from a river – the falls are fed by run-off from the mighty storms and other rainfall across the wide plateau. The water breaks up into tiny droplets about halfway down, and during the dry season sometimes not a drop reaches the bottom. At the foot of the mountain the water collects in the Río Churún, a tributary of the Río Carroa.

1 The Parque Nacional Canaima is a region of unspoiled forests through which flow mighty rivers, such as the Río Carrao. The Salto Hacha near Canaima can be seen in the foreground.

2 The gigantic Parque Nacional Canaima in the highlands of Guyana features numerous waterfalls.

391

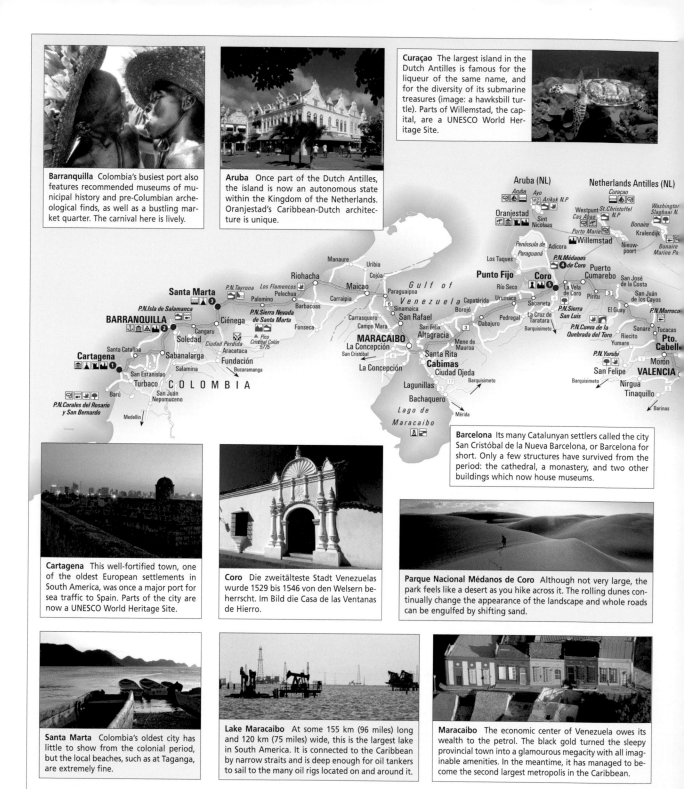

Curaçao The largest island in the Dutch Antilles is famous for the liqueur of the same name, and for the diversity of its submarine treasures (image: a hawksbill turtle). Parts of Willemstad, the capital, are a UNESCO World Heritage Site.

Barranquilla Colombia's busiest port also features recommended museums of municipal history and pre-Columbian archeological finds, as well as a bustling market quarter. The carnival here is lively.

Aruba Once part of the Dutch Antilles, the island is now an autonomous state within the Kingdom of the Netherlands. Oranjestad's Caribbean-Dutch architecture is unique.

Barcelona Its many Catalunyan settlers called the city San Cristóbal de la Nueva Barcelona, or Barcelona for short. Only a few structures have survived from the period: the cathedral, a monastery, and two other buildings which now house museums.

Cartagena This well-fortified town, one of the oldest European settlements in South America, was once a major port for sea traffic to Spain. Parts of the city are now a UNESCO World Heritage Site.

Coro Die zweitälteste Stadt Venezuelas wurde 1529 bis 1546 von den Welsern beherrscht. Im Bild die Casa de las Ventanas de Hierro.

Parque Nacional Médanos de Coro Although not very large, the park feels like a desert as you hike across it. The rolling dunes continually change the appearance of the landscape and whole roads can be engulfed by shifting sand.

Santa Marta Colombia's oldest city has little to show from the colonial period, but the local beaches, such as at Taganga, are extremely fine.

Lake Maracaibo At some 155 km (96 miles) long and 120 km (75 miles) wide, this is the largest lake in South America. It is connected to the Caribbean by narrow straits and is deep enough for oil tankers to sail to the many oil rigs located on and around it.

Maracaibo The economic center of Venezuela owes its wealth to the petrol. The black gold turned the sleepy provincial town into a glamourous megacity with all imaginable amenities. In the meantime, it has managed to become the second largest metropolis in the Caribbean.

Bonaire Part of the Dutch Antilles, the island is flat and hilly by turns. There is excellent diving at Bonaire Marine Park. The image shows old slave cottages.

Caracas The Venezuelan capital enjoys a mild climate owing to its elevation. The Old Town and churches here are recommended, as is the political wall art, known as murales, which offers a critique of contemporary Venezuelan politics.

Trinidad Port of Spain is the capital of the island and state of Trinidad and Tobago, lying in the mouth of the Orinoco delta. This multicultural city has Hindu temples, churches, and mosques, and a wealth of colonial-era buildings. The natural landscape is by turns mountainous, swampy, and prairie, and there is a lake of asphalt in the south-west of the island.

Tobago The second-largest island of the state is largely forested and mountainous. Its charm resides in its luxuriant natural scenery and the variety of the local marine species. The image shows Pigeon Point.

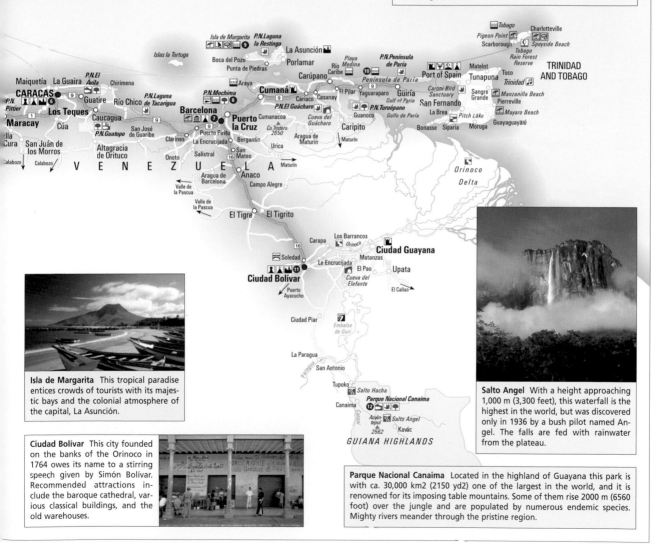

Isla de Margarita This tropical paradise entices crowds of tourists with its majestic bays and the colonial atmosphere of the capital, La Asunción.

Ciudad Bolívar This city founded on the banks of the Orinoco in 1764 owes its name to a stirring speech given by Simón Bolívar. Recommended attractions include the baroque cathedral, various classical buildings, and the old warehouses.

Salto Angel With a height approaching 1,000 m (3,300 feet), this waterfall is the highest in the world, but was discovered only in 1936 by a bush pilot named Angel. The falls are fed with rainwater from the plateau.

Parque Nacional Canaima Located in the highland of Guayana this park is with ca. 30,000 km2 (2150 yd2) one of the largest in the world, and it is renowned for its imposing table mountains. Some of them rise 2000 m (6560 foot) over the jungle and are populated by numerous endemic species. Mighty rivers meander through the pristine region.

Colombia and Ecuador

Following the Panamericana through the northern Andes

The Andes are South America's backbone, and the Panamericana Sur follows this mighty mountain range as it runs the length of the subcontinent from Colombia to the furthest reaches of Patagonia. The road threads its way through indigenous villages and colonial cities, crossing deserts and forests as it passes by mountain peaks and glaciers.

As they pass smoking volcanoes and deep fjords, those who drive the Panamericana will also glimpse evidence of Latin America's glorious but sometimes cruel past. The American states first planned a coherent transport connection as early as 1884, but the original goal of a joint railway line was abandoned at the Pan-American Conference 40 years later and a communally built road was chosen instead. According to the conference's resolution, this gigantic road-building project was also intended to symbolize the concept of general peace and the common goals held by the American peoples. The Panamericana was planned as an all-weather road, which it now is, but the degree to which it has been developed varies considerably in the various countries – although it is one of the main arterial routes of every country it crosses, the road necessarily passes through states with widely varying infrastructures and economic strengths. It has ended up as a motley collection of multi-lane freeways, highways and byways, with side

The villagers of Pasto, Colombia, on "Volcano Road."

Ominous storm clouds scud across the sky over the 16,000 ha (62 sq. miles) of the El Angel nature reserve in northern Ecuador.

Quito at dusk, with the most active volcano in Ecuador, the snow-capped, 5,897-m (19,347-foot) Cotopaxi.

exits to the cities and tourist attractions that lie along our dream route.

The Panamericana is still incomplete: the all-important stretch between Panama and Colombia is broken by the rainforests of north-western Colombia, so there is still no connection with the Panamericana's Central American cousin, the Carretera Interamericana. Both the funds and the political will are lacking for this consummation; trade between the countries has switched entirely to sea transport. Ecologists are not interested in a road either – it would have to go straight through the middle of the Darién National Park in Panama, which has been listed as a UNESCO World Heritage Site for its outstanding animal and plant life.

Colombia is the only South American state with access to both the Pacific and the Caribbean. The fourth-largest country in South America has an area of 1.1 million sq. km (424,712 sq. miles) and a population of about 30 million. It takes its name from Christopher Columbus and is a land of myths – it is the legendary El Dorado, the golden country sought by the Spaniards, and is not short of natural beauty or cultural highlights. Famous for its coffee, it is also infamous for its cocaine and has declined as a tourist destination since the drug cartels, guerillas, and paramilitary factions began a deadly civil war. This is all the more regrettable as Colombia, with its 1,600 km (1,000 miles) of Caribbean and 1,300 km (800

miles) of Pacific coast – not to mention its unspoiled rainforests and snow-capped 5,000-m (16,400-foot) peaks – is one of the most beautiful and diverse lands on the Panamericana.

A Pre-Columbian golden mask from Tierradentro.

The South American section of the Panamericana begins in Bogotá, the capital of Colombia, and crosses the breathtaking mountains of the Andes and a variety of landscapes and cultural regions before reaching Loja in Ecuador.

Colombia is currently a less popular tourist destination, but under more auspicious political circumstances a journey through northern South America might well start in Colombia's capital, Bogotá.

1 Bogotá The country's commercial and cultural hub is situated in a fertile upland valley (2,640 m/8,660 feet) and was founded in 1538. The Plaza de Bolívar in the city's historic center is flanked by the Capitolio Nacional (the national assembly), the presidential residence, the Edificio Lievano (the mayor's residence), the palace of justice, and the supreme court. The cathedral is an early 19th-century, classical creation but the city's greatest tourist sight is the Museo del Oro, with its 30,000 exhibits made of gold, most of which date back to pre-Columbian times.

Bogotá is also a good base for two expeditions north via Tunja to Villa de Leyva and the El Cocuy National Park. Head north-west from Bogotá toward Ecuador on the Panamericana, ascending the Cordillera Oriental, and the next valley will bring you to the town of Honda on the Río Magdalena, a very popular resort with a mild climate. From here the route dips into the Zona Cafetera, where a good half of all Colombian coffee is cultivated; almost every mountain slope between 1,300 m and 1,700 m (4,270-5,580 feet) is covered with coffee plantations.

2 **Manzinales** The Feria Anual de Manzinales, an annual event held in the heart of the region, includes a large international coffee fair and an impressive folk festival.

The city's main attraction is the neo-Gothic 20th-century cathedral, which was constructed out of concrete because of the danger of earthquakes. The Panamericana turns south at Manzaniles to run between the Codillera Occidental and the Cordillera Central, two of the three mighty mountain chains into which the Andes subdivide within Colombia.

3 **Cali** Colombia's second-largest city was founded in 1536 but only began to flourish in the 20th century with the advent of the sugar cane industry. Now the industrial heart of the south-west, the city is well known as a party town and as one of the country's salsa centers, but also infamous as the seat of the Cali Cartel, one of the most pernicious gangs of producers, dealers, and smugglers in the global cocaine and heroin market. The mountains extend close to the south of Cali, with peaks reaching some 1,700 m (5,580 feet). To the south-east of Cali but hard to access lies the Nevado de Huila National Park, with the volcano of the same name (5,750 m/18,865 feet) at its center.

At Río Blanco, shortly before Popayán, there is an exit leading to the Parque Arqueológico Tierradentro (see sidebar, page right).

4 **Popayán** Founded in 1536, the "White City" is a major religious center in Colombia, with magnificent monasteries and churches as well as colonial townhouses that feature wrought-iron balconies and rather beautiful patios. It lies at an elevation of 1,740 m (5,710 feet) and is the best base from which to explore the surrounding mountains. To the south you will find the Parque Nacional Puracé with its three imposing volcanoes: Puracé (4,800 m/15,750 feet), Pan de Azucar (4,800 m/15,750 feet), and Sotará (4,580 m/15,030 feet).

An excursion from Popayán to the Parque Arqueológico San Agustín is definitely recommended. Pasto, the largest city in southern Colombia, is only a short distance further along the Panamericana and as you travel on to Quito you will see the 4,764-m (15,630-foot) peak of Volcán Cumbal to the west as you cross the border into Ecuador at Ipiales. It is the southernmost historically active volcano of Colombia.

1 The southern summit of the Volcán Cumbal (4,764 m/15,630 feet) near Túquerres is an extinct crater, but smoke rises almost continually from several craters and vents around the active northern summit.

2 The high-rise skyline of modern-day Bogotá.

The Cascada de San Rafael waterfall (also known as the Cascada del Coca) on the road from Quito to Lago Agrio via Baeza is at the highest altitude of any falls in the country, and is also one of the most magnificent on the eastern slopes of the Andes. Here the crystal-clear

waters of the Río Coca – a tributary of the Río Napo and thus of the Amazon itself – crash into a gorge 150 m (490 feet) deep. The falls are located not far from the very active 3,562-m (11,686-foot) Volcán El Reventador, and are a mecca for ornithologists.

1

⑤ Otavalo The most beautiful and best-known market in Ecuador is held every Saturday in Otavalo. A cattle market is held a little out of town, while the town center is principally devoted to the sale of textiles: there are ponchos, blankets, jackets, and caps in every shade, shape, and size, all made traditionally from wool and dyed with natural pigments. There is craft work as well: jewelry, wood, and ceramics, all originating from the workshops of the Otavalo people.

Cotacachi, to the west of Otavalo, is one of Ecuador's main producers of leather goods and is the gateway to the Reserva Ecológica Cotacachi-Cayapas. The heart of the park is formed by the Laguna de Cuicocha (3,070 m/10,070 feet), a water-filled impact crater. The lake is dominated by the 4,939-m (16,204-foot) peak of the extinct Volcán Cotacachi.

The Panamericana now follows an extended highland valley that runs the length of Ecuador from north to south, and you will soon see the majestic backdrop of the snow-capped summit of Volcán Cayambe (5,790 m/18,996 feet).

⑥ La Mitad del Mundo Not far from the village of San Antonio de Pichincha you will find a red strip that leads to a concrete pyramid topped with a metal globe – this is the Mitad de Mundo ("half the world"), where you can stand with one foot in the southern hemisphere and the other in the northern. Nearby there is a museum devoted to national ethnography.

⑦ Quito Many visitors begin their journey along the Panamericana in this capital city of millions, home to a tenth of the entire Ecuadorian population. It is also the administrative and cultural center of the country, although Guayaquil is larger, and thanks to its port is the most important commercial conurbation. The air is already quite thin up here at 2,800 m (9,200 feet) above sea level, and if you were to arrive by air, you shouldn't be surprised if climbing only a few steps is enough to leave you out of breath.

The best view of the city is to be had from the Panecillo hill to the west of the historic center, which affords a panorama of the colonial Old Town – now a UNESCO World Heritage Site – and the new town to the north. On clear days you can even see Cotopaxi to the south.

The heart of the Old Town is the Plaza de la Independencia, around which the cathedral, the bishop's palace, the parliament building, and the town hall all huddle. The cathedral contains the sarcophagi of two national heroes: Antonio José de Sucre, one of Simon Bolívar's brothers in arms, and Juan José Flores, the country's first president. A few paces from the Plaza you will find the Spanish baroque of the Iglesia El Sagrario, as well as the Jesuit church of Iglesia la Compañia. The falls at Cascadas San Rafael on the road to Lago Agrio to the east of Quito are also recommended.

⑧ "Volcano Road" South of Quito, the Panamericana crosses the lofty mountains of central Ecuador. Imposing mountain peaks rise up to left and right, including Antisana (5,705 m/18,717 feet), Cotopaxi (5,897 m/19,347 feet; see sidebar page right), and Chimborazo, the highest mountain in the country at 6,310 m/20,702 feet. Alexander von Humboldt (1769–1859), who visited Ecuador in 1802 and climbed Chimborazo to a height of 5,759 m (18,894 feet), christened the highland valley between the two mountain chains "Volcano Road."

The Panamericana runs straight down this valley and passes close to all of Ecuador's important highland cities: Ibarra, Quito, Ambato, Riobamba, Cuenca, and Loja; those wishing

2

to visit the Cotopaxi National Park should take the exit for Pedregal just south of Quito at Machachi.

As the road winds south, the rather unattractive provincial capital of Ambato marks the end of this highland section and we turn east. Beyond Pelileo, the road follows a series of little rivers before running parallel to a valley gouged out of the rock over millions of years by the Río Pastaza, a tributary of the Amazon. The vegetation becomes ever more luxuriant as we descend, and after about 30 km (19 miles) the town of Baños is reached.

9 Baños The town lies at an elevation of 900 m (2,950 feet) and is dominated by the 5,016-m (16,457-foot) peak of the active Tungurahua volcano, whose name means "little hell" in the Quechua language. Its breathtakingly beautiful surroundings, including the steep summits of the Cordillera Real and areas of jungle, its mild climate, and its mineral springs have made this one of the most popular tourist resorts in Ecuador. The Tungurahua volcano in the Sangay National Park is responsible for both the warm thermal springs and the tropical rainforest.

10 Riobamba Returning to the Panamericana will soon bring you to the provincial capital Riobamba in the Chamba Valley. Lying at 2,750 m (9,020 feet) above sea level, the city has only a few attractions to offer – including a cathedral with an ornate façade and the little Museo de Arte Religioso in the Convento Concepción – but there is plenty of authentic highland life, with any number of local tribespeople pouring into the city at the weekend to buy and sell. On clear days, there is a wonderful view of Chimborazo from the Parque 21 Abril in the center of town, and the volcano can be reached by turning off the Panamericana (first head to-

ward Guaranda, then exit right). Riobamba is also a good starting point for a trip to the Parque Nacional Sangay, whose main attractions include three volcanoes: Sangay (5,230 m/17,160 feet), Tungurahua (5,016 m/ 16,457 feet), and Altar (5,319 m/ 17,451 feet).

11 Volcán Chimborazo This 6,310-m (20,700-foot) volcano, whose five peaks rise to a height of some 3,000 m (9,850 feet) above the surrounding highland plains, is a mountain of superlatives: because of the way the earth bulges out near the equator, the summit is the furthest point on the surface from the earth's exact middle.

The snow line begins at about 4,800 m (15,750 feet) and here there is also a rescue hut (and another at 5,000 m/16,400 feet) which is accessible with four-wheel drive vehicles. The climb to the summit takes about 12 hours and needs a good preparation.

12 Alausí The Panamericana Sur divides at Riobamba: the western arm passes through El Triunfo on its way to Guayaquil, but a detour to the port town of Alausí could also begin on the eastern arm.

The town is a station on what is claimed to be the steepest stretch of railtrack in the world (built between 1874 and 1908). The railroad is a technical miracle: in places, the course for the tracks had to be blasted from the rocks with explosives and it now descends from the mountains around Alausí to the coast over a distance of only 130 km (81 miles). The steepest stretch (the "Devil's Nose") sees

1 The 5,790-m (18,996-foot) Cayambe volcano rises majestically above the highlands north-east of Quito.

2 With 5319 m (17,450 feet) the volcano Altar tops all other sommets in Sangay National Park.

1

the track ascend 500 meters (1,640 feet) in the course of only 2 km (1.2 miles)!

⑬ **Ingapirca** The largest and most important Inca ruin in Ecuador is located to the south of Alausí on a 3,160-m (10,370-foot) mountain just off the main road. Ingapirca means "stone wall of the Inca" in the Quechua language; the site was built from large stone blocks neatly fitted together without any mortar, but unfortunately, many of these stones have since been taken away by local people to build houses and churches.
The Inca town was built about 1500 but abandoned only 30 years later, and may have been either a temple or a fortress, to judge from the poor remnants. For the next 80 km (50 miles) the Panamericana crosses a highland basin with the colourful and lively Cuenca at its center.

⑭ **Cuenca** Founded by the Spanish in 1557 on the ruins of the ancient Inca city of Tomebamba, the city possesses the finest collection of colonial architecture in Ecuador, with the possible exception of Quito. There are magnificent churches, interesting museums, and cobbled streets lined with colonial buildings that boast ornate balconies and shady patios. Two cathedrals face one another across the central Plaza: the old cathedral (begun in 1557) is a small, plain building with a low bell-tower, whereas the new cathedral (begun 1885) is a mighty brick structure with two still incomplete façade spires and three blue domes. The marble-clad interior is impressive for its sheer size: a congregation of nearly 10,000 are said to fit into its 105 m by 42.5 m (345 feet by 140 feet) nave. This university town is a peaceful haven of lit-

tle markets and two recommended museums: the Museo del Banco Central, built near the ruins of an old sun temple and the palace of the last Inca ruler, displays finds from Tomebamba, the greatest Inca city in southern Ecuador, while the Museo del Monasterio de las Conceptas has collections of religious folk objects, furniture, and colonial-era art.

⑮ **Parque Nacional El Cajas** About 30 km (19 miles) to the west of Cuenca there is an area of mountainous uplands lying at an elevation of more than 4,000 m (13,100 feet) and with no less than 250 lakes of different sizes. There is a wealth of plant and animal life. With luck you may see toucans and hummingbirds in the western mountain forests or eagles and condors on the open, grassy uplands. Between Cuenca and Loja, the Panameri-

cana runs through typical Páramo scenery, with shrubs and tussock grasses lining the road and moorland and canyons to right and left. The next town is Saraguro, the capital city of a small indigenous tribe, after which the route climbs to Loja at 2,225 m (7,300 feet) above sea level.

⑯ **Loja** Loja's main attraction is the cathedral on the main square. The statue of the Virgen del Cisne (16th century) is kept here from August until the beginning of November, and for the rest of the year resides in the pilgrimage site at El Cisne about 30 km (19 miles) northwest of Loja.

1 The gleaming blue domes of the new cathedral dominate the skyline of Cuenca.

Bogotá Colombia's capital lies at an elevation of 2,640 m (8,660 feet) above seal level. The Museo Fundacion Botero and the gold museum with its pre-Columbian exhibits are world-famous.

El Cocuy National Park This park in the north-east, which has been largely turned over to eco-tourism, is still inhabited by descendants of the U'wa. El Cocuy mountain is 5,493 m (18,020 feet) high.

Villa de Leyva The whitewashed houses of this idyllic little village near Tunja to the north of Bogotá make it one of the colonial jewels of Colombia. It is famous for its wild festivals.

Cali Founded on the Río Cauca in 1536, this city of two million inhabitants at the foot of the western Cordillera is the second-largest in the country. It is famous for its bullfighting traditions, adopted from Spain.

Tierradentro The site had its heyday between 500 BC and 500 AD, and boasts impressively ornate burial chambers.

San Agustín Central Colombian religious and burial site, in use between 3300 BC and 1400 AD.

Sangay National Park A nature reserve near the equator; its volcanoes reach heights between 1,000 m and 5,230 m (3,300 feet and 17,160 feet).

Loja Founded in 1548, Loja is one of the oldest Spanish settlements in Ecuador and also the southernmost. The Old town of this provincial capital of 130,000 inhabitants boasts several charming colonial-era buildings, including the cathedral on the Plaza. The Museo del Banco Central archeological museum is also recommended.

Manizales This charming coffee town has a population of about 400,000. The theater festival and the feria (bullfighting season), which ends with the crowning of the Coffee Queen, are famous throughout the country.

Cumbal Although this volcano near the Ecuadorian border is an impressive 4,764 m (15,630 feet) high, it is considered an easy climb.

Quito The colonial-era buildings of Ecuador's capital are now a UNESCO World Heritage Site.

Cascada de San Rafael Ecuador's highest falls are situated in an area of great interest to birdwatchers.

Cuenca A University city with one of Ecuador's most beautiful Old Towns, numerous colonial-era buildings, and two cathedrals.

Volcán Cotopaxi The 5,897-m (19,347-foot) summit of the highest active volcano in the world is a "relatively easy" climb, even for the inexperienced.

Guayaquil Situated on the Río Guaya river delta, Ecuador's largest city is also its principal port. The Museo del Banco Central records Ecuador's pre-Columbian past.

Ingapirca The "stone wall of the Inca" is the largest Inca ruin in Ecuador; it is thought to have been a fortress or a religious site.

Chimborazo Ecuador's highest mountain (6,310 m/20,700 feet) is a giant extinct volcano with five sister summits of heights around 3,000 m (9,850 feet).

Galápagos Islands

Noah's Ark in the Pacific

When Hermann Melville, the author of Moby Dick, visited the Galápagos in 1841 he described them as "enchanted islands" that were unlike anywhere else in the world in terms of their surreal appearance. Piles of volcanic ash cover the landscape, which appears as the earth might look after a terrible, global fire.

The Galápagos Islands are a surreal and rather inhospitable place, with hills and mountains of lava and sparse forests instead of sandy beaches and palm groves, not to mention the cold water that surrounds them. The average sea temperature in August is a chilly 19°C (66°F), only rising by another 10 degrees or so in March and April, so this is no tourist's dream tropical destination. However, the islands form a truly unique natural paradise for animal and plant life, with species that do not exist anywhere else on earth, including sea lions, reptiles, and water birds. The animals and birds are also unique in that they have no natural enemies on the islands, and, having no fear of humans either, they do not automatically run or fly away when humans approach them.

It is vitally important that this natural world be protected, but inevitably the large numbers of people who now visit the islands represent a threat to its extraordinary wild life. In an effort to preserve the islands, the Ecuadorian government declared them a national park in 1959, and in 1978, the Parque Nacional y Reserva Marina Galápagos became the first area to

Tortoise on the island of Santa Cruz.

be designated a UNESCO World Heritage Site.

The islands are located almost 1,000 km (620 miles) from the coast of Ecuador between 90 and 92°W longitude and 1.4°N and 1.3°S latitude. The group comprises thirteen main islands and around fifty smaller ones. The largest island is Isabela, with a surface area of 4,855 sq km (1,874 sq miles). The volcano of Cerro Azul (1,689 m/5,542 ft), the highest mountain in the island group, is a distinctive landmark. The north-westerly islands of Fernandina and Isabela, the youngest islands geologically-speaking, have the most active volcanoes.

The islands were formed as a result of volcanic activity. They lie on a hotspot, a zone beneath the earth's crust where there is

The Sally Lightfoot crab is the most striking of the three types of crab that live on the islands. In contrast to the mature crabs, the young are gray-black.

A glowing sunset sky over Puerto Villamil on the island of Isabela.

known volcanic activity, with magma rising up from the earth's inner core. Due to continental drift, part of the the earth's crust, in this case the Nazca plate, is moving slowly to the south-east toward the South American continent.

The islands were formed around nine million years ago and were initially an empty wasteland, but today they are famous for their animal and plant life. So how did plants and animals reach these islands so far from the mainland? The majority of the plants were brought here in the form of seeds and spores on the wind, while birds such as albatrosses and terns, and some insects could naturally fly here. Seals, penguins, and sea tortoises could reach the islands by sea, assisted by strong ocean currents. Driftwood and clumps of vegetation floating on the sea may have served as a means of transportation for animals from South America, including the land-dwelling tortoises and lizards. However, only animals that can survive for a long period of time without food and water have been able to survive on the archipelago, explaining why some species are common on the island and others are rare. There are, for example, many sea birds, sea mammals, and reptiles, but no land mammals except for two species of bat (and also rats and goats, introduced by man). For many people the islands are inextricably linked with just one man, Charles Darwin, the English naturalist who, after visiting them in 1835 while on his five-year voyage aboard the Beagle, proposed his theory of evolution. In his seminal work On the Origin of the Species (1859), Darwin proposed that through a process of natural selection all species of life have evolved over time from one or a few common ancestors.

A shoal of yellowfin surgeonfish in the rich waters around the islands.

1

To make the most of a visit to the Galápagos Islands, you really need to spend several days cruising the islands. Not all of them can be visited, however, the national park administration has set up numerous official visitor sites that are open to the public and can be explored with a guide. As a province of Ecuador, the official names of the islands are Spanish (as used here), but they also have English names: Albemarle for Isabela, Narborough for Fernandina, Indefatigable for Santa Cruz, Charles for Floreana, etc.

❶ Santa Cruz Almost all the cruises start on Santa Cruz. It is the second largest island in the archipelago and has not only the most diverse vegetation and the largest town, Puerto Ayora, but is also the location of the Charles Darwin Research Station, the islands' center for scientific research. The creation and evolution of life on the islands is explained at the museum there. The largest tortoise in the world, the Galápagos giant tortoise, endemic to several of the islands, is one of the main attractions here. The station has established a breeding program in an effort to preserve the breed and increase its numbers. As soon as the tortoises have reached a certain size, they are released into the wild, many into the tortoise reserves near Santa Rosa and Santa Cruz, where they lie in the meadows, motionless like large rocks.

In the north of the island is the Caleta Tortuga Negra, a cove with mangroves where a large number of pelicans nest and sea turtles, small whitetip sharks, and rays can be seen in the water.In the smaller and most interesting areas of the cove it is prohibited to use a motor.

❷ Islas Plaza Sur To the east of Santa Cruz are the two Plaza islands, though tourists are only allowed to visit Plaza Sur. Several rare species live here so it is one of the early highlights of the cruise. Sea birds such as the red-billed tropic bird and the swallow-tailed gull nest on ledges along the steep coast and sea lions slide off the rocks to frolic in the water. The Galápagos sea lion, one of the six mammal species that live on the islands, is a subspecies of the Californian sea lion. They live in colonies of around twenty to thirty females to one bull. The males are considerably larger and can weigh up to 250 kg

Travel Information

Route profile
Length: approx. 1,000 km (620 miles)
Duration: at least 1 week
Start and end: Puerto Ayora (Santa Cruz)
Itinerary (main locations): Santa Cruz, Islas Plaza Sur, Floreana, Española, Isabela, Fernandina, Santiago, Bartolomé, Genovesa, Santa Cruz

Travel tips
The cruise ships travel at night and visit the islands during the day when passengers are taken to the islands for excursions. All boats have at least one guide on board. Tourists on package deals who book in Europe or Ecuador are met by the organizer at the airport. Cruises can also be booked in Puerto Ayora on Santa Cruz.

Tourist information
www.visitecuador.de
www.darwinfoundation.org

(550 lbs). They have a strong skull and a massive, thick neck. Usually playful and curious, young sea lions are often encountered in the water by divers.

Under the Opuntia (fig cacti), seemingly lethargic iguana sit in a motionless state. They are small, dragon-like lizards, typically with an orange-yellow back and a red-brown stomach and a ridge of spines running down the neck and back. However, do not be fooled by their apparently quiet demeanor; male land iguanas will defend their territory and females against rivals very aggressively. The only natural enemy of adult land iguanas, which grow to around 1 m (3 ft) in length and weigh around 13 kg (29 lb), are their own kind.

❸ **Floreana** One of the few inhabited islands in the archipelago is Floreana. The first European to set foot on the Galápagos was the Spaniard Tomás de Berlanga. Having failed to find fresh water there he thought them worthless, just a pile of rock inhabited by strange animals. Until the early 1800s the islands were mostly used by English pirates who ambushed Spanish galleons on their way from South America to Spain. Then whalers arrived around 1790 and used the islands as a base from which to hunt not only whales but tortoises until around 1870. They sometimes took live tortoises on

1 This land iguana on the island of Plaza Sur looks like a strange prehistoric creature.

2 Curious sea lions are not afraid to swim close to visitors under the water.

3 Mist shrouds the peaks of the volcanoes on the island of Santa Cruz.

4 A brown pelican's nest, protected by mangroves.

board ship with them to ensure a fresh supply of food. On some of the islands, the tortoises were completely wiped out.

Floreana has an interesting history. The first person to settle here permanently was an Irishman called Patrick Watkins. Stranded on the island in 1807, he made a cave near Post Office Bay his home for several years. He grew vegetables and traded them for rum from passing whalers, but eventually had his fill of the solitary life, stole a dinghy and persuaded five sailors to take him to the mainland. After Ecuador annexed the islands in 1832, Floreana was initially used as a penal colony. In the 1930s, a group of German and Austrian bohemians arrived, dreaming of a life lived close to nature.

However, disputes arose and some of the group died in mysterious circumstances, leading to much speculation in the press at the time. In World War II,

Ecuador granted the US navy permission to establish a base on the islands to guard the approaches to the Panama Canal. Today, only Santa Cruz, San Cristóbal, Floreana, and the south of Isabela are inhabited, but now tourists are arriving in numbers, bringing money to the islands and boosting their economy which otherwise relies on agriculture and fishing.

One of the visitor sites on Floreana is Punta Cormorán to the north of the island, where flamingos can often be seen in the lagoon.

At nearby Post Office Bay you can see a ragtag of mailboxes marking the spot where English whalers first set up a post box in the 18th century. Sailors passing back and forth would stop off to leave mail here to be taken by ships on their way home, or collect post that had been brought out. Today it is the tourists who use the mailboxes however.

④ Española The southernmost island of the archipelago has several beautiful visitor sites. On the coast at Bahía Gardner in the north-east of Española, you can see a large group of sea lions, while at Punta Suárez in the north-west, you can follow a circular trekking path (around 2 km/11/4 miles), which takes you past colonies of blue-footed and masked boobies.

The birds will often remain quite happily in their nests on the ground as tourist pass by just a few feet away. Elegant in flight but awkward on the ground, albatrosses also nest here, while marine iguanas inhabit the cliffs, whereas in the sea they fall prey to sharks.

1 Flamingos search for food in the shallows of the lagoon on Floreana.

2 Marine iguana in the surf.

Despite being all around the same size, the different types of Darwin finches on the island have all developed different shapes and sizes of beak, to suit their different feeding habits. The cactus finch, shown here, feeds mainly on pollen and the fruit of the Optunia (fig cactus).

Covering an area of 4,855 sq km (1,874 sq m), Isabela is the largest of the Galápagos islands and is more volcanically active than most of the others. Situated slightly east of the Galápagos Hotspot, thought to be near Fernandina, Isabela has five active volcanoes. Arranged

roughly from north to south these are: Wolf (1,646 m/5,400 ft), Darwin (1,280 m/4,200 ft), Alcedo (1,097 m/3,600 ft), Sierra Negra (1,490 m/4,887 ft), and Cero Azul (1,689 m/5,542 ft), which last erupted in Setember 1998. Shown here is the circular crater lake of Cero Azul

5 Isabela This is the largest of the Galápagos Islands but one of the least populated. Its capital city, Puerto Villamil, is in the south-east of the island, with around two thousand inhabitants. Nearby, a short walk away through mangrove forests, is the Laguna de Villamil, a popular feeding-ground for flamingos. Puerto Villamil also has the most beautiful beaches of the islands and a breeding station for Galápagos tortoises. You can see them around the crater of the volcano Alcedo (1,097 m/3,599 ft).

On a trek up to the peak from the eastern side of the island, you will pass through several different vegetation zones before arriving at the top from where you can see down into the huge caldera (around 7 km/4 miles in diameter). These almost circular, very deep craters are a typical feature of the islands' volcanic landscape. They are formed when the magma chamber beneath the cone emp-

ties, causing the rock above the now hollow chamber to collapse.

As on the other islands, there are six different vegetation zones on Isabela, determined by the height above sea level. In the coastal zone, almost all the plants, such as mangroves, are resistant to salt and strong ocean winds. The arid lowland zone extends from the coastal zone to an elevation of around 100 m (328 ft) and is dominated mainly by cacti and palosanto trees, which have no leaves for most of the year.

Thanks to more frequent rainfall, evergreen plants flourish in the next zone, the transitional, which extends to around 200 m (656 ft). Next is the Scalesia zone, which rises to 400 m (1,312 ft) above sea level. It is named after the Scalesia plant, a member of the daisy family endemic to the Galápagos Islands. Some species of Scalesia grow so tall they can be classed as trees. The next level is the Mi-

conia zone (up to 500 m/1,640 ft), named after the Miconia, a type of shrub also endemic to the islands that grows up to 4 m (13 ft) in height and often forms an impenetrable tangle of vegetation with other plants. Beyond the Miconia zone, the Pampa zone is the highest and wettest. There are virtually no trees or shrubs growing here, just ferns, grasses, and sedges.

The Pampa zone is also the preferred habitat of the Galápagos tortoise, which can be seen here in large numbers. There were originally fourteen different

tortoise subspecies on the island, but today only eleven remain, living on different islands. In 1835, when Charles Darwin visited the islands, he met the English governor of Floreana, Nicholas Lawson, who told Darwin he could identify from which island any tortoise had been brought by the shape of its shell. Larger and heavier tortoises have evenly formed and dome-shaped shells, while the slightly smaller tortoises have a saddle-shaped shell. The saddleback tortoises gave the islands their name as galápago means

3

tortoise in Spanish. While the larger subspecies of tortoise eats mainly grass, the saddle-back tortoise feeds on slightly taller vegetation, low-growing leaves, and twigs. This is why their shell is arched high at the neck and their legs and necks are slightly longer.

Land tortoises mate during the rainy season, which on the Galápagos is January to June. Then, at the beginning of the dry season, the female tortoise lays two to sixteen eggs in a hole in the ground around 30 cm (12 in) deep, which she digs with her back legs. After four months, the baby tortoises emerge from their shells. Their gender is determined mainly by the temperature at which they are incubated; males develop when the temperature is low and females when it is high.

The very young tortoises are at risk from predators such as buzzards, but once their shells start to harden they are better protected. If attacked, their defen-

sive strategy is normally passive. Expelling air from their bodies with a hiss, they withdraw their head and legs into their shell.

In addition to the tortoises, there are twenty-two other species of interesting reptiles on the islands, twenty of which are endemic. Reptiles are cold-blooded vertebrates that are unable to regulate their body temperature, but are resistant to extreme changes in temperature. They may sit motionless in the sun to warm themselves up after a cold night or after a spell in cold water, while in very hot weather they spend their time keeping cool in water or in the shade.

The marine iguana is unique to the islands; it is the only iguana that swims and forages in saltwater. "A hideous-looking creature, of a dirty black color, stupid, and sluggish in its movements" is how Darwin described it in disgust. It lives on land, but finds most of its food in the ocean, grazing on algae

at depths of up to 15 m (50 ft), and can even survive underwater for up to an hour. Marine iguanas store oxygen in their tissues, which they then consume when underwater, and can also reduce their heart rate from its normal forty-five beats per minute to only eight to twelve beats, and can sometimes stop it altogether. They are excellent swimmers, holding their legs close to their bodies and propelling themselves forward with their long tails. Untroubled by strong currents, they can cling securely to rocks underwater with their strong claws. The marine iguana has no natural predators on land, but while in the ocean it can fall prey to hungry sharks.

After a spell in the water, the iguanas lie close to each other on rocks in the sun to warm themselves up. They expel the salt that they have taken in with their food by spraying it out through a gland in the head. Nature provides for everything.

⑥ Fernandina The third-largest island of the Galápagos is the youngest and also the most volcanically active, situated almost exactly above the hotspot that created the island group. Fernandina's first major eruption did not take place until 1988, which is why the lava formations are different here. The layers of lava are very thin, causing fresh lava to flow out of the crater rather than erupt explosively, and it solidifies very slowly. Two types of lava are characteristic here: pahoehoe, or skeleton lava, which has a

1 Giant tortoises relaxing in the pampa vegetation zone of the Alcedo volcano on Isabela.

2 Close to some red Sally Lightfoot crabs, a group of marine iguanas, warm themselves up after swimming in the cold water.

3 Impressive volcanic activity on the island of Fernandina.

There are two types of iguana on the Galápagos Islands. As its name suggests, the Galápagos land iguana lives almost exclusively on land, the usual habitat of iguanas, while its cousin, the marine iguana, has developed quite a taste for the sea. As a result of the small

amount of food to be found on land, it forages in the ocean, where temperatures can sometimes fall to below 18°C (64°F). The marine iguana can stay underwater for up to an hour, an unusual length of time for a cold-blooded animal.

lumpy or ropy surpface, and aa lava, which is is rougher and more rubbly in appearance, composed of clinker.

At Punta Espinosa, you can see the flightless cormorant, which is endemic to the islands. Since it has no natural predators, but has a plentiful supply of food available on land, it has lost the ability to fly. The largest colony of Galápagos penguins also lives here, which is incidentally the only species of penguin that lives north of the equator.

Brown penguins are also found on Fernandina. They build their nests in low-lying bushes on the coast or in mangrove trees, of which there are also many on the island. The females lay two to three eggs and both male and female share first the incubation of the eggs and then the feeding of the young.

❼ Santiago

The fourth-largest Galápagos island has a desert-like volcanic landscape. There are a number of official visitor sites on the island. At Sullivan Bay to the east of the island, you can see a fresh lava field that is barely eroded, though fresh in volcanic terms means it is around two hundred years old. You can see the different types of lava here and some of the first pioneer plants

(species that colonize previously uncolonized land) such as the lava cactus, though plant life develops very slowly here.

Southern fur seals live at Puerto Egas, on the west of the island, and many varieties of long-legged wading birds can also be sighted along the coast, searching for food in shallow water or marshes. Some of the most striking are flamingos and red-billed American oystercatchers. Great white egrets, cayenne night-herons, and lava herons also live here.

Punta Espumilla is a good place for snorkeling and exploring underwater, but it can often be quite difficult to identify the different fish; there are around three hundred different types to be seen in these waters. You can also see larger marine creatures such as rays and sharks. Of all the different types of ray, only stingrays are dangerous, but even so they are not likely to attack in aggression. They like to hide on the sea bed, burrowing into the sand. They may sting in a reflex action if stepped on, or if attacked by a predator.

Gold rays and the eagle ray (easily identifiable as it is black with white spots) are both far more vibrant in appearance than the stingray. A diverse range of sharks also live here, some are

harmless, such as the gigantic whale shark, which can grow up to 15 m (49 ft) in length and which is seldom glimpsed by divers, while others should be given a wide berth.

Oceanic whitetip sharks are fairly common here and can be aggressive; hammerhead sharks are also aggressive and are easy to identify from their odd hammer-shaped head; and large tiger sharks, which are very dangerous predators, can also be seen.

Feral pigs and goats were introduced to Santiago by humans but caused a great deal of harm to the endemic species. They are likely to have been introduced fairly shortly after Charles Darwin's visit in 1835.

The pig population was reported to be numerous as early as 1875. As pigs are omnivores they eat both native plants and animals, including green turtles, lava lizards, petrels, and the eggs and hatchlings of tortoises. Since their presence was clearly threatening the survival of these species it was decided that drastic action would have to be taken. An eradication program was launched in 1968, and the island was finally cleared of pigs in 2000, while the goat population is now virtually zero too.

❽ Bartolomé

The landscape on the tiny island of Bartolomé looks desert-like in places, but its two sandy beaches, separated by a narrow isthmus, are perfect for swimming and snorkeling. Climb up Bartolomé's volcanic cone, its highest peak, passing cinder cones and lava tunnels on the way, for some beautiful views over Isla Santiago and the Pináculo (Pinnacle Rock), a volcanic rock formation that rises out of the sea like an enormous shark fin. If you are lucky, and if the water is cold enough, penguins and sea lions. The sandy beaches are also the stomping ground of ghost crabs, with their eyes on stalks they have an excellent field of vision.

❾ Genovesa

This small, horse-shoe-shaped "bird island" north of the equator is of volcanic origin. It covers just 14 sq km (5 sq miles) and its highest point, a volcanic peak, is just 76 m (249 ft) above sea level. Genovesa is home to what is probably the largest collection of red-footed boobies (up to 140,000 pairs).

1 The two beautiful beaches of Bartolomé are separated by a narrow isthmus. On the right is the Pináculo rock formation. The island of Santiago is in the background.

Cerro Azul (Isabela) At 1,689 m (5,542 ft), this is the highest volcano on Isabela and has a round crater lake. As the island is only just east of the Galápagos volcanic Hotspot, earth tremors are quite common.

Alcedo (Isabela) Giant tortoises inhabit the pampa zone on this volcano (1,097 m/3,590 ft), where they feed on grass. The giant tortoise can live for as long as 200 years.

Santiago Vegetation is sparse here, but it is a good diving location; sharks and rays can be seen as well as marine iguanas who brave the cold waters in search of food.

Bartolomé This small island is characterized by its rugged rocky cliffs and isolated beaches. The Pináculo rock rises up in the distance to the right.

Marchena

Bahía Darwin

Genovesa ❾

Roca Redonda

Punta Albemarle

Parque Nacional y Reserva Marina Galápagos

Volcán Wolf
610 ▲ 1646 ▲

Punta Espumilla

Santiago ❼

Bahía Banks

Cerro Cowan 884 ▲

Sullivan Bay

Bartolomé ❽

Volcán Darwin 1280 ▲

Puerto Egas

Punta Espinosa

Cabo Douglas

Seymour

Volcán La Cumbre 1463 ▲

Volcán Alcedo 1097 ▲

Rábida

Caleta Tortuga Negra

Baltra

Fernandina ❻

Pinzon

Santa Cruz ❷

Santa Rosa

Cerro Chacras 864 ▲

Islas Plaza Sur

Bahía Elizabeth

Punta Moreno

Isabela ❺

Volcán Sierra Negra 1490 ▲ ○ Tomás de Borlanga

Puerto Ayora

Santa Fé

San Cristóbal

Puerto Grande

Cerro San Joaquín 896 ▲

Puerto Baquerizo Moreno

Cabo Norte

Punta Cristóbal

Cerro Azul 1689 ▲

Puerto Villamil

Tortuga

Cabo Rose

Floreana ❸

Post Office Bay

Punta Cormorán

Puerto Valesco Ibarra

640 ▲

Española ❹

Punta Suárez

Bahía Gardner

Santa Cruz The second-largest Galápagos Island is the starting point for many of the islands' tours. It is known for its diverse vegetation and its land tortoise reserve.

Puerto Villamil (Isabela) The largest town on Isabela, Puerto Villamil has a small airport and a lagoon. It makes a good starting point for trips to other islands by boat.

Fernandina The youngest and most volcanically active of the Galápagos Islands experienced its last major eruption in 1988. This is a good place to see several of the different types of lava.

Floreana Though now almost deserted, you can still see traces of human activity here, the legacy of early settlers, whalers, and pirates. Flamingos inhabit a lagoon to the north of the island.

Española This island is worth visiting for its rich wildlife, including lava lizards and marine iguanas, and birds such as albatrosses, finches, and boobies.

Peru

With the Panamericana
along the Peruvian Pacific coast

Peru was the heart of the Inca civilization, and its riches also made it the center of the Spanish colonial empire. Cuzco, at an altitude of 3,500 m (11,484 ft) in the Andean highlands, was founded as the Inca capital in the 12th century. From here, the Incas continued to expand until their empire reached from Ingapirca in Ecuador to northern Argentina at the start of the 16th century. The Inca themselves had built a road over 5,000 km (3,107 mi) long, setting up stations (tambos) a day's march apart where the travel-weary could stop get refreshments.

The Inca Road was an important communications and transport artery within the extensive dominions of the Spanish. For the most part it ran through the Andes, but there were also shorter, seemingly insignificant, routes along the Pacific coast in what is modern-day Peru.

The Spanish, who had conquered the Inca empire under Francisco Pizarro in 1532, established the capital of their viceroyalty in Lima, on the coast, as early as 1535. However, for a long time Peru's economic heart remained in the country's interior, in the domains of the fallen Inca. Things have changed since then as the focus of power shifted to Lima. In modern times this shift has also been influenced by the Panamericana, which primarily runs along the coast. The ports and coastal towns (Chiclayo, Trujillo, Chimbote, Lima-Callao or Arequipa) have since become important industrial conurbations. Peru's mineral resources, meanwhile, have become the backbone of the economy and are shipped from those ports.

Peru was the wealthiest and most important of Spain's Latin American colonies. The country's gold and silver mines – the most important of which were situated near Potosí, in the heart of the former Inca empire – yielded immeasurable volumes and hence almost every important colonial town boasts its own resplendent civil buildings as well as magnificent churches.

Then, as now, Peruvian society was characterized by one element: the highly conspicuous contrast between rich and poor. Impoverished shanties stand

Representation of a Mochican chief.

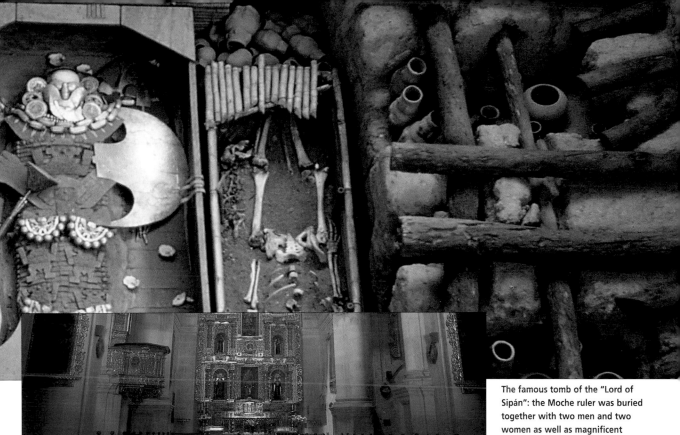

The famous tomb of the "Lord of Sipán": the Moche ruler was buried together with two men and two women as well as magnificent weapons, gold clothing and valuable artworks.

Arequipa, the "White City", is home to numerous baroque monasteries, churches and palaces.

next to magnificent palaces – those of the colonial era and those of the industrial age.

About twenty-seven million people live in Peru, some 70 percent of them in the inhospitable coastal region and 25 percent in the highlands of the Andes. Only five percent live in the Selva, the Amazon lowlands. An astonishing one-third of the population lives within the Greater Lima area alone, and all of the cities continue to grow.

As in most Latin American countries, Spanish is the official language in Peru; many Peruvians however speak a different mother tongue. More than half of the country's inhabitants come from Indian families, so almost one-third of the population speaks Quechua (the language of the Inca empire), and four percent speaks Aymara as their first language, which is another Native American language.

A majority of the poorest people are "indígenas" – indigenous folk. It is estimated that four out of every ten Peruvians live in abject poverty.

Peru is the third-largest country in South America after Brazil and Argentina. It is a country of great contrasts with arid coastal deserts, impressive peaks in the central Andes region and the Selva, and tropical rainforests in the east that form part of the Amazon lowlands.

The Panamericana follows the coast for most of its length, passing through inhospitable scree and sand landscapes. Almost no rain falls here because the humidity coming from the ocean is only released as rain at a height of 800 m (2,625 ft). The coastal deserts are dotted with occasional river oases where earlier civilizations and later the Spanish built their towns.

Thanks to the cold Humboldt Current, however, the entire coast is very rich in fish stocks and it is therefore still a popular area to settle.

View over Huascarán National Park from the statue of Christ in Yungay.

Following the Panamericana through Peru means that you get to know one portion of the country, but will miss out on some mountain regions and rainforest. The coastal route does, however, provide an insight into the country's various cultures, which extend from the adobe pyramids of the Moche people to the desert images of the Nazca civilization and Spanish colonial-era buildings.

① Piura The Spanish conquistadors founded this town on the northern rim of the Sechura Desert in 1532, and some of its colonial-era buildings have survived the years. Mostly, though, it is simply a suitable stopover before crossing the desert on the way to Chiclayo.
From Piura you drive through 220 km (137 mi) of bleak sand and stone landscape.

② Chiclayo The fourth-largest town in Peru is the ideal starting point for visiting the region's archaeological sites. You start in Lambayeque 12 km (7.5 mi) to the north-west, which not only has a number of attractive colonial buildings, but also the Museo Tumbas Reales de Sipán. The museum holds wonderful

collection of ceramics and textiles from Northern Peru, and exhibits from Sipán, Moche and Chan Chan.

③ Sipán With the tomb of the so-called Lord of Sipán, this town 32 km (20 mi) east of Chiclayo, the burial site of the Moche warrior, which has been fully reconstructed, is one of Peru's most interesting excavations. The dead ruler lay on the upper level of a 30-m-high (98-ft), six-storey pyramid, beset by a number of decorative items and skeletons. The landscape soon becomes more fertile south of Chiclayo, with sugar plantations lining the road before the gray desert begins again at Chicama. It extends as far as Chan Chan about 30 km (19 mi) away.

Travel Information

Route profile
Length: about 2,600 km (1,616 mi)
Time required: at least 3 weeks

Start: Piura
End: Tacna
Route (main locations):
Piura, Trujillo, Lima, Reserva Nacional de Paracas, Nazca, Arequipa, Tacna

Special note:
Protests and demonstrations with roadblocks have been a regular occurrence in Peru in recent years. Peru also has a pretty high crime rate (drug-related, robbery, kidnapping). Slum areas should be avoided,

as should nighttime overland journeys. The route follows the Panamericana, which runs parallel to the coast, but there are some worthwhile detours to sights in the country's interior. They bring you from Pisco to Ayacucho, from Nazca to Cuzco/Machu Picchu and from Arequipa to Lake Titicaca.
Roads near the coast tend to be well maintained. Farther inland that changes and you may need four-wheel-drive vehicles to get around.

Information:
travel.peru.com
www.justperu.org
www.peruatravel.com

④ Chan Chan This town was founded in the 12th/13th centuries as the capital of the Chimú realm. The Inca later conquered the Chimú empire in 1460, but its true decline, like

many cultures here, came only with the arrival of the Spanish. Chan Chan comprises ten districts, each with its own temple pyramid which, like the houses, are all built from adobe (clay

bricks). From Chan Chan, one of Peru's many UNESCO World Heritage Sites, it just a short way to the city of Trujillo.

⑤ Trujillo For a city with some 1.2 million residents, Trujillo's Old Town has an astonishingly charming colonial feel. Fortunately, many of the 17th- and 18th-century buildings have survived a number of earthquakes: the cathedral with the magnificent choir stalls is one of them, as are the aristocratic houses in the blocks around the central plaza. South of the town center

there is a bridge over the Río Moche and 6 km (4 mi) further on you reach the adobe pyramids of Moche.

⑥ Moche The largest of the pyramids at the foot of the Cerro Blanco is the Huaca de Sol (pyramid of the sun), built in the 5th century using over 140 million clay bricks. The pyramid covers an area of 55,200 sq m (66,000 sq yds), making it one of the largest pre-Columbian structures in of South America. Its relief walls are ornately decorated with animal and geometric figures.

The route now continues south along the Panamericana via Chimbote as far as Casma. Here you leave the coastal road and travel east to Huarás at 3,028 m (9,935 ft) in the Cordillera Negra (Black Range), almost 100 km (62 mi) away. This town is the gateway to the Huascarán National Park.

⑦ Parque Nacional Huascarán Nevado Huascarán, the highest mountain in the Peruvian Andes, forms the heart of this national park at an elevation of 6,768 m (22,206 ft).

The park contains the core of the Cordillera Blanca (the White Range), a snow-capped chain with more than two dozen peaks over 6,000 m (20,000 ft). Chavín de Huántar, yet another UNESCO World Heritage Site, is also within the park.

⑧ Chavín de Huántar It is still not clear today whether Chavín was a town, a temple area or a pilgrimage site. What is clear, however, is that the complex was built around 800 BC and

belonged to the Chavín civilization, which extended from Piura to Lake Titicaca between 1400 and 400 BC. At the center of the site is a 5-m (16 ft) monolith depicting a deity with clawed hands and a jaguar's head.

The road now takes you via Callejón de Huaylas back to the Panamericana for the journey to Paramonga.

⑨ Paramonga This Chimú temple stands high up above the coast and affords a splendid

1 Only a few of the buildings at Chan Chan still bear evidence of the reliefs that once decorated the houses and walls.

2 Huascarán National Park is home to the Nevado Huascarán (6,768 m/22,206 ft), Peru's highest mountain.

3 Tucume Moche is about 45 km (30 mi) north of Chiclayo. From the Mirador you have a view over twenty-six clay pyramids, unwalled citadels and residential areas.

view of the Pacific Ocean. Its mighty walls made it impregnable.

After a drive through the coastal desert you reach the capital Lima about 200 km (124 mi) away.

⑩ Lima Lima is Peru's cultural, economic and political center with one-third of the total Peruvian population. The city boasts twelve universities as well as the oldest college in the Americas, founded in 1551. Lima is also Peru's capital, and is home to the seats of government and administrative offices. The Port of Callao is the country's most important transport hub. As a city, Lima is literally overflowing: the very heavily populated outskirts are full of shanty towns and slums. After leaving greater Lima you reach Pachacámac another 30 km (19 mi) away.

⑪ Pachacámac This excavation site was once the center of the Cuismancu empire, estab-

lished in around 500 and later subjugated by the Incas. Pachacámac was founded in around 800 and was one of the largest towns in Peru when the Spanish arrived. The Inca built a stepped pyramid around 80 m (262 ft) high over the Cuismancu sanctuary. From the top of the platform you get wonderful panoramic views. The small museum has an interesting model of the now almost completely derelict town.

The Panamericana stays on the Pacific coast for the next 170 km (106 mi), passing a series of seaside resorts that serve as getaway destinations for residents of Lima during the December to April season and on weekends. Towns such as Punta Hermosa, Punta Negra, San Bartolo, Santa María and especially Pucusana, slightly back from the Panamericana, have great beaches.

San Vicente de Cañete, a small market town surrounded by cotton fields, and Chincha Alta are

the next two stops. Chincha Alta is known for its distinctive Afro-Peruvian culture. It is home to a larger number of the descendants of African slaves who were shipped in to work on the plantations in this area.

The road branches off from the Panamericana to Tambo Colorado and Ayacucho, near Pisco.

⑫ Tambo Colorado The Peruvian coast boasts but a few Inca ruins. Tambo Colorado, whose name comes from the traces of red on the walls, is one of the best preserved sites. The ruins are situated at an elevation of 530 m (1,739 ft) about 50 km (31 mi) from the Panamericana. It is not clear today whether Tambo Colorado was a sun temple or a military base.

Anyone looking for adventure can continue along the road to Ayacucho, which climbs up into the mountains to an elevation of 4,600 m (15,093 ft) at Castrovirreyna after roughly 70 km

(43 mi). The Andes here present a superb panorama.

Back on the Panamericana you soon reach Pisco.

⑬ Pisco The town of Pisco would not be as well known if it were not for the famous marc schnapps of the same name. Indeed, the Peruvian national drink, Pisco Sour, has turned the town into a tourist destination even though most of the distilleries are located around Ica, about 60 km (37 mi) farther to the south. The Old Town of Pisco has even developed its own port. It is now 15 km (9 mi) to Paracas, from where the boats sail to the Islas Ballestas.

⑭ Islas Ballestas Because it is a sanctuary for tens of thousands of sea birds, it is prohibited to land on the islands. You are only allowed to observe from the boat. The Islas Ballestas, Isla Sangayan and the nearby Reserva Nacional de

source of great wealth for the region: their guano, meaning dung in Quechua, was the best natural fertilizer and fetched very high prices on international markets before the rise of artificial fertilizers.

⑮ Reserva Nacional de Paracas

This nature reserve is worth a visit not just for nature lovers, but for anyone who is interested in ancient civilizations – the peninsula was settled as early as 3000 BC. People here once lived primarily from fishing and gathering mussels. In around 1000 BC maize, cassava, cotton and beans were cultivated by a community living here. It is considered the earliest example of a complex society on the southern Peruvian coast.

The museum in Paracas details the fascinating history of the settlement of the Paracas Peninsula. On display are the archaeological finds that have been excavated on the peninsula since 1925, including mummies, wrapped in woven shrouds.

Both the graves and the mummies had remained almost completely intact due to the location and the dry climate. Based on the burial grounds, the Paracas civilization was divided into two types: the cavernas graves date from the period 600 to 400 BC, while those from the necropolis date from 400 BC to AD 200.

On a slope north-west of the Bay of Paracas (best viewed from the sea) is the 120-m-tall (394-ft) "Candelabra" geoglyph. It is also known as the "Three Crosses", the "Trident" or the "Tree of Life". Its actual meaning still remains unclear. Was it a navigational aid for ships? A fetish image? Or a stylized sign of the zodiac?

Experts believe that the image derives from the same civilization as the Nazca geoglyphs, while others surmise it was created more recently, in the 19th century.

⑯ Nazca

You can make the comparison yourself with the Nazca Lines (Líneas de Nazca) some 150 km (93 mi) further to the south. They were created in the stony desert soil during the Nazca civilization. The building work involved clearing away the dark gravel of the top layer to a depth of up to 20 cm (9 in) over a width of 1 m (1.1 yds) to form colossal geometric shapes and figures such as a monkey, a 46-m (50-yd) spider, hands and the Colibri, which also often appears on Nazca ceramics. The largest

Paracas to the south (the Islas Ballestas are not part of the park) boast what can be assumed to be the highest density of sea birds in the world. The cliffs of this wild, craggy group of islands, pounded by the foaming blue-green waves of the Pacific, provide ideal nesting grounds – and shelter.

Until the mid-19th century, these sea birds were an indirect

1 The wild, craggy, storm-battered coast of the Paracas Peninsula is a paradise for sea birds.

2 Despite its height, the peak of the Chachani Volcano near Arequipa is generally considered an easy climb at 6,080 m (19,948 ft).

3 The "Candelabra" geoglyph in Paracas, viewed from the ocean.

figures measure up to 200 m (219 yds) and some of them are incomplete. There are more than one hundred overall and around thirty human or animal images in total. From the viewing platform you get a good look at three of the images: the hands, the lizard and the tree.

You are now directly on the Panamericana, but even from the platform the lines, which are up to half a mile long, reveal real images. To really grasp their size and beauty, take a short sightseeing flight from the nearby airfield in Nazca. The figures are best seen from the air.

South of the town of Nazca, the Panamericana initially takes you through a desolate desert landscape and past the Cementerio de Chauchilla, where the Nazca dead were preserved in this arid climate by an impressive method of natural mummification.

After 85 km (53 mi), the road reaches the Pacific again near Puerto de Lomas. To Camaná it is another 300 km (186 mi) through a desert of gravel that skirts the steep coastline. The route takes you up and down hilly stretches, and you roll past a series of bays with beautiful long beaches. There are also a number of sleepy fishing villages on the way that only come to life when the regional bus makes a stop here.

17 Camaná With its attractive beaches, this small town has quickly become a popular seaside resort for the residents of Arequipa. Originally founded as the port for Potosí and Arequipa, the goods produced in Camaná are now shipped from the port further south.

18 Arequipa The "White City", or "Ciudad blanca", is the local nickname for Arequipa, and when you arrive at the central plaza you realize why: the shiny white cathedral and the myriad other white colonial buildings with their two-storey arcades characterize the cityscape. All of them were built from the white volcanic rock sillar quarried in the region and still used as a building material today.

The Old Town of Arequipa, which was founded in 1540 and experienced its peak in the 17th and 18th centuries, has been perfectly restored, an effort that earned it the title of UNESCO World Heritage Site in 2000. The two most important attractions are buildings of religious significance. The Jesuit church dates from 1698, and the decoration of its façade displays distinct Indian influences, as does Santa Catalina monastery, a "town within a town" with fountains, squares and courtyards. It was expanded in the 17th century to its present size of 20,000 sq m (215,2000 sq ft).

Two volcanoes form the backdrop for Arequipa, at an elevation of 2,370 m (7,776 ft): Volcán Misti (5,835 m/19,145 ft), which is constantly smoking, and the higher but much easier to climb Chachaní (6,080 m/19,948 ft).

From Arequipa the route continues through the desert along the Panamericana to the south. Moquegua, a town situated in the river valley of the same name, meaning "quiet place", is worth a short visit and is about 213 km (132 mi) away. It has a lovely Old Town center around the plaza with a number of well-restored churches and other colonial buildings.

Torata, about 24 km (15 mi) away, also has a scenic Old Town with traditional houses featuring mojinete or slanted roofs.
You then come to Tacna after another 185 km (115 mi).

19 Tacna The last of the larger Peruvian towns before you reach the Chilean border used to belong to Chile, from 1880 to 1929. In 1880, during the so-called Saltpeter War, the Chileans conquered large parts of Peru and Bolivia in order to take control of the salt-producing regions of the desert. Chile gave the town of Tacna back to Peru in 1929 following a referendum.

The battlefield from 1880 can be visited on a hill above the town. The town center has two early works by André Gustave Eiffel: the cathedral at the plaza and the fountains.

From Tacna it is then an other 46 km (29 mi) to the Chilean border at Concordia.

1 Palm-lined Plaza de Armas in Arequipa where the 19th-century cathedral takes up the entire north side of the plaza.

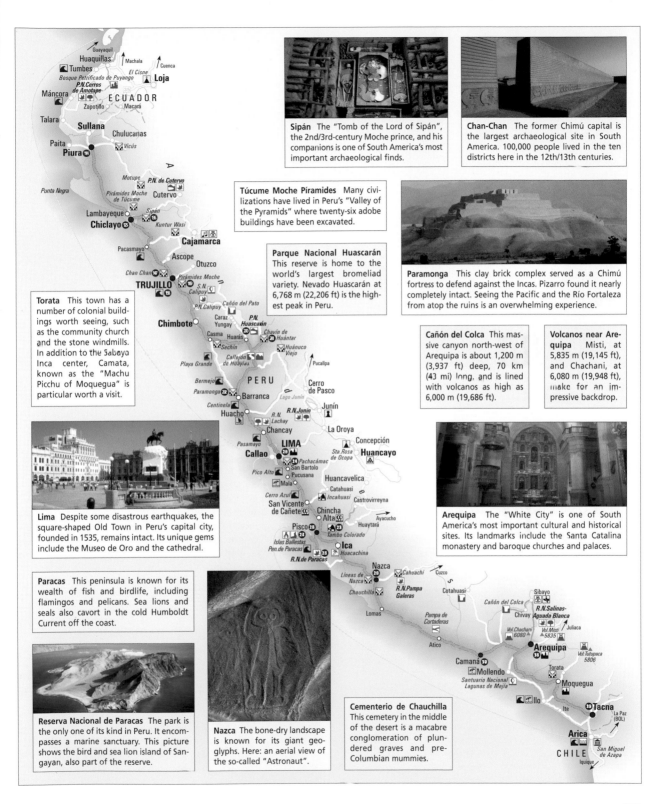

Sipán The "Tomb of the Lord of Sipán", the 2nd/3rd-century Moche prince, and his companions is one of South America's most important archaeological finds.

Chan-Chan The former Chimú capital is the largest archaeological site in South America. 100,000 people lived in the ten districts here in the 12th/13th centuries.

Túcume Moche Pirámides Many civilizations have lived in Peru's "Valley of the Pyramids" where twenty-six adobe buildings have been excavated.

Parque Nacional Huascarán This reserve is home to the world's largest bromeliad variety. Nevado Huascarán at 6,768 m (22,206 ft) is the highest peak in Peru.

Paramonga This clay brick complex served as a Chimú fortress to defend against the Incas. Pizarro found it nearly completely intact. Seeing the Pacific and the Río Fortaleza from atop the ruins is an overwhelming experience.

Torata This town has a number of colonial buildings worth seeing, such as the community church and the stone windmills. In addition to the Sabaya Inca center, Camata, known as the "Machu Picchu of Moquegua" is particular worth a visit.

Cañón del Colca This massive canyon north-west of Arequipa is about 1,200 m (3,937 ft) deep, 70 km (43 mi) long, and is lined with volcanos as high as 6,000 m (19,686 ft).

Volcanos near Arequipa Misti, at 5,835 m (19,145 ft), and Chachani, at 6,080 m (19,948 ft), make for an impressive backdrop.

Lima Despite some disastrous earthquakes, the square-shaped Old Town in Peru's capital city, founded in 1535, remains intact. Its unique gems include the Museo de Oro and the cathedral.

Arequipa The "White City" is one of South America's most important cultural and historical sites. Its landmarks include the Santa Catalina monastery and baroque churches and palaces.

Paracas This peninsula is known for its wealth of fish and birdlife, including flamingos and pelicans. Sea lions and seals also cavort in the cold Humboldt Current off the coast.

Reserva Nacional de Paracas The park is the only one of its kind in Peru. It encompasses a marine sanctuary. This picture shows the bird and sea lion island of Sangayan, also part of the reserve.

Nazca The bone-dry landscape is known for its giant geoglyphs. Here: an aerial view of the so-called "Astronaut".

Cementerio de Chauchilla This cemetery in the middle of the desert is a macabre conglomeration of plundered graves and pre-Columbian mummies.

Peru and Bolivia

The Inca Trail

The Inca Trail connects the capitals of Peru and Bolivia and passes through culturally and historically significant sites in the highlands of the Andes Mountains. Travellers will be amazed by magnificent monuments dating back to early Inca civilization and Spanish colonial times.

The Inca Trail begins in the Peruvian capital of Lima, extends through the western cordilleras (range) of the Andes and runs right across Peru to Lake Titicaca. From there, one of the most spectacular routes in the whole of South America travels over Bolivian territory through the basin scenery of the Altiplano to the south-east and finally terminates in the eastern cordilleras of the Andes, in Sucre, the country's constitutional capital.

A fascinating natural environment, protected in a number of national parks such as the Parque Nacional Manú, provides a stunning backdrop for the region's cultural treasures.

At the beginning of the 16th century, before the arrival of the Spanish, the Inca Empire covered almost the entire Andes region, including parts of the Andean foreland. A large number of the architectural treasures of this advanced civilization have been preserved along the Inca Trail. The architectural highlights include spectacular temples and palaces as well as a series of fortresses built at impressively shrewd locations. Most of these huge buildings, such as the large sun temple at Cuzco, were also built without significant technological assistance. A prime example of the strategic locations selected for Inca settlements is

Highland Indians with their llamas.

Machu Picchu, an extraordinary terraced site and one of the Incas' last places of refuge from advancing colonial troops.

Ironically, the Spanish never actually discovered this well-hidden settlement, which lies at around 2,800 m (9,187 ft). It was an American explorer who first found it in 1911. However, the discovery brought with it more riddles than answers regarding Inca culture.

Lake Titicaca, which still has a healthy fish population, straddles the Peru-Bolivia border. It lies 3,812 m (12,507 ft) above sea level and is not only the largest lake in South America, it is also the highest navigable lake in the world. Close to its southern shores is the town of Tiahuanaco (also known as Tiwanaku) which, up until the 10th century, was

A view of the ruins of Machu Picchu, a glorious terraced Inca city in the high Andes.

In Sillustani, on Laky Umayo, the Colla cultures buried their important citizens under chullpas, or burial mounds.

the religious and administrative center of an important pre-Columbian civilization. The natural environment in the region around Lake Titicaca is also spectacular. Some of the highest mountains in the Andes are here, including the 6,880-m (22,573-ft) Nevado del Illimani, located south-east of Bolivia's largest city and administrative capital, La Paz.

Numerous remnants of the Spanish colonial era can also be seen here, in particular in the area around Lago de Poopó. The Europeans were especially interested in the mineral wealth of the 'New World', and large numbers of Indians were forced to work as slaves in Spanish mines, many of them losing their lives in the process. At the beginning of the 17th century

Potosí was the world's most important center for silver mining. As a result of its historical significance the town has been declared a UNESCO World Heritage Site, together with Cuzco, Machu Picchu and the Old Town of Lima. The listing has been awarded for both the ancient Inca sites and also for some of the architectural achievements of the Spanish colonial rulers.

In addition to these cultural and historical features, the diverse natural environment in this South American region has also been given its share of attention – the Manú National Park, in the transition zone between the Amazon lowlands and the middle Andes, has been declared a biosphere reserve by UNESCO in 1977 and a World Natural Heritage Site ten years later.

With its dramatic differences in altitude, the Inca Trail provides a wonderful cross-section not only of Peru and the northern reaches of Bolivia, but also of the ancient history and the diverse scenery and natural environment of an entire continent.

Women with traditional hats offer their produce at the market in Cuzco.

427

The Inca Trail runs from Lima on the Peruvian Pacific coast through countless Andean passes, majestic mountains and high plateaus on its way to Sucre in Bolivia. The route features both desert landscapes and tropical rainforests as well as high mountain lakes. The well-preserved Inca ruins make the journey an unforgettable experience.

1 Lima Our journey begins in the largest city on the Inca Trail, where traffic is characterized by the expected noise and chaos of a large urban center. Lima was founded by the Spanish in 1535 and they quickly established it as the focal point of their colonial empire in South America. In 1826 Lima replaced Cuzco as the capital and grew into a wealthy metropolis.

Some of the most magnificent buildings from this era – palaces and churches – have since been beautifully restored to their original glory. The main cathedral (1535–1625) is located on Plaza San Martín in the historic Old Town, which itself has been declared a World Heritage Site in its entirety. The tomb of the

conqueror Francisco Pizarro, the founder of Lima, is also said to be somewhere in the city.

Lima is a junction for several important transcontinental routes such as the Pan-American Highway. When you leave Lima heading east you will unfortunately encounter few inviting locations. Due to significant migration from the countryside, sprawling slums have developed on the outskirts of the city. Road conditions in the outer areas can be very bad at times. The multi-lane Pan-American Highway runs past these outskirts before heading south towards Pachacámac.

You will soon leave the coastal flats as the road climbs quickly into the Andean foothills toward

Travel Information

Route profile
Length: approx. 2,000 km (1,243 miles)
Time required: 3 weeks
Start: Lima, Peru
End: Sucre, Bolivia
Route (main locations):
Lima, Ayacucho, Cuzco, Machu Picchu, Lake Titicaca, La Paz, Cochabamba, Oruro, Potosí, Sucre

Traffic information:
Drive on the right side. Road conditions vary considerably. Heavy rainfall and the resulting landslides can make some mountain routes impassable.

When to go:
The best time for travelling to the Andes is during the southern hemisphere winter (May to September), as the southern summer (December to March) is the rainy season. The temperature range between night and day is considerable.

Information:
Peru travel info:
www.peru.info/perueng.asp
Bolivian travel info:
www.boliviaweb.com
Peruvian and Bolivian embassies around the world:
www.embassyworld.com

the market town of La Oroya. There are some steep, winding road sections here. From there a detour (64 km/40 miles) heads north to Junín where several memorials commemorate the

Battle of Junín in 1824 between Simon Bolívar's troops and Spanish soldiers, one of many South American battles for independence. The journey then continues through the narrow but

fertile Mantaro Valley towards the town of Huáncayo.

2 Huáncayo The Mantaro Valley is renowned for its numerous pre-Columbian ruins. It ends in Huáncayo, the largest town in the region. Maize, potatoes and vegetables are grown outside the town using irrigation and in some places the allotments seem to stretch beyond the horizon.

Huáncayo, at an altitude of roughly 3,350 m (10,991 ft), is an important regional trading cen-

ter. Today there is little left as a reminder that the town was once also a center of the Inca Empire. The cityscape is today characterized by Spanish colonial architecture.

The route now heads along a valley towards the south and the climate becomes milder with the decreasing altitude. Prickly pears grow right up to the roadside, their fruit highly prized by the Peruvians.

3 Ayacucho This city, at an elevation of 2,760 m (9,056 ft), is

an interesting combination of past and present. Ayacucho was at one time the capital of the Huari Empire, one of the first advanced civilizations in the Andes and, as such, a predecessor to the Incas.

The city was discovered and refounded in 1539 by Francisco Pizarro. It is known as the 'City of 33 churches' and indeed, religious ceremonies play a major role here. The Holy Week processions (Semana Santa) are among the most important of their kind in South America, drawing visitors from all parts of the country.

4 Huari Approximately 22 km (14 mi) north-east of Ayacucho is Huari, once a key center of the culture of the same name (6th–12th centuries). During the heyday of the Huari Empire in the 9th century nearly 100,000 people lived here. The city was carefully planned and the grid-like layout of the streets can still be seen today. The well-organized

Huari armies had a history of subordinating enemy peoples, but the city was ultimately abandoned in the 10th century.

Back on the main route we now head east past more Andean peaks towards Cuzco, the red tiled roofs of which can be seen from miles away.

5 Cuzco For many travellers, Cuzco is one of the most important destinations in Peru. With its scenic location in the Andes, relaxed atmosphere, easy access to its attractions, and especially as a base for tours to the sacred Urubamba Valley and Machu

1 Rooftop view of the Renaissance-style cathedral in Cuzco (17th century).

2 Near Cuzco, a high-altitude basin framed by snow-capped Andean peaks.

3 Plaza San Martín, the lively center of the Peruvian capital, Lima.

Picchu, the city is indeed a highlight along the Inca Trail.

For the Incas, Cuzco was the focal point of their empire and therefore the center of the world as they knew it. They established the city as a political, religious and cultural hub. Upon their arrival the Spanish knew of the city's importance but they were dazzled by its wealth and grandeur. Unlike in other Inca strongholds, the Spanish destroyed only a few of the buildings when they invaded Cuzco, and only the most significant structures with political or religious functions were razed. On those earlier foundations the colonial rulers then erected a series of their own buildings, some stately in scale, others of religious importance.

The Plaza de Armas, for example, was constructed on the site of the former main square, Huacaypata, at the time 600 m (1,969 ft) long. Santo Domingo monastery was built from the ruins of the Coricancha sun temple. The Jesuit church La Compañía (1571) was constructed on the foundations of the grand Inca palace, Huayna Capac.

In 1950, parts of the city were destroyed by a strong earthquake. Fortuitously, however, the quake actually unearthed a number of Inca remains and ruins that had been previously hidden from view.

Cuzco's importance remains unchanged for the descendants of the Inca. The Quechua-speaking Indians hold colourful ceremonies in the city, in which the customs and traditions of their forebears are relived, and yet Christian festivals are also celebrated with great enthusiasm. The annual Corpus Christi processions in particular attract much attention. In 1983 the Old Town was declared a UNESCO World Heritage Site.

6 Sacsayhuamán Situated above Cuzco – about 3 km (2 mi) north of the city – are the remains of a mighty fortress. Between 1440 and 1532 the Inca built an imposing citadel here encircled by three concentric rings of walls.

Sacsayhuamán can be reached on foot from Cuzco in just under half an hour. The path leads from the Plaza de Armas via the Calle Suecia, past San Cristobal church and via the old Inca path up to the fortress.

In their time the stone blocks, which are up to 5 m (16 ft) high and weigh 200 tonnes (220 tons), intimidated many a would-be attacker and thus fulfilled their purpose as a demonstration of the power of their owners. The fortress is a main attraction in the Cuzco area. Today it is assumed that it was built to control the most vulnerable entrance to the city. The complex includes a number of store rooms for food and an armory for weapons.

During the Spanish invasion, hundreds of Inca warriors barricaded themselves within the walls of Sacsayhuamán, right up until the bitter end. In addition to the heavy fighting, strong earthquakes have also caused significant damage to the structure. Today only about one-third of the fortress remains.

7 Pisac On a 32-km-long (20-mile) detour to the north you are led along a scenic road via the cult site Kenko, the 'Red Fortress' (Puca Pucara), and the sacred spring of Tambo Machay in the idyllic village of Pisac, which can be reached by a metal bridge. Inca influences clash here with colonial era flair.

Market days in Pisac are full of activity. Souvenirs such as flutes, jewellery, and clothing made from llama wool are traded on the central plaza. Just as attractive, however, are the ruins of an Inca ceremonial site located 600 m (1,969 ft) above the village and holding a sacred shrine.

8 Ollantaytambo At the end of the Sacred Valley, 19 km (12 miles) beyond the main town of Urubamba, is the

village of Ollanta (2,800 m/ 9,187 ft), named after Ollantay, an Inca military leader. The fortress, with its spectacular stone terraces, stands on a bluff above the village. The Inca began construction on the well-fortified complex in 1460, but the project took much longer than planned. Ollantaytambo was not yet complete when the Spanish attacked in 1523.

Despite that, residents of Ollanta are still enjoying the benefits of the irrigation system developed

back then by the Inca. Even during the dry season there was, and is, enough water available for agriculture.

Costumes worn by local residents are especially eye-catching and have hardly changed from those worn by their forefathers 500 years ago. The last few steps to the fortress have to be covered on foot.

While the landscape in the Cuzco hinterland is characterized by sparse vegetation, the scenery changes drastically as you head

towards Machu Picchu. It becomes more tropical and the monotone flora of the highlands gives way to dense rainforest. The road starts to wind pretty heavily now, with tight curves and an occasionally hair-raising climb up to Machu Picchu.

9 Machu Picchu The 'City of Clouds', as Machu Picchu is also known, is about 80 km (50 mi) north-west of Cuzco. Surrounded by imposing mountains and set in the midst of a dense forest is the most significant and fascinating archaeological site in South America. It is spectacularly located on a high mountain ridge nearly 600 m (1,969 ft) above the Urubamba River. There is hardly any other site where the technical and mechanical skills of the Inca are demonstrated more tangibly than Machu Picchu, and it is therefore no surprise that the site was declared a UNESCO World Heritage Site in 1983. It is also no surprise that myths and

legends still surround this magical place today. In fact, its very origins remain unknown.

It is assumed that Machu Picchu was built in the 15th century. One theory holds that Machu Picchu served as a place of refuge during the Spanish invasion. Another theory supposes that the Inca relocated their political center to this barely visible and even more inaccessible site. One thing remains certain, however – the colonial Spanish were fully unaware of the existence of this city. The site was first discovered in 1911.

The city's structure is still easily recognizable today. Stone houses comprise one room only and are arranged around small courtyards. What might appear

1 The walls of the Inca fortress Sacsayhuamán were intended to command the respect of attackers.

2 The sun temple and stone terraces of the Ollantaytambo fortress.

simple at first is in fact the result of considerable technical and mechanical skill on the part of the builders. The structures are grouped around a central, more or less quadratic formation. The most striking buildings include the temple tower, or Torreon, and the Sintihuatana sun temple, with seventy-eight stone steps leading up to it.

From Machu Picchu you first need to return to Pisac via the same road, where another road then branches off toward Huambutiyo. On a narrow, gravel road you will then come to Paucartambo and Atalaya, jumping-off point for a visit to the Manú National Park, a biosphere reserve popular with birdwatchers. From Pisac back on the Inca Trail you soon branch off onto a signposted side road heading north to Tipón. The gravel road here is typically in good condition. After about 4 km (2.5 miles) you will reach the ruins of the old city of Tipón at an altitude of about 3,500 m (11,454 ft).

⑩ Tipón Especially noteworthy are the well-preserved terraces, where a sophisticated system of irrigation still enables productive cultivation of the land. It is now surmised that the Inca used the site as an experimental area for acclimatizing plants that otherwise only grew in lower-lying areas. On the onward journey from Tipón towards the southeast you pass the little village of Andahuaylillas where the 17th-century baroque church is worth a brief visit. The peak of Nudo

Ausandate towers 6,400 m (20,998 ft) above you on the left.

⑪ Raqchi Located at the base of the Quinsachata volcano, this town hosts an important traditional festival every year on the third Sunday of June. From a distance, the temple, which is dedicated to Viracocha, the most important Inca god, resembles a viaduct because of its 15-m-high (49-ft) walls. It provides an impressive backdrop for the festivities.

⑫ Sillustani The well-built road from Raqchi now leads south-east towards Lake Titicaca. Near the northern shore of the lake a road branches off to the right towards one of the architectural attractions on this section of the route – the pre-Incan burial mounds of Sillustani, a peninsula in Lake Umayo.

The mounds, known as chullpas, were constructed out of clay and are up to 12 m (39 ft) high. They served as the burial sites of regional rulers. Some chullpas

1 The ruins of Machu Picchu are even impressive when shrouded in mist. Yet they lay hidden for several centuries without the help of this natural veil. Situated as it is 600 m (1,969 ft) above the Urubamba River on a high mountain bluff, this surprisingly well-preserved Inca ruin is reached only with difficulty.

2 On the Inca Trail, the Nudo Ausandate (6,400 m/20,998 ft) rises out of the high Andean plateau.

It is hard to imagine how the Inca could have transported the stone blocks to Machu Picchu that were used to build the magnificent structures. Both the buildings and the site itself are testimony to their advanced skills and craftsmanship.

The Sacsayhuamán fort is the most important sight in the area around Cuzco, the historic capital of the Inca Empire. It is presumed that around twenty thousand people were put to work on the 70-year project. The fort protected a number of vital supply routes to the former

Inca capital. Because of its strategic importance, Sacsayhuamán was extremely well built and it took a number of heavy battles before the Spanish conquistadors were able to break the resistance of the Inca and take the fort. An earthquake also left its marks here.

1

seem to defy gravity, with base diameters smaller than those of their tops.

It is known that the material for the burial mounds comes from quarries near the lake. Particularly noticeable here, too, is the precise working of the stone blocks, which were put together without the use of joints.

It is possible to drive around Lake Titicaca to the north and the south, and both roads run close to the shores almost all the way. You will reach Puno after about 32 km (20 miles) on the southern route of the Inca Trail.

13 Puno The location of this town, directly on Lake Titicaca, is striking enough in itself, giving you the impression that you are at the coast.

Puno is considered to be a cradle of Inca civilization. One legend has it that the first Inca rose from the lake here to create the empire. The surrounding area used to be ruled from Tiahuanaco. Puno, at an elevation of

3,830 m (12,566 ft), was founded by the Spanish in 1668 and then quickly equipped with a number of Christian churches intended to evangelize the Indians living here. Part of this religious center remains today. Many Peruvians associate Puno with colourful folklore – it is known as the folkloric capital of Peru. Every year in February, residents stage one of the best-known festivals in the country, named after the Virgen de la Candelaria. Lively markets are held on the Plaza Mayor, which is flanked by the cathedral completed in 1757. Boats depart from Puno's port to some of the islands on the lake.

The region around the city is used intensively for agriculture, and pastures for the llama and alpaca herds extend almost to the edge of the road. Nearby is Chucuito, a charming Aymara village with two colonial churches and an Inca fertility temple.

2

14 Lake Titicaca This is a lake in a class of its own. With a surface area of 8,300 sq km (5,158 sq mi), Lake Titicaca is the largest lake in South America and the border of Peru and Bolivia runs right through it. The water level lies at 3,812 m (12,507 ft), making it also one of the highest navigable lakes in the world.

But it is not only these record features that characterize this unique body of water. The scenery and the remains of Inca civilization in the area around

the crystal-clear 'Andean Sea' constitute the real attraction of the lake, which belongs to both Peru and Bolivia.

Ruins and ritual sites exist on the Isla del Sol (Island of the Sun) as well, which rises nearly 200 m (656 ft) out of the lake. The Incas created a variety of myths that proclaimed the island as their place of origin. The Templo del Sol (sun temple) in particular, situated on the highest point of the island with view on the lake, is still shrouded in mystery. Isla de la Luna (Is-

land of the Moon) is also worth a brief visit. In addition to the 'stationary' islands there is also a series of 'floating' islands, designed by the Uros people in the pre-Inca era and still surviving today (see sidebar on the right).

⑮ Copacabana Turn off the southern coastal road to the border town of Yunguyo. On the Bolivian side, between the Cerro Calvarío and Cerro Sancollani mountains, is the fishing village of Copacabana, located on the peninsula of the same name

extending far out into Lake Titicaca. Excursion boats to the islands of the sun and moon depart from here. The climate is rough and the water temperature is usually quite cool.

Copacabana is an important pilgrimage destination for Bolivians. On 4 August every year a large procession of pilgrims arrives for the Fiesta de la Virgen de Copacabana. The Virgin is also sanctified in the Moorish-style basilica (1820). From Copacabana you can either return to the southern route via Yun-

guyo (crossing the border for the second time), or continue your journey without the border crossing by taking the northern route around the lake towards the city of La Paz.

⑯ Tiahuanaco The ruins of this city (also called Tiwanaku) lie about 20 km (12 miles) from the southern end of Lake Titicaca. The site used to be directly on the lake shore but the lake has become smaller over the centuries. Very close to the former ceremonial site is present-day Tiahuanaco, just a short drive from the ruins.

The first traces of settlement here have been dated back to approximately 1500 BC. Tiahuanaco was probably founded in around AD 300. It subsequently developed into the center of an empire that covered most of the region and whose cultural and religious influences extended far beyond Peru, even as far as northern Chile and Argentina. The civilization experienced its

heyday between 300 and 900. It is meant to have been the most advanced civilization in the central Andes. Around 20,000 residents lived together on only a few square kilometers.

Agriculture was the most important economic activity in Tiahuanaco, with nearby Lake Titicaca providing water for effective cultivation. Using an advanced system of canals, farmers here channelled lake water to their fields, which extended over an area of 80 sq km (50 sq mi).

1 Many of the massive stone tombs in Sillustani, which are visible from great distances, have been partially destroyed by grave robbers or lightning.

2 Lake Titicaca on the Altiplano has a total of seven large islands.

3 A colonial church in Puno, at an altitude of 3,830 m (12,566 ft), on the western shore of Lake Titicaca.

Most of the temples, pillars and monoliths were built between 700 and 1200. An important place of worship, in this case a step pyramid about 15 m (49 ft) high, is situated in the middle of the city. The most famous construction, however, was the sun gate, sculpted out of one stone that weighs almost 44 t (48 tons). Many buildings were removed by the Spanish who needed ready-made stone blocks for the construction of their own showcase buildings. Blocks from Tiahuanaco were used to build a number of churches in La Paz, for example.

Only a few remains of the site survived the centuries of destruction and overall disregard for their cultural significance. It was not until at the beginning of the 20th century that extensive excavations began. The site was reconstructed as precisely as possible to the original plans once archaeologists were able to clear sufficient remains of the ancient buildings.

Ultimately, the site was declared a UNESCO World Heritage Site in the year 2000. However, there are still many unanswered questions. Why was the city abandoned? Was it due to climate change, or had the population become too large? Without any doubt, the stonemasonry in Tiahuanaco is among the most skilled in South America. Shortly before La Paz the road following the eastern shore of Lake Titicaca joins National Road 1.

⑰ La Paz The largest city in Bolivia, and the highest city in the world, La Paz is nestled impressively among the slopes of a steep valley. The metropolis is not the constitutional capital but it is the seat of the Bolivian government – and the heartbeat of the country.

The city's neighbourhoods seem to cling to the mountain slopes and are striking even from afar. La Paz is situated at an elevation of between 3,650 and 4,000 m (11,976 and 13,124 ft). Those

who can afford it choose to live in the low-lying suburbs as the climate is somewhat milder in the 'lower city' and the residents are more protected from the Altiplano winds.

If you arrive from the west, the road passes the international airport of El Alto. Temperatures in this now independent suburb are often up to 10°C (50°F) cooler than in the city center. From El Alto the road crosses a basin where many stop to enjoy the view of the city.

On the onward journey the colourful markets of the famous

'Indio neighbourhood' pop up on the right. Behind that is the Old Town, which has been able to retain its colonial-era feel. A wide boulevard passes straight through the entire inner city and while the various sections of it have different names, the locals simply refer to this central road as the 'Prado'.

From here it is not far to the sightseeing attractions such as the cathedral, which was completed in 1933 and has capacity for 12,000 people. The Bolivian metropolis is a good base for tours to the Nevado del Illimani,

3

the highest mountain in the country, to the east of the city.

18 Nevado del Illimani The journey to this 6,880-m-high (22,573-ft) mountain in the Cordillera Real can be tedious as the road leading directly to the base of Illimani is occasionally closed. The road to the small Indian village of Comunidad Uno is recommended as an alternate route. Climbers can start the ascent of the mountain from here too, and base camp is reached in about five hours of hiking.

For locals the mountain is not only a symbol, it also represents an image of their country. With a little imagination you can recognize the outline of an Indian with wife, child and llama in the three peaks of the Nevado del Illimani. The southernmost of the three peaks is the highest and easily the most accessible, but it takes several days to complete the challenging hike.

Another awe-inspiring peak, the Mount Sajama volcano, lies to

the west of the Inca Trail. From La Paz travel south-east to Patacamaya. From there a well-paved road branches off to the south-west. After about 150 km (93 miles) on this road you reach the Sajama National Park in the center of which is the majestic 6,520-m (21,392-ft) volcano of the same name.

Back in Patacamaya, follow the National Road 1, which has oil and gas pipelines running parallel to it. After 90 km (56 miles) turn off to the south-east at Caracollo, taking National Road 4 towards Cochabamba. The road passes a vast expanse of fertile farmland where grain, fruit and vegetables are cultivated.

19 Cochabamba In contrast to the raw climate of the highlands, the weather is much milder in Cochabamba, which is situated at 'only' 2,570 m (1,597 ft) above sea level. This city on the eastern slopes of the Andes has appropriately earned the name 'the city of eternal springtime'.

The name Cochabamba, however, derives from the Quechua language and basically means 'swampy flatland'. It is home to a renowned university and, with about 600,000 residents, is one of the largest cities in Bolivia.

Unlike most of the cities along the Inca Trail Cochabamba has no precolonial history, having been first founded by the Spanish in 1574. Many Spanish immigrants settled here because of the comfortable climate. In the center of the city there are a number of houses and churches dating from the city's early days. A poor-quality road leads from Cochabamba to the Tunari National Park, a natural protected area which extends to the mountain of the same name.

20 Oruro Back in Caracollo, continue for a few kilometers through some pretty bleak scenery until you reach the city of Oruro, elevation 3,710 m (12,173 ft). At the height of the tin-mining era, from the early

19th century to the middle of the 20th century, Oruro was one of the most important economic locations in Bolivia. That, however, has changed since the mines were closed.

Yet the locals' zest for life remains undiminished and Oruro continues to be the center of the eight-day Bolivian carnival, which is celebrated here with sophisticated revelry. The dancers adorn themselves with colourful, ornately carved devil and ghost masks.

1 Tiahuanaco, the sacred site and capital of an Andean culture of the same name that experienced its heyday between the 3rd and 9th centuries.

2 Salar de Uyuni and Salar de Coipas, the two largest saltwater lakes in the Bolivian Altiplano.

3 View over La Paz with snow-capped volcano.

㉑ Lago de Poopó Only a short distance beyond Oruro is Lake Poopó. With a surface area of 2,800 sq km (1,740 sq mi), it is the second-largest lake in Bolivia after Lake Titicaca. Lake Poopó receives some of its water from the outflow of Lake Titicaca from the Río Desaguadero. The lake is very shallow in comparison to the up to 280-m-deep (919-ft) Lake Titicaca, with a depth of just a few meters. High levels of evaporation over the decades have caused a slow but consistent drop in the water level and surface area of the lake. Its swampy shores are only sparsely populated.

㉒ Laguna Tarapaya The road now heads south-east to another scenic highlight of the region, an almost perfectly circular lake with a diameter of some 100 m (328 ft) located in the crater of an extinct volcano, Laguna Tarapaya. This thermal pool, already used by the Inca, boasts a temperature of 35°C (95°F). The Balneario de Tarapaya, at 3,400 m (11,155 ft), is a perfect place to

relax, especially after long hikes at this altitude.
The onward journey is a steep climb towards teh city of Potosí, about 25 km (15 miles) away.

㉓ Potosí At just below 4,000 m (13,124 ft), Potosí was one of the wealthiest cities in all of South America between the 16th and 18th centuries. The wealth came from a mountain with relatively unspectacular looks, but of spectacular intrinsic value – the conical, 4,830-m-high (815,847-ft) Cerro Rico ('Rich Mountain').
The Spanish colonial rulers were fortunate enough to discover extensive silver reserves within this mountain, which they then proceeded to mine mercilessly. Tens of thousands of tonnes of silver were extracted over time but the lucrative mining activities had another side to them, namely Indian slave labour that led to countless deaths.
The silver mines have since been abandoned but tin-mining has become increasingly important in recent decades. Unfortunately

for the people of Potosí, tin is not as lucrative as silver.
Several traces of the former wealth can be found in the city center – stately homes and churches from the Spanish colonial era, some of which have striking façades. The city and the neighbouring silver mines were declared a UNESCO World Heritage Site in 1987 n recognition of its rich history and architectural treasures. A bumpy road leads to the visitors' mine, located at an altitude of 4,300 m (14,108 ft).
Beyond Potosí the road (No 5) winds its way north. En route to the much lower-lying city of Sucre you descend some 1,400 m (4,593 ft) in altitude over a relatively short distance, with very steep gradients in places.

㉔ Sucre On the approach to the capital, at an altitude of about 2,600 m (8,531 ft), the glittering buildings of the 'White City' are visible even from a distance. Ivory-coloured baroque churches and religious buildings, whitewashed houses,

mansions and regal palaces define Sucre, which was founded in 1538.
There are only a few Spanish colonial cities that are as well-preserved as this one. Buildings with stylish balconies and lovely arcades characterize the Old Town, which became a UNESCO World Heritage Site in 1990. Even though Sucre has been the capital of Bolivia since 1828, there are only a few civil authorities based here. The government and its ministries all have their seats in La Paz.
The university, founded in 1624, is one of the oldest in South America. Celebrated as the jewel of Bolivian colonial architecture, reflecting the Andalusian style, Sucre makes a fitting and faboulous conclusion to the Inca Trail, which traverses two countries and two worlds.

1 A view over Potosí, the 'Silver City', towards the snow-capped peak of Cerro Rico.

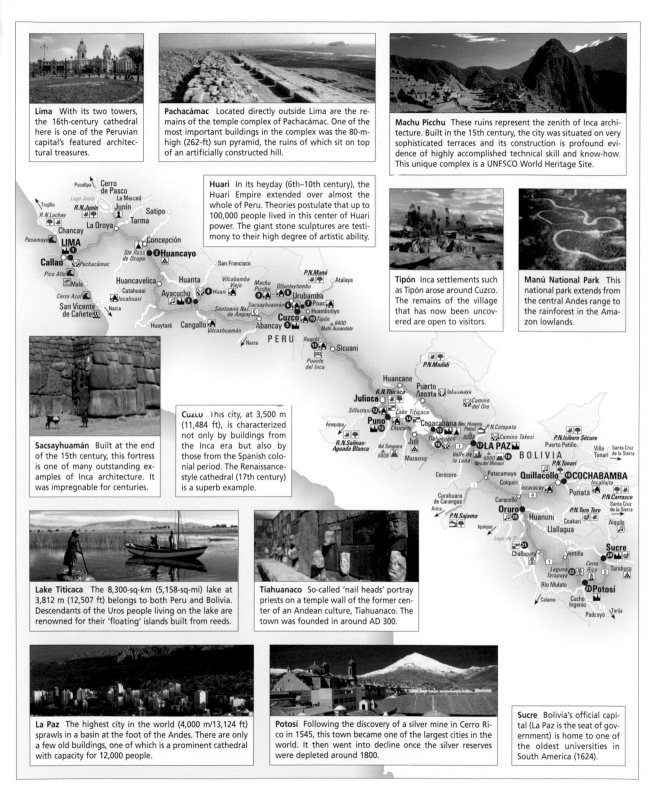

Lima With its two towers, the 16th-century cathedral here is one of the Peruvian capital's featured architectural treasures.

Pachacámac Located directly outside Lima are the remains of the temple complex of Pachacámac. One of the most important buildings in the complex was the 80-m-high (262-ft) sun pyramid, the ruins of which sit on top of an artificially constructed hill.

Machu Picchu These ruins represent the zenith of Inca architecture. Built in the 15th century, the city was situated on very sophisticated terraces and its construction is profound evidence of highly accomplished technical skill and know-how. This unique complex is a UNESCO World Heritage Site.

Huari In its heyday (6th–10th century), the Huari Empire extended over almost the whole of Peru. Theories postulate that up to 100,000 people lived in this center of Huari power. The giant stone sculptures are testimony to their high degree of artistic ability.

Tipón Inca settlements such as Tipón arose around Cuzco. The remains of the village that has now been uncovered are open to visitors.

Manú National Park This national park extends from the central Andes range to the rainforest in the Amazon lowlands.

Sacsayhuamán Built at the end of the 15th century, this fortress is one of many outstanding examples of Inca architecture. It was impregnable for centuries.

Cuzco This city, at 3,500 m (11,484 ft), is characterized not only by buildings from the Inca era but also by those from the Spanish colonial period. The Renaissance-style cathedral (17th century) is a superb example.

Lake Titicaca The 8,300-sq-km (5,158-sq-mi) lake at 3,812 m (12,507 ft) belongs to both Peru and Bolivia. Descendants of the Uros people living on the lake are renowned for their 'floating' islands built from reeds.

Tiahuanaco So-called 'nail heads' portray priests on a temple wall of the former center of an Andean culture, Tiahuanaco. The town was founded in around AD 300.

La Paz The highest city in the world (4,000 m/13,124 ft) sprawls in a basin at the foot of the Andes. There are only a few old buildings, one of which is a prominent cathedral with capacity for 12,000 people.

Potosí Following the discovery of a silver mine in Cerro Rico in 1545, this town became one of the largest cities in the world. It then went into decline once the silver reserves were depleted around 1800.

Sucre Bolivia's official capital (La Paz is the seat of government) is home to one of the oldest universities in South America (1624).

Chile

On the Panamericana Highway down the Chilean Pacific coast

"When God looked at the world He had created in seven days, He realized that there were a number of things left over: volcanoes, primeval forests, deserts, fjords, rivers and ice. He told the angels to stack them up behind a long mountain chain. Those mountains were the Andes – and that is how Chile came to be the most diverse country on earth."

That is how a legend describes the creation of Chile, also referred to by some as the "country with the craziest geography". Indeed, its proportions are record-breaking: the country covers more than 4,300 km (2,672 mi), from Arica in the north on the border with Peru to the border post in the southern Tierra del Fuego, and is never wider than 180 km (112 mi).

Chile covers a surface area of 756,629 sq km (470,169 sq mi). The Panamerican Highway, known as the Panamericana in Chile, is the backbone of the country's infrastructure. It links the most important cities and, for the most part, runs straight through the central Chilean valley. Two roads branch off from the Panamericana to the east and the west, leading either into

the mountains or out to the coast. The majority of the more than fifteen million Chileans live in the three main regions: the so-called "Small North", central Chile around the capital, Santiago de Chile, and the so-called

Guanacos are prized for their coats.

"Small South" between Temuco and Puerto Montt.

The "Great North" region is a desert that extends for more than 1,000 km (621 mi) from Arica to the south of Antofagasta.

It is a desert with ocher-colored mountains, snow-covered volcanoes, deep blue lagoons, green oases and white shimmering salt lakes. Known as the Atacama, it is one of the driest and most hostile regions on the planet. The aridity is caused by the cold Humboldt Current, an ocean current off the Pacific Coast of South America that flows northwards from the Antarctic. The low water temperatures result in the regular build up of fog, which largely prevents precipitation. Life exists here only at a few oases, but this coastal desert is definitely one of the

Lago Chungara in the Parque Nacional Lauca is at an elevation of 4,570 m (14,994 ft), making it the highest lake in the world. It is home to over 130 species of bird.

The majority of the high-rises in Santiago de Chile are in the newer areas of the city, such as here in Providencia.

most interesting destinations in Chile. It has also been one of the country's most economically important regions since the 19th century. The rich saltpeter deposits here were the catalyst for the so-called Saltpeter War between Chile on the one side, and Peru and Bolivia on the other. Other mineral resources are mined here as well, such as copper in Chuquicamata west of Calama, the world's largest opencast copper mine.

Rainfall increases towards the south so that the desert landscape in the "Small North" is scattered with rivers and some agricultural production.

Central Chile around Santiago is the primary wine-growing and agricultural region as well as the most industrialized area. Coastal towns like Viña del Mar, are popular summer resorts and Valparaíso is the country's most important port.

The "Small South" is known as the lake district, with lakes strung from north to south along the Andes like a chain of pearls: Lago Villarrica, Lago Llanquihue and Lago Todos Los Santos – to name just a few of the major ones. Most of them are accompanied by towering volcanoes and surrounded by thick forests where the rare araucaria conifers grow.

The "Large South" is also referred to as the "wild south". South of Puerto Montt and the Isla Grande de Chiloé is the beginning of a remote, almost uninhabited region filled featuring glaciers, islands, fjords and cold rain forests – and of course a chilly climate. The best way to get there is via the Carretera Austral, a road built in the 1970s, that cuts through wilderness, skirts majestic fjords and lakes, traverses raging whitewater rivers, climbs mountains and sweeps across vast meadow landscapes, swamp areas and pristine forests before coming to an end in Puerto Yungay at the mouth of the Río Bravo on the Pacific coast.

A covered well in Parinacota in the Parque Nacional Lauca in northern Chile.

1

Chile is an "island on the mainland". In the north it is bordered by the driest desert on the planet; to the west are the crashing waves of the Pacific Ocean; to the east are the towering peaks of the Andes. In the south the narrow strip of land breaks up into islands and islets that seem to get lost in the Antarctic Ocean. Anyone looking to experience the beauty of this country should travel along the Panamericana.

1 Arica The northernmost town in Chile is one of the country's oldest settlements. People have lived here at the mouth of the Río San José on the Pacific coast for thousands of years. The Spanish built a port here to ship the silver from the Potosí mines. The best view of town is from Morro, a 200-m-high (656 ft) rocky peak south of the center where can look down at the bustling fishing port and the Iglesia San Marcos (1875), one of Gustave Eiffel's early works. Beaches stretch for miles south of the town.

The Museo Arqueológico in the suburb of San Miguel de Azapa is worth a visit. It has Chinchorro mummies on display that are thought to be over 7,500 years old. During the mummification process, the Chinchorro removed all soft tissue and muscles from the corpse, hollowed out the skull and rebuilt the skeleton. The head was fixed to the body by means of a wooden stick and all cavities were filled and padded with straw and wool.

There are two options for the onward journey south from Arica. The shorter one follows the Panamericana (Ruta Nacional 5) which often hugs the Pacific coast and rolls over the coastal mountains towards the south. You reach Humberstone after 265 km (165 mi). From there it is

Travel Information

Route profile
Length: approx. 4,300 km (2,672mi)
Length: at least 5 weeks

Start: Arica
End: Puerto Yungay
Route (main locations):
Arica, Iquique, Valparaíso, Santiago de Chile, Temuco, Villarrica, Valdivia, Puerto Montt, Coihaique, Lago General Carrera, Puerto Yungay

Traffic information:
The Panamericana is in good condition pretty much throughout, and parts of it even of highway quality. Difficult dirt roads are mainly in the north on the detours to

and in Parque Nacional Lauca. The Carretera Austral is a dirt road of good quality in all weather conditions. BUT, it is only accessible along its full length in summer because the necessary ferries only operate between the months of December and February.

Health:
Tiredness and headaches are the initial, still harmless symptoms of elevation sickness. You should descend to the lower regions as soon as the first signs appear.

Information:
www.sernatur.cl
www.turismochile.com
www.geographia.com/chile

40 km (25 mi) to Iquique. The longer, more interesting option takes you through the Chilean Altiplano, past 6,000-m (19,686-ft) volcanoes, salt lakes, geysers and some tiny villages. From

444

Arica, Ruta 11 follows the Río Lluta Valley and initially runs parallel to the railway line that links Arica with La Paz, Bolivia. After a little more than 12 km (7.5 mi) you will be able to see the gigantic geoglyphs on the mountainsides depicting llamas, humans and other figures.

You soon reach Poconchile with its attractive adobe church built in 1605. Like most of the village churches in Northern Chile, it has a freestanding, tiered bell tower. The roof and the door are made from the wood of the large candelabra cactuses that are visible all along the route.

❷ Putre The scenic village of Putre at an elevation of 3,500 m (11,484 ft) is a green oasis in an otherwise desolate landscape and is the most important stop on the route from Arica near the Bolivian border. It is also the gateway to the Parque Nacional Lauca. Many visitors use a stop in the village to acclimatize to the elevation. Soroche, or alti-

tude sickness, can make itself felt as of 3,000 m (9,843 ft). The village has about 1,200 residents, the majority of whom are Aymara Indians. The village church was built in 1670. At 6,825 m (22,393 ft), the Nevado de Putre towers impressively over the village.

❸ Parque Nacional Lauca The road continues to climb the mountain into the national park and affords a terrific mountain panorama, particularly once you get to Lago Chungara at an elevation of 4,570 m (14,994 ft) on the border with Bolivia. The lake often reflects Las Payachatas, the twin icy volcanoes Pomarape in Bolivia that rise more than 6,000 m (20,000 ft) above the Altiplano plateau.

From the national park the route continues south along the border, initially through the Reserva Nacional Las Vicuñas to Salar de Surire, a salt lake at an elevation of 4,200 m (13,780 ft) where you often see flamingos.

The Parque Nacional Volcán Isluga covers an area of 174,744 ha (431,792 acre) and begins south of the Salar. The park includes part of the Cordillera Occidental and is dominated by the still active volcano of the same name (5,530 m/18,144 ft). You'll pass through a number of villages such as Isluga before reaching the southern edge of Baños de Puchuldiza National Park, a geyser field at an elevation of over 4,000 m (13,124 ft).

❹ Gigante de Atacama The "Desert Giant" geoglyph is on the Cerro Unitá just before Huara. The ground drawing is 86 m (94 yds) long and presumably depicts an Indian ruler or a deity. From here it is just 70 km (43 mi) to Humberstone.

❺ Humberstone Once a boomtown and the economic center of the region, Humberstone is no more than a ghost town now. It was here that the saltpeter required to make gun-

powder and artificial fertilizers was mined after 1872.

After a descent of 15 km (9 mi) down to the coast you reach the port of Iquique.

❻ Iquique The largest town in northern Chile, with about 150,000 inhabitants, sprawls out on a narrow plain between the Pacific and the wall of coastal cordilleras rising up more than 600 m (1,969 ft) from the ocean. Above Iquique is a gigantic sand dune. The port is of economic

1 The Parque Nacional Lauca on the Chilean Altiplano lies at an elevation of 4,000 m (13,124 ft) and is dominated by several 6,000-m (19,686-ft) peaks such as Parinacota.

2 A herd of llamas with Las Payachatas in the background, two volcanoes in the Chile-Bolivia border region. To the left is the 6,282-m (20,611-ft) Pomarape; to the right is the 6,342-m (20,808-ft) Parinacota.

Two panoramic views from the Parque Nacional Lauca: herds of alpacas and llamas make use of the varying vegetation comprising tufts of grass on the more than 4,000-m-high (13,124 ft) plateau. The plano is dominated by a number of magnificent 6,000-m (19,686 ft) peaks.

the most famous of which include the perfectly shaped Pomarape volcano (to the left in the lower picture) and Parinacota (top picture and below right), both of which belong to Bolivia. The Lago Chungara is one of the national park's major attractions,

significance as a reloading point, initially for guano, later for saltpeter and today for fishmeal. The center of Iquique is very compact, but atypical for South America as its cathedral is not right on the main plaza. Instead, the plaza boasts buildings that are testimony to the wealth created from saltpeter mining: the classicist Teatro Municipal, opened in 1890, the clock tower that has adorned the plaza since 1877, and the Centro Español with its elegant restaurant built in 1904. South of the plaza is Calle Baquedano, a street with the town's loveliest wooden buildings as well as the Museo Regional. The latter provides an outstanding overview of the history of the "Great North".

The distance from Iquique to Antofagasta is about 480 km (298 mi). You have a choice of two routes: one climbs directly up into the coastal range from Iquique and follows the Panamericana. You can make detours from the main road to the

Atacama and San Pedro de Atacama at the María Elena turnoff (Ruta 24). The other option is to take Ruta 1 along the coast, which cruises past the seemingly endless white sandy beaches.

⑦ La Portada On the coastal route about 20 km (12 mi) north of Antofagasta you reach La Portada, a rocky arch towering up out of the Pacific surf. The steep coast here is made up of shell limestone and is eroded away by the ocean. La Portada, however, is on top of the coastal cliffs, enabling it to withstand the waves. The area around the arch is a great place for watching pelicans and other seabirds.

⑧ Antofagasta The largest town in the north, with around 225,000 people, owes its wealth and development to the port from which Chile's abundant natural resources from the desert are shipped throughout the world – formerly guano and saltpeter, today copper. There is

no mistaking the English influence from the saltpeter era on the Plaza Colón in the town center where a miniature Big Ben stands. The plaza is surrounded by attractive neo-Gothic buildings such as the cathedral and the town theater.

Just over 900 km (565 mi) of desert open up south of Antofagasta. The Panamericana climbs up over the plateau before heading down again to the coast passing Parque Nacional Pan de Azúcar near the seaside

town of Chañaral. The reserve offers sandy beaches and desert areas for penguins, cormorants, pelicans and seals.

This is followed by the port of Caldera and the Panamericana then heads for the interior, passing through the mining town of Copiapó, which has an outstanding Museo Mineralógico. After 350 km (217 mi) you reach the Pacific again near La Serena.

⑨ La Serena Thanks to its expansive beaches, this town of 100,000 has developed in recent

decades into one of Chile's most popular seaside resorts. But it is not only swimmers and sunbathers who head for La Serena. Founded in 1544, the town has a great deal of colonial character and yet owes much of its charisma to the conversions of the 1950s. The center boasts a total of twenty-nine churches, most of them from the 17th to 19th centuries, an attractive market as well as a mineralogical and an archaeological museum.

⑩ Valle del Río Elqui The Río Elqui Valley extends east of La Serena and is a tropical paradise in the midst of the desert, with grapevines, fig and papaya trees growing between the largely barren mountains. The valley is scattered with small towns like Vicuña, the birthplace of Nobel Prize winner for Literature, Gabriela Mistral. Vicuña also boasts another major tourist draw: the Planta Capel where the country's best Pisco, Chilean schnapps, is distilled.

⑪ Parque Nacional Bosque de Fray Jorge South of La Serena, the onward journey takes you by Parque Nacional Bosque Fray Jorge, encompassing a wetland forest area close to the coast. The park has a distinctive microclimate due to the rising coastal fog and the resulting humidity. On the stretch from the national park to Viña del Mar, wide beaches and charming seaside resorts like Los Vilos await you.

⑫ Cristo Redentor de los Andes Shortly before Viña del Mar it is worth taking a detour to the east on Ruta 60, which takes you high up into the Andes before crossing the border with Argentina. At an elevation of 4,000 m (13,124 ft) the statue of Christ, Cristo Redentor de los Andes, marks the national border in this rugged and majestic mountain landscape. Just a short distance down the road, on the Argentinean side, you will be able to enjoy probably

the best view of the Aconcagua peak at 6,959 m (22,832 ft).
Leaving the mountain world of the Andes to return to the Pacific, two very different but equally appealing towns await your arrival and visit.

⑬ Viña del Mar and Valparaíso These two towns have nearly merged into one larger entity. Viña del Mar is Chile's best-known coastal resort with wide beaches, lovely parks and expensive hotels. Valparaíso, on the other hand, is the country's largest port and the seat of the Chilean parliament. It stretches along a large bay and extends high up the mountain. The steep hillsides in town can be navigated by rickety funicular elevators that date back to the second half of the 19th century.

⑭ Isla Negra "Black Island" is a fishing village around 80 km (50 mi) south of Valparaíso. The largest and loveliest house in town belongs to the Chilean

winner of the Nobel Prize for Literature, Pablo Neruda. It is an imaginative structure directly on the Pacific coast, half family home, half castle.
From Isla Negra there is a road that connects you with the highway to Santiago.

⑮ Santiago de Chile The Chilean capital is the country's undisputed center. Founded in 1541, it is not only home to one-third of the entire population of Chile (around five million) but

1 The icon of the Antofagasta region is La Portada, an archway of shell limestone.

2 The old town of Valparaíso extends right up the hillside. The steeper slopes are sometimes bridged by elevators.

3 The center of Santiago de Chile at dusk. In the foreground to the right is the Moneda, the seat of government.

449

The heart of the Atacama is the second-driest place on earth. Part of the reason for this is the Humboldt Current, an ocean current that flows along the Pacific coast carrying cold water from the Atlantic northwards. That, combined with an absence of wind, the towering

coastal range and coastal fog, prevents moisture from reaching the interior. Géiser el Tatio is one of the highest geysers on earth, most active in the early morning (top). Bottom: The name says it: the Valle de la Luna near San Pedro de Atacama looks like a moonscape.

1

also to almost all of the country's important political, economic and cultural institutions. On a clear day, Santiago, affords wonderful panoramic views of the snow-covered peaks of the Andes and the rich green expanse of the plains. It also boasts a number of especially lovely colonial buildings around the lively plaza, whereas the sea of buildings downtown is dominated by high-rise blocks.

It is easy to list the most important sightseeing attractions: the plaza with the cathedral, completed in 1789; the Palacio de la Moneda, which was built as a mint in 1799, but has been the presidential palace since 1846; and the Iglesia de San Francisco with its accompanying convent, which were built in the 16th century and are today the oldest buildings in Santiago. The city has suffered many earthquakes and outbreaks of big fires over the centuries. It is worth taking a day's excursion to the Maipo Valley (Cajón del Maipo), best

known for its fine wineries and well-balanced red wines, including Chile's best Cabernets.

South of Santiago, the Panamericana traverses the long valley running through the center of Chile – the country's orchard and bread basket. The road is lined with vast plantations and large storage warehouses where it is not uncommon to see lines of trucks being loaded with the apples, grapes and other fruit grown in the area.

You pass Talca and Chillán before reaching a superb waterfall after 400 km (249 mi).

16 Salto del Laja The Panamericana crosses the Río Laja about 25 km (16 mi) north of Los Angeles. Just above the bridge, the river, which is roughly 100 m (109 yds) wide at this point, drops nearly 50 m (164 ft) over a high rocky plateau, forming the Salto del Laja, Chile's largest waterfall. A short walk takes you directly to the falls,

one of the most scenic falls in the world.

17 Temuco The town of Pablo Neruda's birth has a population of about 250,000 residents, making it one of the largest towns in the south and the economic center of this primarily agricultural region. You can get a taste of Chilean country life at the Feria Libre, the huge market to the south-west of the railway station where many Mapuche Indians from the region's more remote villages sell their wares. The Mercado Municipal is more tourist-oriented and mainly has handicrafts on offer. The Museo Regional de la Araucania offers details of the culture and history of the region and its inhabitants, the Mapuche.

Temuco is the starting point for excursions into the Andes and so, instead of following the Panamericana further south, it is worth taking a detour through the Andes and the various national parks with their volca-

noes, lakes and lagoons, briefly crossing over into Argentina.

18 Villarrica South of Temuco, near Loncoche, there is a road that branches off the Panamericana to the east that will take you to Villarrica. This town's location on a lovely lake has made it into one of the country's most popular tourist destinations. From here you can enjoy a wonderful view of the active volcano of the same name (2,847 m/ 9,341 ft) with its nearly symmetrical cone and tidy collar of snow beautifully reflected in the sizable lake. Lago Villarrica is the northernmost of a string of lakes that extend south as far as Lago Llanquihue.

After passing the tourist town of Pucón, and between the Villarrica and Huerquehue national parks – the latter has extensive araucaria forests –, you will cross the border into the Argentinean Parque Nacional Lanín and come to San Martín de los Andes, a small town that is a perfect jumping off point for exploring

2

the Argentinean Andes. Not only does the "Seven Lakes Road" take you to more than seven lakes, it also passes torrential waterfalls and travels through thick forests to the Parque Nacional Nahuel Huapí.

⑲ Parque Nacional Nahuel Huapí This national park is one of the largest and most popular of its kind in Argentina. Lago Nahuel Huapí, a sizable glacial lake that covers an overall surface area of 500 sq km (193 sq mi), forms the heart of the park. The route continues past another lake to yet another Andes park back in Chile.

⑳ Parque Nacional Puyehue The highest peak in this park is Puyehue, a still active volcano that rises 2,236 m (7,336 ft) and last erupted in 1960. The park is home to pumas and pudús (a type of small deer).
Passing the small town of Entre Lagos, "between" Lago Puyehue and Lago Rupanco, you will

get back on the Panamericana at Osorno. Anyone still wanting to visit the port of Valdivia will need to continue about 100 km (62 mi) further north.

㉑ Valdivia Founded and named after the Spanish conquistador Pedro de Valdivia in 1552, this is one of the loveliest towns in Chile. Valdivia today boasts a modern skyline after having been almost completely leveled by a series of earthquakes, including submarine, or offshore, earthquakes, in 1960. The main attraction here is the Mercado Fluvial on the banks of the river where you will find all kinds of fish and seafood on offer.
The next stop is Lago Llanquihue, 70 km (43 mi) south of Osorno. This marks the south end of the Chilean lake district.

㉒ Lago Llanquihue Covering 877 sq km (339 sq mi) this is the second-largest lake in Chile after Lago General Carrera. The deep-

est point in the Llanquihue is 350 m (1,148 ft) and, like most of the country's lakes it is glacial in origin, a so-called moraine basin edged with detritus deposited by the glaciers.
Towering above the lake is the 2,652-m-high (8,701-ft) Osorno volcano which, like the Villarrica volcano, has a nearly flawless cone shape. There are a number of popular tourist towns along the lake, a couple of which were founded by German immigrants in the 19th century including Puerto Varas and Fruillar, mostly famous for its open-air museum. Only a stone's throw away is Puerto Montt, a harbor town on the Seno de Reloncaví, the north end of the Golfo de Ancud.

㉓ Puerto Montt This town itself is not particularly attractive for visitors but it is a handy starting point for journeys into Chile's "wild south" as well as the island of Chiloé. On the outskirts of town it is worth visiting Angelmo, where one of Chile's

largest handicraft markets is held. You will find mountains of thick, knitted pullovers, wood carvings, as well as regional delicacies such as cheese, honey, liqueur, dried mussels and dried algae on offer. All kinds of seafood is also served from bubbling pots in the fishing port.
From Puerto Montt it is another 60 km (37 mi) to Pargua and Calbuco, where the ferries embark to Isla Grande de Chiloé. If you are lucky, you may be accompanied by dolphins.
For anyone wanting to skip this island detour, the journey continues along the east coast of the gulf to the Parque Nacional Alerce Andino.

1 Salto del Huilo Huilo is the most spectacular of Chile's waterfalls, plunging 100 m (328 ft).

2 The Villarrica volcano is 2,847 m (9,341 ft) high and has a near perfect conical shape.

24 Parque Nacional Alerce Andino The Alerce Reserve extends along the Seno and the Estuario de Reloncaví. This pristine forest features the Alerce, or Patagonian Cypress (related to the redwood), large trees that can reach diameters of up to 4 m (13 ft), and heights of up to 50 m (164 ft). Many of the trees are around 1,000 years old. Puerto Montt is also the starting point of the famous Carretera Austral, Chile's most scenic route into the remote south. For the most part, Ruta 7 is unpaved for over 1,000 km (621 mi) taking you through forests, around lakes, past fjords and by snow-capped peaks. There are only some 100,000 people living in the region, which covers about 150,000 sq km (57,900 sq mi).
Even the first 200 km (124 mi) of the Carretera Austral from Puerto Montt to Chaitén are a tough haul. There are two wide estuaries to be crossed: the one from Caleta La Arena to Puelche takes 30 minutes and the one from Hornopirén to Caleta Gonzalo takes about five hours and also takes you into the Parque Natural Pumalín.

25 Parque Natural Pumalín This 270,000-ha (667,170-acre) nature reserve was created by Douglas Tompkins, a successful American businessman focused on environmentalism. The sanctuary includes spectacular Pacific coast fjords, steep mountains and pristine forests. With 4,500 to 6,000 mm (177 to 236 in) of rain a year, the lichens and ferns compete with bamboos and fuchsia plants, while centuries-old giant alerce conifers tower among the southern beech trees. There are hiking trails leading deep into this magical forest.
Next comes the small town of Chaitén before the road passes Lago Yelcho in the Río Yelcho Valley and heads on to some expansive meadowlands. The next point of reference is the settlement of La Junta, about 150 km (93 mi) south of Chaitén, followed by Puerto Puyuhuapi. This storybook pioneer village is the starting point for a visit to Queulat National Park and Isla Magdalena. It is also home to a handful of large wooden houses.

26 Parque Nacional Queulat This nature sanctuary encompasses 154,000 ha (380,534 acres) of unspoilt forest with wonderful ferns and lianas, bamboos and pangue plants. The latter are similar to rhubarb, with leaves easily reaching the size of an umbrella. The park rises up from the ocean in several plateaus until it reaches an elevation of 2,225 m (7,300 ft). There is a hiking trail to the Ventisquero Colgante glacier, or "hanging glacier". Its tongue protrudes threateningly over a saddle between two mountains. On the way to Coihaique almost 200 km (124 mi) away it is worth taking a detour to Puerto Aisén, a port and starting point for boat cruises through the fjords, including the Laguna San Rafael. After the turnoff to Puerto Aisén the road follows the Río Simpson as far as Coihaique. The river's southern catchment area is protected in the Reserva Nacional Río Simpson.

27 Coihaique "The land between the water" is what the indigenous inhabitants called this place at the confluence of two rivers. Today it has 50,000 residents. A hiking trail leads to the Verde and Venus lagoons near the Reserva Nacional Coihaique. After driving about 200 km (124 mi) through dense forest you then come to Lago General Carrera near Puerto Murta. It is just less than 3 km (2 miles) from town.

28 Lago General Carrera With 1,840 sq km (710 sq mi) of coverage, this body of water on the border with Argentina is the largest lake in Chile and in the Patagonian Andes. The Chilean part of the lake is surrounded by the breathtaking peaks of the southern Andes: Cerro Campana (2,194 m/7,199 ft), Pico Sur (2,190 m/7,185 ft), Cerro Hyades (3,078 m/10,099 ft) and Cerro San Valentín (4,058 m/13,314 ft). The smaller Argentinean part, known as Lago Buenos Aires, is imbedded in the Patagonian lowlands. Following Río Baker you reach Cochrane after about 150 km (93 mi).
From there it is another 120 km (75 mi) to Puerto Yungay.

29 Puerto Yungay This settlement at the mouth of the Rio Bravo in the Mitchell Fjord was only founded in the 1990s for the construction of the Carretera Austral. Its port provides an important link with the north. The place also marks the end of your journey.

1 The Carretera Austral road in the Río Baker valley.

The Río Simpson nature reserve west of Coihaique attracts hikers with its high-elevation scenery (up to 1,900 m/6,234 ft). River valleys and several waterfalls are hidden amid dense forests here – the impressive Cascada de la Virgen crashes down over a series of drops.

Parque Nacional Lauca This nature sanctuary is on the vast, 4,000-m-high (13,124-ft) Altiplano, featuring snow-covered 6,000-m (19,686-ft) peaks. The shores of one of the highest lakes in the world, Lago Chungará (4,570 m/14,994 ft), are home to over 130 bird species.

Géiser el Tatio These geysers at an elevation of 4,300 m (14,108 ft) are always active in the early morning hours. Swimmers can enjoy a warm water basin in the middle of the steppe landscape while icy temperatures prevail all around.

Chañaral This area around a mining town has numerous canyons and is influenced by the cold Humboldt Current. Due to the frequent coastal fog the interior is constantly dry.

Observatories Low humidity, clean air and starry nights prevail in the Chilean Andes, ideal conditions for observatories such as the Cerro Tololo Inter-American Observatory seen here.

Viña del Mar The "Vineyard at the Sea" is Chile's most famous seaside resort, with lovely beaches, old palaces, magnificent parks and the Casino Municipal. It is reminiscent of Nice and Monte Carlo.

Valparaíso "Paradise Valley", Chile's largest port, sprawls over a great many hills. The differences in elevation within the city are sometimes overcome with elevators.

Reserva Nacional las Vicuñas The vast vicuña herds are what gave this sanctuary on the Altiplano its name. The smallest of the Andean camel species (shoulder height 85 cm/33 in) and related to the alpaca, it produces fine, light wool and has thus far resisted all attempts at domestication.

Licancábur On the border with Bolivia, this volcano is 5,916 m (19,410 ft) high. The deep crater lake and the sacrificial sites on the crater's edge make it an unusual peak in the chain of Atacama volcanoes.

San Pedro de Atacama This adobe village on the northern shore of the Salar de Atacama is home to a church made partly of cactus wood. There is also an informative museum. The bizarre landscape is magnificent, with glowing deserts and snowy mountains in the background.

Valle de la Luna "Moon Valley" is aptly named as it boasts a wealth of fantastic sand, salt and clay formations which, at sunset, appear indeed to be otherworldly.

Aconcagua The best view of Aconcagua, one of the highest mountains in the Andes at 6,959 m (22,832 ft), is from the pass where a number of Chilean winter sports resorts are located.

Santiago de Chile One-third of all Chileans live in the capital city. Only a few colonial-era buildings remain, such as the Casa Colorada or the Posada del Corregidor. On a clear day you have an impressive view of the snow-covered peaks of the Andes, the city's spectacular backdrop.

PERU
La Paz
Nevado de Putre 5825 m
P.N. Lauca
Pomerape 6282
Pta. Chungará
Tambo Quemado
Lima
Tacna
Oruro
Arica 1
Poconchile
San Miguel de Azapa
M.N. Salar de Surire
Sabaya
Pisagua
Vol. Isluga 5530
Isluga
P.N. Vol. Isluga
Baños de Puchuldiza
R.N. Pampa del Tamarugal
Gigante de Atacama
Chuzmiza
BOLIVIA
Mamiña
Iquique
Humberstone
Seremeño
Salar de Pintados
Potosí
Collahuasi
Chiguana
Vol. Chiguana 5291
R.N. Pampa del Tamarugal
Escalerilla
Ollagüe
Alota
El Loa
Vol. S. Pedro 6159
Tocopilla
San Pedro
Chuqui-camata
Quetena Grande
Géiser el Tatio
Reserva Nacional de Fauna Andina Eduardo Avaroa
María Elena
Calama
Pedro de Valdivia
San Pedro de Atacama
Vol. Licancábur 5916
Co. Zapaleri 5653
Carmen Alto
Reserva Nacional Los Flamencos
Valle de la Luna
Mejillones
Baquedano
Arenales
Laguna Chaxa
Socaire
Laguna Miscanti
Salar de Atacama
Laguna Miñique
Tarija
La Portada 7
Antofagasta 8
Varillas
Ea. Pan de Azúcar
Catúa
Viaducto la Polvorilla
Socompa
Cauchari
Salta
San Antonio de los Cobres
Paranal Observatory
Caipe
CHILE
R.N. Paposo
Paposo
P.N. Llullaillaco
Vol. Llullaillaco 6739
ARGENTINA
Taltal
Azufrera
Planta Esmeralda
Altamira
P.N. Pan de Azúcar
El Salvador
Chañaral
Diego de Almagro
La Rioja (RA)
Caldera
P.N. Nevado Tres Cruces
Tres Cruces
Copiapó
P.N. Nevado Tres Cruces
Barranquillas
P.N. Llanos de Challe
Juntas
Huasco
Vallenar
Alto del Carmen
Las Campanas Observatory
La Silla Observatory
P.N. San Guillermo
La Serena 9
Coquimbo 10
Valle del Río Elqui
Vicuña
Tongoy
Andacollo
Gemini South-Observ.
La Rioja
Ovalle
Monte Patria
P.N. Bosque de Fray Jorge 11
M.N. Valle del Encanto
Combarbalá
R.N. Las Chinchillas
Illapel
Salamanca
Los Vilos
Chincolco
Mendoza
La Ligua
Los Andes
Co. Aconcagua 6963
Puente del Inca
M.N. Isla Cachagua
P.N. La Campana
Llay-Llay
Cristo Redentor
Co. Tupungato 6800
Viña del Mar 13
Valparaíso
La Campana
R.N. Lago Peñuelas
SANTIAGO DE CHILE 15
Isla Negra 14
San Antonio
Paine
Cajón del Maipo
El Volcán
Rancagua

456

Cajón del Maipo This valley in the foothills of the Andes is highly regarded by wine lovers for its excellent Cabernet wines.

Chillán The valleys between Santiago and Osorno are popular among trekking and skiing fans. The town was destroyed by an earthquake in 1751, but the small market for handicrafts and fruit is still a worthwhile attraction today.

Valdivia Despite damage from fires and an earthquake, this university town is one of the loveliest in Chile. Its various markets, in particular, still show the influence of German colonists and have a great deal of flair and charm.

Puerto Varas The legacy of immigrant German speakers in the Lago Llanquihue area is clearly visible.

Isla Grande de Chiloé This island is 180 km (112 mi) long and 50 km (31 mi) wide. It is inhabited mainly by farmers and fishermen, and is famous for more than 150 wooden churches built by the Jesuits.

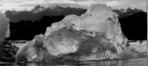

Laguna San Rafael A boat cruise from Puerto Aisén provides a close-up look at the impressive glacier tongue and the icebergs in the fjord.

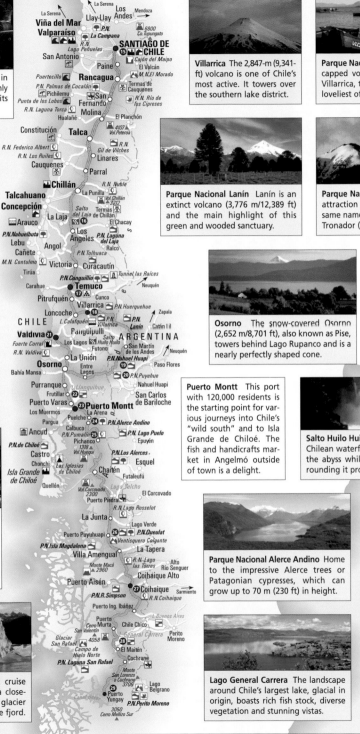

Villarrica The 2,847-m (9,341-ft) volcano is one of Chile's most active. It towers over the southern lake district.

Parque Nacional Villarrica With the snow-capped volcano as a backdrop on Lago Villarrica, this national park is one of the loveliest of its kind in Chile.

Parque Nacional Lanín Lanín is an extinct volcano (3,776 m/12,389 ft) and the main highlight of this green and wooded sanctuary.

Parque Nacional Nahuel Huapí The main attraction here is a glacial lake of the same name. The highest peak is the Cerro Tronador (3,554 m/11,661 ft).

Osorno The snow-covered Osorno (2,652 m/8,701 ft), also known as Pise, towers behind Lago Rupanco and is a nearly perfectly shaped cone.

Lago Llanquihue Chile's second-largest lake covers 877 sq km (338 sq mi) and is up to 350 m (1,148 ft) deep. It is situated in the "Switzerland of Chile". The town of Frutillar still has many old colonial buildings as well as the "German Colonists' Museum".

Puerto Montt This port with 120,000 residents is the starting point for various journeys into Chile's "wild south" and to Isla Grande de Chiloé. The fish and handicrafts market in Angelmó outside of town is a delight.

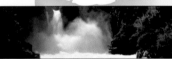

Salto Huilo Huilo One of the most spectacular Chilean waterfalls plunges 100 m (328 ft) into the abyss while the dense virgin forests surrounding it provide some fascinating hiking.

Isla Magdalena This barren island is inhabited by about 250,000 Magellanic penguins that breed in large flocks in October and March.

Parque Nacional Alerce Andino Home to the impressive Alerce trees or Patagonian cypresses, which can grow up to 70 m (230 ft) in height.

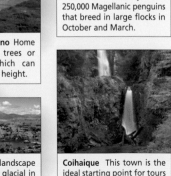

Lago General Carrera The landscape around Chile's largest lake, glacial in origin, boasts rich fish stock, diverse vegetation and stunning vistas.

Coihaique This town is the ideal starting point for tours to the spectacular Cascada de la Virgen, pictured here.

Argentina and Chile

Through the Pampas and Patagonia

Argentina is characterized by three major geographical regions that could scarcely be more different from one another – the endless Pampas, the high peaks of the Andes, and the plains of Patagonia with their steep isolated mountains and glaciers. Part of the Andes and some of the southern foothills of Patagonia near the Tierra del Fuego belong to Chile.

Covering an area of more than 2.8 million sq km (1 million sq mi), Argentina is the second-largest country in South America after its significantly larger neighbour Brazil. The Pampas, which make up the heartland of Argentina, are a vast green expanse on which isolated mountain ranges emerge like islands in an ocean, from Buenos Aires all the way to the western border with Chile.

One such 'island' is the Sierra de Córdoba, a range that rises west of Córdoba in the Cerro Champaqui to a height of 2,884 m (9,614 ft), indeed a considerable height, but that is nothing compared to the awe-inspiring peaks west of Mendoza. There, the Cerro Aconcagua, or 'Stone Sentinel', towers to 6,963 m (23,000 ft) and is the highest peak in the Andes and the highest mountain in the Americas.

The Andes mark the natural border between Argentina and neighbouring Chile. National parks have been established on both sides of the border in magnificent mountain landscapes containing virgin forests interspersed with shimmering blue and green lakes and rivers of cloudy glacier water. The areas are a paradise for hikers and include the Lanín National Park, where dense forests of araucaria and Antarctic beech engulf the mighty Lanín volcano. At the base of this 3,747-m (12,290-ft)

An Argentinian gaucho herding his cattle on the Pampas.

The tongue of the Perito Morena Glacier in Los Glaciares National Park is some 70 m (233 ft) high.

Like an impregnable fortress, the granite towers of the Torres del Paine in Chile rise from the plains of southern Patagonia. They are a favourite destination for trekkers from all over the world.

volcano is a deep blue lake called Lago Huechulafquén.

While northern Patagonia occasionally offers gentle landscapes such as that of the Nahuel Huapi National Park, in the south the terrain becomes progressively more windswept and barren. The constant Westerlies bring humidity from the Pacific, falling as rain on the Chilean side of the Andes. The winds then sweep over the icy inland regions, glaciers and ice fields of Patagonia, which chill them before they whip over towards the eastern plains.

The Andes open up here and there, revealing gaps between the peaks like the ones at Lago Buenos Aires – known as the Lago General Carrera on the Chilean side – and at the Los Glaciares National Park. Also typical of southern Patagonia are the isolated granite peaks that dominate the plains: the FitzRoy Massif and the Torres del Paine, for example.

It was not until the last ice age that the Strait of Magellan, once just a cleft in the Andes, split off from the mainland and created the island of Tierra del Fuego. This main island in the archipelago is 47,000 sq km (20,000 sq mi) with a landscape that clearly resembles that of Patagonia. In the north is a broad plateau while in the south the last foothills of the Cordilleras reach heights of 2,500 m (9,000 ft), finally sinking spectacularly into the sea at the notorious Cape Horn, whose perpetually stormy seas have been the bane of the lives of so many brave sailors.

The impressive gorges and ravines east of San Carlos de Bariloche.

1

From the Pampas over the mountains, past the granite massifs and glaciers of Patagonia, through the Strait of Magellan to Ushuaia, this dream route leads you all the way down Argentina along the Pan-American Highway to the southern tip of Tierra del Fuego on Lapataia Bay.

❶ Córdoba Argentina's second-largest city, with 1.5 million inhabitants, is frequently called 'La Docta', 'the Erudite', and it bears the nickname with pride. It was here in 1614 that the country's first university was founded, and still boasts excellent university faculties.
Founded in 1573, Córdoba's center is surprisingly tranquil. The plaza contains the beautifully arcaded Cabildo, the colonial-style government building, and the cathedral, built in 1574 in a mixed baroque and neoclassical style. A few steps further along, through the pedestrian zone, you come to the Manzana Jesuítica, the Jesuit quarter, with a Jesuit church and the first university buildings.

Passing through the suburbs, we leave Córdoba on Ruta 20 in the direction of Carlos Paz and reach the Sierra de Córdoba, which rises impressively from the Pampas to a height of 2,884 m (9,614 ft) in the Cerro Champaqui. At Villa Dolores, some 170 km (105 miles) south-west of Córdoba, you will leave the mountains behind and enter a flatter landscape that remains as such for the next 500 km (310 mi) until Mendoza.

❷ Mendoza The green countryside around Mendoza is deceptive, as this city of around 600,000 is in a desert known as the Cuyo, which means 'sandy earth'. Plentiful water from the nearby mountains has allowed

Travel Information

Route profile
Length: approx. 5,300 km (3,315 miles)
Time required: 4 weeks
Start: Córdoba
End: Ushuaia
Route (main locations):
Córdoba, Mendoza, Puente del Inca, San Carlos de Bariloche, Parque Nacional Los Glaciares, Parque Nacional Torres del Paine, Punta Arenas, Parque Nacional Tierra del Fuego

Traffic information:
The trip mostly follows the Argentinian Ruta 40, which runs north-south along the eastern edge of the Andes. The highway is mostly surfaced, although a few of

the side-roads in southern Patagonia are gravel. You will need to watch for oncoming traffic and pass close to it, otherwise loose stones flying up from the road could damage the windshield. It is generally not advisable to drive at night outside the main cities.

Strait of Magellan:
There is a good ferry connection from the mainland to Tierra del Fuego; in summer, the ferries operate hourly.

More information:
www.ontheroadtravel.com
www.parquesnacionales. gov.ar
www.travelsur.net

the desert to bloom, and it is here that the finest Argentinian wines are produced.

Although Mendoza was founded as early as 1561, the center of the city is mostly modern.

Older buildings have been repeatedly razed by earthquakes, most severely in 1861. All that remains is the Church of San Francisco, dating from 1638. The pedestrian area of the Calle Sarmiento, with its cafés and restaurants, and the suburb of Maipú, with bodegas that offer wine tastings, are worth a visit. From Mendoza, take a detour to the stunning Puente del Inca.

❸ Puente del Inca The 'Inca Bridge', at a height of 2,720 m (9,000 ft), is a natural arch over the Río Mendoza that was formed by mineral deposits. Following the road westwards, you soon come to the best view of Aconcagua (see sidebar left).

A dirt road then leads up to the old border zone on the Bermejo Pass at 3,750 m (12,500 ft). From there your climb will be rewarded by a wonderful view over the High Andes.

From Mendoza, Ruta 40 leads south. After about 300 km (190 miles) through the Cuyo, a road branches at El Sosneada to the west towards Las Leñas,

Argentina's greatest skiing area. You will then head another 490 km (310 miles) south, parallel to the Andes, to Zapala.

This city has a museum displaying beautiful local minerals and fossils. The distances are great in Argentina, but after another 156 km (100 miles) on Ruta 40 there is a road turning off to the west, leading to San Martín de los Andes, a little mountain town with the best approach to Lanín National Park.

❹ Lanín National Park This park surrounds the extinct volcano after which the park was named. The 3,747-m (12,490-ft) ice-clad volcano, which has a perfect formed cone peak, is mirrored in Lago Huechulafquén. It is the ideal scenic backdrop for extended hikes. Back on Ruta 40, San Carlos de Bariloche is not far away.

❺ San Carlos de Bariloche Bariloche was founded by Swiss immigrants, and is the 'Swiss side' of Argentina. The Centro Civico, the community center, is built to resemble a Swiss chalet. Best of all, the main shopping street features one chocolate factory after another, and all the restaurants have cheese fondue on the menu.

The first settlers sought and found a rural idyll here. Bariloche lies on one of Argentina's most beautiful lakes, Lago Nahuel Huapi, at the heart of the national park of the same name. The road leads further south through a magnificent mountain landscape.

You then reach the Los Alerces National Park near Esquel.

1 Steppe as far as the eye can see – beginning just east of San Carlos de Bariloche, the vast Patagonian plains extend all the way out to the Atlantic Ocean.

2 A peak in the southern Pampas – the 3,680-m (12,266-ft) Cerro Payún south-east of Bardas Blancas.

461

The granite peaks of the Fitz Roy Massif rise almost 3,000 m (9,840 ft) above the plains of Patagonia. The highest of them all, the Cerro Fitz Roy, reaches a height of 3,375 m (11,070 ft); it is considered to be one of the most difficult mountains in the world to climb. You will

rarely be lucky enough to have such a clear view of the peak – as here across Lago Sucia – because thick clouds often obscure the summit. Anyone hiking in the Los Glaciares National Park must be prepared for sudden changes in weather conditions.

1

2

6 Los Alerces National Park
This park was created in 1937 and covers an area of 260,000 ha (650,000 acres). It is dedicated to the preservation of the alerces, gigantic and spectacular evergreen trees that can reach heights of 70 m (235 ft) with diameters of 4 m (14 ft). Some of the trees are believed to be 3,500 years old. In the center of the park is the 78-sq-km (30-sq-mile) Lake Futalaufquén. From the national park, Ruta 40 continues to the south. It is 381 km (237 miles) from Esquel to Río Mayo, but shortly before this, Ruta 26 branches to the east towards Colonia Sarmiento via the petrified forests.

To the west, Ruta 26 winds through the Andes to the Chilean city of Coyhaique. From there it is another 129 km (80 mi) south to Perito Moreno.

7 Perito Moreno is the starting point for excursions to the teal-coloured Lake Buenos Aires, the second-largest lake in South America after Lake Titicaca. The Argentinean side of the lake lies in the middle of the Patagonian plains; the Chilean side is surrounded by snow-covered peaks. You can cross the Chilean border at Los Antiguos, on the southern edge of the lake.

Some 56 km (35 miles) south of Perito Moreno, the road forks, one branch leading to Cueva de las Manos (see page 469).

It is another 239 km (148 miles) from Perito Moreno through the desolate, Patagonian plains edged by snowy mountains to the next settlement, Hotel las Horquetas, a handful of houses in the Río Chico Valley.

At an intersection here, a gravel road branches off to the west in the direction of Estancia la Oriental and Lake Belgrano. This is the route to the Perito Moreno National Park.

8 Perito Moreno National Park This is one of Argentina's most isolated and spectacular national parks. There are glaciers and shimmering mountain lakes with floating blocks of ice, and the park is teeming with wildlife such as pumas, wildcats, guanacos and waterfowl.

The second-highest mountain in Patagonia, Monte San Lorenzo (3,706 m/12,159 ft), is the home of the condor. The park can only be explored on foot or horseback. As there are few roads or facilities for travellers – only basic campsites are found along this route – make sure you have emergency supplies. Tres Lagos is the name of the next crossroads on Ruta 40, about 235 km (146 miles) further on. At this point, Ruta 288 goes east towards the Atlantic Ocean.

After 45 km (28 miles) heading south is the elongated Lake Viedma which was formed by melting glacial ice. The road on this lake's northern bank leads directly westward and, on cloud-less days, there is a fantastic view of the FitzRoy Massif in the far distance.

The biggest of these giants is the Upsala Glacier, with a surface area of 595 sq km (230 sq mi). The most popular spot, however, is the Perito Moreno Glacier about 80 km (50 mi) from El Calafate, whose glacial tongue pushes out into Lake Argentino to such an extent that every few years it completely seals off the Brazo Rico, one of the lake's offshoots.

⑪ Puerto Natales Founded in 1911 and situated on the Ultima Esperanza Estuary, this town was the last hope of sailors who had got lost in the countless channels of southern Patagonia in their search for an east-west passage. Puerto Natales is the best starting point for a visit to nearby Torres del Paine National Park, and also a worthwhile stop for arranging various excursions. For example, you could take a boat ride on Seno de la Ultima Esperanza (Last Hope Sound) up to the border of the Bernardo O'Higgins National

Park to Cerro Balmaceda 2,035 m (6,676 ft) with its impressive glaciers. Bird lovers should visit the town's old pier in the late afternoon. It's a meeting place for hundreds of cormorants.

⑫ Cueva del Milodón En route to the Torres del Paine National Park, take the a time to visit Cueva del Milodón. Travel 8 km (5 miles) north of Puerto Natales and then west.

1 The drastic edge of the Perito Moreno Glacier in Los Glaciares is up to 70 m (230 ft) high. With a great roar, ice chunks the size of houses continually break off from its walls.

2 The icy blue-green waters of Lake del Grano in the Perito Moreno National Park.

3 Colourful sandstone cliffs near Sarmiento between Lake Musters and Lake Colhué Huapí.

⑨ El Chaltén This town is the northern access point for Los Glaciares National Park, a dream destination for mountaineers from all over the world as it is home to the 3,375-m (11,072-ft) Mount FitzRoy. But it is not just for climbers. Hikers will also find a plethora of activities. You can organize one-day or multi-day excursions from El Chaltén.
Back on Ruta 40, you pass through the Leona Valley and along the eastern bank of Lake Argentino, the largest lake in

Patagonia, which leads to the junction to El Calafate.

⑩ Los Glaciares National Park There is more activity at the southern end of this park, near El Calafate, than in the northern part. This is due to the spectacular glaciers that can be much more easily accessed from here than anywhere else. Large slabs of ice frequently break from the 70-m (230-ft) glacial walls, landing in the lake with an immense crash.

After 5 km (3 miles) you reach the cave where German immigrant Hermann Eberhard found remains of a huge dinosaur, a 4-m (13-ft) megatherium, in 1896. A replica of the creature stands by the entrance to the cave to show how it may have looked.

⑬ Torres del Paine National Park The peaks of the majestic Torres del Paine Massif rise dramatically from the windswept plain. These steep, seemingly impregnable mountains have granite peaks, the highest of which is Cerro Torre Grande at 3,050 m (10,007 ft), surrounded by Paine Chico, Torres del Paine and Cuernos del Paine.

This is Chile's adventure paradise. Visitors can choose between embarking on long hiking trails in the park, day-long tours, or a hiking trail around the entire massif. All these trails pass by bluish-white, opaque, glacial lakes with floating icebergs. They include Grey Glacier and the amazing Río Paine,

which plummets into Lake Pehoe as a cascading waterfall.

The stunted trees brace themselves against the wind here, but in early summer the plains form a sea of flowers. In addition to guanacos, you will likely spot condors and sundry waterfowl. Remember to take warm clothing and sturdy boots.

To the south of Puerto Natales, the route continues straight through the plains. Stubby grass grows on both sides of the road. You'll often see guanacos, rheas (flightless birds) and sheep. This is Ruta 9 to Punta Arenas.

Some 34 km (21 miles) before the city, a road branches westwards. After 23 km (14 miles) you reach Otway Sound, home to a large penguin colony.

⑭ Monumento Natural Los Pingüinos There is another large penguin colony to the north-east of Punta Arenas, right on the Strait of Magellan. In the summer months, some 2,500 Magellan penguins, the

smallest of the species, live in this colony. They only grow to between 50 and 70 cm (20 and 28 in) tall and weigh a mere 5 kg (11 lbs). They can be easily recognized by their black-and-white heads and the black stripe running across the upper part of their torsos.

⑮ Punta Arenas This city, which was founded in the mid 19th century as a penal colony, grew quickly and was an important port for ships plying the west coast of America until the construction of the Panama Canal in 1914. Patagonia's prof-

itable sheep-farming also made its contribution to the city's success, allowing wealthy inhabitants to build sheep estancias (ranches) around the city center. The Palacio Braun-Menéndez, today a museum, shows how the upper class lived in those days: walls elegantly covered in fabric imported from France,

1 Guanacos, relatives of the llama, in a flowery meadow in the Torres del Paine National Park.

2 Rider on the Patagonian plains north of Punta Arenas.

One of the wonders of nature – a cluster of flowers, mainly lupins, in the Torres del Paine National Park, with snowy peaks in the background. This magnificent sight can be seen only in late spring and early summer.

billiard tables from England, gold-plated fireguards from Flanders and Carrara marble decorations from Italy. Burials were no less regal here. The Punta Arenas cemetery contains the enormous mausoleums of the city's wealthier families. The Museo Regional Mayorino Borgatallo is also worth a visit.

From Punta Arenas, drive 50 km (31 miles) back to the intersection of Ruta 9 and Ruta 255. Then follow Ruta 255 in a northeast direction until you reach Punta Delgada. From there, Ruta 3, which originates in Argentina, leads south and soon reaches the Strait, where a ferry transports travellers to Puerto Espora in Tierra del Fuego.

16 Strait of Magellan/Tierra del Fuego In 1520, Fernando de Magellan, a Portugese sea captain and explorer, was the first person to sail through the Strait which was later named after him. As he skirted the mainland and the islands, he saw fire and smoke, hence the archipelago's name. The island group covers 73,500 sq km (28,378 sq miles). Its main island, the western part of which belongs to

Chile, covers an area of about 47,000 sq km (18,147 sq mi). It is some 280 km (174 mi) from Puerto Espora to the Río Grande through vast, open countryside. At San Sebastián Bay, you can cross the border to Argentina. South of the Río Grande, the landscape changes – the valleys become narrower, the hills higher, and dense forests come into view. After about 250 km (155 mi), you reach Ushuaia and the Tierra del Fuego National Park.

17 Tierra del Fuego National Park Hikers will enjoy Tierra del Fuego National Park, which begins some 18 km (11 mi) west of Ushuaia. It is easily accessible in its southern part but inaccessible in the north, and stretches

along the Chilean border offering marshes, rocky cliffs and temperate rainforests.

Ruta 3, the Argentinean part of the southern Pan-American Highway, leads directly into the park and ends picturesquely at the Bahía Lapataía.

18 Ushuaia The southernmost city in the world is set between the icy waters of the deep Beagle Channel and the peaks of the Cordillera which, despite being only 1,500 m (4,921 ft) high, are always covered in snow. Originally founded as a penal colony, the city thrives mostly from tourism these days. The Museo Fin del Mundo has a collection depicting the early and colonial history of the area. If the weather

is clement, take a boat trip to the glorious end of the world, Cape Horn.

Another of the town's attractions is the Ferrocarril Austral Fueguino, a beautifully elegant and antique steam locomotive, which will take you on an 8-km (5-mile) tour leaving from the End of World Station up to the Tierra del Fuego National Park.

1 The Tierra del Fuego National Park entices adventurous travellers with its expansive steppe, mountainous landscape and impenetrable jungles and rainforests.

2 Punta Arenas port in the Strait of Magellan.

Aconcagua The highest mountain in the Americas at 6,963 m (23,000 ft), Aconcagua is near Mendoza on the Chilean border. It was first 'officially' climbed in 1897. 2,000 to 4,000 mountaineers enjoy it every year.

Mendoza This modern city of 600,000 also has a colonial past, although many buildings have been destroyed by earthquakes. Mendoza has now become the hub of Argentina's flourishing grape growing and wine industry. It has many wineries and bodegas where visitors can savour the delicious local wine amid the area's stunning landscape.

Los Alerces National Park Gigantic alerces trees, some estimated to be over 3,500 years old, grow to a massive height and girth.

Los Glaciares National Park This park consists of two formations, the high mountain landscape in the north, with the FitzRoy Massif, and the inland glaciers in the south, with the Upsala and Perito-Moreno Glaciers.

The Torres del Paine National Park The highest peak in the park is the 3,050-m-high (10,007-ft) Cerro Torre Grande, surrounded by Paine Chico, Torres del Paine and Cuernas del Paine.

Ushuaia This city, the southernmost in Argentina, lies on the Beagle Channel. The Museo del Fin del Mundo (End of the World Museum) displays exhibits from the prehistoric and colonial history of Tierra del Fuego.

Cueva de las Manos In a sizeable cave in the Río Pinturas Canyon. The original inhabitants of this area left behind the oldest indications of human settlement in South America.

Córdoba Argentina's second-largest city (1.5 million inhabitants) is home to the country's oldest university. The picture shows the cathedral and Cabildo in the central plaza of the town.

Nahuel Huapi National Park This park near Bariloche has several different landscape zones including the High Andes, rainforest, transitional forest and steppe.

Perito Moreno National Park The national park surrounding Lake Belgrano (the picture shows the broad Belgrano Peninsula) showcases the diverse Patagonian nature. Numerous indigenous animals live here, including pumas, guanacos, nandus, flamingos and condors.

Tierra del Fuego National Park This national park, close to Ushuaia in Terra del Fuego, runs to the Chilean border with its lakes, glaciers and rainforests.

Punta Arenas Until the Panama Canal was built in 1914, this port town was of great importance at the tip of South America. Some of the typical houses from that era remain to the present day.

The Los Pingüinos and Seno Otway Penguin Colonies Thousands of Magellan penguins live here near Punta Arenas in the summer. They are the smallest species of penguin in South America.

469

Brazil

A whole continent in one country

Idyllic beaches and coastline, colonial cities and futuristic architecture, sweeping wetlands and breathtaking waterfalls – this route through Brazil offers an amazing array of cultural and natural treasures.

Our enthralling journey into the heart of Brazil starts in one of the country's most beautiful big cities. From the very beginning of the trip, the roots of Brazil's unique charm become clear: the wealth and diversity of its peoples and cultures.

For many years Salvador da Bahía was the entry point for African slaves, and its state has a large black and mixed-race population. You can hear and see that influence on popular culture everywhere, especially in the African-influenced music.

From Salvador, our journey leads west. The BR 242 crosses the state of Bahía from one side to the other, climbing through Brazil's coastal mountains where the peaks can reach heights of 1,700 m (5,580 ft) and are surrounded by spectacular canyons, such as those in the Chapada Diamantina National Park. Descending to the plains, the route crosses the Rio São Francisco at Ibotirama, where the river is 1.5 km (1 mile) wide. After passing the regional center of Barreiras, the route turns south, running parallel to the Serra Geral do Parana chain before reaching Brasilia. The broad prairies and pastureland of the state of Mato Grosso do Sul stretch away to the west. This waterlogged area, bounded by the Rio Paraná to the east and the Rio Paraguay to the west, is part of the largest wetland on earth: the Pantanal, a paradise almost without equal for plant and

A woman sporting traditional African-style headwear in Salvador.

Colonial architecture in southern Brazil: just one of the baroque-influenced buildings in Ouro Preto.

The baroque church of Igreja de Nossa Senhora do Rosario on the Largo do Pelourinho in Salvador's upper town stands among streets of houses painted in shades of bright pastel colours.

animal life, spreading over a vast area of 230,000 sq. km (88,800 sq. miles) and crossing several countries' borders.

The next stop on this Brazilian route is the 1,320-km (820-mile) Iguaçu River which crashes down over two waterfalls with a total height of 72 m (236 ft), at a spot close to where the borders of Argentina, Brazil and Paraguay converge. From this spot, the road continues east through the lush forests, meadows, and thriving coffee plantations of the state of Paraná to eventually reach São Paulo, Brazil's largest and most commercially important city and the centre of its industrial heartland. (See page 480).

Rio de Janeiro, previously the country's capital city, boasts two of the most famous beaches in the world, but Praia Copacabana and Praia Ipanema are not much more than crowded catwalks where people dress up and go to see and be seen.

Our journey begins in a region drenched in history and it ends in one too: there are several jewels from the country's colonial past to be discovered to the north of Rio. The modern state of Espírito Santo has its origins in the Portuguese capitania (province) founded in 1534, and the first Jesuit priests arrived in 1551. They were followed by Franciscans and other religious orders, and soon parishes such as Congonhas do Campo and Ouro Preto boasted ecclesiastical buildings which are regarded among the most beautiful creations of Brazilian architecture. (See page 486).

The Salvador carnival is not quite as famous as Rio's but just as lively.

1

The route connects Brazil's first capital, by the sea, with its modern one in the interior, before continuing past bustling cities and little colonial towns as it crosses broad pasture land and plantations. Spectacular national parks and Atlantic beaches offer plenty of opportunities for rest and relaxation.

1 Salvador What a start to the journey and what an awe-inspriing location! The Portuguese sailors who arrived on this recently discovered continent on November 1, 1501, must have been equally impressed by this magnificent bay. To commemorate the day, they named the spot Baia de Todos os Santos (All Hallows Bay) and soon established their first settlement here; this was christened Salvador and became the original capital of the Portuguese colony of Brazil in 1549.

Salvador soon flourished as monasteries and churches were founded and residences and fortifications were built up. The city was divided into an upper town, with churches and the colonial rulers' townhouses, and a lower town, the preserve of merchants and the docks. The wealth of the new capital stemmed from trading the sugar cane cultivated in what is now the modern state of Bahía. This was difficult and dangerous work and Salvador soon became the principal importer of slaves from Africa. The stocks where the slaves were whipped stood on the Praça Pelourinho, the central square of the upper town, in full sight of the cathedral and other churches.

Salvador has a over 12 colonial church buildings, most of which have been built and decorated in the distinctively Brazilian baroque style. Almost all have a façade flanked by two towers, a triangular tympanum, and a long nave bereft of the dome which might be expected in European baroque. Salvador's upper town has several excellent examples of such churches, including the cathedral (begun in 1657) with its beautifully gilded coffered ceiling, the Convento de Nossa Senhora do Carmo with its church of Largo do Carmo, the austere church of Nossa Senhora do Rosarió dos Pretos with its very characteristic blue tones, and the Franciscan church of São Francisco, built between 1708 and 1723, whose interior is decorated with gilded carvings.

The lower town is reached by an elevator and here the main attraction is the Mercado Modelo, not just for the market's range of products – which include extremely good-value leather goods – but also for its bustling atmosphere. Built just outside the town center in 1598, the Fort Santo Antônio da Barra with its museum is also well worth visiting.

② Chapada Diamantina National Park From Salvador the road turns west, climbing into the mountains that line Brazil's coast and to an exciting landscape of forested upland plains punctuated with canyons. Scattered across elevations between 800 m and 1,200 m (2,600 ft and 3,900 ft), the 152,000 ha (587 sq. miles) of the Chapada Diamantina National Park make up the heartland of this mountainous territory. Among the forest's many waterfalls are the highest falls in Brazil (the 422-m/1,385-ft Cachoeira Glass, named after George Glass, the American pilot who discovered them) and

falls with cave systems containing clear streams, and little lakes. The ideal base for excursions is the colonial town of Lençois, whose smart colonial-era houses and municipal buildings were paid for with diamonds discovered locally; these also gave their name to the park. A short-lived diamond rush broke out here in 1844. An excursion to the Chapada dos Veadeiros National Park is recommended before moving on to Brazil's capital.

③ Brasília In 1763 Salvador ceased to be Brazil's capital and Rio de Janeiro was given the role. Then the provisions of a new constitution unveiled in 1891 included the removal of the capital once more, to the country's interior, in a bid to counteract the influence of the developed cities along the Atlantic coast. However, the foundation stone for the project was not laid until 1922, and it was only 34 years later, in 1956, that

tenders were invited by President Juscelino Kubitschek de Oliveira for the design of a city to be called Brasília, and which was officially confirmed as the capital of Brazil on 21 April 1960. With Lúcio Costa planning the overall layout of the city and Oscar Niemeyer designing most of the buildings, it is a city that has sprung straight from the drawing-board, and it is best appreciated from the air. Costa conceived the city as an aircraft, with the government, supreme court, and president in the cockpit, the general populace in the

1 A golden dream – the interior of the beautiful church of São Francisco in Salvador.

2 The forests, canyons, and mesas of the Chapada Diamantina National Park.

3 The square of the three powers – legislative, judiciary, and executive – in the capital, Brasília.

Above: The bridge was named after Juscelino Kubitschek de Oliveira, the former president of Brazil, who in the late 1950s, decided to create Brasília as the country's new capital. Below: The Blue Church is famed for its blue stained glass walls.

Above: The 28-storey twin towers of Parliament House, behind the Senate. Below: Another remarkable church in the city is the Cathedral

wings, and the municipal buildings and administrative district in the tail, with a 250-m (820-ft) wide central axis running north-south for 6 km (4 miles). Brasília has all the strengths and weaknesses of modern town planning. On one hand it has the benefit of imaginative architecture of glass and concrete – for example, the converging arches and circular floorplan of the cathedral make its concrete ribs resemble Christ's crown of thorns, and whilst its exterior looks uninviting, the interior is full of light and space, striving for heaven. On the other hand, the entire zone can at times lack any human scale; the buildings are so big that an individual human being is lost beside them. Structures such as the twin 28-storey tower blocks of the government buildings can appear pristine and cold, symbolizing technology and power. The two chambers of Brazil's two parliaments are accommodated directly in front of these, in two

semi-circular buildings housing the House of Representatives in the lower half and the Senate in the upper half. Initially rejected by the population, the city has now been accepted as the country's capital of the interior.

④ Chapada dos Guimarães Named after the upland plains that surround it, the little town of Chapada dos Guimarães lies some 1,100 km (685 miles) to the west of Brasília. The road crosses the cerrado savannah region, through a landscape of low shrubs and trees that slowly gives way to prairie and pasture land. En route, there are many canyons, plateaus, caves, rivers, and waterfalls –the greatest being the Véu-da-Noiva, with a drop of some 80 m (265 ft).

⑤ Pantanal Lying some 80 km (50 miles) to the west, Cuiabá is the ideal base from which to explore the Pantanal, the gigantic wetland of western Brazil. The Pantanal has a total area of

about 230,000 sq. km (88,800 sq. miles), of which some 35,000 sq. km (13,500 sq. miles) is a protected national park. Although the word Pantanal literally means "swamp," this is misleading: only certain sections of the region are marshland, the rest are a low-lying plain of many shallow depressions which fill with water during the rainy season between November and March, creating numerous lakes and flood plains of all sizes. The earth soaks up the water like a sponge and by the end of the rainy season, four-fifths of the total surface area lie under water, with only a few isolated hills, clumps of trees, and areas of undergrowth to be seen above the floodwaters. Copses of trees resemble small dark green islands in a light green sea, while the narrow gallery forests are like ribbons of vegetation along unseen rivers. This giant wetland drains into countless tiny streams which soon converge into the Rio Paraguay,

a tributary of the mighty Rio Paraná. The Pantanal is heaven on earth for animal lovers and is home to a great wealth of species. There are some 250 different kinds of freshwater fish, including piranhas, as well as water-dwellers such as the Yacare caiman (jacaré), and rodents such as the capybara – not to mention anacondas, otters, toucans, blue parrots, hummingbirds, and the occasional glimpse of a jaguar. Unfortunately, the road does not follow the river, as this would the route things much easier; instead, we must circumnavigate the Pantanal on the BR 163, first heading east and then south. After 690 km (430 miles) we pass Campo Grande, the capital of the state of Mato Grosso.

1 Abrupt, jagged cliffs, canyons, forests, and caves are typical features of the Chapada dos Guimarães highlands.

Above: The chestnut-eared aracari is a cousin of the toucan and a protected species. It lives mainly on forest fruits. **Below:** The stork-like jabiru (known to the locals as the tuiuiu) is synonymous with the Pantanal and can achieve a wingspan of up to 2.5 m (8 feet).

In the language of the Guaraní people, Iguaçu means "great water," but given the dimensions of the waterfalls, even this name sounds rather modest: roaring savagely, the river hurls 1,700 m³ (60,000 cubic ft) of water over the cliff every second, creating cascades and

individual waterfalls that reach depths of up to 72 m (236 ft). The falls are 2,700 m (8,860 ft) wide. Allocate several days to explore one of the most impressive waterfalls in the world. Dinghy trips which take visitors up close to the cascades are particularly exciting,

After another 480 km (300 miles) we arrive in Mundo Novo on the Paraguayan border. A further 270 km (170 miles) of Paraguayan highway brings us to Ciudad del Este, a paradise for merchants and smugglers. Returning to Brazil across the "Friendship Bridge" over the Paraná, which marks the border here, the route continues on to Foz do Iguaçu, the town after which the Iguaçu Falls, one of South America's greatest attractions, is named.

6 Iguaçu Several days should be set aside to visit Iguaçu, not least as you should see the falls from both sides of the river; the Brazilian side offers a gigantic panorama in wide-screen format and the Argentinian side provides the close-up. You can even walk between the waterfalls on the Rio Iguaçú or take dinghy trips to the cascades. Afterward, a trip to the Jesuit missions is highly recommended. (See page 471).

7 São Paulo No one is quite sure where the city really starts; you are just suddenly in the middle of the bustle. Some 20 million people live in the greater São Paulo area, and this number is growing by thousands every day. The city is the most important commercial, financial, and cultural center, and a transport node with universities, colleges, theaters, and museums. It is the largest industrial conurbation in Latin America and the most important manufacturing site in the Third World. Its rather modest origins lie in a tiny settlement founded on 25 January 1554 by José Anchieta, a Spanish padre. After initially unproductive sugar cane cultivation, the locals experimented with growing wheat in the 17th century. The town was incorporated in 1711 and Brazil's independence from Portugal was proclaimed here on 7 September 1822. However, things only really started to change for this sleepy little town in the mid-19th cen-

tury, when coffee, a product dear to the heart of the European market, was planted in the São Paulo highlands. Immigrants came to work on the plantations, principally from Italy, but also Germany, Japan, and Lebanon, and from the 1920s onward, more immigrants powered the industrialization of the area. São Paulo's population explosion – in 1940 there were just about one and a quarter million inhabitants, and now there are more than ten million

– has brought its own problems, and the city is extremely overcrowded: some parts of the suburbs have 2,371 inhabitants per sq. km (a third of a square mile), in São Paulo itself the figure is 6,580, and in the town of Diadema on the city limits it has reached 12,724. The Paulistanos, as the inhabitants of São Paulo are known, suffer the consequences of inadequate or absent infrastructure, air pollution, insufficient water supply, noise, traffic, and poor refuse

3

disposal and sanitation. The Praça da Se, the main square in the city center, is graced by a few fountains, but the stores and apartment buildings that surround it are functional rather than beautiful. Standing just opposite, the gigantic neo-Gothic cathedral was completed in 1954 and can accommodate a congregation of about 8,000. The nearby Casa de Anchieta is a reproduction of the house lived in by the city's founder, and the church of the Ordem Terceira de São Francisco, built in 1676, houses a gilded altar dating back to 1735 which is certainly worth seeing.

The Convento Nossa Senhora da Luz now houses a museum of sacred art, and the Museu Paulista is to be found on the same hill in the Parque de la Independência, a little beyond the city center, from which Emperor Dom Pedro proclaimed independence in 1822. It has large collections in the fields of anthropology and ethnography, with exhibits from all over Brazil. Those seeking peace in the heart of the city should head for the Parque Independência or the larger and more popular Parque Ibirapuera to the south; established in 1954 on the 400th anniversary of the city's foundation, this green lung in the middle of the metropolis has two small lakes and several museums. Along with its treasures of 20th- and 21st-century European and Brazilian art, the Museu de Arte Contemporânea has also hosted the São Paulo Biennale since 1951, and the Museu de Tecnica Populares has interesting collections of folk art and craft work. The Museu de Arte de São Paulo has a selection of Old Masters and European Impressionists.

⑧ Parati Beyond São Paulo, the road continues to the ocean, but the city has already spread to engulf Santos, its port. As you head north-east along the coast you will gradually leave the suburbs behind you and there are plenty of beaches to tempt you down to the sea along this peaceful road. The prettiest place to stop is at Parati, a well-manicured little town that was once only accessible by boat. The town center is closed to traffic, which is a bonus on top of the beaches and the refined and relaxed atmosphere.

⑨ Rio de Janeiro See page 484.

⑩ Nationalpark Serra dos Órgãos This small park slightly to the north of Rio de Janeiro occupies only 10,000 ha (39 sq. miles) of uplands about 800 m (2,600 ft) above sea level, and its tallest peak, the Pedra de Sino, is 2,263 m (7,425 ft) high. Its south-west face is considered one of the most difficult climbs in Brazil and the peak attracts mountaineers from all over the world. They also come to scale other formations in the park, such as the sheer summits of Dedo de Deus (1,692 m/5,551 ft), Escalavrado (1,300 m/4,265 ft), Dedo de Nossa Senhora (1,320 m/4,330 ft) and Nariz do Frade, the "monk's nose" (1,980 m/6,496 ft). The park is also good for hiking, with trails such as the 30-km (19-mile) Travessía from Petrópolis to Teresópolis, and you can expect to see mountain peaks, steep cliffs, bare slopes, countless rivers and waterfalls, streams and plunge pools, and forests of cinnamon and guama trees, fuchsias, acacias, soap bark trees, and cedars.

1 A glittering metropolis of 20 million inhabitants, São Paulo is Brazil's commercial center.

2 The Serra dos Órgãos National Park near the metropolis of Rio de Janeiro is fantastic for both hikers and climbers.

3 The traffic never sleeps: the city freeways of São Paulo.

The view at dusk from Corcovado hill across the Praia do Botofago to the 394-m (1,293-ft) Sugarloaf Mountain, the symbol of Rio de Janeiro. The name of this striking mountain – Pão de Açúcar in Portuguese – is said to come from a misunderstanding on the part of

Portuguese explorers. The local people called the spot *paundaçuqúa*, a word referring to the jagged coast here, but the Portuguese heard "pão de açúcar" and took it to refer to the rock formation which does indeed bear a striking resemblance to a loaf of sugar.

Rio de Janeiro

Very few cities in the world have such a breathtaking location and skyline as that of Rio de Janeiro – the view from Corcovado hill or the Sugarloaf Mountain down to Rio and the world-famous Atlantic beaches will stay with you for the rest of your life.

When the Portuguese explorer André Gonçalvez sailed his ships into the wide waters of the Bay of Guanabara on New Year's Day 1502, he thought he had discovered an estuary and called the supposed river the Rio de Janeiro – the January River. Although this proved not to be the case, the name stuck and the settlement established on 1 March 1564 was named Cidade de São Sebastião do Rio de Janeiro. Rio has been famed for its beauty since its foundation; inhabitants of Rio de Janeiro, known as Cariocas, maintain that of the seven days of Creation, God needed two alone to make their city. It is easy to believe this was the case when you stand on Corcovado hill

(704 m/2,310 ft) beneath the 30-m (98-foot) concrete and granite statue of Christ with the arms spread out to bless the city. An unforgettable

panorama is laid out before you, from the Bay of Guanabara in the west, to the Sugarloaf Mountain, a 394-m (1,293-ft) granite monolith that after the statue of Christ has become the second emblem of the city; from the tall apartment blocks of the Copacabana suburb to the south, to Ipanema, the most famous beach in Brazil, further to the east. Despite its magnificent natural anchorage, Rio

de Janeiro did not really begin to flourish until the 18th century: then, when gold and precious stones were discovered in what is now the modern state of Minas Gerais, Rio was the nearest port and grew rich. When profits exceeded those brought in by the sugar cane of the north, Rio replaced Salvador as the capital of the colony, remaining so until Brasilia had been completed.

1 Christ in blessing with out-stretched arms on the Corcovado hill, one of the most famous symbols of Rio de Janeiro.

2 The beach at Ipanema was already famous before Antonio Carlos Jobim wrote the well-known bossa nova song *The Girl from Ipanema*.

3 The cable car to the Sugarloaf Mountain.

3

The wealth of animal species includes insects and birds such as spotted nightingale-thrushes and hummingbirds, in addition to deer, and monkeys.

⑪ Congonhas do Campo Leave Rio de Janeiro heading north, and after about 350 km (217 miles) of freeway through verdant mountains you will reach the little town of Congonhas do Campo, whose principal attraction for visitors is its baroque pilgrimage church. The Basilica do Senhor Bom Jesus de Matosinhos was built on a hill above the city in 1757 and to reach it, visitors must first pass seven stations of the cross before climbing to a terrace where they are met by statues of the 12 apostles, carved from the same soapstone which went to make the portal of the twin-towered church. The ornate interior features six side chapels containing no less than 66 figures from the Passion story, all of which have their origins in the 18th-century sculptural workshop of "Aleijadinho," a major artist whose real name was Antônio Francisco Lisboa. He received the name by which he is now known ("little cripple") in childhood because of the leprosy which deformed his hands and feet.

⑫ Ouro Preto This, the most beautiful and best-preserved baroque city in Brazil, marks the end of the route. Sudden prosperity here in the 18th century was followed by a relatively steep decline in the 19th, meaning that a number of baroque structures were built and then abandoned. Despite ebeing in ruins, ins the buildings were allowed to remain standing. The city's landscape of baroque architecture has earned it UNESCO World Heritage status.

Ouro Preto was originally founded as Vila Rica – "Rich Town" – by the thousands of emerald and gold prospectors who flocked to the region in the 17th century, but the capital of the newly founded province of Minas Gerais had to cede this honour to the up-and-coming Belo Horizonte when the gold and gemstone deposits began to run dry toward the end of the 19th century. The best view of the cobbled streets and white, two-storey houses of this cramped little city are to be had from the local mountain, the 1,753-m (5,751-ft) Pico do Itacolomi. Of the 23 churches that have survived, Nossa Senhora do Monte do Carmo is the most striking for its sheer size, but the most magnificent is the Igreja São Francisco de Assis, which is Aleijadinho's masterpiece – he not only contributed the overall design, but is believed to have personally created the pulpit.

The Praça Tiradentes at the heart of the city is named after José da Silva, the "tooth-puller," who led a conspiracy in 1790 that strove to liberate Brazil from Portugal, for which he was hanged the following year. All of Ouro Preto's main sights lie in close proximity, including the Antigo Paço Municipal, the old governor's residence, which now belongs to the university, the Museu da Inconfidência, which commemorates da Silva's insurrection and has an exhibition of sacred art, and the Teatro Municipal, Brazil's first theatre which was built between 1746 and 1770.

1 A view of Ouro Preto, the home of Brazilian baroque.

2 The Basilica do Senhor Bom Jesus de Matosinhos pilgrimage church in Congonhas do Campo.

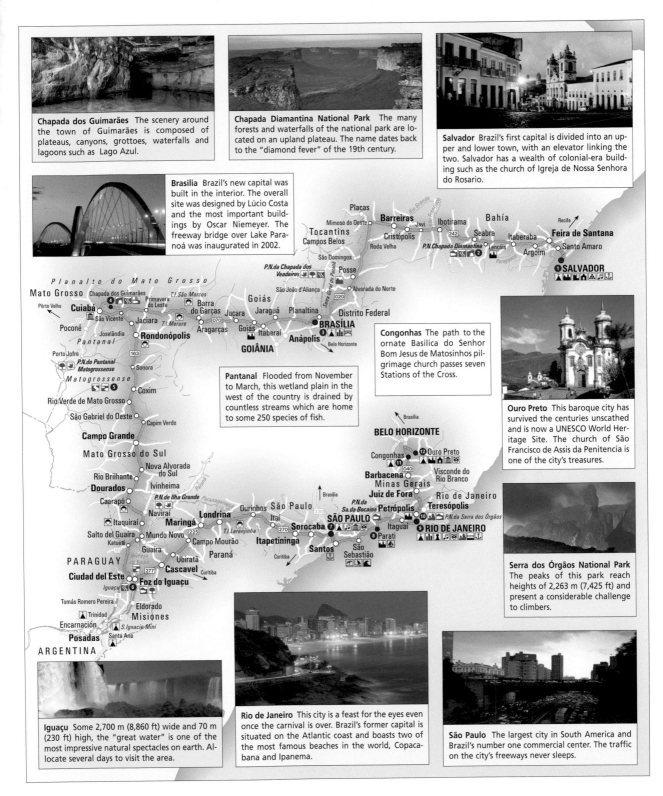

Chapada dos Guimarães The scenery around the town of Guimarães is composed of plateaus, canyons, grottoes, waterfalls and lagoons such as Lago Azul.

Chapada Diamantina National Park The many forests and waterfalls of the national park are located on an upland plateau. The name dates back to the "diamond fever" of the 19th century.

Salvador Brazil's first capital is divided into an upper and lower town, with an elevator linking the two. Salvador has a wealth of colonial-era building such as the church of Igreja de Nossa Senhora do Rosario.

Brasilia Brazil's new capital was built in the interior. The overall site was designed by Lúcio Costa and the most important buildings by Oscar Niemeyer. The freeway bridge over Lake Paranoá was inaugurated in 2002.

Congonhas The path to the ornate Basilica do Senhor Bom Jesus de Matosinhos pilgrimage church passes seven Stations of the Cross.

Pantanal Flooded from November to March, this wetland plain in the west of the country is drained by countless streams which are home to some 250 species of fish.

Ouro Preto This baroque city has survived the centuries unscathed and is now a UNESCO World Heritage Site. The church of São Francisco de Assis da Penitencia is one of the city's treasures.

Serra dos Órgãos National Park The peaks of this park reach heights of 2,263 m (7,425 ft) and present a considerable challenge to climbers.

Iguaçu Some 2,700 m (8,860 ft) wide and 70 m (230 ft) high, the "great water" is one of the most impressive natural spectacles on earth. Allocate several days to visit the area.

Rio de Janeiro This city is a feast for the eyes even once the carnival is over. Brazil's former capital is situated on the Atlantic coast and boasts two of the most famous beaches in the world, Copacabana and Ipanema.

São Paulo The largest city in South America and Brazil's number one commercial center. The traffic on the city's freeways never sleeps.

Antarctica

A cruise to the world's most southerly continent

This cruise to the ice world of the Antarctic sets off from the city of Ushuaia in the Argentine province of Tierra del Fuego, and heads toward the Falkland Islands. Sailing past icebergs and colonies of penguins, it continues on to the South Shetland Islands and the Antarctic Peninsula.

Norwegian explorer Roald Amundsen described the Antarctic as "more wild than any other country on earth" in his diary written in 1911.

On December 14, 1911 he became the first person to reach the South Pole, after a dramatic race against the British explorer Robert Falcon Scott who, after reaching the Pole one month later tragically lost his life with several of his companions on the return journey. Antarctica is the fifth largest and most southerly continent in the world. The Antarctic Circle lies 66°33' south of the equator. South of it, at the December solstice the sun never sets, and at the June solstice it never rises. The Antarctic Convergence, better known as the Antarctic Polar Frontal Zone, is where the cold, northward-flowing Antarctic waters meet and mix with the relatively warmer waters of the sub-Antarctic.

At the center of the land mass usually referred to as the Antarctic, lies the South Pole. Most of the land is covered with ice and snow. Just one-sixth of its surface area, 12,393,000 sq km (4,783,698 sq miles) (or 13,975,000 sq km (5,394,350 sq miles) including the ice shelves) is free of ice. On average the ice sheet is 2,500 m (8,203 ft) thick, but in places it is more than

Falkland Islands: a southern elephant seal hidden in the seaweed.

488

King penguins spend their entire lives in the Antarctic and breed in locations sheltered from the wind.

The bizarre shapes of icebergs eroded by the wind and water are a familiar sight south of the Antarctic Polar Circle.

4,500 m (14,765 ft) thick. However, the term "sheet" is misleading, as this desert of ice is often not flat, and it boasts several mountain ranges. The Transantarctic Mountain range is one of the longest in the world, stretching for over 4,800 km (2,983 miles) diagonally across the continent, from the Ross Sea to the Weddell Sea. Only the highest peaks, such as the 4,897-m (16,067-ft) high Mount Vision, break free from this enormous mass of ice. The South Pole itself is some 2,804 m (9,200 ft) above sea level (including the ice).

Conditions in the Antarctic are extremely hostile. The very low temperatures (Russian researchers estimate -88°C/-126°F) are made even more extreme by ice storms carrying winds of over 350 km/h (217 miles/h). The only forms of life visible on ground that is free from ice, providing welcome glimpses of green, are mosses, lichen, and algae. The only land-dwelling creatures here are insects and nematode worms.

However, things are surprisingly different in and around the cold waters that surround the continent. Full of nutrients, they provides ideal living conditions for many sea creatures and those who forage for food in the sea: algae, seaweed, fungi, krill, sea urchins, jellyfish, seals, whales, and penguin all flourish, and albatrosses, petrels, and seagulls soar above the coastline.

The Antarctic has never fully been colonized by man. Around four thousand people live here during the summer, in the continent's 80 research stations, dropping to around a thousand in winter. The largest research station, the American McMurdo Station at Hut Point on Ross Island, can accommodate up to 1,100 residents during a snow-free summer. McMurdo Station is about 5 km (3 mi) from Scott Base, New Zealand.

A yacht in a storm in Drake Passage between Cape Horn and the Antarctic.

1

The number of passengers wishing to take Antarctic cruises increases each year, but, just as for the polar explorers of a century ago, the weather and ice conditions restrict today's tourists, determining when and how far they can go. Decisions as to which islands and coves can be visited and where passengers can step ashore are normally made only shortly before departure.

1 Ushuaia Most of the cruises through the South Pacific and many Antarctic expeditions start in Ushuaia, which claims to be the southernmost town in the world, though there are other contenders for the title. The capital of the Argentine province of Tierra del Fuego has an impressive backdrop formed by the snow-covered Darwin Mountains and the Beagle Channel. There is an excellent view of the city from the 1,328-m (4,357-ft) high Mount Olivia and its glacier. Cruise ships leave the Beagle Channel heading eastward to begin their journey to the Antarctic. After

sailing just a few miles, you reach Puerto Williams on the northern coast of Isla Navarino.

2 Puerto Williams This Chilean port and military base competes with Ushuaia for the coveted title of the most southerly town in the world. If you make a stop here, you can visit the Martín Gusinde Anthropological Museum, or do a stage of one of the trekking trips offered, if time allows. The waterfalls Cascada de la Virgen and Cascada Los Bronces are not far away. The last of the remaining Yamana Nutivo Americans live in the village Villa Ukkika. A little

Travel Information

Route profile
Length: approx. 2,000 km (1,243 miles)
Duration: min. 2 weeks
Start and end: Ushuaia
Itinerary (main locations): Ushuaia, Falkland Islands, Paulet Island, Deception Island, Port Lockroy, Lemaire Channel, Paradise Bay, Cape Horn, Ushuaia

When to go
Cruises operate during the southern hemisphere's summer (Nov–Feb). In November, there is still pack ice to contend with and the shores are covered in snow. The penguin breeding season begins at this time. It is light for just four hours a day from December to January when the first penguins are born. The best time for whale-watching is February and March, when it is also possible to land and visit the Antarctic Peninsula farther south.

Tourist information
Falkland Islands:
www.falklandislands.com
www.tourism.org.fk
www.antarcticaonline.com/ antarctica/home/home.htm

farther on, the cruise continues past Puerto Toro with a population of around fifty. It is the southernmost settlement to be occupied permanently.

3 Beagle Channel The narrow Beagle Channel, only 5–13 km (3–8 miles) wide, divides Tierra del Fuego from Isla Navarino to the south. It is a

490

natural waterway and provides a route from the Atlantic to the Pacific Ocean. Today, Faro del Fin del Mondo marks the end of the Beagle Channel and the beginning of the open sea, the South Atlantic. The Falkland Islands crossing takes about two days.

④ Falkland Islands Known as the Islas Malvinas in Spanish, the Falkland Islands lie around 500 km (311 miles) off the coast of Patagonia. The two large islands called West Falkland and East Falkland, divided by the Falkland Sound, are the most well known. In addition to these, there are innumerable smaller islands. The total surface area of the archipelago is 12,173 sq km (4,699 sq miles), a rugged landscape that reminds many of the Scottish Highlands. At 705 m (2,313 ft), Mount Usborne on East Falkland is the highest point of the island group. The

Falklands have belonged to Britain since 1833, but during that time Argentina has sought to regain its former power over the islands, both diplomatically and through an unsuccessful military campaign in 1982. Nowadays, the population is around two thousand. The Stanley Museum provides a good insight into the islands' history. It has served as a sealing and whaling base, and a coaling station for the British Royal Navy. Today, the island's sheep still produce wool as they have done in the past and a sheep features on the islands' heraldic seal.

The wildlife is surprisingly diverse and in addition to penguins and egrets, giant petrels also nest here. You may also see colonies of cormorants, and seals or dolphins playing at the water's edge.

The small capital city, Stanley (formerly Port Stanley), chosen

for its deep anchorage for shipping was founded in 1844.

The cruise from here to the South Shetland Islands takes one and a half to two days.

⑤ Elephant Island This is the best-known of the South Shetland Islands, named after the southern sea elephants that live on the rocky shores of the islands. British whaler George Powell was the first to discover the island, which is just 10 km (6 miles) long and in places only 2 km (1¼ miles) wide. The island is most famous as being the place where Ernest Shackleton and his crew took refuge in 1916 after their ship Endurance had been lost. Nowadays, it is inhabited by several species of animal, including gentoo penguins and seals.

⑥ Paulet Island The narrow Antarctic Peninsula is the most easily accessible part of the con-

tinent. Around 1,300 km (808 miles) long, it divides the Weddell Sea from the Bellingshausen Sea. Approaching from the South Atlantic, most ships cross through the Arctic Sound, which divides Dundee Island from the north point of the Antarctic Peninsula, lying to the west. Huge icebergs can often be seen here in "Iceberg Alley" as the waterway has been appropriately nicknamed. Cruise ships usually head for the circular Paulet Island with its summit crater; it is home to one of the

1 A view of Ushuaia in Tierra del Fuego, the southernmost city in the world. Mount Olivia and the Marcial Glacier majestically rise up in the background.

2 Large colonies of blue-eyed cormorants can be seen on the Falkland Islands.

Antarctic's largest colonies of Adelie penguins.

A stone hut was built on a hill here by the shipwrecked crew of a Swedish expedition in 1903 (led by Otto Nordenskjöld). Their expedition ship Antarctic, which gave the Antarctic Sound its name, sank 40 km (25 miles) off the coast of the island.

⑦ Deception Island This horseshoe-shaped South Shetland island is the caldera of a volcano which last erupted in 1970. The flooded crater at the center of the island is entered via a strait named Neptune's Bellows. The big attraction here is bathing in the warm springs of Pendulum Cove, a surreal experience when surrounded by the cold Antarctic landscape. The island's highest point is Mount Pond, at some 539 m (1,768 ft).

The British research station in Whalers Bay and a Chilean station were both damaged during the volcanic eruption in 1967, but the British finally abandoned their station in 1969 following a second eruption. A derelict hangar and the wreck of an airplane can still be seen. The most southerly whale-oil processing plant operated here from 1910 to 1931 in Whalers Bay, a maar (low volcanic crater) that forms a natural port. At Baily Head look out for tens of thousands of chinstrap penguins as well as a number of fur seals.

⑧ Paradise Bay Islands and peninsulas of land form a picturesque bay here, bordered on one side by mountains over 1,100 m (3,609 ft) high. Towering glacial walls shelter the bay, sometimes shedding pieces of ice as fissures and cracks widen and break open. In some places, ice tongues (long narrow sheets of ice projecting from the coastline) and icebergs narrow the waterway, making negotiating this part of the route an exciting experience. The Argentinian research station, Almirante Brown, on the Antarctic mainland is a bright red smudge on the blue-white glacier landscape. It was set on fire in 1984 by a station doctor who could not bear the thought of another winter in such a place, but was restored in 1996. The Gonzalez Videla station, also located in the bay, can only be accessed by ship and has now been taken over by gentoo pen-guins. It was built by Chile to stake its claim on the Antarctic. Since the end of the 1950s, around a dozen countries have claimed the Antarctic as their own. The reason for this is simple: large amounts of natural oil, gas, coal, iron ore, gold, silver, platinum, copper, and other valuable minerals can be found here. Several countries have based their claims on geographical proximity, including Chile, Argentina, and Britain, via the Falkland Islands. Other countries referred to the role they played in discovering the continent or used other strategic arguments.

The journey continues past Anvers Island (with the US-owned Palmer Station) and through the Neumayer Channel to the old whaling station Port Lockroy.

⑨ Port Lockroy Whalers and seal hunters were the first to plunder the natural resources of the Antarctic. Between 1930 and 1950, whales were slaughtered on a huge scale in the Southern Ocean and each year around 400,000 were killed. Since then, whale numbers have recovered well as a result of environmental protection in the area, but the whales are now being threatened by the over-fishing of krill, the most important and nutritious food for the whale.

A British research station was built in 1944 on Goudier Island at the only anchorage point used by the whalers. Station A in the Neumayer Channel, was abandoned in 1962, but is now open to tourists and is one of the most frequently visited destinations for Antarctic cruises. After it was abandoned, it was taken over and restored by the British Antarctic Heritage Trust. Nowadays it is a museum, and an old kitchen, common room, and research laboratory give an impression of what everyday life was like at the station. The Heritage Trust staff maintain the station and also run a postal service for the Antarctic. Gentoo penguins and king cormorants nest not far from the station.

⑩ Lemaire Channel The narrow Lemaire Channel, discovered by Captain Eduard Dallmann in 1873, is one of the great natural wonders of the Antarctic Peninsula. It is 11 km (7 miles) wide at its broadest section, narrowing to just 500 m (1,700 ft) at one point. This is a particularly difficult navigational challenge for the cruise ships because of the drifting ice floes and icebergs. The channel entrance to the north on the mainland side is marked by the 747 m (2,450 ft) twin peaks of Cape Renard and Booth Island, providing a barrier between the channel and the sea. Tall cliffs rise up somewhat menacingly from the ocean and give the channel the feeling of a gorge. They are partially covered by snow, but in places are so steep that not even snow and ice can cling to them. The Three Sisters, an immense rocky formation with smooth, almost vertical peaks rising straight out of the Bellinghausen Sea next to a glacier, is also a beautiful sight. The journey southward through the Lemaire Channel is often hampered by more than just icebergs. Navigation is generally difficult here, requiring special equipment such as sonar and radar. The narrowness of the passage and the rocks hidden beneath the water can make it quite dangerous. Ice conditions permitting, the ship may now chart a course for Petermann Island south of the channel.

① Petermann Island Named after August Petermann, the German geographer, this island was discovered by a German expedition in 1873. It is one of the myriad tiny islands that form the Wilhelm Archipelago, off the west coast of the Antarctic Peninsula. A large colony of Adelie penguins lives on the island and many fin and humpback whales can be spotted in the surrounding waters. A colony of blue-eyed cormorants also lives here. As the island is relatively free of ice, crabeater seals and leopard seals have also made this their home.

Drake Passage, almost 1,000 km (621 miles) wide, between the Southern Shetland Islands and the tip of South America, is named after the English sailor Sir Francis Drake (16th century). Winds and treacherous currents can make this part of the cruise quite uncomfortably turbulent as the ship makes its way toward Cape Horn and then back to Ushuaia. If you are lucky, you will see whales and dolphins making their way though the nutrient-rich waters.

② Cape Horn (Cabo de Hornos) If the weather is good enough to land using an inflatable dinghy, cruise ships drop anchor at South America's southernmost point or if conditions prevent landing, slow down to allow passengers to take photographs.
A lighthouse, the Chilean military station Cabo de Hornos,

and the Cape Horn memorial sculpture created the shape of an enormous flying albatross can be seen on a 50 m (164 ft) high plateau.
The large waves, and strong winds and currents have made the treacherous waters around Cape Horn a graveyard for shipping. Over eight hundred ships and more than ten thousand people have been claimed by the sea here.
In 1945, Cape Horn and the surrounding islands were made a national park. From Cape Horn, the ship makes the return journey to Ushuaia at the bottom of Tierra del Fuego and proud to be the Southernmost city in the world.

1 The Antarctic mountains at Port Lockroy resemble a perfect picture-book landscape.

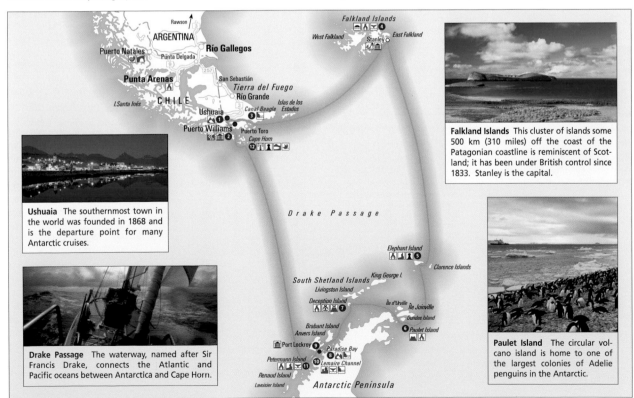

Ushuaia The southernmost town in the world was founded in 1868 and is the departure point for many Antarctic cruises.

Drake Passage The waterway, named after Sir Francis Drake, connects the Atlantic and Pacific oceans between Antarctica and Cape Horn.

Falkland Islands This cluster of islands some 500 km (310 miles) off the coast of the Patagonian coastline is reminiscent of Scotland; it has been under British control since 1833. Stanley is the capital.

Paulet Island The circular volcano island is home to one of the largest colonies of Adelie penguins in the Antarctic.

456 r. 5. C/Macduff Everton, 457 l. t. C/Charles O'Rear, 457 l. m. C/Wolfgang Kaehler, 457 l. b. C/Wolfgang Kaehler, 457 m. 1. C/Galen Rowell, 457 m. 2. C/Hubert Stadler, 457 m. 3. C/Macduff Everton, 457 m. 4. C/Anthony John West, 457 m. 5. C/Hubert Stadler, 457 r. 1. C/Hubert Stadler, 457 r. 2. C/Ric Ergenbright, 457 r. 3. P, 457 r. 4. C/Douglas Peebles, 458 C, 458/459 P/Pan Images, 459 t. G/Stone/Klevansky, 459 b. C/Hubert Stadler, 460/461 C/Peter Johnson, 461 C/Yann Arthus-Bertrand, 462/463 N. N., 464 C/Anthony John West, 464/465 P/Maywald, 465 C/Modic, 466 t. C/Galen Rowell, 466 b. C/Hubert Stadler, 467 C/Galen Rowell, 468 t. C/Anthony John West, 468 b. C/Macduff Everton, 469 l. 1. C/David Keaton, 469 l. 2. C/Galen Rowell, 469 l. 3. C/Ecoscene/Graham Neden, 469 l. 4. C/Galen Rowell, 469 l. 5. ifa, 469 m. t. C/Hubert Stadler, 469 m. b. C/Sergio Pitamitz, 469 r. 1. ifa, 469 r. 2. C/Ric Ergenbright, 469 r. 3. C/Anthony John West, 469 r. 4. C/Ric Ergenbright, 469 r. 5. C/Craig Lovell, 470 L/hemis, 470/471 L/Tjaden, 471 t. L/REA, 471 b. L/Piepenburg, 472 L/hemis, 473 t. L/Piepenburg, 473 b. A/Worldwide Picture Library, 474 t. L/Christian Heeb, 474 b. L/Christian Heeb, 475 t. L/Christian Heeb, 475 b. L/Christian Heeb, 476 L/Christian Heeb, 477 t. L/Christian Heeb, 477 u. L/Sasse, 478/479 P, 480 t. L/Kreuls, 480 u. P/Minden/Lanting, 481 L/Christian Heeb, 482/483 P, 484 t. L/Christian Heeb, 484 u. L/Christian Heeb, 485 C/Sergio Pitamitz, 486 t. L/Piepenburg, 486 u. Das Fotoarchiv/Claus Meyer, 487 l. t. L/Christian Heeb, 487 l. m. L/Christian Heeb, 487 l. u. P, 487 m. t. L/Piepenburg, 487 m. u. L/Christian Heeb, 487 r. t. L/Tjaden, 487 r. m. t. L/REA, 487 r. m. u. P/Minden/Lanting, 487 r. u. L/Christian Heeb, 488 P, 488/489 P, 489 t. L/Arcticphoto, 489 u. L/Heidorn, 490 L/Gonzalez, 491 P, 492 L/IML, 493 l. t. L/IML, 493 l. u. L/Heidorn, 493 r. t. L/Hoa-Qui, 493 r. u. L/IML.

Cover: Premium

The publisher made every effort to find all of the copyright holders for the images herein. In some cases this was not possible. Any copyright holders are kindly asked to contact the publisher.

Imprint

MONACO BOOKS is an imprint of Verlag Wolfgang Kunth

© Verlag Wolfgang Kunth GmbH & Co.KG, Munich, 2010

Translation: JMS Books LLP, Silva Editions Ltd., Emily Plank, Katherine Taylor
Editor: Kevin White for bookwise Medienproduktion, Munich

For distribution please contact:

Monaco Books
c/o Verlag Wolfgang Kunth, Königinstr. 11
80539 München, Germany
Tel. (49) 89 45 80 20 23
Fax (49) 89 45 80 20 21
info@kunth-verlag.de

www.monacobooks.com
www.kunth-verlag.de

Printed in Slovakia

All facts have been researched with the greatest possible care, to the best of our knowledge and belief. However, the editors and publishers can accept no responsibility for any inaccuracies or incompleteness of the details provided. The publishers are pleased to receive any information or suggestions for improvement.